Anonymous

**Coursing and Falconry**

Anonymous

**Coursing and Falconry**

ISBN/EAN: 9783337717858

Printed in Europe, USA, Canada, Australia, Japan

Cover: Foto ©ninafisch / pixelio.de

More available books at **www.hansebooks.com**

# COURSING AND FALCONRY

COURSING

BY HARDING COX

FALCONRY

BY THE HON. GERALD LASCELLES

*WITH ILLUSTRATIONS by JOHN CHARLTON, R. H. MOORE LANCELOT SPEED, G. E. LODGE, and from PHOTOGRAPHS*

LONDON
LONGMANS, GREEN, AND CO.
1892

# *DEDICATION*

*TO*

# *H.R.H. THE PRINCE OF WALES*

BADMINTON : *May* 1885.

HAVING received permission to dedicate these volumes, the BADMINTON LIBRARY of SPORTS and PASTIMES, to HIS ROYAL HIGHNESS THE PRINCE OF WALES, I do so feeling that I am dedicating them to one of the best and keenest sportsmen of our time. I can say, from personal observation, that there is no man who can extricate himself from a bustling and pushing crowd of horsemen, when a fox breaks covert, more dexterously and quickly than His Royal Highness; and that when hounds run hard over a big country, no man can take a line of his own and live with them better. Also, when the wind has been blowing hard, often have I seen His Royal Highness knocking over driven grouse and partridges and high-rocketing pheasants in first-rate workmanlike style. He is held to be a good yachtsman, and as Commodore of the Royal Yacht Squadron is looked up to by those who love that pleasant and exhilarating pastime. His encouragement of racing is well known, and his attendance at the University, Public School, and other important Matches testifies to his being, like most English gentlemen, fond of all manly sports. I consider it a great privilege to be allowed to dedicate these volumes to so eminent a sportsman as His Royal Highness the Prince of Wales, and I do so with sincere feelings of respect and esteem and loyal devotion.

BEAUFORT.

BADMINTON

# PREFACE

A FEW LINES only are necessary to explain the object with which these volumes are put forth. There is no modern encyclopædia to which the inexperienced man, who seeks guidance in the practice of the various British Sports and Pastimes, can turn for information. Some books there are on Hunting, some on Racing, some on Lawn Tennis, some on Fishing, and so on ; but one Library, or succession of volumes, which treats of the Sports and Pastimes indulged in by Englishmen—and women—is wanting. The Badminton Library is offered to supply the want. Of the imperfections which must be found in the execution of such a design we are conscious. Experts often differ. But this we may say, that those who are seeking for knowledge on any of the subjects dealt with will find the results of many years' experience written by men who are in every case adepts at the Sport or Pastime of which they write. It is to point the way to success to those who are ignorant of the sciences they aspire to master, and who have no friend to help or coach them, that these volumes are written.

To those who have worked hard to place simply and clearly before the reader that which he will find within, the best thanks of the Editor are due. That it has been no slight labour to supervise all that has been written, he must acknowledge; but it has been a labour of love, and very much lightened by the courtesy of the Publisher, by the unflinching, indefatigable assistance of the Sub-Editor, and by the intelligent and able arrangement of each subject by the various writers, who are so thoroughly masters of the subjects of which they treat. The reward we all hope to reap is that our work may prove useful to this and future generations.

THE EDITOR.

# CONTENTS

## *COURSING*



## *FALCONRY*

# ILLUSTRATIONS

Reproduced by J. D. Cooper and Messrs. Walker & Boutall.
Photographs by G. Mitchell.

## PLATES

## ILLUSTRATIONS IN TEXT

# COURSING

BY

HARDING COX

THE WATERLOO CUP

A frolic

# INTRODUCTION

COURSING, as a national field sport, holds its own for antiquity with any other that is now followed. How far back it dates cannot, indeed, be precisely said, but it is at least certain that very nearly nineteen hundred years ago coursing was practised very much in the same manner as it is in the present day ; for Arrian, A.D. 150, wrote a long and elaborate treatise on the subject, from which the student may ascertain that in all essentials the sport was what it remains ; though it may be added that in its leading features it is not easy to see how it could be otherwise conducted.

Arrian describes coursing with an appreciation of sport which will be cordially recognised. He insisted on letting the hare have her start, creep from her form as if unperceived, and recover her presence of mind. Then, he says, 'if she be a racer she will prick her ears and bound away from her seat with long strides;' and he grows enthusiastic over the sight that ensues when the greyhounds stretch out at full speed after her. The spirit in which this ancient Greek wrote will warmly commend itself to readers of to-day. Those coursers who are true sportsmen, Arrian asserts,

do not take their dogs out for the sake of catching a hare, but for the contest or sport of coursing, and they are glad if the hare escapes. If she fly to any thin brake for concealment, where they see her trembling and in the utmost distress, they will call off their dogs. Often, indeed, when following a course on horseback, have I come up to the hare as soon as caught, and have myself saved her alive, and then have taken away my dog, fastened him up, and allowed her to escape. And if I have arrived too late to save her, I have struck my head with sorrow that the dog had killed so good an antagonist.

All this is as it should be, and in passing on with a tribute of respect to the good sportsman who wrote it nearly two thousand years ago, it need only be incidentally added that he says nothing about testing the relative merits of greyhounds. These old coursers went out merely to see their dogs run a hare, and, though Arrian enforces the rule that more than a brace of greyhounds should never be slipped at a time, this is because he thought two greyhounds to one hare made a fair encounter.

The date when matches were first made between dogs is not easily to be traced, but it was certainly before the time of Elizabeth, during whose reign, by special command of the Queen, certain 'laws of the Leash or Coursing' were drawn up and 'allowed and subscribed by Thomas, Duke of Norfolk.' They will be of much interest to the coursers of the present time, and are therefore here quoted:—

1. That he that is chosen Fewterer, or that lets loose the greyhounds, shall receive the greyhounds matched to run together, into his Leash, as soon as he comes into the field, and

follow next to the hare-finder, *or he who is to start the hare* until he come unto the form ; and no horseman or footman is to go before, or on any side, but directly behind, for the space of about forty yards.

2. You ought not to course a hare with more than a brace of greyhounds.
3. The hare-finder ought to give the hare three so-ho's before he puts her from her form or seat, that the dogs may gaze about and attend her starting.
4. They ought to give twelve score yards law before the dogs are loosed, unless there be danger of losing her.
5. The dog that gives the first turn, if after that there be neither cote, slip, nor wrench, wins the wager.
6. If the dog give the first turn, and the other bear the hare, he that bears the hare shall win.
7. A go-by, or bearing the hare, is equivalent to two turns.
8. If neither dog turn the hare, he that leads last to the covert wins.
9. If one dog turn the hare, serve himself, and turn her again, it is as much as a cote, and a cote is esteemed two turns.
10. If all the course be equal, he that bears the hare shall win, and if she be not borne, the course shall be adjudged dead.
11. If a dog take a fall in a course, and yet performs his part, he may challenge the advantage of a turn more than he gave.
12. If a dog turn the hare, serve himself, and give divers cotes, and yet in the end stands still in the field, the other dog, if he turn home of the covert, although he gives no turn, shall be adjudged to win the wager.
13. If by misfortune a dog be ridden over in his course, the course is void, and to say the truth, he that did the mischief ought to make reparation for the damage.
14. If a dog give the first and last turn and there be no other advantage between them, he that gives the odd turn shall win.
15. A cote is when a greyhound goeth endways by his fellow, and gives the hare a turn.
16. A cote serves for two turns, and two tripplings or jerkings for a cote ; and if she turneth not right about she only wrencheth. The first version has it thus :—A cote shall be more than two turns, and a go-by or bearing the hare equal to two turns.

17. If there be no cotes given between a brace of greyhounds and that the one of them serves the other as turning, then he that gives the hare most turns wins the wager; and if one give as many turns as the other, he that beareth the hare wins the wager.
18. Sometimes the hare doth not turn but wrencheth, for she is not properly said to turn, unless she turns as it were round; and two wrenches stand for a turn.
19. He that comes in first to the death of the hare, takes her up and saves her from breaking, cherishes the dogs and cleanses their mouths from the wool, is adjudged to have the hare for his pains.
20. Those that are judges of the leash must give their judgment presently, before they depart the field.

The earliest coursing seems to have been private, but in the reign of the first Charles matches were decided in public, and they have increased in popularity till the present day, when the Waterloo Cup is recognised as one of the chief events of the sporting year, even by those who are in no way enthusiastic about the greyhound.

It is not the purpose of this work to trace the history of coursing as related in the works of Dame Juliana Berners, Wynkyn de Worde, Daniel, and other authorities, nor will space be occupied with well-worn quotations from Shakespeare and elsewhere. It is rather the object to describe the method in which coursing is carried on, so that any reader who has a fancy for the leash may be provided with information which will help him to join the ranks of the coursers with some knowledge of what is done, and some perception of (what the writer's experience has induced him to regard as) the best way of attaining success. Those who are curious as to the progress and development of coursing may be referred to the third volume of 'The Greyhound Stud Book,' in which an exhaustive chapter on the subject appears.

Much misconception prevails about coursing. Comparatively few men really appreciate the niceties of the sport, and many persons have no ideas beyond a vague belief that two greyhounds run after a hare, one kills her—if she does not get away—and wins in consequence. This is, of course, by no means the case. Very often the dog that actually kills loses, the winner being the one that 'does most towards killing the hare;' it has even been estimated by some devotees of the sport that as often as nine times out of ten the worse of the two dogs kills.

Judging a course is, therefore, a somewhat elaborate business, requiring special knowledge and aptitude, the keenest eyes and quickest observation, on the part of the official who undertakes the duty. He is guided by Rules set down by the National Coursing Club; but, for the better appreciation of the sport by those who are altogether unacquainted with the subject, it may here be briefly said that the points of the course are six in number, and include 'speed,' the 'go-by,' the 'turn,' the 'wrench,' the 'kill,' and the 'trip.' For a full explanation of these terms the reader is referred to the aforesaid Rules, which are quoted in an Appendix to this portion of the volume.

So much will, it is hoped, serve for general introduction. Before closing these preliminary remarks, the author desires to add his acknowledgments to Mr. CHARLES RICHARDSON, for his chapter on Coursing Clubs, and for various other aid kindly furnished.

We now proceed to a detailed examination of the sport.

# CHAPTER I

## THE WATERLOO CUP

MENTION of public coursing is to be found as far back as the middle of the seventeenth century, but it is only in comparatively recent years that public stakes have become a sporting institution. In an admirable article by that sterling authority, 'Robin Hood,' in the 'Field Quarterly Magazine and Review' of February 1870—an article to which I am indebted for much valuable information on the coursing of the past—the writer estimates that at least 50,000*l*. was run for in stakes in the preceding year. This was in the palmy days of Lords Sefton, Craven, Lurgan, Grey de Wilton, and a host of others, for the sport was then a thoroughly popular one, and was supported by the highest in the land. We have already spoken of the origin of coursing. For a long while greyhounds were used as a means of catching hares, apart from relative merit, and a dog that ran cunning and could account for fur with unfailing regularity was regarded as a real friend, instead of being promptly put out of the way—a fate that generally overtakes rogues since stakes were instituted By-and-by owners would match their dogs against each other ; but for a long time the killer was considered the winner, apart from any points of merit as calculated nowadays. When these points had been adopted small stakes were run for, and no better illustration of the progress and development of the sport can be found than a reference to the historical records of the Waterloo Cup, which is rightfully called 'The Blue Ribbon of the Leash'—for is it not the summit of a coursing-man's ambition to be returned the winner of the great event? and should he be fortunate enough to have bred and trained his successful nomination, the achievement will rank as a red-letter performance in the pages of his life's history. The Waterloo Cup finds its parallel on the turf. In these days of 10,000*l.* stakes a man may win a prize of greater pecuniary value than the Derby; but even the most mercenary of racing-men and those who look upon the sport as a profession would in all probability, if asked, tell you they would rather win one Derby than two Eclipse Stakes. So it is with the great trophy of Altcar; richer stakes are to be found, but none is so sought after. A Gosforth Gold Cup is won and forgotten, but a Waterloo triumph is a living memory.

Let us then look to the foundation of this popular stake, and, again adopting 'Robin Hood' as our authority, unearth its records. The year 1836 saw its beginning. That beginning was modest in the extreme, for we find in the 'New Sporting Magazine' a record of the event described as an eight-dog stake at 2 sovs. each. The contest was conducted under the auspices of a Mr. Lynn, and resulted in a win for that gentleman's nomination, Melanie, though the owner of the bitch was none other than Lord Molyneux, eldest son of the Earl of Sefton, who had kindly given permission for the stake to be run on the now classical plains of Altcar. In addition to the stakes, a trophy, in the form of a silver snuff-box, was presented to the winner. The following year saw the nominations increased to sixteen at 5*l.* each; and the eight dogs beaten in the first round could compete for 'the Altcar Plate,' an equivalent to the Waterloo Plate of to-day. The next celebration found thirty-two nominations at 25*l.* each, and no alteration occurred for twenty years, with the exception of a distinct stake called 'The Waterloo Purse,' which was added to the card. It was not until 1857 that the stake attained its full dimensions as follows :—

The Waterloo Cup, sixty-four subscribers at 25*l.* each = 1,600*l.*, which is allotted as follows : 1,240*l.* to the thirty-two dogs left in the Waterloo Cup proper, comprising 500*l.* to the winner, 200*l.* to the second, 50*l.* each to the third and fourth, 30*l.* each to the next four, 20*l.* each to eight, and 10*l.* each to the other sixteen. The thirty-two dogs beaten in the first round to run again for the Waterloo Purse, for which 260*l.* is reserved, the winner getting 100*l.*, the second 50*l.*, two dogs 15*l.* each, four dogs 10*l.* each, and eight dogs 5*l.* each respectively. For the Waterloo Plate 100*l.* is reserved for the sixteen dogs beaten in the second round of the Cup, the winner receiving 45*l.*, the second 20*l.*, two dogs 7*l.* 10*s.* each, and four others 5*l.* each.

Now, having regard to these conditions, it is easily gathered that the owner of a smart dog stands a fair chance of drawing a prize of some sort, even should he fail to win the laurel crown and its substantial concomitant ; so no wonder that the nominations are eagerly sought after, and that the fact of one being allotted is considered a high honour in the coursing world.

A short account of some of the more remarkable winners of this trophy may here prove acceptable to the reader, and amongst the older generation may recall many half-forgotten scenes of interest and excitement.

1847.—This was the first year in which Lord Sefton competed on his native soil, and he won ; what is more, he bred the winner, Senet, himself, and also his sire and dam.

1854.—Lord Sefton repeated his triumph with Sackcloth, a son of Senet, a victory that must have been specially gratifying.

1850-52-53.—In these years the winner was Cerito, who was only a puppy on the first occasion. Altogether this smart bitch was slipped fifty-three times and won forty-five courses.

1855 saw the victory of Judge, a dog who subsequently proved of inestimable value at the stud, and who was runner-up in the following year.

1857 was the first year that the stake attained its full dimensions, and the winner proved to be King Lear, the runner-up being Sunbeam, who was backed to win an enormous stake.

1858 saw a rank outsider in Neville victorious; another greatly fancied one, named Deacon, running up.

1859.—In this year the stakes were divided; and when 'Robin Hood' wrote the article to which I have referred, this was a record; but in late years we have three examples of a division of stakes: by Miss Glendyne and Bit of Fashion, by Herschel and Greater Scot, and by Fullerton and Troughend, further allusion to which will be made in the proper sequence. On the occasion under notice the dividers were Clive and Selby; the latter, whose success was expected, was the property of Mr. Jardine, while Clive was by the 1855 winner, Judge—a good example of the transmission of merit.

1861 saw the victory of a sterling greyhound in Canaradzo, whose name is conspicuous in most of the tabulated pedigrees of our present-time celebrities. A sister of Canaradzo, called Cioloja, was believed to be a perfect wonder, and became a very hot favourite for the Cup; but, as ill luck would have it, she broke her thigh a few days before the event.

1863 was remarkable for the victory of Chloe, another daughter of Judge, the favourite and runner-up being Rebe, the property of Messrs. Heywood and Raester.

1864.—Rebe again ran up, being unluckily beaten in the final by King Death, a son of Canaradzo, and in

1865 she divided the Purse with Beckford. In

1866 she ran into the last four, this proving the finale to a remarkable but luckless career.

1865.—In this year Brigadier was returned the winner, a dog that had previously shown wretched form and had cost his owner the modest sum of twenty-five shillings—a most profitable investment as it turned out; for Mr. Gorton had backed his nomination to win a good round sum, having an idea that a bitch called Wild Geranium (believed to be very smart) would fill it. So he won his money, as it were, against his will.

1866.—Here again was a *dea ex machinâ*, to the great benefit of Mr. Stocker, who had secured the Newmarket Champion Puppy Stakes winner, Saucebox, to fill his nomination. This bitch went wrong after a trial with Lobelia, but so smartly did the latter run that Mr. Stocker sent her to fill his nomination, and, moreover, threw a fresh commission into the market. 'Lobelia,' says 'Robin Hood,' 'ran her first three courses somewhat unsteadily; but settling down to her work she won the remainder most brilliantly: her decisive victory over Royal Seal in the last course being one of the smartest performances imaginable. She took part in the Waterloo Cup in the two subsequent years, and won four courses each time, but was compelled twice to lower her colours to the invincible Irishman.'[1] She was a small wiry greyhound by Sea Foam, weighing a shade over 44 lbs. 'When Lobelia secured her memorable victory, so great was the enthusiasm at Southport that a messenger was despatched from Altcar with instructions that the bells of the parish church were to be rung in honour of the event.'

We now come to what may be termed the Master McGrath era—viz. from 1868–1871, for this prodigy made a mark on the records of coursing which is quite indelible, and stamped it with a public interest which reaches far beyond the limits of the true votaries of the sport. His was a name to conjure by, and many a one who had never seen a course, who would not know a greyhound from a lurcher, would discourse of the prowess of this canine giant—giant only in achievement, for he was by no means a big dog; nor was he a remarkably handsome one, having a short, even sour, head; but he was compactly built, and stood on the best of feet and legs. In another

[1] Master McGrath.

portion of this volume, when discussing breeding theories, we shall enter into an analysis of Master McGrath's pedigree, which cannot fail to be of interest to students of the subject. For the present we must return to his career as affecting the history of the Waterloo Cup.

1868.—In this year Brigade was favourite, and though the Irishmen were very sweet on their puppy, and entrusted him with solid support, the fact remained that the coveted trophy had never crossed the Channel, and the English division were in happy ignorance of the sort of goods that was to be slipped. Prior to leaving his native soil, Master McGrath had won the Visitors' Cup at Lurgan, and those who witnessed his victory did not forget him when he went to the slips. His first opponent was Belle of Scotland, and he began moderately by running an undecided, but at the next time of asking he polished her off in decisive style, and made quite an example of Kalista, Marionette, the favourite, Brigade, and the previous year's winner, Lobelia. For the final he met Mr. Lister's Cock Robin. In the previous round this dog had tumbled on his sister Charming May, who was drawn in his favour, though she ran the bye with him, and, strange to say, easily beat him, so that when he made a very respectable show against the Irish crack, Mr. Lister must have been sorry that he did not leave the bitch in. This year was also remarkable for the *début* in the stake of Bab at the Bowster, whom contemporary critics considered second only to McGrath. She came from Scotland with a great reputation untarnished by defeat, and won two courses in brilliant fashion; but then she met Lobelia and went down after an undecided.

The following year (1869) was full of interest, for both the Irish dog and the Scotch bitch had added to their laurels since the last meeting. The bitch's record was indeed brilliant, for she won the Scarisbrick Cup (128), the Douglas Cup (64), the coveted Altcar Cup (20), and the Elsham Cup (32). In the Douglas Cup she had had her revenge on Lobelia, for on a strong outside she led her former conqueror three lengths and gave her a good beating. Notwithstanding this the British public would not be stalled off their idol, and McGrath was steadily backed down to 6 to 1, whilst 'tens' were procurable about Bab, who ran in Mr. R. Paterson's nomination. As luck would have it, the great rivals were drawn well apart, so that as the contest progressed excitement waxed higher and higher, until it culminated in their going to slips together for the final. Lobelia, who had grandly worked her way into the last four, had met the Irishman in the morning. At one moment in the course it looked as if the idol would be shattered, as Lobelia fairly held him, and had she killed at the drain when she made her great effort, McGrath would never have been hailed winner of a triple Waterloo. No sooner,

A long jump

however, had the hare crossed than the leviathan came like great guns and snatched the verdict in a brilliant finish. Meanwhile Bab at the Bowster had settled Ghillie Callum, who made no show against her. Then came the tug of war: away they went to a splendid slip and to a stout hare, and a shout arose as it was seen the bitch was slightly leading. On approaching the drain McGrath steadied himself, and clearing it more smartly than the bitch, he scored first and second; Bab soon joined issue, and brilliant exchanges ensued; then McGrath drew out, and concentrating his forces in the marvellous way so often noticed, he dashed in and effected a grand kill, thus winning his second, but not his last, Waterloo.

In 1870 the meeting was interrupted by frost, and an objection was lodged by Mr. Borrow against the nominations of

Lord Lurgan and Mr. Jones on the ground that they had not named by the time fixed. As Master McGrath represented his owner, there was a deal of excitement; but the objection was overruled by the stewards, and was similarly treated on appeal to the National Coursing Club. On Wednesday the frost gave, and a start was made the following day. Although the Irish champion had not been seen in public since his previous triumph, he went to the slips a hot favourite, as little as 7 to 2 being accepted about his chance. What then was the general dismay when it was seen that Lady Lyons was not only holding him, but giving him a severe dressing. She drew right out, and the course ended at the river Alt, still covered with rotten ice. In following the hare it gave way, and McGrath was in imminent peril, but was rescued by Wilson, the Irish slipper. The next morning the poor dog was in a pitiable state, and Lord Lurgan, in the heat of the moment, expressed his opinion that he had been poisoned, and swore that he should never run again; but the general impression was that the crack was short of work, and that he was upset by the treacherous state of the ground. Meanwhile Bab at the Bowster had won three courses, and was then put out by Cataclysm, but the winner turned up in Sea Cove, a bitch with very fair credentials. Bed of Stone and S. S., two sterling greyhounds, competed in this stake. The latter, having been unluckily put out in the first ties, scored decisively in the Plate, and it is the general opinion that, had he got clear of his first course, the Cup would again have gone to Ireland by aid of her second string.

Lord Lurgan, repenting of his hastiness, put McGrath into training again, and won the Brownlow Cup, when it was seen that the old dog had lost none of his dash, so that on the night of the draw for the Waterloo Cup (1871) he was again installed favourite, but this time at the extended odds of 10 to 1. It was soon apparent that he would make it as hot as usual for the best of his opponents. His first course against Wharfinger was not particularly brilliant, and many expected a repetition of last year's *fiasco*; but he improved as he went on, and when he met the puppy Pretender in the final he crowned a very smartly run trial with one of those dashing kills which went so far to uphold his fame. In this Cup, Bed of Stone had the bad luck to run no less than three undecideds with Bendimere, which of course destroyed her chance; but she came out like a giantess refreshed, and polished off her opponents in the Plate in grand style. This was the last course that the great dog ran in public, and, as we have said before, his name became a household word. Even Her Majesty the Queen commanded him to appear at Windsor Castle, and expressed a lively interest in his performances. He did not long survive his retirement, for he died of heart-disease two years after. In the chapter of this volume entitled 'Famous Greyhounds of the Past' will be found the measurements of this remarkable greyhound, whose running weight was 54 lbs.

1872 found Bed of Stone victorious. She was a sterling bitch, and had previously won the Purse in 1870 and the Plate in 1871, so that this last performance set a seal on her fame, and as a matron she was a decided success (see chapter on 'Celebrated Greyhounds'). The runner-up was Peasant Boy, who occupied the same berth the following year (1873), when Muriel was successful. On this occasion there was a disgraceful demonstration against the judge, Mr. Warwick. It having got wind that he had judged a private trial of Peasant Boy, an idea prevailed that he meant pulling that dog through at all hazards; consequently, when he went to the slips with Muriel for the final, Mr. Warwick was literally mobbed, and although Muriel fairly won at the finish, there were not wanting those who declared that the judge had been intimidated; these were probably the disappointed backers of Peasant Boy. Mr. Warwick had judged the Waterloo Cup thirteen years, and had given every satisfaction; but this was the last time he officiated.

1874 was remarkable for being the first year in which Mr. Hedley acted as judge; he had every qualification for the post, which he has held up to the present time. Magnano, the winner, was a rank outsider, and he put out Muriel in the first ties; she, however, making amends by winning the Purse.

In 1875 the Irish were again successful with their much-fancied representative Honeymoon, the favourite Sirius going down the first round.

The next year (1875) Honeymoon, who in the interim had won the important Brownlow Cup, started a hot favourite at 11 to 2. She beat in grand style Warren Hastings, Handicraft,

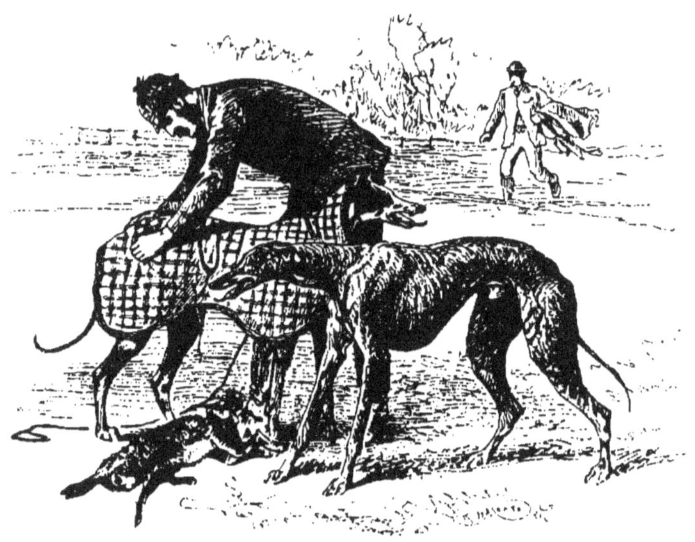

He's had enough

and Lucetta, but in the next round fell foul of her compatriot and kennel companion, Donald, who succeeded in lowering her colours, and eventually proved the winner of the Cup. After his victory Donald was sold for 300*l.*, and was immediately put to the stud.

1876.—Now once more we have to deal with a canine marvel, for the winner was the diminutive Coomassie, who made very short work of all her early opponents, with the exception of Master Sam. This dog, who was a regular electric flash, led the little bitch, but he had one conspicuous failing, which was his utter inability to kill his hares. On this occasion it cost him the course, as Coomassie, getting a chance, put in some telling points, and wound up with a brilliant kill; for she was as clever with her teeth as her opponent was deficient. When it came to the final, the fawn had a hard nut to crack in Braw Lass, who was favourite for the stake; but she led her, and though the latter was very busy afterwards, Coomassie, finishing with another brilliant kill, gained the award.

The next year (1878) Coomassie, who had not been seen

Too many hares

out since her previous victory, was naturally enough installed favourite at 9 to 1, with a point longer odds accepted about her old opponent Braw Lass. Now it appears that Coomassie had been amiss, but the secret was well preserved, and did not leak out till she had run her first two courses in anything but her old form; however, she pulled through, and improving as she went on, she went to slips for the last time with Zazel, who had been somewhat hard run. She made a fair show against the crack; but, killing too soon, settled her chance, and gave Coomassie her second Waterloo Cup.

This year witnessed Tom Wilkinson's *début* as slipper, a

post he filled most efficiently until 1890, when Wright handled the slips.

As the time approached for the next Waterloo (1879), it was thought that the little wonder Coomassie had a chance of rivalling the feats of Master McGrath, but these hopes were disappointed. She had the ill-luck to fracture a small bone in her leg during training, so that she never ran again. Coomassie was the smallest greyhound that ever won the Waterloo Cup, as she weighed but 44 lbs.; but, with the exception of Master McGrath, Fullerton, and possibly of Miss Glendyne, she stands out from other winners as an animal of exceptional merit. She was bred by Mr. Cafley, of Runham, near Yarmouth, and when at walk at a butcher's there, might have been purchased for a few shillings. It was not until she ran in, and won, the Newmarket Champion Puppy Stakes that her merit was discovered.

1879.—The way now being clear for Zazel, she was made favourite for the great event; but she was not destined to recompense her owner for the previous disappointment. The winner sprang from the extreme outside division, viz. Misterton, a dog who was to make a great name for himself at the stud. He started at the remunerative price of 1000 to 6, which is rather odd, considering that in the Newmarket Champion Puppy Stakes he had won four courses in grand style, and had been most unluckily put out. The final with Commerce was a close affair, and she had none the best of the luck against Mr. Miller's dog.

1880.—Misterton had a rare gruelling in his first course, and was put out by Devastation next round. Honeywood and Plunger (100 to 1 chance) were left in for the final, and after the former had made a strong beginning, he ran roguishly, and Plunger all but succeeded in snatching the verdict out of the fire.

A very smart and clever greyhound won in 1881, viz. Princess Dagmar: she was a big bitch (58 lbs.), and disposed of all her opponents with considerable ease. The next year (1882) she made but a poor show, having been amiss, and the winner turned up in Snowflight, who fought out the issue with the aged Hornpipe. The last-named had had a hard time of it, having run an undecided with Banchory, and defeated Glenlivet, Death or Glory, Sut and Leader. In the final, after a stiffish course, the hat came off, and at the second go a fresh hare crossed them and they separated ; so that, when at last they were fairly off, the poor old bitch was spun out, and, to add to her misfortunes, the hare favoured Snowflight throughout the course.

1883.—Snowflight was within an ace of repeating her victory, but it was snatched from her by Wild Mint, who had the luck of the contest, and who is generally considered the worst greyhound that ever won the trophy.

In 1884 Mineral Water won, and the runner-up was that good game but unlucky greyhound Greentick, a dog that has made a name for himself as a sire that is not likely to be eclipsed. Here again it was thought that a bad dog had won ; but Mineral Water's subsequent performance in the Gosforth Gold Cup went far to remove that impression, though his defeat in the Waterloo Cup of 1885 was easily brought about in the first ties. Here we had another division when Bit of Fashion and Miss Glendyne were left in for the final. These bitches represented one interest, though owned respectively by Mr. E. Dent and Mr. C. Hibbert. Had they run it off, it would have been, bar accidents, a very one-sided affair, as Miss Glendyne was quite a class above her kennel-companion, though the latter has subsequently been immortalised as the dam of Fullerton.

That Miss Glendyne was a really peerless bitch was proved the next year (1886). In the summer she had the misfortune to break a toe, and as the time approached for her preparation it was found she was constantly falling lame. The late eminent surgeon, Mr. Hutton, however, performed a most successful operation, and though the bitch was brought to the slips very big and made a slovenly exhibition of herself in her first two courses, she ran herself into condition and wound up with a brilliant victory over the midget, Penelope II., who was even smaller than Coomassie, and weighed no more than 41 lbs. To see the two bitches in the slips together was really comical, and to look at, it was 20 to 1 on one; nevertheless, the pigmy could go a great pace, and was as clever as a monkey; she rendered an excellent account of herself, and only just lost one of the grandest trials ever run. We remember asking Mr. Hedley, during one of the intervals this year (1890), what was the finest course he ever witnessed, and he immediately said the one under notice.

In 1887 a division once more occurred, the heroes being Greater Scot and Herschel. The latter was a particularly brilliant all-round performer, and would in all probability have beaten his kennel-companion, especially as the latter was very hard run with Jenny Jones.

1888 witnessed the victory of Burnaby. The original fixture had to be abandoned owing to frost, and the draw was declared void. This year is indelibly fixed on our memory, as, for the first time, we held a nomination and journeyed to Liverpool to see her (it was a bitch) run; but, owing to the postponement, we returned to town after a bootless journey. At the second time of asking, Herschel and Miss Glendyne were drawn together, and there was great excitement when they went to slips; but the dog led and beat her decisively. though she eventually won the Purse, one of her victims being our above-mentioned hope and joy, who had won two courses in great style before tumbling up against the crack. Curiously enough, when the hare to which Miss Glendyne and Herschel had been slipped was picked up, it was found to have but three legs, though this mutilation was not apparent when the dogs were slipped, and she seemed to go strongly and well. Greater Scot raised but one flag; but Herschel survived until meeting Burnaby, when he was seen to be spun out, and Mr. Pilkington's dog won rather easily. The runner-up was Duke McPherson, an Irish dog that had recently been purchased by Colonel North, who had just risen on the horizon of the coursing world. His blue dog made a good show against the winner; but, to add to the bitterness of the defeat, the Colonel had the bad luck to lose his dog. Since then Fortune has come with both hands-full, as in 1889, 1890, 1891, and 1892 he has had it all his own way in the Waterloo Cup. In 1889 he sprung a mine on us in the shape of his puppy Fullerton, by Greentick—Bit of Fashion. Whatever may have been the opinion of the critics after the division between this dog and his kennel-companion, Troughend —and it is not unlikely that his colours would have been

On his own account

lowered by Herschel, who was going in his best form, had not the latter got away with a demon hare that ran him as stiff as the proverbial poker—nevertheless, there could be no mistaking his quality after his brilliant performance in 1890 and the two following years.

As for Troughend, the divider in 1889, he did very badly, and was very lucky to get as far as he did in the Purse. The runner-up, Downpour, was a sterling little bitch, very fast and clever withal; with Fullerton out of the way she would have easily accounted for the stake.

In the Waterloo Cup of 1892 Fullerton set a seal on his fame and broke all records by winning outright for the third year running—after having divided with his kennel companion

FULLERTON

Troughend (whom he could assuredly have beaten) in his puppy season. On this occasion great interest was centred in the event; the eyes of all coursers, and a vast concourse of those who, as a rule, pay little attention to the affairs of the leash, were bent on the contest, and all items of news connected with it were greedily scanned.

At one time a feeling of uneasiness and dissatisfaction prevailed, because at the first draw Colonel North had announced his intention of drawing any or all of his dogs that might meet Fullerton, in the latter's favour. On the first blush Colonel North was to be commended for a very natural desire to smooth the path for his matchless favourite; but when the pros and cons were fairly weighed, it was obvious that the proceeding was *not* a sportsmanlike one. In the first place, it would be grossly unfair on the nominators who were represented by his other dogs; and, secondly, were the great brindle to pull through under such circumstances, a substantial handle would be afforded his detractors for dragging in a host of 'ifs' and 'perhapses.'

Fortunately, it soon dawned on Fullerton's owner that he had made a mistake, and having arrived at such a conclusion, he lost no time in altering his tactics, and the result must have left him heartily thankful that he did so, though, as it happened, the old dog did not meet any of his kennel companions.

For the third time in the history of the contest a postponement on account of frost was found necessary; but the following Tuesday (February 23) a beginning was made. In both draws Colonel North may be said to have been favoured by fortune. In his first course, Fullerton made short work of Likeness, for he raced away quite six lengths and ran clean into his hare; and Maggie Miller in the first ties fared no better when opposed to him; for she failed to score a point, as the brindle led four lengths, and though momentarily thrown out at a dyke, managed to keep possession until the end.

The following day he came out like a giant refreshed, and then came across a foeman worthy of his steel in Rhymes—

indeed, there is no disguising the fact that his neck was fairly stretched, and at one time his opponent had won the course; but just failing to kill at the critical moment, the never-to-be-denied champion put in some of his finest work and pulled through. The course was one of the most interesting that the Cup contest has produced—which is saying a great deal—and the enthusiasm at the result was unbounded. It is thus technically described:—

To a good slip Fullerton led nearly three lengths and scored thrice; but Rhymes shot up as the hare broke away and rapidly put together a sequence of strong points and soon had matters equalised; he then made a bold attempt to kill and just failed; this let up Fullerton, who again scored twice, but he was not left in possession long, as his opponent joined in, and the hare taking them over some rough ground, quick exchanges followed; but at last the crack drew out, and scoring twice, smartly picked up his hare, and won.

His next victim was the puppy Patrick Blue, who had previously disposed of Great Fly and Burlador in smart fashion before being favoured by a bye through the withdrawal of Pleasant Nancy, who was lame; and though the white and black actually got his head in front when nearing the hare, he pecked and let up Fullerton, who flew the drain in grand style, and got up quite two lengths to the good. The puppy now crossed behind and managed to score a little one, but the other soon clinched matters by spinning round him, wrenching, and killing brilliantly.

The following day Fullerton was due to meet Racecourse, a very highly-fancied dog belonging to, and nominated by, Mr. Russel; but as he (Racecourse) had got away with a fresh hare after defeating a very smart puppy in Ivan the Great, and had been run to a standstill, odds of 7 to 1 were laid on the old dog, whilst 2 to 1 that he won outright was freely betted by his supporters. The former odds were fully justified, for whatever chance Racecourse may have possessed before the mishap alluded to, he now failed to make any impression on his opponent, who led three lengths, and running a magnificent course, ended with a particularly brilliant kill. The hare having broken across a drain, he was round on her scut like lightning, and pinned her down on landing before she could recover herself. Now came the final course, and excitement ran high when Fullerton and FitzFife were delivered to Bootiman. Certainly two more strikingly handsome greyhounds have never gone to slips to fight out the final stage of the great contest; well matched in size and symmetry, but not in colour, for FitzFife shows a deal of white—is, in fact, a white and brindle. He ran remarkably well in the 1891 Cup, but had the misfortune to be run to a complete standstill early in the contest. Seeing how he acquitted himself on this occasion, the Messrs. Fawcett are surely to be condoled with that, through her going amiss, they were unable to run Faster and Faster (the 1891 runner-up), who at home was always reckoned a good two lengths in front of FitzFife and quite as clever; albeit, Fullerton had already lowered her colours, and on form should have done so again, though great improvement was claimed for the bitch, whereas it was reasonable to suppose that the champion had lost some of his speed and dash. All this is a matter of speculation, for the question now to be settled was not, *Could* he beat Faster and Faster? but, *Would* he beat FitzFife? The latter had run quite well enough to promise an interesting struggle, having beaten successively Sir Sankey, Woodcote Green, Silver City, and Texture—the last-named, who is evidently an exceedingly smart bitch, somewhat luckily, as she was easily leading, but made a slight mistake at the drain, and FitzFife, making the most of his opportunity, had just won, when Texture shot up for a mutual kill; had the hare lived, in all probability the verdict would have been reversed—another case of 'if.'

To a good hare Bootiman despatched them on their fateful journey on capital terms, and everyone held breath as it was seen that the younger dog was holding his own for pace; but, nearing the hare, Fullerton put on a great spurt, drawing clear he reached her nearly two lengths ahead, and staying there scored the second; but puss, breaking round, gave FitzFife an opening, which he used to great purpose, as he shot up, scored once, and effected a very fine kill, Mr. Hedley's hat coming off, rather to the surprise of the skilled spectators,

The judge

for it certainly looked a good thing for Fullerton. However, the old coursing adage that no one can decide a trial but the judge is a good one, and doubtless on this occasion Mr. Hedley must have seen something that was lost to the general body of beholders. Anyhow, the excitement was protracted, and had lost none of its fever-heat when, for the second time, the doughty pair went to the slips, odds of 4 to 1 being laid.

This time the old dog was on his legs quickest and, making the best of his way, drew out a good four lengths for the turn and again scored decisively twice, the third being gained by his brilliantly sweeping round his opponent; a slight scrimmage now took place, out of which the younger dog came best, and he began to run up such a smart sequence that the odds were in jeopardy; but, not to be denied, the crack came again, a series of exchanges followed, and then FitzFife had an innings of small points. Meanwhile the hare had ringed, and they were approaching the slipper's shelter. With one of those mighty efforts that have distinguished him throughout his career, the great dog now drew past, and driving the hare before him very strongly over the bank, swept her up on the other side, and thus won what may fairly be termed his fourth successive Waterloo Cup.

Had the voting circulars as to the merits of greyhounds that form another chapter been sent out subsequent to this great achievement, surely Fullerton would have stood at the head of the poll, instead of occupying third place to Master McGrath and Bab-at-the-Bowster? That his equal has been seen we doubt—his superior we deny. Surely his detractors are now silent; where is the flaw in his reputation? In his early days he was decried as not being smart with his teeth: but this theory has been completely falsified by a succession of really brilliant kills. Long will it be before we see such another, and in bidding him farewell, we can only hope that he will live to reproduce a modicum of his own brilliancy in a long line of offspring; and that his stud achievements may rival if not outstrip those of his remarkable parents.

## WATERLOO CUP.—WINNERS

| Date | Winner | Colour | Sire | Dam | Owner |
|---|---|---|---|---|---|
| 1836 | Milanie | r. b. | Milo | Duchess | Lord Molyneux |
| 1837 | Fly | bk. b. | Tommy Roads | Fly | Mr. Stanton |
| 1838 | Bugle | be. d. | Batchelor | Nimble | Mr. Balls |
| 1839 | Empress | r. b. | Tramp | Nettle | Mr. Robinson |
| 1840 | Earwig | bk. d. | Hailstone | Pastime | Mr. Easterby |
| 1841 | Bloomsbury | r. d. | Redcap | by Walton (Sister to Preserve) | Mr. King |
| 1842 | Priam | f. w. d. | Emperor | Venus | Mr. Deakins |
| 1843 | Major | f. d. | Moses | Melon | Mr. G. Polloks |
| 1844 | Speculation | r. w. b. | Sandy | Enchantress | Mr. N. Slater |
| 1845 | Titania | bk. b. | Driver | Zoe | Mr. Temple |
| 1846 | Harlequin | bk. w. d. | Emperor | Lady | Mr. Sampson |
| 1847 | Senate | r. d. | Sadek | Sanctity | Lord Sefton |
| 1848 | Spade | bk. w. b. | Nonchalanee | Margery | Sir St. G. Gore |
| 1849 | Magician (Long) | bk. d. | King Cob | Magic | " |
| 1850 | Cerito (late Lucy | f. w. b. | Lingo | Wanton | Mr. G. F. Cooke |
| 1851 | Hughie Graham | f. d. | Liddesdale | Queen of the May | M. W. Sharpe |
| 1852 | Cerito | f. w. b. | Lingo | Wanton | Mr. G. F. Cooke |
| 1853 | " | " | " | " | " |
| 1854 | Sackcloth | bk. d. | Senate | Cinderella | Lord Sefton |
| 1855 | Judge | r. d. | John Bull | Fudge | Mr. Jefferson |
| 1856 | Protest | f. b. | Weapon | Pearl | Mr. W. Peacock |
| 1857 | King Lear | w. f. d. | Wigan | Repentance | Mr. W. Wilson |
| 1858 | Neville | f. d. | Autocrat | Catherine Hayes | Mr. S. Cass |
| 1859 | Clive | bk. b. | Judge | Moeris | J. Jardine |
| | Selby | bk. d. | Barrator | Ladylike | |
| 1860 | Maid of the Mill | r. b. | Judge | Bartolozzi | Mr. J. Blackstock |
| 1861 | Canaradzo | w. d. | Beacon | Scotland Yet | Mr. I. Campbell |
| 1862 | Roaring Meg | bk. b. | Beacon | Polly | Mr. Gregson |
| 1863 | Chloe | w. bk. b. | Judge | Clara | Mr. T. T. C. Lister |
| 1864 | King Death | w. bk. d. | Canaradzo | Annoyance | Dr. Richardson |
| 1865 | Meg | r. or f. b. | Terrona | Fanny Fickle | Mr. G. Carruthers |
| 1866 | Brigadier | bk. w. d. | Boreas | Wee Nel | Mr. Foulkes |
| 1867 | Lobelia | w bd. b. | Sea Foam | Lilac | Mr. W. J. Legh |
| 1868 | Master McGrath | bk.w.d.p. | Dervock | Lady Sarah | Lord Lurgan |
| 1869 | " (Covet) | " | " | " | " |
| 1870 | Sea Cove (late | r. b. p. | Strange Idea | Curiosity | Mr. J. Spinks |
| 1871 | Master McGrath | bk.w.d.p. | Dervock | Lady Sarah | Lord Lurgan |
| 1872 | Bed of Stone | f. b. | Portland | Imperatrice | Mr. J. Briggs |
| 1873 | Muriel | r. w. b. p. | Fusilier | Portia | Mr. R. Jardine |
| 1874 | Magnano | r. d. | Cauld Kail | Isoline | Mr. C. Morgan |
| 1875 | Honeymoon | bk. w. b. | Brigadier | Hebe | Mr. W. F. Hutchinson |
| 1876 | Donald | bk. d. | Master Burleigh | Phoenia | Mr. R. M. Douglas |
| 1877 | Coomassie | f. w. b. p. | Celebrated | Queen | Mr. R. Gittus |
| 1878 | " | " | " | " | Mr. T. Lay |
| 1879 | Misterton | bk.w.d.p. | Contango | Lina | Mr. H. G. Miller |
| 1880 | Honeywood | r. w. d. | Cavalier | Humming Bird | Earl of Haddington |
| 1881 | Princess Dagmar | w. b. d. b. | Ptarmigan | Gallant Foe | Mr. J. S. Postle |
| 1882 | Snowflight | bk. b. p. | Bothal Park | Curiosity | Mr. G. Hall |
| 1883 | Wild Mint | r. b. | Haddo | Orla | Mr. M. Osborne |
| 1884 | Mineral Water | w. bk. d. | Memento | Erzeroum | Mr. L. Mayer |
| 1885 | Bit of Fashion | bd.w.b.p. | Paris | Pretty Nell | Mr. E. Dent |
| | Miss Glendyne | b. d. b. p. | " | Lady Glendyne | Mr. C. Hibbert |
| 1886 | Miss Glendyne | " | " | " | " |
| 1887 | Greater Scott | bk. d. | Macpherson | Madge | Mr. R. F. Gladstone |
| | Herschel | r. d. p. | " | Stargazing II. | Mr. T. B. Hornby |
| 1888 | Burnaby | bk. w. d | Be Joyful | Baroness | Mr. L. Pilkington |
| 1889 | Fullerton | bd. d. p. | Greentick | Bit of Fashion | Colonel North |
| | Troughend | " | " | Toledo | " |
| 1890 | Fullerton | bd. d. | " | Bit of Fashion | " |
| 1891 | " | " | " | " | " |
| 1892 | " | " | " | " | " |

## WATERLOO CUP.—RUNNERS-UP

| Date | Runner-up | Colour | Sire | Dam | Owner |
|---|---|---|---|---|---|
| 1836 | Mocking | [illegible] d | Harvest | Fly | Mr. Morris |
| 1837 | Dr. Fop | bk. w. d. | Bob Logic | Spitfire | Mr. Sparel |
| 1838 | Bird (late Village) | r. b | [illegible] | Minion | Mr. [illegible] |
| 1839 | Frenchi | [illegible] h. | Jupiter | Bellmaid | Mr. Russell |
| 1840 | Emperor | [illegible] d | Hailstone | Fly | Mr. Easterby |
| 1841 | Needler | [illegible] w. d | Old Sailor | Fanny | Mr. Brooks |
| 1842 | Rustic | r. d | Bingarn | Lady | Mr. Bradley |
| 1843 | [illegible] | [illegible] d | Monarch | Nysie | Mr. N. Slater |
| 1844 | Drummer | bk. w. b | [illegible] | [illegible] | Mr. Cruise |
| 1845 | Sheriff | bk. d | Kestwick | [illegible] | Mr. B. Smith |
| 1846 | Oliver Twist | [illegible] | [illegible] | [illegible] | Mr. Ormsall |
| 1847 | Fan | r. b | Marquis | Coquette | Mr. W. Webb |
| 1848 | Smut | bk. w. b. | [illegible] | [illegible] | Mr. [illegible] |
| 1849 | Forward | bk. d | [illegible] | [illegible] | Mr. Temple |
| 1850 | [illegible] | r. [illegible] d | Sam | [illegible] | Mr. [illegible] |
| 1851 | Stewmaker | bk. d | Foremost | [illegible] | Lord Sefton |
| 1852 | Lampton | [illegible] d. | Calderwade | [illegible] | Mr. G. F. Henderson |
| 1853 | Movement | bk. w. b | [illegible] | [illegible] | Mr. [illegible] |
| 1854 | [illegible] | [illegible] d | [illegible] | [illegible] | Mr. [illegible] Henderson |
| 1855 | [illegible] | [illegible] | Wigan | [illegible] | Mr. Campbell |
| 1856 | Judge | [illegible] d | John Bull | Fudge | Mr. Jefferson |
| 1857 | Sunbeam | [illegible] d | [illegible] | [illegible] | [illegible] |
| 1858 | [illegible] | [illegible] | Ben | [illegible] | Mr. T. D[illegible] |
| 1859 | Divided | — | | — | — |
| 1860 | [illegible] | [illegible] | Sky Rocket | [illegible] | Lord Sefton |
| 1861 | [illegible] | [illegible] | Wilton | Fanny | Mr. J. [illegible] |
| 1862 | [illegible] | bk. w. b | Judge | [illegible] | Mr. J. [illegible] |
| 1863 | Rota | [illegible] | [illegible] | Lady | Mr. H. Haywood |
| 1864 | | | | | |
| 1865 | King Lear | [illegible] d | Canaradzo | [illegible] | Mr. [illegible] |
| 1866 | [illegible] | [illegible] | [illegible] | [illegible] | Mr. F. [illegible] |
| 1867 | [illegible] | bk. b | Patent | [illegible] | Mr. Haywood |
| 1868 | [illegible] | [illegible] | King Death | [illegible] | Mr. T. J. G. Lister |
| 1869 | [illegible] | [illegible] | [illegible] | [illegible] | Mr. [illegible] |
| 1870 | Bendimere | [illegible] | Cardinal [illegible] | [illegible] | Lord [illegible] |
| 1871 | [illegible] | [illegible] | [illegible] | [illegible] | Mr. W. H. [illegible] |
| 1872 | Peasant Boy | [illegible] | [illegible] | [illegible] | Mr. A. Smith |
| 1873 | | — | | | |
| 1874 | [illegible] | [illegible] | Sir William | [illegible] | Mr. [illegible] |
| 1875 | Corby Castle | [illegible] | [illegible] | [illegible] | Mr. [illegible] Cunningham |
| 1876 | Lord Glendyne | [illegible] | [illegible] | [illegible] | Mr. [illegible] |
| 1877 | Braw Lass | [illegible] | [illegible] | [illegible] | Mr. [illegible] |
| 1878 | [illegible] | [illegible] | Master Frederick | [illegible] | Lord [illegible] |
| 1879 | Commerce | [illegible] | [illegible] | [illegible] | Mr. [illegible] Carruthers |
| 1880 | Flower | [illegible] | [illegible] | [illegible] | Mr. J. [illegible] |
| 1881 | [illegible] | [illegible] | Barleycorn | [illegible] | Mr. [illegible] |
| 1882 | [illegible] | [illegible] | [illegible] | [illegible] | Earl of Haddington |
| 1883 | [illegible] | [illegible] | [illegible] Park | [illegible] | Mr. [illegible] |
| 1884 | [illegible] | [illegible] | [illegible] | [illegible] | Mr. [illegible] |
| 1885 | Divided | | — | — | |
| 1886 | Penelope II | [illegible] | Macpherson | [illegible] | Mr. R. [illegible] |
| 1887 | Divided | — | | | |
| 1888 | Duke Macpherson | [illegible] | Macpherson | [illegible] | Colonel North |
| 1889 | Divided | | — | | |
| 1890 | [illegible] | [illegible] | — | — | Mr. [illegible] |
| 1891 | [illegible] | [illegible] | Northern Express | | [illegible] |
| 1892 | [illegible] | [illegible] | [illegible] | | |

# CHAPTER II

## A TREATISE ON BREEDING

In giving Misterton a place amongst greyhounds of the past, we must use him as a connecting link with the dogs of the day, or his blood is intimately intermingled with the running strains, and his puppies were so recently running with success. Later on we shall give a table of this remarkable dog's winning progeny, together with those of Macpherson and Greentick, the former of whom predeceased Misterton; but the latter still flourishes and adds laurels to his crown as a sire as surely as the seasons come round. Now, as a basis for breeding winners, we should take these three dogs as primary sires, representing as they do a long line of highly successful ancestors, and on them we should ring the changes and embody the Glendyne and Clyto family. An indiscriminate use of these dogs or their representatives would, of course, be futile, and due regard must be had to size, constitution, temperament, faulty points, points of excellence and other details that command a breeder's closest attention; but when once a successful 'nick' has been discovered, it should be closely adhered to, if not on identical, at any rate on similar, that is to say collateral, lines; such, for example, as the union of Beacon with Scotland Yet, one to which we shall have to make frequent reference in a subsequent chapter, which produced Canaradzo, Sea Foam, Sea Pink, Cioloja, Bugle, and through them a host of high-class winners. In recent times we have good examples in the produce of Misterton and Lady Lizzie, Misterton and Gulnare II. (which includes Mullingar, Habeas Corpus, Ayala,

Glenmahra, Hibernian, &c.), Macpherson and Rota (Happy Rondelle, Have a Care, Iulus, Rotula, &c.), Macpherson and Stargazing II., Ptarmigan and Gallant Foe, Greentick and Tonic, Greentick and Bit of Fashion (Fullerton, Jupon Vert, Kate Cuthbert, Young Fullerton, Simonian, Netherwitton, &c.), Greentick and Governess (Greengage, Greengoose, Greenhouse and Greenstick).

It will be interesting to scan the respective pedigrees of these well-mated ones, and try to discover to what the success of their progeny is attributable. To begin with, let us take the Misterton-Gulnare II. combination. Gulnare II. was bred by Mr. Horner, and was by his dog Harfagar out of his Herrenhausen. Now here is a bitch possessed of good stout blood, traceable to the strains that are most noticeable in the pedigrees of Waterloo winners. Harfagar was by Harold (sire of Saxon King) by Farrier by Cavalier, son of Cauld Kail; whilst Gulnare, dam of Harold, was a granddaughter of Master McGrath on her sire's side, and a great-granddaughter of Canaradzo on her dam's side. Herrenhausen owns a different infusion altogether, but is a descendant of Cock Robin (grandson of Canaradzo) and Glimpse of Glory (Goodlake's strain). Turning back to Misterton's pedigree, we find it full of Canaradzo blood, whilst his maternal grandsire is Cock Robin, so that the cross is identical with that which produced Saxon King, whose dam, Locomotion, was a granddaughter of Contango. Here is an example of constant but discreet inbreeding to a famous strain, but when the performances of the produce are looked to a curious fact presents itself. The *pace* of the family is concentrated in Mullingar, whose great *forte* was speed; all the rest are deficient (as regards first class) in that respect, though all are stout honest runners. In conformation they are of good size and strongly built, with plenty of bone and good legs and feet, though some show a tendency to coarseness.

Now that Misterton is dead, breeders who want to follow up the line indicated must make choice of a successor, and that choice will naturally fall on Mullingar, as his performances will bear looking into, and his speed is undeniable; moreover, such of his stock as we have seen are full of promise. In fact, we are convinced that a carefully selected combination of Mullingar with Macpherson bitches will assuredly produce high-class winners. Our own dog Habeas Corpus was a sticker of the first water with fair speed, and he kept on winning. That Mullingar was a dog of very great courage we take leave to doubt, and on one occasion we saw him deliberately 'cut it.' Next we will analyse the Macpherson-Rota combination. MacPherson himself was got by Master Sam, son of Contango, and one of the speediest dogs ever slipped, whilst his dam, Annie Macpherson, was by Fusilier (a grandson of Judge), so that there is no doubt about his running blood. Rota was by Balfe (a son of Contango) out of Ruby III. Now it may be held that the cross between a Misterton dog and a Macpherson bitch is carrying inbreeding to a dangerous extent; but, supposing there is no constitutional weakness on either side, and taking care that the Misterton dog has a fresh strain on his dam's side, and that the Macpherson bitch has a like advantage, we maintain that the happiest results may be expected.

We will now pass on to the Ptarmigan-Gallant Foe combination, which includes a Waterloo winner in Princess Dagmar, Paris (sire of Miss Glendyne and Bit of Fashion, hence grandsire of Fullerton), and Jester (sire of Huic Holloa and other winners noted for speed). Here, indeed, we have a grand running strain. Ptarmigan was by Contango, and his dam is inbred to the Canaradzo strain, with a telling admixture of Cauld Kail's desirable blood. Gallant Foe also has plenty of the grand vein, but one remarkable fact in her pedigree is that her dam, Maggie Smith, is descended from a union of Beacon, not with his ever-successful and legitimate spouse, Scotland Yet, but with Miss Nightingale. A careful study of Princess Dagmar's pedigree (p. 122), and a comparison with that of Misterton and Macpherson, will show how similar they are, and how the same telling blood stands out clearly defined in each. Paris is dead, but this variety of the strain is ably represented by Jester, who is a remarkably fine handsome dog, and whose stock, as we have remarked above, are nearly always possessed of a fine turn of speed. Gay City, too, is bred on similar lines, being by Paris—Lady Glendyne, hence own brother to Miss Glendyne. His first batch of saplings, or rather such as we have seen of them, are hardly to our liking; but it seems as if this dog, himself a brilliant performer, is absolutely certain to get some big winners in the future. He is a remarkably handsome dog, but his back is as level as a billiard board, his tail is set on too high, and he carries it badly. We remember judging at a show where he was a competitor, and he had to put up with second place to a dog of Dr. Salter's, faultless in conformation, but who in these running days would have had to 'look on' from a respectful distance if he had been slipped with the dashing red. So much for show points.

Now we come to Greentick, and we take the union of that game and honest dog with Bit of Fashion (a speedy, though somewhat flashy bitch, but one of the best-looking ones we have ever seen) as productive of indubitably the best greyhound of our time. Bit of Fashion's dam, Pretty Nell, was by Country Man out of an unnamed f. w. bitch by Willie Wylie—Miss Johnson (a granddaughter of Canaradzo), whence it will be seen that she is outbred to a considerable extent, and as her dam produced London (a good winner and sire of winners) to Pathfinder (by Ptarmigan—Gallant Foe) we may feel assured that the cross is a successful one. Besides Fullerton and Bit of Fashion in her first litter, she threw Yooi Over (Jupon Vert), Yo Doit and Kate Cuthbert, all winners, her second lot including Young Fullerton, Simonian, Netherwhitton, Over the Alt, &c. From a cross of Greentick with Miss Glendyne great things were naturally expected, but the result was rather disappointing. One of the progeny, a blue brindle dog called Cagliostro, ran in the Waterloo Cup of 1890, and after cleverly defeating Hughie Fearon in the Purse, was put out by the speedy Plymouth Rock, though, had the hare lived a bit longer, the verdict might have gone the other way. Struck by the dog's good looks and his clever performance in the previous round, Mr. William Ingram and the writer purchased him from Mr. Hibbert.[1]

Unfortunately Macpherson himself is dead, but he has left four good dogs to represent him—viz. Herschel and Lance Macpherson (out of Stargazing II.), Jock Macpherson, and Greater Scot (out of Madge). Of these our choice would fall on the first and last named, though their puppies have yet to make their *début*, and Jock and Lance have already sired several good winners. We have never seen Jock, but some of his saplings have not the best of legs.

Having rung the changes on these three branches of the Canaradzo family, we may find it necessary to breed out again, and we must look out for a strain that is fairly remote, though it is hard to find any good greyhound that has not the Scotland Yet quarterings on his coat-of-arms ; but a few years back Mr. Crosse owned a good greyhound in Clyto. A short study of his pedigree shows a digression from the strongly marked line that we have indicated, and he was a dog that got a large number of winners, though few if any were of the very first order. The most promising of his sons was perhaps Holmby, and next to him Clytorus, who, after dividing the Plumpton Stakes and showing a fine turn of speed, fell and injured himself so badly at Kempton that he could never be trained again. His dam, Mabel, was by the Canaradzo dog Crossfell, which proves the efficacy of the cross. Clyto himself was by Caleb Garth, a dog inbred to David and going back through his sire, Racing Hopfactor, to Senate, Hannah, and Tollwife, and through his dam, who was by Brigadier, to Figaro. Clyto's dam was Clytie by Howden out of Acute, the former being a grandson of David and the latter a great-granddaughter of the

[1] In her next litter by Fullerton, Miss Glendyne threw Not Out, a useful dog. Miss Glendyne died in 1891.

same dog, so he was well inbred to a good old-fashioned strain, while the only trace of Scotland Yet blood is through Sea Foam, maternal grandsire of Howden. Hence, if a dog by Misterton out of a Clyto bitch were crossed with a bitch by Greentick out of a Paris or Jester bitch, we should get a grand concentration of running blood. The value of Clyto as a stud dog was evidenced by his getting 33 winners and dividers from his first season's puppies, and eight saplings out of a Misterton bitch fetched 600*l.* at auction ; so the cross was evidently appreciated.

The difficulty is to find a Clyto dog whose efforts at the stud have met with marked success. We cannot say we altogether like the running of the progeny of Clytorus, but we should have no hesitation in using Holmby, and his first batch of puppies were decidedly smart. His dam, High Opinion, was by Good Authority out of H. P., and through the latter (a granddaughter of King Death) he has a dash of Canaradzo blood. Fury, dam of H. P., was a granddaughter of David, and as Good Authority was by Howden (sire of Clytie, Clyto's dam), we find very close inbreeding to the Tollwife strain, which is very stout, physically and morally. This, then, is, in our opinion, the dog to use to Misterton bitches ; he was a sterling greyhound and won forty courses in public, setting a seal to his performances by securing the Kempton Park Grand Champion Prize. All the Clytos are distinguished for quality, a matter of great consideration when we have in view the tendency to coarseness shown by some of the Greenticks, especially those inbred to Contango.

Another useful dog by Clyto is Clyto IV., who has size and substance, and is free from Contango blood, his dam being Governess, a thorough winner-producer, as when put to Greentick she threw Greengage, Greenstick, and Greenhouse, who between them won over sixty courses their first season : hence Clyto IV. should suit either Misterton or Greentick bitches or those that combine their blood. A very valuable strain is that of Cui Bono, who was a decided success at the stud. He was by Gone, by Strange Idea—Gaudy Poll, and his dam was Ruby (sister to Rota), a most remarkable bitch, as she was not only a fine performer, but as a matron she threw such first-class performers, besides Cui Bono, as Rhodora, Romney, Rufina, Rufus, Radiant (dam of Fluttering Fersen and Happy Omen), Hector, Edwina Balfe, &c.

Calix and Clamor are both by Cui Bono, and though neither is free from Canaradzo blood, the strain that they have will prove beneficial, even with bitches that are inbred thereto. A dog that possesses this blood already fused with that of Greentick is Edwin Greentick, and as he combines two crosses of Bab-at-the-Bowster and one each of Bed of Stone, Ruby and Rebe, he may be considered one of the best-bred dogs of the day, and should not want for patronage. We are under the impression that he never ran, having met with an accident when in training; his dam was that flying bitch Edwina Balfe, own sister to Hector.

Of course there are numerous high-class dogs worthy the attention of breeders of to-day, and in making the foregoing remarks we have but indicated certain strains that we opine should never be lost sight of, and have pointed out a few of the choicest dogs available for carrying out the theory we uphold. Before touching on the practical procedure of greyhound breeding, we must not omit to mention a noticeable failing, and a very serious one, to be observed in the produce of Greentick. For the time he has been at the stud this dog has sired more winners than any greyhound that preceded him, and the number of sons and daughters which he has had running for him in 1890 was something remarkable. His puppies kept winning good stakes; but his second-season produce, with a few notable exceptions, trained off to an extraordinary extent. Troughend is an example of this, and a score of others could be mentioned; the one marked exception that proves the rule being the mighty Fullerton, who, good as he was as a puppy, went to slips for his second Waterloo Cup a better greyhound in every respect. We do not think that a search through Greentick's pedigree will expose the weak spot, but we feel confident that the cause is not far to seek, and that it is because the dog's physical powers have been overtaxed, for his early successes at the stud did not escape notice. As a rule his stock are particularly robust and stout in their early days, and the decline of energy and vital power is not noticeable until their second season comes round. It will be interesting to watch the future progress of his progeny, and it is devoutly to be hoped that the same falling off will not be apparent when the seasons come round. As a useful index to those crosses that have proved most efficacious, we give a table of winners of sixteen dog stakes and upwards with names of their dams, got by Misterton Macpherson, and Greentick respectively; following this will be found the tabulated pedigrees of some of the most celebrated stud dogs of the day, and of those that are dead but that are directly represented.

After perusing the tables of winners springing from the loins of Misterton, Macpherson, and Greentick, the intending breeder can have little doubt as to the success that has constantly attended the strains that have been indicated. We have already thrown out a few hints as to inbreeding, in fact our whole argument as followed out in this chapter is entirely in favour of the practice if not carried too far, and if conducted not only with common sense, intelligence, and a general knowledge of physiology, but with what is of still greater service, experience. Take a dog and bitch descended from a common ancestor of marked type or peculiarity; neither may show the remotest trace of its origin, neither may they resemble each other in any way, yet the produce of their union are usually reproductions of the aforesaid common ancestor, sometimes wonderfully like, but always recognisable. The natural inference is that any great greyhound can be reproduced simply by mating descendants, and that all a breeder has to do is to follow this theory and produce a succession of Master McGraths, Coomassies, Miss Glendynes, and Fullertons; but such is not the case, and for this reason.

The *general resemblance* of the product of your sagacity to his (or her) illustrious ancestor may be striking in a degree; but take measurements and you will find wide discrepancies, and even when points are well balanced and measurements in due proportion, there is often something wanting when the subject is asked to display his prowess; when the weak point, moral or physical, is discovered, our breeder must search for it amongst his *other* ancestors; and with a view to the next generation must mate him (or her) with one claiming descent sufficiently remote from the same common ancestor and being entirely free from the blood of that dog or bitch from whom he (or she) inherited the fault.

A perusal of the tabulated pedigrees herein printed will show that certain strains bear inbreeding very much better than others. Where a particular dog or bitch is concerned success may almost invariably attend the experiment, and yet an attempt to inbreed to a brother or sister of that dog or bitch may meet with hopeless failure, the probability being that some constitutional weakness exists in the latter which is accentuated by the process of inbreeding. Notable instances of success in this particular are Scotland Yet, King Cob, Tollwife, Cauld Kail, and Judge. Of these Scotland Yet is the most striking example, for not only was inbreeding to this bitch herself eminently successful, but it seems to be possible to carry it to any extent, as witness the results of in-breeding to Canaradzo, Bab-at-the-Bowster, and Contango. Several great greyhounds have had four and five crosses of Tollwife, generally through her son David; and the blood of King Cob, Cauld Kail, and Judge generally lends itself readily to the experiment. The question is where to stop; and we are far from advocating incestuous union, though we have known even that productive of winning greyhounds. In most cases puny rickety whelps would be the result, which, if they escaped the ravages of distemper—a most unlikely contingency—would never be worth training, and might probably exhibit signs of mental deficiency or highly timid and nervous temperaments. There might be exceptions, and supposing a sound, strong bitch to be produced by the incestuous intercourse of a brother and sister, a father and daughter, or a son and mother—supposing this bitch to turn out a fairly good performer and eventually to be mated with a dog of a distinct strain—it is possible, nay, probable, that the progeny would distinguish themselves; that is, if their incestuous grandparents were the representatives of a robust and successful strain. Personally we are testing this theory, and so far it has been borne out to the letter; but the difficulty in procuring a strong and healthy bitch as the result of too close inbreeding is so great that we do not advise our readers to follow our example; for in our case the original dam was the result of an accidental union of brother and sister, and we should not have thought of deliberately setting about such an experiment; but having thus produced a winning bitch that was likewise blessed with a hardy constitution, we bred out, and in her first litter she produced a winner, and in her next (to Greentick) she had four. There is one noticeable peculiarity in this bitch which may be attributable to her origin: she has had three litters, but twice she has only thrown two puppies and once four.

Having now discussed the theory of breeding, we will proceed to the practical part, which is quite as important, though it does not afford so much food for reflection, certain data being always present, and years of experience having immutably fixed the mode of procedure.

## MISTERTON

| NAME | DAM | WON |
|---|---|---|
| Aberbrinnt | Promotion | — |
| Aber Menai | Truthful | — |
| " | " | — |
| " | " | — |
| Away | Merry Heart II. | Quarrington Stakes |
| Allegroist | Ettrick | Westraw Purse |
| Alice Daisy | Graceful Girl | — |
| Apperley (late Shipley) | Mermaiden | Tenant Farmers' Stakes |
| Bermondsey | Lady Lizzie | Durling Stakes |
| " | " | — |
| " | " | — |
| Bessie May | Flywheel | — |
| Braggart | Merry Maid II. | — |
| Bronze | Speculation | — |
| Bloomsbury | " | — |
| Bog Oak | " | Wandon Lodge Stakes |
| Bouquet of Beauties | Nell | — |
| Blink | Sister to Alec Halliday | — |
| Brewer's Boy | Graceful Girl | — |
| Bank Street | Fairation | Redshank Stakes |
| Branston | Burglary | — |
| Baseball (vide Go Bang II.) | — | — |
| Cherry | Clytie | — |
| Coronet | Hark Forward | — |
| Cotillon | Waltzing Kate | — |
| " | " | — |
| Cymbeline | Merry Heart II. | Brough Cup |
| Clamontes | Ripe Cherry | — |
| Cottage Nymph | Cottage Maid | Hassocks Stakes |
| Countess Lilian | Lady Macbeth | — |
| Countess Dudley | " | — |
| Crown Point | Rose Marie | — |
| Donington | Deborah | — |
| Eltham Lad | Durable | — |
| Freewill | Village Girl | — |
| Fusilier II. | Foam Belle | Tenants' Cup |
| Gaily | Tennis Ball | — |
| " | " | — |
| Gladsome | Merry Maid II. | — |
| " | " | Craven Cup |
| Glenbloom | Mary Hill | Brighton Cup |
| " | " | — |
| Glencotho | Glengowan | — |
| " | " | — |
| " | " | Scarisbrooke Cup |
| " | " | Hesketh Cup |
| Glenkirn | " | — |
| Glaucus | Hilda | October Stakes |
| Glenmahra | Gulnare II. | Olanteigh Stakes |
| Glenmaid | Redemption | — |
| Gorse | Hertha | — |
| Giuseppe | Mascotte | — |
| Go Bang II. | Tennis Ball | Adderley Stakes |
| " | " | — |
| Glenkirk | Glengowan | — |
| " | " | — |
| Happy Hampton | Corsica | Ashford Stakes |

## MISTERTON

| Meeting. | [illegible] | Meeting. | Season. |
|---|---|---|---|
| | Misterton Stakes | Haydock | [illegible] |
| — | [illegible] Stakes | Lichfield | [illegible] |
| — | Anglesey Cup | | 1884–6 |
| — | [illegible] Stakes | Wappenbury | [illegible] |
| Stratford | | | [illegible] |
| Carmarthen | | | [illegible] |
| | New Grange Stakes | [illegible] | 1887 |
| Dickensmiths | Second [illegible] | Kelmarsh | [illegible] |
| | [illegible] Stakes | | |
| Cliffe and Hundred of Hoo | [illegible] Stakes | Wye | [illegible] |
| — | " | " | [illegible] |
| | Hythe Stakes | " | [illegible] |
| | South Lancashire Stakes | Kilgrove Club | 1880–6 |
| | Maiden Stakes | Wye | [illegible] |
| | [illegible] Stakes | Lichfield | [illegible] |
| | Counties Stakes | Cliffe | [illegible] |
| Lichfield | | | [illegible] |
| — | [illegible] Cup | Corbrook | 1879–6 |
| — | [illegible] Stakes | Mid Annandale | [illegible] |
| | Lichfield Stakes | Lichfield | [illegible] |
| Lanark Pen | | | [illegible] |
| | [illegible] Stakes | [illegible] | [illegible] |
| | [illegible] Stakes | Hoddington | [illegible] |
| | [illegible] Derby | [illegible] | [illegible] |
| | [illegible] Stakes (Jun.) | Wye | [illegible] |
| — | (Aber.) | " | 1880–8 |
| Darlington Club | | | [illegible] |
| | [illegible] Stakes | Plumpton | [illegible] |
| Plumpton | | | [illegible] |
| | Wye Oaks | Wye | 1887–8 |
| | [illegible] Stakes | | 1887–9 |
| | [illegible] Stakes | Haydock | [illegible] |
| — | [illegible] Stakes | Plumpton | [illegible] |
| — | [illegible] Stakes | Wye | [illegible] |
| | Monmouth Stakes | Berkeley | [illegible] |
| Corne | | | [illegible] |
| — | [illegible] Stakes | Mid Annandale | [illegible] |
| | [illegible] Stakes | South Lancashire | 1880 |
| — | [illegible] Stakes | Lichfield | [illegible] |
| Ashdown | | — | [illegible] |
| Plumpton | | | [illegible] |
| | [illegible] Stakes | [illegible] | [illegible] |
| | Border Union Stakes | Border Union | [illegible] |
| — | St. [illegible] Cup | Mid Annandale | [illegible] |
| Southport | | | 1887–8 |
| Kelford | | | [illegible] |
| | [illegible] Stakes | Haydock | 1884–6 |
| Haydock | | | [illegible] |
| Wye | | | [illegible] |
| | [illegible] Stakes | [illegible] | [illegible] |
| | Wye Derby | Wye | [illegible] |
| — | [illegible] Stakes | [illegible] | [illegible] |
| Market Drayton | | | [illegible] |
| | Second [illegible] Stakes | Market Drayton | [illegible] |
| — | [illegible] Stakes | Haydock | [illegible] |
| | [illegible] Gold Cup | [illegible] | [illegible] |
| Wye | | | [illegible] |

## MISTERTON—

| Name | Dam | Won |
|---|---|---|
| Harraby . . . | Hook | — |
| Hieland Fly . . | Sall o' the Mill | Ashdown Stakes |
| " | " | Scarisbrooke Cup |
| " | " | Burscough Cup |
| Hibernian . . . | Gulnare II. | Cowley Cup |
| " | " | Wallasea Stakes |
| Homers' Claim . . | Hilda | — |
| Hone Lassie . . | Go | Dover Stakes (No. 1) |
| Heavy Cavalry . . | Hilda | — |
| Habeas Corpus . . | Gulnare II. | — |
| " | " | — |
| Ivy Green . . . . | Arama | — |
| Jealous Squaw (late Wild-girl) | Woodsdown | Bagley Cup |
| " | " | Westminster Stakes |
| " | " | — |
| Jolly Mystery (late Bonny Glen) | Mermaiden | — |
| Kilkoo . . . | Koriata | Roche's Point Stakes |
| Kilkiel . . | " | — |
| King Cole . . | Lyonese | — |
| " | " | Quarrington Stakes |
| Knockshea . . | Koriata | Second Southern Club Stakes |
| Kilchief . . . . | " | — |
| " | " | Scarva Stakes |
| " | " | — |
| Longest Day . | Flywheel | — |
| " | " | — |
| " | " | Buccleuch Cup |
| Mada . . . . | Mermaiden | Southminster Oaks |
| Magic . . . . | Arama | Beaudesert Stakes |
| " | " | — |
| Maid of Kellena . . | Madcap Violet | — |
| Maidstone . . . . | Princess Dagmar | — |
| Matin Bells . . . | Joyful | — |
| " | " | Tenants' Cup |
| " | " | — |
| Miranda . . . | Promotion | — |
| Miss Baxter . . | Flywheel | St. Mungo's Cup |
| " | " | Queensberry Stakes |
| Mullingar . . . | Gulnare II. | Cardinal Wolsey Stakes |
| " | " | Gold Cup |
| " | " | — |
| Master Tom Harbison . | Mrs. Eliza | — |
| " | " | September Stakes |
| " | " | — |
| " | " | — |
| " | " | — |
| " | " | — |
| Miss Avon . . . . | Avon Beauty | Conington Stakes |
| Miss Harries . . . | Romanoffski | — |
| " | " | — |
| Missing Son . . . | Now or Never | — |
| Maggie Park . . . | Glengowan | — |
| Mid Lincoln . . | Memorial | — |
| My Dear . . . | Ma Chère | — |
| Northern Express . | Prenez Garde | — |
| Phantom II. . | Speculation | Lady Hill Stakes |

*continued*

| Meeting | Divided | Meeting | Season |
|---|---|---|---|
| — | Dinnington Stakes | Gosforth | 1888–9 |
| Haydock | — | — | 1885–6 |
| — | — | — | 1886–7 |
| Burscough | — | — | 1887–8 |
| Southminster | — | — | 1888–9 |
| Rochford Hundred | — | — | 1888–9 |
| — | Dullingham St. Leger | Dullingham | 1885–6 |
| Wye | — | — | 1888–9 |
| — | Hasting Stakes | Plumpton | 1887–8 |
| — | Hassocks Stakes | " | 1888–9 |
| — | Brook Stakes | Wye | 1889–90 |
| — | Cliffe Stakes | Cliffe and Hundred of Hoo | 1889–90 |
| Bagley | — | — | 1884–5 |
| Kempton | — | — | 1885–6 |
| — | Leamington Stakes | Wappenbury | 1886–7 |
| — | Second Gold Cup | Haydock | 1889–90 |
| Southern Club Ireland | Needham Purse | North of Ireland Union | 1884–5 |
| — | " | " | 1884–5 |
| — | Maiden Stake | Wye | 1884–5 |
| Sleaford | — | — | 1886–7 |
| Southern Club Ireland | — | — | 1884–5 |
| — | Downshire Stakes | Banbridge | 1887–8 |
| Banbridge | — | — | 1888–9 |
| — | Purdysburn Stakes | Purdysburn | 1889–90 |
| — | Carmichael Cup | Carmichael | 1884–5 |
| — | Carmichael Stakes | " | 1887–8 |
| Upper Nithsdale | " | " | 1885–6 |
| Southminster | — | — | 1889–90 |
| Lichfield | — | — | 1884–5 |
| — | Beaudesert Stakes | Lichfield | 1885–6 |
| — | Earlstown Stakes | Haydock | 1884–5 |
| — | Garrick Stakes | Kempton | 1885–6 |
| — | Eldon Stakes | Gosforth | 1885–6 |
| Lower Gosforth | — | — | 1886–7 |
| — | Prestwick Stakes | " | 1887–8 |
| — | Tibbers Castle Stakes | Upper Nithsdale | 1885–6 |
| Mid-Annandale | — | — | 1885–6 |
| Upper Nithsdale | — | — | 1885–6 |
| Kempton | — | — | 1885–6 |
| Gosforth | — | — | 1886–7 |
| — | Kilmorey Cup | Mourne Park | 1888–9 |
| — | " | " | 1886–7 |
| Northern Club | — | | 1887–8 |
| — | " | " | 1887–8 |
| — | Killingworth Stakes | Gosforth | 1887–8 |
| — | Kilmorey Stakes | " | 1887–8 |
| — | Blagdon Stakes | " | 1887–8 |
| Carmichael | — | — | 1886–7 |
| — | Paget Stakes | Lichfield | 1886–7 |
| — | Southport Stakes | Southport | 1886–7 |
| — | Newton Stakes | Haydock | 1886–7 |
| — | " | " | 1886–7 |
| — | Dudley Maiden Stakes | Gosforth | 1888–9 |
| — | First Club Stakes | Cliffe and Hundred of Hoo | 1889–90 |
| — | Trabolgan Stakes | Trabolgan | 1886–7 |
| Haydock | — | — | 1884–5 |

## MISTERTON—

| Name | Dam | Won |
|---|---|---|
| Phantom II. | Speculation | |
| Penalty | Durable | |
| Possum | Glengowan | — |
| " | " | — |
| " | " | Sefton Stakes |
| Rainbow | Rosemary | — |
| Rebound | Gulnare II. | — |
| Royal Prince | Regal Court | — |
| " | " | — |
| Ruby IV. | Hopper | — |
| Run Forward | Hark Forward | — |
| Revolt | Cottage Maid | — |
| Sewing Maid | Stitch in Time | — |
| " | " | Carmichael Cup |
| " | " | — |
| Soprano | Adelaide | Cowley Cup |
| " | " | — |
| Sorcerer (late Shopwalker) | Lady Lizzie | Heath Stakes |
| " | " | — |
| " | " | — |
| Spider II. | Star of Woodcote | Hordley Stakes |
| " | " | Anglesey Cup |
| Spinage | | — |
| Settling Day | Sally Day | — |
| " | " | — |
| " | " | — |
| " | " | — |
| Sister Eliza | Lady Jessie | — |
| Stronghow | Graceful Girl | — |
| " | " | — |
| Sarah Day | Sally Day | Rufford Stakes |
| Sallie Day | " | De Grey Jubilee Cup |
| Swaffham | Star of Woodcote | Craven Challenge Cup |
| Startaway | Go | First Club Cup |
| Stonebow | Fairation | — |
| " | " | — |
| Swan | Graceful Girl | Farmers' Stakes |
| Talbot | Ladybird | — |
| Très Bien | Truthful | — |
| Twenty Five | Lady Lizzie | — |
| The Guv'nor | Redemption | Isle of Grain Stakes |
| " | " | — |
| The Slut | The Squaw | The Oaks |
| " | " | — |
| The Bard | Gulnare II. | — |
| " | " | — |
| " | " | — |
| Veracity | Truthful | — |
| Wainfleet | Lady Lizzie | Hamsey Stakes |
| Welsh Gem | Gulnare II. | — |
| Willoughby | Wheel of Fortune | — |
| Woman in Black | Promotion | — |
| Wine Bottles | Madcap Violet | — |
| " | " | — |
| Westrup | Lyonese | Old Sleaford Stakes |
| Winchelsea | Redemption | Preston Stakes |
| Woodcote | " | Chapel Bridge Stakes |
| " | " | — |

continued

| Meeting | [illegible] | [illegible] | [illegible] |
|---|---|---|---|
| — | Westminster Stakes | Ecclestone | [illegible] |
| — | Lytham Cup | Lytham | [illegible] |
| — | Lancashire Stakes | Haydock | [illegible] |
| | [illegible] Stakes | | [illegible] |
| Altcar | Derby Stakes | Hookersiffe | [illegible] |
| — | [illegible] Stakes | Gosforth | [illegible] |
| — | St. Leger | Cliffe and Hundred of Hoo | [illegible] |
| — | | | |
| | Chiltern Stakes | Wye | [illegible] |
| — | Wye Stakes | " | [illegible] |
| — | Champion Stakes | [illegible] | [illegible] |
| — | [illegible] Stakes | Wye | [illegible] |
| — | Gravesend Stakes | Cliffe and Hundred of Hoo | [illegible] |
| — | Corrie Cup | Corrie | [illegible] |
| Cambridge | | | [illegible] |
| — | Lytham Cup | Ridgway | [illegible] |
| Southminster | | | [illegible] |
| | [illegible] Stakes | Lytham | [illegible] |
| Haydock | | | [illegible] |
| — | [illegible] Stakes | [illegible] | [illegible] |
| | [illegible] Stakes | " | [illegible] |
| Barby | | — | [illegible] |
| Lichfield | — | — | [illegible] |
| — | [illegible] Stakes | | [illegible] |
| — | [illegible] Stakes | South Lancashire | [illegible] |
| | [illegible] Stakes | | [illegible] |
| — | Royal Plate | Yorkshire Club | [illegible] |
| | Wye Stakes | Wye | [illegible] |
| — | [illegible] Cup | Lichfield | [illegible] |
| | [illegible] Produce Stakes | Haydock | [illegible] |
| — | [illegible] Stakes | " | [illegible] |
| [illegible] | | | [illegible] |
| Yorkshire Club | — | | [illegible] |
| — | | | [illegible] |
| Cliffe and Hundred of Hoo | — | " | [illegible] |
| — | Old [illegible] Stakes | [illegible] | [illegible] |
| — | [illegible] Stakes | [illegible] | [illegible] |
| [illegible] | | | [illegible] |
| | [illegible] Stakes | Haydock | [illegible] |
| — | [illegible] Stakes | [illegible] | [illegible] |
| — | [illegible] Stakes | Plumpton | [illegible] |
| Cliffe and Hundred of Hoo | [illegible] Cup | Cliffe and Hundred of Hoo | [illegible] |
| | [illegible] Stakes | " | [illegible] |
| Southminster | | | [illegible] |
| | [illegible] Cup | Southminster | [illegible] |
| — | [illegible] Cup | [illegible] | [illegible] |
| — | Newton Stakes | Newton | [illegible] |
| — | [illegible] Stakes | Gosforth | [illegible] |
| — | [illegible] Stakes | Lichfield | [illegible] |
| Plumpton | — | — | [illegible] |
| | [illegible] Stakes | Kingston | [illegible] |
| | [illegible] Stakes | [illegible] Park | [illegible] |
| — | [illegible] Stakes | Gosforth | [illegible] |
| — | [illegible] Stakes | Market Weighton | [illegible] |
| | Dawney Jubilee Cup | Leeds and County | [illegible] |
| Sleaford | | — | [illegible] |
| Plumpton | — | — | [illegible] |
| Whittlesea | — | — | [illegible] |
| — | [illegible] Stakes | Sleaford | [illegible] |

## MACPHERSON

| NAME | DAM | WON |
|---|---|---|
| Be at Home | Baby | Manor Stakes |
| Be Good | " | — |
| Bird's Head | Stargazing II. | — |
| " | " | — |
| " | " | Watlass Cup |
| " | " | — |
| Bonny Dick | Bal Gal II. | — |
| Brave Scot | Duchess of Delvin | — |
| " | " | — |
| Buxton Lad | Baby | — |
| Carratze | Patella | — |
| Caterham Usher | Hush | — |
| Charming Sally | Avon Conway | — |
| Christmas Day | Christmas Box | — |
| " | " | Trabolgan Stakes |
| Companion | Hush | November Stakes |
| Dingwall | Œnone | Produce Stakes |
| " | " | Scarisbrooke Cup |
| Duke Macpherson | Prenez Garde | — |
| " | " | Holestone Derby |
| Faliant Fhairshon | Strawberry Girl | — |
| Fenton Fairy (late Charming Sally) | Avon Conway | Needham Stakes |
| Flattering Fersen | Radiant | — |
| " | " | — |
| " | " | — |
| Flora Scotica | Strawberry Girl | Ashton Stakes |
| Footboard (late Backbiter) | Peppercorn | — |
| " | " | — |
| Gentle Eva | Bal Gal | — |
| Greater Scot | Madge | — |
| " | " | — |
| " | " | — |
| Half a Chance | Sing Song | — |
| Half a Scot | Agnes | — |
| Hamilton Palace | Heart of Oak | — |
| Happy Rondelle (late Rondelle) | Rota | Members' Cup |
| Harpoon | Hush | February Stakes |
| Hartington | Prenez Garde | — |
| Have a Care | Rota | Burradon Stakes |
| Hayleaf | Hush | — |
| " | " | — |
| " | " | — |
| Haytime | " | — |
| " | " | — |
| Helice | Starlight | Newton Stakes |
| " | " | — |
| Herschel | Stargazing II. | Sefton Stakes |
| " | " | — |
| " | " | — |
| " | " | Haydock Grand Prize |
| Highland Laddie | Holein Lass | — |
| " | " | Scarisbrooke Cup |
| Hostia | Lady Agnes | Golbourne Stakes |
| Hush Money | Hush | — |
| " | " | — |

## MACPHERSON

| Meeting | Division | Meeting | Season |
|---|---|---|---|
| Southport | — | — | 1887-8 |
| — | Christmas Produce Stakes | Haydock | [illegible] |
| — | Tenants' Cup | North of England | [illegible] |
| | Kendon Stakes | Gosforth | [illegible] |
| Thornton Watlass | Brancepeth Stakes | Willington | [illegible] |
| | Tenants' Stakes | Windlestone | [illegible] |
| | Farmers' Stakes | Halewood | [illegible] |
| | Valentine Stakes | Haydock | [illegible] |
| | Burrough Cup | Burrough | [illegible] |
| | Lady Hill Stakes | Haydock | [illegible] |
| | Sefton Stakes | Altcar | [illegible] |
| | Rosehill Stakes | Gosforth | [illegible] |
| | Gosforth Oaks | | [illegible] |
| | Southern Club Stakes | Cork | [illegible] |
| Trafalgar | | | [illegible] |
| Haydock | — | | [illegible] |
| Plumpton | — | | [illegible] |
| Southport | | — | [illegible] |
| — | Winnerlow Stakes | Mourne Park | [illegible] |
| Northern Club | | — | [illegible] |
| — | Pages Stakes | Lichfield | 1887-8 |
| Mourne Park | — | — | [illegible] |
| — | Gosforth Oaks | — | [illegible] |
| — | Netherby Cup | Border Union | [illegible] |
| | Balmoray Stakes | Mourne Park | [illegible] |
| Haydock | — | | [illegible] |
| | Club Cup | West Cumberland | [illegible] |
| | " | " | [illegible] |
| | Farmers' Stakes | Hale | [illegible] |
| | Waterloo Cup | — | [illegible] |
| | Champion Produce Stakes | Haydock | [illegible] |
| | Produce Stakes ([illegible]) | " | [illegible] |
| | St Leger | [illegible] | [illegible] |
| | " | Cliffe and Hundred of Hoo | [illegible] |
| | Ark Stakes | Stokesby | [illegible] |
| Altcar | | | [illegible] |
| Haydock | Border Union Stakes | Border Union | [illegible] |
| — | City of London Stakes | Kempton | 1887-8 |
| Gosforth | | — | [illegible] |
| | Match Maiden Stakes | Haydock | [illegible] |
| | Club Cup | West Cumberland | [illegible] |
| | Springhill Stakes | Springhill | [illegible] |
| | Border Union Stakes | Border Union | [illegible] |
| | Gosforth Stakes | Gosforth | [illegible] |
| Haydock | | | [illegible] |
| — | Spring Stakes | Haydock | [illegible] |
| Altcar | Champion Produce Stakes | " | [illegible] |
| — | Waterloo Cup | — | [illegible] |
| | Members' Cup | — | [illegible] |
| | | Altcar | [illegible] |
| — | Consolation (Maiden) Stakes | Haydock | [illegible] |
| South Lancashire | | | [illegible] |
| Haydock | Sefton Stakes | Altcar | [illegible] |
| | South Lancashire Stakes | Ridgway | [illegible] |
| | Sefton Stakes | Altcar | [illegible] |

MACPHERSON—

| NAME | DAM | WON |
|---|---|---|
| Jinne Macpherson (late Black Lass) | Stargazing II. | Rainham Stakes |
| " | " | — |
| " | " | Newby Stakes |
| " | " | Catterick Stakes |
| " | " | — |
| " | " | — |
| " | " | — |
| Iulus | Rota | — |
| " | " | — |
| Just Asleep | Hush | Maiden Stakes |
| Lacerta | Starlight | — |
| " | " | — |
| Lance Macpherson (late Blackman) | Stargazing II. | Hutton Stakes |
| " | " | Blaydon Stakes |
| Last of the Macs | Œnone | Bristol Stakes |
| Little Giant (late Sailor V.) | Bugle | — |
| Meol's General (late Colin Campbell) | Sweet Daughter | April (Maiden) Stakes |
| Meol's Hero | Meol's Vixen | Waterloo Plate |
| " | " | — |
| Miss Webster | Lilac | — |
| " | " | Tenants' Cup |
| Penelope II. | Stitch in Time | Altcar Club Cup |
| " | " | Members' Cup |
| " | " | — |
| " | " | — |
| " | " | — |
| Porcia | Patella | — |
| Prince Alexander | Brighton Lady | — |
| " | " | — |
| " | " | March Stakes |
| " | " | — |
| " | " | — |
| " | " | Leamington Stakes |
| " | " | Downshire Stakes |
| " | " | Foyle Stakes |
| Prince Napoleon | Lady Agnes | — |
| " | " | — |
| Rags and Feathers | Cosy | — |
| Relentless | Baby | Scarisbrooke Cup |
| Ripe Berry | Strawberry Girl | — |
| Rose Macpherson | Stargazing II. | Brafferton Stakes |
| " | " | — |
| Rhoda Macpherson (late Flossie) | Cosy | Paget Stakes |
| " | " | Queensberry Stakes |
| " | " | — |
| " | " | — |
| Rotula | Rota | — |
| " | " | — |
| Scotch Pearl | Sea Maid | — |
| Silence | Hush | — |
| Simba | Salamis | Mourne Park Plate |
| Sir E. K. | Sister Ada | — |
| Sparkling Gem | Œnone | Sleaford Stakes |
| Step Aside | Salamis | — |
| Strathpeffer | Nuit Blanche | — |
| Warden | Mazurka | — |
| Willie Macpherson | Duchess of Delvin | Ewerby Stakes |

*continued*

| MEETING | DIVIDED | MEETING | SEASON |
|---|---|---|---|
| North of England | Prestwick Stakes | Gosforth | 1884–5 |
| — | Selby Stakes | Selby | 1884–5 |
| Newby | — | — | 1885–6 |
| Catterick | — | — | 1885–6 |
| — | Willington Stakes | Willington | 1886–7 |
| — | Ravensworth Cup | North of England | 1886–7 |
| — | " | — | 1887–8 |
| — | Wye Derby | Wye | 1887–8 |
| — | Members' Produce Stakes | Plumpton | 1887–8 |
| Haydock | — | — | 1888–9 |
| — | Rainton Stakes | Rainton | 1887–8 |
| — | Royal Stakes | " | 1888–9 |
| North of England | Plessy Stakes | Gosforth | 1884–5 |
| Gosforth | — | — | 1885–6 |
| Sleaford | Westminster Stakes | Kempton | 1888–9 |
| — | Earlstown Stakes | Haydock | 1884–5 |
| Haydock | — | — | |
| — | — | — | 1885–6 |
| — | Gosforth Stakes | — | 1887–8 |
| — | Oaklands Stakes | Longtown (Local) | 1888–9 |
| Corrie (Tenants) | — | — | 1887–8 |
| Altcar | — | — | 1885–6 |
| " | — | — | 1885–6 |
| — | Lytham Cup | — | 1885–6 |
| — | Ravensworth Cup | North of England | 1886–7 |
| — | Clifton Cup | Ridgway | 1886–7 |
| — | Covington Plate | Carmichael | 1884–5 |
| — | Scarva Stakes | Banbridge | 1887–8 |
| — | Champion Produce Stakes | Haydock | 1887–8 |
| Haydock | — | — | 1887–8 |
| — | Holestone Stakes | Northern Club | 1888–9 |
| — | October Stakes | Haydock | 1888–9 |
| Wappenbury | — | — | 1888–9 |
| Banbridge | — | — | 1889–90 |
| Black Brae | — | — | 1889–90 |
| — | Lady Hill Stakes | Haydock | 1885–6 |
| — | October Stakes | " | 1887–8 |
| — | Barnton Stakes | Barnton | 1888–9 |
| South Lancashire | — | — | 1888–9 |
| — | Valentine Stakes | Haydock | 1889–90 |
| Heworth Park | Ripon Stakes | North of England | 1886–7 |
| — | Prestwick Stakes | Gosforth | 1886–7 |
| Lichfield | — | — | 1888–9 |
| Upper Nithsdale | — | — | 1889–90 |
| — | Paget Stakes | Lichfield | 1889–90 |
| — | Molyneux Stakes | Altcar | 1889–90 |
| — | Quarrington Stakes | Sleaford | 1889–90 |
| — | Keymer Stakes | Plumpton | 1889–90 |
| — | Gordinnog Stakes | Bangor | 1886–7 |
| — | March Stakes | Four Oaks Park | 1885–6 |
| — | — | — | 1888–9 |
| — | Bickerstaffe Stakes | Bickerstaffe | 1888–9 |
| Sleaford | — | — | 1887–8 |
| — | Gordinnog Stakes | Bangor | 1887–8 |
| — | Burscough Cup | Burscough | 1888–9 |
| — | December Stakes | Kempton | 1888–9 |
| Ewerby | — | — | 1887–8 |

*continued*

| Meeting | Divided | Meeting |
|---|---|---|
| North of England | Prestwick Stakes | Gosforth |
| | Selby Stakes | Selby |
| Newby | — | — |
| Catterick | — | — |
| — | Willington Stakes | Willington |
| — | Ravensworth Cup | North of England |
| — | " | — |
| — | Wye Derby | Wye |
| — | Members' Produce Stakes | Plumpton |
| Haydock | — | — |
| | Rainton Stakes | Rainton |
| — | Royal Stakes | " |
| North of England | Plessy Stakes | Gosforth |
| Gosforth | — | — |
| Sleaford | Westminster Stakes | Kempton |
| | Earlstown Stakes | Haydock |
| Haydock | — | — |
| — | — | — |
| — | Gosforth Stakes | — |
| — | Oaklands Stakes | Longtown (Local) |
| Corrie (Tenants) | — | — |
| Altcar | — | — |
| " | — | — |
| — | Lytham Cup | — |
| — | Ravensworth Cup | North of England |
| — | Clifton Cup | Ridgway |
| — | Covington Plate | Carmichael |
| — | Scarva Stakes | Banbridge |
| — | Champion Produce Stakes | Haydock |
| Haydock | — | — |
| — | Holestone Stakes | Northern Club |
| — | October Stakes | Haydock |
| Wappenbury | — | — |
| Banbridge | — | — |
| Black Brae | — | — |
| — | Lady Hill Stakes | Haydock |
| — | October Stakes | " |
| — | Barnton Stakes | Barnton |
| South Lancashire | — | — |
| — | Valentine Stakes | Haydock |
| Heworth Park | Ripon Stakes | North of England |
| — | Prestwick Stakes | Gosforth |
| Lichfield | — | — |
| Upper Nithsdale | — | — |
| — | Paget Stakes | Lichfield |
| — | Molyneux Stakes | Altcar |
| — | Quarrington Stakes | Sleaford |
| — | Keymer Stakes | Plumpton |
| — | Gordinnog Stakes | Bangor |
| — | March Stakes | Four Oaks Park |
| — | — | — |
| — | Bickerstaffe Stakes | Bickerstaffe |
| Sleaford | — | — |
| — | Gordinnog Stakes | Bangor |
| — | Burscough Cup | Burscough |
| — | December Stakes | Kempton |
| Ewerby | — | — |

## GREENTICK

| Name | Dam | Won |
| --- | --- | --- |
| Blue Tick | Cayenne II. | Spoonley Stakes |
| Brief Bliss | Lady Macpherson | — |
| Cagliostro | „ | — |
| Cheque Book | Cayenne II. | — |
| Coca Water | Madeline | Maiden Stakes |
| „ | „ | — |
| Cunningarth | Ecumenical | — |
| Dove Cot | Maid of Taunton | — |
| Equivocal | Ecumenical | — |
| Full of Fashion | Bit of Fashion | — |
| Fräulein II. | Waterwitch | — |
| Fullerton | Bit of Fashion | — |
| „ | „ | Waterloo Cup |
| Germanic | Governess | Stanley Stakes |
| Goldfinder | Cosy | Wye Stakes |
| Green Cot | Baby | — |
| „ | „ | — |
| „ | „ | — |
| Green Fern | Jinne Macpherson | — |
| „ | „ | — |
| „ | „ | — |
| Greengage | Governess | Haydock Derby |
| „ | „ | — |
| Greengoose | „ | Covington Stakes |
| „ | „ | Caledonia Cup |
| Green Hat | Jinne Macpherson | — |
| Green Hay | Jinne Macpherson | — |
| „ | „ | — |
| Greenhouse | Governess | — |
| Green Moss | Jinne Macpherson | — |
| Greenshanks | Rufina | — |
| Greenstick | Governess | November Stakes |
| Green Stone | Jinne Macpherson | — |
| Hammock | Hedge Rose | — |
| „ | „ | — |
| „ | „ | — |
| Happy Fun | Suppliant | — |
| Hellebore | Hedge Rose | — |
| Herrick | Hostia | — |
| Highland Green | Œnone | — |
| Howitzer | Suppliant | — |
| „ | „ | — |
| Huddler | Diadem II. | Southminster Derby |
| Ivy Green | Arausa | — |
| „ | „ | — |
| Jupon Vert (late Yooi Over) | Bit of Fashion | — |
| Kaiser II. | Waterwitch | — |
| Kate Cuthbert | Bit of Fashion | — |
| Lecturer | Madeline | — |
| Manilla | „ | Roche's Point Stakes. |
| Marsayas | Miss Edith II. | — |
| Mespilus | Madeline | — |
| Mickleton | Miss Edith II. | — |
| „ | „ | — |

## GREENTICK

| Meeting | Divided | Meeting | Season |
|---|---|---|---|
| Market Drayton | — | — | 1889–90 |
| — | Manor Stakes | South Lancashire | 1888–9 |
| — | North Seaton Tenants' Stakes | Bothal and North Seaton | 1889–90 |
| — | Berkeley Stakes | Berkeley | 1888–9 |
| Haydock | — | — | 1888–9 |
| — | Second Waterloo Plate | Waterloo | 1889–90 |
| — | Portland Stakes | North of England Club | 1889–90 |
| — | Wye Oaks | — | 1888–9 |
| — | Second Tenants' Stakes | Widdrington | 1889–90 |
| — | Valentine Stakes | Haydock | 1888–9 |
| — | Manor Stakes | Second South Lancashire | 1889–90 |
| — | Waterloo Cup | — | 1888–9 |
| — | — | — | 1889–90 |
| Bickerstaffe | — | — | 1888–9 |
| Wye | — | — | 1889–90 |
| — | Haydock Oaks | Haydock | 1889–90 |
| — | Christmas Produce Stakes | " | 1889–90 |
| — | Second Members' Cup | Altcar | 1889–90 |
| — | Christmas Produce Stakes | Haydock Park | 1889–90 |
| — | Haydock Oaks | " | 1889–90 |
| — | Second Members' Cup | Altcar | 1889–90 |
| — | — | — | 1888–9 |
| — | Scarisbrooke Cup | Second South Lancashire | 1889–90 |
| Carmichael | — | — | 1888–9 |
| Scottish National | — | — | 1888–9 |
| — | Second Haydock Derby | Haydock | 1889–90 |
| — | Second Sefton Stakes | — | 1889–90 |
| — | Haydock Oaks | Haydock Park | 1889–90 |
| — | Champion Produce Stakes | " | 1888–9 |
| — | Haydock Oaks | " | 1889–90 |
| — | Dunmore Stakes | East Stirlingshire Club | 1888–9 |
| Haydock | — | — | 1889–90 |
| — | Champion Produce | Haydock | 1889–90 |
| — | Border Union Stakes | — | 1888–9 |
| — | Spring Stakes | Haydock | 1888–9 |
| — | Sunbury Stakes | Kempton | 1889–90 |
| — | Produce Stakes | Newmarket | 1888–9 |
| — | Blundell Cup | Little Crosby | 1889–90 |
| — | Valentine Stakes | Haydock | 1889–90 |
| — | Old Sleaford Stakes | Sleaford | 1888–9 |
| — | Wye Stakes | Wye | 1889–90 |
| — | Ashford Stakes | " | 1889–90 |
| Southminster | — | | 1889–90 |
| — | Wye Oaks | Wye | 1888–9 |
| — | De Grey Plate | Yorkshire Club | 1888–9 |
| — | Sefton Stakes | Altcar | 1888–9 |
| — | Old Place Stakes | Sleaford | 1889–90 |
| — | Gosforth Gold Cup | | 1888–9 |
| — | Brownlow Stakes | Mourne Park | 1889–90 |
| Trabolgan | — | | 1889–90 |
| — | Newton Stakes | Haydock | 1888–9 |
| — | December Stakes | Kempton Park | 1889–90 |
| — | City of London Stakes | Kempton | 1887–8 |
| — | Olanteigh Stakes | Wye | 1888–9 |

## GREENTICK—

| NAME | DAM | WON |
|---|---|---|
| Mickleton | Miss Edith II. | |
| Mixed Affair | Waterwitch | |
| Restorer | Tonic | Kilmorey Cup |
| " | " | Clifton Cup |
| Sweet Home | Sally Day | — |
| Sweet Music | " | — |
| Terms | Tonic | — |
| " | " | — |
| Thetis | " | |
| Thicket | " | |
| Toboggan | Toledo | |
| " | " | |
| Townend | Tonic | |
| " | " | — |
| " | " | — |
| Troughend | Toledo | November Maiden Stakes |
| " | " | — |
| " | " | — |
| Whaup | Whim | — |

*continued*

| Meeting | Divided | Meeting | Season |
|---|---|---|---|
| — | Sunbury Stakes | Kempton | 1889-90 |
| | Old Place Stakes | Sleaford | 1889-90 |
| Mourne Park | — | — | 1889-90 |
| Ridgway | — | — | 1889-90 |
| — | Sleaford Stakes | Sleaford | 1889-90 |
| — | Newton Stakes | Haydock | 1889-90 |
| — | Portland Stakes | North of England Club | 1888-9 |
| — | Second Tenants' Stakes | West Rainton | 1889-90 |
| — | Christmas Produce Stakes | Haydock | 1888-9 |
| — | Pettinain Stakes | Carmichael | 1889-90 |
| | Spring Stakes | Haydock | 1888-9 |
| | Second Kilmorey Cup | Mourne Park | 1889-90 |
| | Gosforth Derby | — | 1888-9 |
| | St. Leger | Gosforth | 1888-9 |
| | Port Victoria Stakes | Cliffe and Hundred of Hoo | 1888-9 |
| Gosforth | Christmas Produce Stakes | Haydock | 1888-9 |
| — | Waterloo Cup | — | 1889-90 |
| — | Second Waterloo Purse | — | 1889-90 |
| — | Ashford Handicap | Wye | 1888-9 |

# CHAPTER III

## PRACTICAL GREYHOUND BREEDING

THE greyhound-breeder having now made up his mind as to which particular strains he will patronise, and having his theories as to certain crosses and inbreedings that may be calculated to produce desirable stock, must look to individual merit and characteristics; for a certain 'hit' in breeding may be clearly established both in theory and practice, and yet in some cases may fail, not through any miscalculation of genealogy, but owing to some defect, physical or mental, on the part of the immediate parents, a defect that will surely be accentuated if inbreeding is included in the programme. It therefore behoves him to be very careful in the selection of his brood-bitches, and in mating them he must always keep in view their individual peculiarities as well as their inherited characteristics.

To begin with, we think it a mistake to breed from a very big bitch; rather would we choose a medium or even a small one, provided she came of a family that usually produced fair-sized animals. Very often it occurs that in a large litter three or four of its members greatly distinguish themselves, but one little bitch may fail to follow their example, simply and solely on account of size. Such a one can usually be bought for a few sovereigns, and we would as soon breed from her as from her larger sister, who had perchance won the Waterloo Cup; in fact, it is seldom that a hard-run bitch ever distinguishes herself as a matron, though there are notable exceptions to this rule, such as Bab-at-the-Bowster, Tollwife, Bed of Stone, Ruby, Rebe, and Bit of Fashion.

In breeding from such a bitch as we have described, when mated with a dog of size and substance, there would be little fear of the produce being undersized ; but she must not, of course, be weak in bone, rickety, splay-footed, or in any way misshapen. As we said before, size must be the sole supposed objection.

When this bitch has her litter she will, in all probability, be found a good mother. Big bitches are prone to lie on and

The nursery

otherwise injure their whelps. It might be argued that in like manner it is better to breed from an own brother to a great winner than from the dog himself.

A list of winners would not, at first sight, show this to be the case ; but we think the reason is that the distinguished dog gets more and better chances, and unless an unknown dog, by accident as it were, produces some great winner, he will not, however well bred, be generally patronised by breeders. This is so with thoroughbred stock ; unless a horse is 'fashionable,' he gets few chances, and hardly ever a first-class mare. We feel certain there are at the present moment not a few grandly bred horses covering half-bred mares at five guineas that, if they had a fair chance, would produce as good an average of winners as those that stand at 50 and 100 guineas. In the preceding chapter we mentioned a greyhound that would come under this category, viz. Edwin Greentick. We have not the remotest interest in him, but from his breeding and all we have heard of his individual merit (in appearance), we do not doubt his proving a successful sire if provided with a sufficient number of suitable dames.

Having procured our brood-bitches, and premeditated a line of breeding that we must closely adhere to, we must try to get our puppies introduced to the world at a suitable season. Unfortunately the exigencies of nature forbid us producing whelps whenever we want them, but at any rate we can determine when *not* to have them. Those who breed for public auction count themselves fortunate when they have a goodly proportion of January litters. A *sapling* is a greyhound whelped on or after January 1 of the same year in which the season of running began, and no greyhound is to be considered a *puppy* which was whelped prior to January 1 of the year preceding the commencement of the season of running. So that obviously a litter born from August to December is practically worthless for coursing purposes; but a January puppy when brought in front of the rostrum has a pull over those born in the spring or early summer. Those, however, who breed to run may well consider the advisability of getting their litters in March and April. We do not mean to say that a bitch coming in season in the first part of November should be 'passed,' for early puppies come in handy for early produce stakes, and meet their younger opponents at a distinct advantage. But it will be found easier to rear, say, a March litter than one born in January; for just as they are fit to be reared the spring will be well advanced, and the months of May and June, so admirably adapted for the development of all young things, will lend powerful aid to the breeder; whereas the rigours of March and the uncertainty of April are calculated to retard the growth and impair the well-doing of the January puppy.

Those who are anxious to see their charges in the slips as early as possible would do well to avoid breeding from a bitch that comes in use later than May 1, because dogs born in July and August are seldom of much account during their puppy season; but we have known very late ones, that have not run at all as puppies, come out in good form the following season.

During pregnancy the bitch should have plenty of exercise; it is not everyone who finds it convenient to let her wander about at her sweet will, though this is the most desirable course; but, at any rate, she must be taken out for slow exercise, which must be gradually decreased as she nears the time of labour. For those that run loose a suitable place must be provided for whelping, and for early bitches it will be found necessary to call in the aid of artificial warmth. A loose box in a warm but well-ventilated stable is an excellent accouchement chamber, and if the bitch is shut in every night she is sure to betake herself thither when the time of her trouble comes. Great care must be taken that she has constant and uninterrupted access thereto, or we may have the chagrin of finding that our best bitch has whelped a fine litter to a 25-guinea dog under a neighbouring stack of firewood or behind a haystack, and that they have all been frozen to death.

A bedding of good oat straw sprinkled with Keating's insect powder should be placed on a low bench not raised more than six inches from the ground, and guarded by an edging of matchboard four inches in depth, and this should be placed in the corner of the stall. Many people allow their bitch to whelp in an old wine case or other box; but this is dangerous, especially if it be her first litter, as she is prone to injure her babies when she jumps out or in. The reason for providing a low bench is obvious: not only might the whelps fall off, but, in her naturally weak condition after whelping, it would be highly injurious for the mother to have to jump up to, or down from, a height.

If a bitch is permitted to whelp on straw thrown into a corner of the box, it will be found that in a day or two the whelps will have scratched about until they lie on the bare floor, which is not at all conducive to their welfare. Some place a piece of carpet and throw the straw on that ; but it quickly absorbs the urine and becomes foul and unwholesome. Of course care must be taken that all draughts are excluded, and that there is sufficient light and ventilation. For our own part we have converted a row of loose boxes that were used for brood mares, and fitted them with movable benches, under which we have run a two-inch hot-water pipe ; this is fed from a boiler erected in the furthest partition, and the same furnace heats it and the boiler wherein the food is prepared. The doors of these boxes are divided in the centre, and when the top portion is open a sheet of galvanised netting secures the inmates.

It is not everyone, however, who can find the facilities at hand, but in most country places there are buildings that can be converted to the purpose, and a bay of a barn or a clean and well-drained pigsty is not to be despised as a substitute for a more commodious lying-in hospital.

So far we have said nothing about the medical treatment of a pregnant or suckling bitch, and if dosing can be avoided by all means let it be ; but there are circumstances under which it is necessary to have recourse to physic. Foremost amongst these is when the bitch shows signs of irritant skin disease, whether it be follicular mange or eczema, and she should be very carefully watched ; for should she litter down with her blood or skin disease, her whelps will assuredly contract the complaint, and a load of anxiety will fall on the breeder. What is born in the blood will come out in the flesh, and although the little creatures may appear sound and clean up to the time of weaning, they will, nevertheless, break out subsequently, and a deal of care and attention will be necessary to restore them to health; often, indeed, every effort will prove futile, and they will become masses of corruption. In cases of follicular mange, during pregnancy, the bitch should be isolated at once, and well dressed with one of the lotions in vogue. That of Messrs. Spratt is good. A more cooling diet should be resorted to, and a mild aperient administered. Most people prescribe castor-oil, but for our part we prefer to use flower of sulphur, or one of Norton's camomile pills given every other night till six have been taken. These are mild in their action, and stimulate instead of exhausting the digestive organs, whereas castor-oil always causes a certain amount of griping. The dressing should be applied once a week, and continued until the skin presents a healthy appearance and all humid spots have entirely disappeared. In the case of a bitch who has broken out subsequently to the birth of her puppies a somewhat different course must be pursued, for it would not do for them to take in with their mother's milk a large percentage of strong dressing, or to be in continued contact therewith. Therefore the spots and sore places must be well anointed and rubbed in, and the superfluous dressing removed with a dry cloth; after which the back and sides may be covered with a light mixture of sulphur and vaseline, and the same concoction may be applied to the puppies themselves when they are upwards of a fortnight old. If it be possible to obtain a foster-bitch, of course this plan should be adopted, and an exchange of puppies will minimise the risk of infection as regards the little greyhounds, while the other puppies will serve to draw the milk from the tainted bitch and keep her from fretting.

It often happens that a bitch after whelping shows a certain amount of eruptiveness during her suckling period. This is generally the result of too heating food, and must not be confounded with mange or eczema, as it will disappear on change of diet and a cooling draught. When the bitch is suffering from true eczema the internal treatment is more severe, though we have found the mange lotion very efficacious, even when the disease is entirely sanguineous and no parasites exist in the epidermis. Here we recommend a strong dose of sulphur or fluid magnesia to begin with, and a teaspoonful of concentrated essence of sarsaparilla placed in the water daily, whilst all meal must be removed from the food, which should consist of lean meat and gravy mixed with brown bread, and well boiled and mashed carrots, turnips, beetroots or tomatoes, the two last for choice. In many cases eczema proves a stubborn enemy, and its cause and cure vary so that fixed rules for treatment are impossible, and the breeder must be guided by circumstances

Constipation is often present in pregnancy and during nursing, and here the camomile pill or sulphur may be employed; but if obstinate and continual an enema of glycerine and Castile soap may be administered. Other ailments may trouble the breeder ; but, as a rule, a brood-bitch, if constitutionally strong, is exempt from serious contagion. It is always as well, however, to give a bitch a worm powder in the middle of her pregnancy, for we are strongly of opinion that internal parasites are often contracted in the womb, and not always acquired with the food after weaning.

The bitch should be left almost entirely to herself during parturition : in ninety-nine cases out of a hundred Nature is far the best midwife, and any interference is calculated to do more harm than good, though exceptional cases may occur when the veterinary surgeon should be called in, as any attempt at an operation by an inexperienced hand is to be deprecated. After she has pupped and has made herself comfortable, the bitch should be quietly provided with a bowl of gruel, and no attempt should be made to count or overhaul her whelps. Gruel, sheep's-head broth, beef-tea, or some extract of beef should form the sustenance for the first week, during which time no solid food should be given ; but after that the diet may be varied, though very little, if any, meat should be included. If there is a scarcity of milk, the gruel must be continued ; fresh fish carefully freed of all bones will be found very beneficial, and half a teaspoonful of cod-liver oil, with the same quantity of Parrish's chemical food, can be mixed in the feeding-trough.

Greyhounds are very prolific, and have been known to throw upwards of twelve puppies at a birth, nine and ten being of frequent occurrence; but such numbers are more than any ordinary bitch can manage with justice to herself and them. When practicable, a foster-bitch should be ready at hand, and this provision should not be left to the last moment, for they are often very hard to procure. It is better to get a healthy spaniel, poodle, pointer, or other bitch of suitable size, served at the same time as the greyhound bitch, and then you know that the time will fit in conveniently; a maiden bitch, however, should not be chosen, but one who has already performed her maternal duties creditably. However much milk the greyhound is apparently blessed with, she ought not to be asked to bring up more than five whelps at the most; for often the lactine flow will suddenly cease, and it will be necessary to rear the whelps by hand, always a risky undertaking, and even those that survive are heavily handicapped for months to come.

Some breeders are inclined to believe that the moral attributes of the foster-mother are assimilated with the milk. For our part we do not accept this theory; but, were it true, a bull or bull-terrier bitch would be a most desirable wet nurse, likely to impart some of her courage to her charges.

In changing the puppies from the real to the foster-mother it will be as well to do so gradually, and always to leave at least one of her own pups with the latter. Should it be impossible to procure a foster-mother, and should your greyhound produce a large litter of, say, nine, it will be necessary to harden your heart and doom three or four of them to destruction. We are quite aware that this requires Spartan fortitude, especially when a large fee has been paid for some celebrated sire to your choicest bitch, and when the whole litter presents an appearance of level excellence. If, as sometimes happens, there are three or four obviously weakly ones, smaller than their brothers and sisters, and very deficient in bone, then the choice of victims is easy enough; but otherwise there is always the thought present that you may be destroying an embryo Waterloo Cup winner. Experienced greyhound breeders have various methods of selecting choice whelps, and they are guided by general appearance; but the tiro may easily be deceived. 'Stonehenge' gives a hint which is certainly worth attention. Let the puppies remain with their dam for a week, then hold each up by the tail; the best ones will bring their legs well over their head, and you can see which possess length, and the promise of good ribs. And here we would impress on the reader that a well-chosen pup of this age, even if he subsequently deteriorates, will eventually assert his superiority; and however much a grand-looking puppy goes off, he should never be despaired of until he has arrived at full maturity, unless, of course, he has been disabled by accident, or has become 'chink-backed'—an axiom that applies not only to greyhounds, but to foxhounds, and, indeed, to all members of the canine race.

With regard to early whelps (January and February), it will be necessary to keep them in their compartment until they are well over their weaning; but if the place of their birth is small and cramped, or not sufficiently lighted, they must be placed in the warm bay of a barn or an old loft for an hour or two daily, where they will exercise themselves. Great attention must be paid to cleanliness; during the suckling period the bitch will see to these sanitary measures if she is allowed sufficient liberty, but after weaning the room or box must be regularly cleansed. In the case of a loose box, it should be washed out, but must on no account be allowed to remain wet, or even damp; a good supply of Sanitas sawdust should overlie the bricks or tiles, and on this should be spread short clean oat straw. The tin containing the food should be placed on a slab, or, at any rate, the straw and sawdust should be cleared from around it, as the whelps persistently pull their food out of the vessel and would devour a considerable quantity of sawdust, which is very irritating to the intestines.

But now we must speak of the process of weaning, which we have somewhat anticipated. Should it unfortunately happen that the mother's milk dries up suddenly and that no foster-bitch is at hand to continue the nursing—a mishap that may occur as early as the first week—recourse must be had to the feeding-bottle, and Dr. Ridge's food and Swiss milk will be found as good as anything. Cow's milk, we feel convinced, is not a good food for dogs, but if given it should be first boiled and then diluted with a fifth part of water. The bottle-feeding must be very carefully attended to, and should only be temporary; for in the case of valuable whelps—and we trust no man would be so foolish as to breed those that are not presumably valuable—the country should be scoured for a foster-bitch; but when the milk supply fails in the fifth week or later, an attempt at hand-rearing is more likely to prove successful, as by that time the little ones will make an effort to feed themselves. As soon as their noses have been dipped in the basin, and their appetites thus whetted, many dog-breeders would begin to give them bread and milk; a hopeless diet, and one that would, in a very brief space of time, produce what are vulgarly termed 'pot-bellies' and bowed backs—a state of things brought about by the internal parasites whose presence is, our experience tells us, directly traceable to raw cow's milk. Dr. Ridge's food, to which glycerine in the proportion of a teaspoonful to a pint has been added, will prove staple food, and after the sixth week Brand's extract of beef (in the jelly form) may be given; but bread, meal, soaked biscuit or solid meats are carefully to be avoided until after the eighth week, when the weaning proper begins; then brown bread with shreds of well-boiled sheep's head may be made into a partially solid mess with the broth of the latter, and even the Swiss milk should cease. Now is the time when a careful look-out for internal parasites must be kept, and the attendant must not cease his vigilance because the fæces contain none of these pests, as they are sometimes present for months in the intestinal canal without signs, except those produced on the patient by their baneful influence. If, then, the puppies, after weaning, grow emaciated, their backs round, and the vertebræ distinctly limned; if the ribs are tucked and easily counted; if the nose is dry, the coat staring, the breath fœtid, then the natural conclusion will be arrived at, and prompt measures taken to remove the pests: but if no portions have come away with the motions, it is difficult to determine the variety of parasite with which the victims are infested. There are two varieties frequently met with in recently weaned puppies. First, the common tapeworm (*Tænia serrata*), which in its disjointed existence is held by many writers to be identical with the maw-worm, though 'Stonehenge' is inclined to an opposite opinion, which we share, and for the same reason—viz. because the maw-worm is almost innocuous, whereas the tapeworm proper produces the marked symptoms of constitutional disturbance mentioned above.

Of still more frequent occurrence is the round-worm (*Ascaris marginata*), which, unlike the *Tænia serrata*, is acquired from liquids, especially cow's milk. Very few puppies escape a visitation of these pests at some period or other of their youth, but they are more easily got rid of than their flat cousins, and the effects of their ravages soon disappear. Even if puppies fail to show any signs of their presence, it is as well to dose them all round a fortnight after weaning, and the agent to employ is santonine. The patients should be kept without food for at least twelve hours, when enough of the powder to cover a sixpence, made into a bolus with butter, should be administered; half an hour later a dessert-spoonful of castor-oil must be given, and the puppies taken out for exercise; and they should be carefully watched to see if they void any worms. When the attendant is satisfied that round-worms are present, he has nothing to do but to repeat the treatment after the lapse of a week or so; if, however, none are passed and the symptoms of internal parasites continue to be marked, the existence of the tapeworm may be suspected. In this case the same preparation for medicine by fasting must be practised, but freshly grated areca nut must take the place of santonine, and enough of it to cover a shilling. This dose must be followed, as in the case of round-worm, by castor-oil.

The breeder, as soon as he feels confident that his charges are entirely freed from the unwelcome presence of these parasites, should give cod-liver oil and Parrish's chemical food—one teaspoonful of each daily to each puppy ; or he may administer half a tonic ball, as described later on. The former may be mixed in the feeding-trough, and in a very short time he may expect to see a marked improvement in his charges ; the eye will become bright, the nose cold and wet, the body well nourished, the coat soft and sleek, and the spirits exuberant ; failing this desirable state of things, he will have cause to fear some undiscovered malady.

To cure worms is, in our experience, easier than to prevent them. The tapeworm usually comes from the use of raw animal food, and he who allows the cooked meat to be placed in a vessel that has previously contained the raw material runs the risk which is also attendant on the picking up of offal during exercise. The danger arising from round-worms may be avoided by using nothing but boiled water in the kennels ; but if these measures are attempted at all they should be most strictly carried out, for one lapse will render abortive the care of months. About this time that dire disease, the bugbear of all cynophilists—distemper—must be looked for ; though we certainly do not subscribe to the old-fashioned theory that every dog must necessarily pass through the ordeal. Nevertheless, the frequent appearance of the plague, despite the most stringent measures and the strictest quarantine, is undoubted, and the breeder must be ever prepared and strongly armed against it. Every whelp should be overhauled daily, and on the slightest symptom of a disordered state of health should be immediately isolated and a careful examination made.

When the whelps are thoroughly weaned and in good health, the question of 'walks' arises, and here we must begin to discuss the *pros* and *cons* of a very important step. Personally we have no hesitation in advising the breeder to keep his youngsters under his own watchful eye, if he is so fortunate as to be able to afford them his undivided attention, and if he has the space, accommodation, and exercise-ground necessary to rear them to the pitch of strength and vitality to which they must be brought before they enter upon their training. Cramped quarters and overcrowding are fatal, and space is a *sine quâ non* when any number of young greyhounds are to be considered. Presuming that the advantages we speak of are at the command of our breeder—in the shape of a dozen acres of paddock land—he cannot do better than enclose six pieces of about half an acre each with iron fencing of a sufficient height to imprison the inmates securely; for, as the youngsters wax big and strong, they develop marvellous jumping powers. The grass in the enclosure should be cut, and a roomy kennel on four small stout wheels should be placed within. If it is convenient to enclose a tree, this should be done, as the shade afforded thereby will be grateful during the hot summer days; failing a tree, a sheet of bevelled zinc coated with whitewash may be shelved in one corner of the yard. Such a place will hold half-a-dozen greyhounds from three to nine months old; but the whole paraphernalia must be so constructed that it is easily taken down and re-erected on another site. The youngsters should never be kept on the same spot for more than a month at a stretch, nor must they be left there when long-continued wet weather has rendered the ground soaked and slushy; in that case they must return to their barn or stall, or wherever they have been placed after leaving their dam, and road exercise in batches for at least two hours daily must be the rule. We say advisedly in batches, for several six-months-old greyhound puppies are a rare handful for anyone to manage. Even when penned out in the way described above, the road exercise must not be neglected, or bad feet, and legs far from straight, may be expected.

With regard to food, it should be varied occasionally: good old hound-meal, carefully and freshly prepared, with an admixture of flesh, and well-soaked biscuits mashed up with beetroot or cabbage, are the staples, and the changes may be rung thereon. Some extravagant breeders think that no greyhound can be put into training with any hope of winning a stake unless it has been reared on prime joints of mutton and beef; but this is all rubbish, as good sound horseflesh contains quite sufficient nourishment to develop the bone and muscle of any dog that was ever born. Another useful article of food, when properly combined with the others, is plain suet pudding, and after all it is not a very expensive one, and in rearing greyhounds, as also blood stock, it never does to economise food, lest we prove penny wise and pound foolish. After our remarks about beef and mutton, we may appear to contradict ourselves, but in the case of prime joints the extravagance is thrown away and no good purpose is served.

The danger attached to the rearing to maturity of one's greyhounds is this. We have, so to speak, all our eggs in one basket; the outbreak of distemper in its most malignant form may have fatal results, and the first victims are sure to be our most cherished youngsters. Moreover, to do the thing properly, quite a staff of servants is required, and, unless these are trustworthy lads and have learnt their duties under a competent master, they will be found as great a trouble to their employer as the young greyhounds are to them. Unless all circumstances are favourable, it will be as well to send the whelps out to walk at ten weeks old, and let them remain there until they are a year old, or until their delinquencies are so marked that they can no longer be kept in a state of freedom. To puppies reared in this way there are innumerable risks, and the breeder may deem himself fortunate if a third of those sent out are returned to him sound and well. If a sufficient number of 'walkers' who have any real knowledge of dogs, and of greyhounds in particular, can be found, the risks are minimised, and the puppies fare better at walk than they do at home.

Butchers form a class that are in great request, and if they have the necessary knowledge, and take a personal interest in their charge, no better can be found, because they have plenty of good food at hand, and can prepare it properly; but if, on the other hand, one's puppy is stuffed with raw scraps and offal, he is a pretty sure victim of mange and eczema, and distemper will hardly pass him by. The crime of chaining a greyhound up is one that must be condemned most forcibly, and the watchful eye must see that it has not been committed; for the wife of our friend, having had a dozen of her chickens demolished one fine morning, is prone to insist on the culprit being so treated, and by-and-by a rheumatic, twisted-legged, splay-footed, and useless creature is sent in. Unless a puppy walker has had any real experience with dogs, he should communicate with the owner or his kennelman directly he becomes aware of the fact that his charge is ailing, when the matter should be seen to without a moment's delay. A little knowledge is a dangerous thing; and save us from the man who, on the appearance, or supposed appearance, of distemper, forces salt, tobacco, and other such nostrums down our puppy's throat. Another danger that threatens puppies that are walked in villages and towns is that of being run over, an accident of far too frequent occurrence; there are brutes in human shape who will not trouble to turn their cart-wheels aside to avoid crushing to death an innocent and valuable dog standing in the road or basking in the sun.

At least once a week the head kennelman, or trainer, having armed himself with a good supply of worm powders, mange lotion, and other products of the canine pharmacopœia, should drive round and thoroughly overhaul all the 'walks,' and, if he finds ailing puppies, should there and then supply the necessary drugs and give careful instruction as to feeding. In this way much mischief is avoided. Very often greyhound-puppy walkers take a keen interest in their charges, not only during the time they are under their care, but also when the time comes for the animal to go to the slips for an important stake; and those who breed greyhounds on a large scale might do worse than follow the example of M.F.H., in giving a dinner to the walkers and awarding a prize to the best walked puppy. For our own part we rear a few choice puppies, to which we have taken a particular fancy, at home, allowing them to roam about at their own sweet will, and smiling cheerfully when a list of their delinquencies (murdered cats, fowls, ducks, torn clothes, and homesteads laid waste and devastated) is placed before us, putting our hand in our pocket and paying the piper cheerfully, always hoping that some day a good tune may be played whilst we drink from the mythical cup that hails from Altcar, and is called Waterloo. The rest we send out, and fortunately can congratulate ourselves on a long list of safe billets.

Exercise

# CHAPTER IV

## TREATMENT OF SAPLINGS

WHEN the greyhound sapling has reached the age of nine months, a course of treatment which will fit him to begin active training must be put in force. With those that have come in from walk, the first step is a thorough overhauling, carefully looking for signs of accidents, such as scars, enlarged joints, &c. Being satisfied of their freedom from outward weaknesses, the skin should be closely examined for symptoms of mange, eczema, or vermin; should such be discovered, the youngster must be isolated and treated accordingly, and under any circumstances a thorough washing with soft soap in tepid water is recommended, care being taken to thoroughly dry with a rough towel and rub down with a hair glove. The practised eye is pretty certain to detect the presence of internal parasites in a large percentage of the saplings that come in from walk unless they have been constantly attended by the kennelman on the system mentioned in the previous chapter. Anyhow we strongly advocate a general course of physic all round as soon as the youngsters have been cleaned up and have settled to their new abode. A dessert-spoonful of castor-oil, or, better still, a full teaspoonful of German liquorice powder, is first given, and this alone will often betray the presence of worms in the individual. A couple of days later they should be deprived of their evening meal, and on the following morning a dose of freshly grated areca-nut—as much as will lay on a shilling—should be given in butter ; in short, the same process is to be gone through as was practised in the days when they were weaned ; but now the doses must be stronger. If the presence of tapeworm is discovered, those suffering from it should be put aside and dosed again with areca-nut after the lapse of a week, but those which betray no sign of parasites should after a like interval be treated with santonine. When the owner is satisfied that his saplings are purged of all such pests, a tonic treatment will be found most desirable, and with this and regular feeding on suitable food, plenty of exercise and warm clean quarters, he will be pleasantly surprised at the rapid improvement that takes place in his charges. We have already given a description of tonics that are most beneficial, and also general directions for feeding, so we need only point out that the attendant must be guided by circumstances in his choice. Cod-liver oil, for instance, which is most valuable where there is lack of flesh and the patient remains thin and 'tucked up,' must not be administered too freely in the summer months, as it is very heating, and is apt, moreover, to develop an undesirable quantity of internal fat ; if sufficient and regular exercise is not given, it is sure to damage the liver and cause a complication of diseases, so that a watchful eye and common sense should be the guides that must determine the quantity to be used and the duration of the course. These remarks apply with equal force to Parrish's Food, a most useful agent both in wasting of tissue and where there is a tendency to rickety limbs and weak joints.

Now is the time when both home-reared saplings and those that have been sent in from walk must be removed to the kennels proper and rendered amenable to discipline : but on no account must this be done till they are outwardly and inwardly free of all ailments. The number of saplings placed in each department depends, of course, on the size thereof, but in no case should more than five be left together, and, if possible, they should already have been accustomed to one another's society, as greyhounds are apt to be nasty to a 'new chum.'

As a rule it is not advisable to place saplings with the old ones of either sex, or they may be terribly bullied; but a quiet, well-behaved old brood-bitch or young dog of well-tried and exemplary respectability is a most desirable kennel companion for the youngsters, and the force of example is never lost on them. Under no circumstances must a dog who has been used for stud purposes be placed with any of his own sex.

Most owners, in registering their dogs for running purposes, give them fancy names, such as would be both unwieldy and absurd for ordinary everyday work; so it is customary to bestow such appellations as Dick, Tom, or Harry on the saplings as soon as they have been relegated to the kennels, unless some name has been used at walk, in which case a deal of trouble is saved. The kennelman should always make a point of inquiring into this. At feeding-time they should be 'drawn' singly by name, and the allowance of food regulated according to the constitution and appetite of the individual. In fact, no better lesson can be learnt by the beginner at coursing than is obtained by a visit to a neighbouring kennel of foxhounds, always provided that the hounds have the reputation of being properly and methodically managed.

The greyhound is not half such a fool as he looks or is popularly supposed to be. If properly treated he will develop into an intelligent, affectionate and tractable animal, sometimes, indeed, suffering from an overflow of spirits, but he never need be either vicious, disobedient, or treacherous. Comparing his behaviour in kennel and his amenity to discipline with that of the foxhound, the balance is in his favour. There is an old adage that a greyhound cannot be a good one unless he is a fool; but we beg to differ, and most strongly object to the employment of fools for any purpose save that of making wise men laugh. The idea is that an intelligent dog is prone to run cunning, which may in some instances occur ; but, on the other hand, a real fool of a dog does not possess the spirit of emulation that prompts him to 'cut out' his opponent, nor does he show the fire, devil and dash that enable him to dust his hare in the style so taking to the eyes of experienced coursers.

One of the first cares of the attendant will be thoroughly to

Rioting

accustom his charges to the couplings and leads, for now they must be led on the roads in the cool of the morning for at least two hours at a brisk pace. If a quiet cob or pony can be procured, and the attendant is competent to stick on its outside, the youngsters can easily be taught to follow with commendable docility. They can then be taken from ten to fifteen miles five times a fortnight : they should be allowed to settle down to a slow steady running trot, and should be carefully prevented from galloping. In this manner a large number of all ages may be exercised together; but, if possible, a lad should ride fifty yards in the rear armed with a very light hound whip with a long fine lash. He should be sparing in the use of this weapon, but if he possesses a modicum of tact and intelligence he will be able to check any rough play or exuberance of spirits the greyhounds may be inclined to indulge in, and will be handy in case of the sudden rebellions which sometimes occur, and which are certainly a standing difficulty in the way of exercising on horseback. The harmless, necessary cat promenading the road or fleeing at their approach is a sight that no greyhound can bear with equanimity, and away they all go, despite the ratings of their attendant. Then the fun begins: pussy pops over a wall; over go the demons after her pell-mell; she seeks shelter in the cottage of her birth; in rush her pursuers; over go tables, chairs, plates, dishes; the goodwife is distracted and has hysterics, whilst her natural protector seizes a hatchet, and in righteous wrath may deal death and mutilation amongst the valuable but unruly desperadoes before the lads can dismount and appease their wrath; sometimes poor puss is caught and torn to shreds before help arrives, and sometimes she sets her claws in the eye of your most promising sapling. Nor are cats the only victims. A fugitive collie-dog is doomed, but one that stands his ground will probably escape unless an old dog of vicious propensities sets on him at once, when all the others may follow suit. Fowls, ducks, and other poultry run risks, especially from the jaws of saplings that have been reared at home in grass pens; for, as a rule, puppies are cured of this class of riot at their walks. All this kind of thing is very annoying, and even if the owner is prepared to dip generously into his pocket to make good the casualties, a deal of unpleasant feeling is engendered in the countryside, and he and his dogs are looked on as unmitigated nuisances. The only remedy, and that but a partial one, is to muzzle the dogs, an objectionable proceeding from many points of view: first, because of the difficulty of accustoming them to the restraint; and, secondly, because even the best patterns of muzzle must interfere to a great extent with free respiration and perspiration, and, as we have remarked, it is not entirely a safeguard, for muzzled greyhounds may cause as much mischief by terrorisation as with their teeth. Happy, then, is the trainer who has at his disposal a large tract of down-land intersected by sound roadways, where cats, fowls and ducks are not met with, and where a collie dog is an event.

In exercising on downs, in parks, or paddocks, a smaller number of greyhounds must be taken out at a time. Dogs that have trotted quietly enough at the horse's heels will now rush about and play, and these romps are sure to degenerate into bickerings and quarrels, sometimes indeed ending in bloodshed. Nor must old dogs be exercised with young ones under these circumstances; for, instead of leading them in a gallop, they will content themselves with hanging back and nipping the youngsters in the haunches; in fact, one of the most difficult tasks of a trainer is to keep his charges' skin whole and free from scars.

Having a due regard to the difficulties and dangers attending horse exercise, perhaps the safest plan is to *lead* the greyhounds for two or three hours' exercise on the roads, and give them an hour's galloping and play on the grass alternate days. Three months of this treatment (the saplings now being about a year old) will find most of them fit to be tried, and this point should be absolutely assured before they are allowed to see a hare. If on passing the hand from the point of the shoulder down the back to the stern, and then over the thighs, the muscles appear firm and wiry, if the coat is smooth and glossy, the eye bright, the nose cold and wet, and the pads of the feet hard and strong, there need be no hesitation, and it only remains to find a suitable place for the trial to take place, a difficulty that is very often hard to solve. The ideal trial-ground for young greyhounds is a fair sized, flat water meadow or a soundly turfed park if the space in the latter is not too great, an objection that would apply to marsh land, and such flats as those found at classic Altcar—for here our saplings run the danger not only of a terrible gruelling from one hare, but may get on to another before they can be picked up, thus being run to a standstill, and receiving a shock to the system from which they may never recover, and in such cases those of highest courage and promise are likely to be the first victims. Very hilly country is to be avoided, and a flinty soil, such as is found in Bucks and Herts, utterly forbids the slipping of a valuable greyhound, as one course would be sufficient to cut him to ribbons. Stubbles, too, are dangerous, and very apt to produce sore feet. Suitable ground being forthcoming, the question as to the advisability of trying a sapling with an old dog arises, and we have no hesitation in condemning the practice—that is, for the first time of asking, for saplings are easily discouraged. An old dog has an immense pull over one of this age, and is pretty sure to take every advantage; whereas if two saplings run together they meet on even terms, and will vie with one another, thus fostering the spirit of emulation which is so necessary in a dog that is asked to win stakes.

Should it be found impossible to obtain suitable trial-ground, recourse must be had to sapling stakes, affairs that are regarded with righteous horror by a large section of old-fashioned coursers, who maintain that to run a sapling is to ruin him. No doubt this prejudice arose before the days of enclosed meetings, when there was always the risk of a dog being clean pumped out; for these stakes were held at large open meetings, on the ground used for all-aged and puppy stakes. Moreover, many coursers would send their saplings to the slips unfit to gallop across a meadow, and how much more so to dust a hare! But at such enclosures as Haydock and Wye most useful trials for saplings can be had, and nothing but benefit is likely to accrue, providing the youngsters have been properly prepared for the ordeal. By this we do not mean *thoroughly trained*, a proceeding that would certainly ruin any sapling, but brought to such a pitch of physical welfare and freedom from external and internal fat, by the *régime* that we have indicated, as to render him capable of putting forth his powers of speed and endurance without an undue strain on his constitution.

In such sapling trials a shorter slip is given, and the escape is brought half way up the ground, by which means the severity of the course is greatly modified. Moreover, the stakes are limited to four dogs, and if a sapling wins his first course, but shows symptoms of distress, a division can generally be agreed upon, or he can be withdrawn.

Thus a good line can often be obtained, and a dog that has acquitted himself well when pitted against a fancied one of

Feeding

another kennel will later on serve as a useful trial-dog for his kennel companions.

It will now be found an excellent plan to divide the saplings into three classes, keeping them in separate compartments, and placing the best accommodation at the service of Class I., which will consist of well-tried youngsters and those who from their quality, conformation, breeding or style of moving promise great things. Class II. will contain promising but backward ones, in whom time may work wonders, and who, as they come on in looks, or win a satisfactory trial, may be promoted to the superior class. Class III. will consist of very backward ones, and such as lack size and substance, or show but little quality, but whom one is loth to part with, living in hopes that they may see a better day; and it is far from improbable that a gem may suddenly be discovered in this ragged company. It is wonderful what strides very late puppies take when once they begin to improve, and the ugly duckling may yet develop swan's plumage. But the maim, the halt, and the blind, and such as have, with every advantage thrown in, failed signally in their trials, should be destroyed, or bestowed on a neighbouring farmer who enjoys a sporting course on his own land; for a greyhound that 'is not good enough' is good for nothing from a courser's point of view. We are quite aware how difficult it is to make up one's mind thus summarily to dispose of a dog of whom from his earliest days great things have been expected, and whom we have trotted out with pomp and pride. We make all sorts of excuses for his failure, and are always giving him 'another chance.' Undue precipitancy may once in a way lead us to dispose of what subsequently proves to be a smart dog, but in nine cases out of ten we shall not repent the loss, and a long bill for food, entrances, travelling expenses, with zero on the credit side, will be avoided.

When the season has finally closed and the erstwhile saplings (now puppies) have been thoroughly weeded out, a good dose of sulphur or fluid magnesia can be given, and a dressing of black sulphur and vaseline applied from head to foot. They can now rest awhile from long exercise on the roads, but should be taken out for at least an hour daily and allowed to stretch their legs on the grass. At this period the food must not be of too heating or fat-producing a nature, and cod-liver oil must be eschewed; but old hound-meal, dog-biscuits, lean horseflesh, with carrots, turnips, vegetable marrows or beetroots, will form the staple diet, and if a tonic is required iron pills may be used; also Parrish's food mixed with the pudding, in the proportion of one teaspoonful to each dog, will be found most beneficial. Now that the youngsters begin to look like business, attendants are fond of polishing their coats up too much; but this should be delayed for three or four months, as the benefit is only temporary, and is calculated to produce a ragged and thin jacket later on.

After a month's rest the road-work should begin once more, and must be continued at an increased ratio till the puppies are ready to enter upon strict training.

The leisure can be employed in mapping out a campaign for the coming season, and nominations must be taken for suitable produce stakes. The season generally opens about the middle of September, when a big and well-conducted meeting is held at Haydock Park. Here all the choicest and most forward puppies are entered, and if such high game is aimed at, it will be necessary to find our best puppies and exert every energy to bring them to the slips trained to the hour. For these early produce stakes it would obviously be useless to enter anything born later than March, or April at the outside; for the more mature ones, that saw the light at the ushering in of the new year, hold an advantage that can only be wiped out by phenomenal merit, though the May or June puppy may turn the tables in a stake run in the ensuing spring, if not earlier. These facts will therefore guide the courser in taking his nominations, and his plan for the season being satisfactorily decided, he should not trouble himself about the puppies until the beginning of July, beyond seeing that they are properly fed, exercised and kept in a state of boisterous health.

# CHAPTER V

## THE GREYHOUND IN TRAINING

'STONEHENGE,' in his standard work on the greyhound, gives very explicit directions for the reduction of fat and weight, whereby a dog that was absolutely unfit may be hurriedly prepared for a stake. With such we shall not deal; but rather we shall presume that both puppies and older dogs have by degrees been prepared for the final touches by the regular and gradual treatment that we have advocated in the preceding chapters. Hurried preparations are seldom satisfactory, and though in some instances a dog thus treated may see the end of an important stake, it is generally more by good fortune than by reason of his training; even if his first two courses are brilliant, a sudden collapse is likely to occur in the third. If the dogs are thoroughly well exercised and carefully fed during the summer months, very little extra work is needed to complete the winding-up process; nevertheless, the trainer must be very careful that he does not 'bring on' his charges too quickly; if a dog, and especially a puppy, is prematurely wound up to concert pitch, he is sure to run down and become stale before he is wanted.

In this treatise on training we shall only deal with dogs that are presumably fit to begin work, that are in themselves sound and well, and that will eat with relish what is given to them. It may be the lot of many a trainer to have a dog to prepare that is gross and fat, with soft feet and long nails, or one that is so upset by strong work that he goes off his feed.

These are exceptional cases demanding exceptional treatment from practised hands: for ourselves, we repeat, we shall presume that we start with our team in good health, and more than half prepared by summer exercise. We are greatly in favour of a very gradual preparation, a belief that has been engendered by our experience of foxhounds, whose work calls for training such as will produce the physical state so desirable

[illegible]

in the greyhound: for to account for his fox the hound must be possessed of pace, dash, and stamina relatively as great as may enable the greyhound to win an important stake. It has, therefore, struck us that what is sauce for the goose is sauce for the gander; and since we have possessed a pack of foxhounds that could travel fifteen miles to the meet, hunt from 11 A.M. to 4 P.M., return to kennel with sterns up and could repeat this performance with variations five days a fortnight throughout the season, we fail to see why a similar *régime* applied to greyhounds should not prove eminently successful. We say similar, because the nature of the hound and his conformation are not identical with those of 'the long dog.' Nor has the fostering of top speed to be considered in the preparation of the former.

In the early days, say from the beginning of July, slow exercise on the roads in the early morning, and a frolic on the grass in the evening, will be sufficient. As time goes on, the duration of exercise must be increased; but if any member of the string is footsore on his return to kennel, or appears inert and jaded, he must be eased in his work. On returning from road exercise the trainer should wash the feet of his charges in strong brine or a saturated solution of alum. If any inflammation or soreness is visible, an application of Friar's Balsam will give relief; but the individual must not go again on the roads until the symptoms have entirely disappeared. If a gash has been cut by a flint or piece of broken glass, the application of Spratt's Locurium—a most valuable preparation—will be found efficacious.

The next proceeding is thoroughly to rub down each dog with a horsehair hand-glove. This massage should begin at the shoulder and forelegs, be carried down the back and loins to the root of the stern, and end with the thighs, stifles, and hocks; after which a clean chamois leather may be applied. The usual time for feeding greyhounds in training is the middle of the day; but we much prefer it on their return from evening exercise, for two reasons: first, the dogs are more likely to curl themselves up and pass a restful night if fed late; whereas, if they are given their meal earlier they are prone to prowl about and sing choruses that, however charming to their own ears, are not at all calculated to call forth blessings from their human friends who have the misfortune to dwell within hearing. Secondly, dogs that are accustomed to a midday meal will be upset by the want of it when engaged at a coursing meeting; for, of course, conditions may not be favourable for them to be indulged.

The question of gallops is one that requires more thought and tact than that of road-work, as with the former there are many matters to be considered and many theories to be advanced; with regard to the latter, the duration of the exercise, and the pace, are all that need trouble the trainer. If a horse is employed for the purpose, we should advise a walk of a mile, then a steady increase of pace for two miles, taking care that the dogs do not gallop but settle down, like hounds, to a slinging trot, then walk again, and so on alternately until at least

The toilette

twelve miles have been traversed. As condition improves the trotting can be increased and the walking lessened. Many trainers are of opinion that this style of road exercise is calculated to 'slow' a greyhound; and we are hardly prepared to contradict the theory emphatically, though our opinion is not in accord. What we do assert is, that the effect on stamina is most marked, and the advantage that dogs thus trained have over those that have only been *walked out* is very manifest at open meetings where hares are strong and courses long. We have always held that, where a dog is being trained for an enclosed meeting, a preparation widely different is necessary; but as this style of coursing is practically moribund, it would serve no good purpose to enter upon the subject at any length.

True, Haydock Park still exists and flourishes; and in Ireland there are more than one of these enclosures; but an English or Scotch dog that runs at Haydock must, for the rest of the season, look for his laurels in the open.

Stamina, then, is as important as pace, and many a half-trained flyer is out-counted by a plodding dog who means 'being there' as long as the hare lives.

Now comes the question of gallops, and, to begin with, it will be necessary to find a strip of sound turf on the decline, or slightly undulating. With young greyhounds it is a fatal mistake to gallop them uphill; for that, we have no doubt, is highly prejudicial to speed, and induces an undesirable shoulder action, whereas a gallop on a decline is calculated to produce speed and develop the shoulder. There are several ways of galloping greyhounds, and the one usually practised is for a boy to take the string some three furlongs from the trainer. The latter then holloas or whistles, and the boy releases one that is sure to go straight; when this one has traversed a couple of hundred yards another is slipped, and so on until the whole string is under weigh—each one will strive to overtake the dog in front of him, and will thus be properly extended. If sufficient interval is not allowed they overtake one another, and rough play begins, generally ending in torn flanks and perforated thighs.

When the gallops are increased in length, the trainer must mount his horse and gallop away whistling, when in like manner the dogs are slipped one by one, and in their eagerness to overtake the horse they will refrain from interfering with one another.

It is very important that the horse selected for this duty should be thoroughly quiet, or disastrous results may ensue.

The most likely animal is a hunt servant's horse, that is thoroughly accustomed to hounds crowding round his legs ; such a one is not only free from kick, but will carefully avoid treading on them, whereas one that has not been accustomed to hounds is almost sure to let fly when they come racing up to his heels—bounding and barking as is their wont—and even if he refrains from so doing, is likely by clumsiness and fidgetting to put his hoofs on their precious toes.

Those who have closely followed 'Stonehenge's' directions for galloping greyhounds, and now turn to these pages, will be struck by the fact that the great sporting writer advocates up-hill galloping and long work. In fact, he goes so far as to say that the trainer should mount his horse and gallop his charges *for four miles at top speed*. This, we confess, is positively astounding. Perhaps the greyhounds of the day are a degenerate lot ; but we fancy that there are very few whose constitution would stand such an ordeal. And what about the horse ? The days of Beacon courses and rides to Ghent, not to mention York, are over, and if greyhounds are not what they were, the same applies to horses yea, even to trained racers.

Exercise in the paddock

No, we opine that stamina should be induced by road work, and speed by short gallops, six furlongs being quite the limit at

the dogs are fully extended. It is true that greyhounds have to cover long distances when contesting a course in public; but the very bends, wrenches, and turns afford relief that is not obtained in a straight-away gallop, in the same way that a racehorse, who cannot stay home in a five-furlong sprint, is often seen to advantage in a race of two miles over hurdles.

When we advised that the first gallops should take place on a decline, we did not mean that this should apply to the whole period of training. As condition improves and the date of 'cherry-ripeness' approaches, undulating ground will be desirable, so as to bring into play all the muscular powers; but we still object to a long incline.

Every day the trainer must overhaul his charges, and the first spot on which he must place his hand is the chest and brisket. If these, and particularly the former, are soft and flabby, then is the subject far from fit, and increased work will be necessary; but if they are firm and hard to the touch, a near approach to fitness is indicated. Next, the hand is passed down the neck, back, and quarters, and second thighs, and here the eye will aid the touch; but experience alone will guide the two.

The question of weight is a most important one, and every kennel should be supplied with a machine for the purpose. A weighing-machine has been invented of late which is much in vogue at dog shows, where the exhibits are classified by weight, and this is well adapted to the purposes of the greyhound trainer. It consists of a cage or cradle of galvanised iron in which the dog is easily placed, when the exact weight is registered on a dial.

It is almost an axiom with trainers that the weight of a twelve-months-old sapling, when in full and lusty condition, but not fat, is the weight at which that dog should run as a puppy when trained to the hour. There are frequent exceptions to this rule, as some dogs train lighter than others, while some show to greater advantage when running big; but the rule is a good one to keep in view when reducing flesh, and is for the most part approximately correct. When once the trainer has found the weight at which a mature dog shows to greatest advantage, the weighing-machine will always answer the important question as to ripeness, and will frequently check a tendency to over-train.

The advice we have given as to the final preparation of greyhounds must only be taken generally, as it is impossible to lay down any hard and fast rule, for the simple reason that the constitutions and temperaments of greyhounds vary to a remarkable degree. The old saying that 'What is one man's meat is another man's poison,' is peculiarly applicable to greyhounds; a preparation necessary to enable one dog to stay to the end of a big stake would send another to the slips jaded and 'over-marked.' Here is where the ability, experience, and intelligence of the trainer are tested. It is his duty to mark the running of each of his charges most carefully, and when he sees one display fire and dash, together with stamina, he will know that he has had a preparation that suits his constitution. But when a kennel companion that has had identical work shows speed and smartness in his first or first two courses, but, without undue pumping, or any unforeseen contingency such as a cut or a sprain, fails to raise a gallop, and lobs along behind his opponent without attempting to share the work, he may reasonably suspect that the dog is over-trained, and on a future occasion it will be as well to send him to the slips a pound or two heavier.

There are many greyhounds who, starting in a stake a bit above themselves, yet manage to survive a couple of courses, and, improving as they go on, run themselves into perfect condition, and wind up brilliantly. Examples of this are very frequent, and a notable one is Miss Glendyne, who was decidedly 'jolly' when she went to the slips for the Waterloo Cup the year following that in which she had divided with Fullerton's dam, her half-sister Bit of Fashion. She ran her first two courses in very slovenly style; but by the time she met Penelope II. in the final she was thoroughly fit, and her display was one of the grandest ever seen.

The adage that we have quoted as applied to work is of still greater force when the all-important question of food is to be considered; and here, again, observation and study of the individual must constantly occupy the trainer's mind. It used to be considered a *sine quâ non* that the only way to prepare a dog was to stuff him with unlimited mutton, on the principle adopted by domestic servants, I suppose, who fancy that they will drop down dead or faint over their menial tasks if they fail to consume a sufficient poundage of 'butcher's meat.' We are quite opposed to this idea, and feel convinced that nothing upsets a dog's stomach and renders him stale and useless more than a continued use of toasted mutton, without a variety of other food. A greyhound will stand his road-work and gallops for several months, and flourish thereon; but stuff him with a surfeit of animal food for one month only, and the chances are he will utterly lose his form. It is very easy to ascertain when a dog has had too much animal food—on examination the fæces will be found to be black; if, on the contrary, there has not been a sufficient quantity, the motions will be almost colourless; when they are the colour of ochre the proportion is correct.

When a dog has been trained and run for a stake, and is wanted again in, say, three weeks' time, it is a good plan to 'let him down,' i.e. his exercise should be gentle and only sufficient to keep him healthy and active, and his food should consist of old meal, brown bread, vegetables, trotter jelly, and broth of sheep's heads. No more solid animal food should be given till within ten days of his running again. As soon as he returns from the first meeting he should have a dose of Epsom salts or German liquorice powder, to be followed by a tonic ball. It is wonderful how this treatment and the cessation of solid animal food will freshen the stomach, and prepare the dog for another ordeal. The resumption of solid mutton for a week previously to running will be found ample; even if he went to the slips on the former occasion rather stale and over-trained, he may now appear in totally different colours, and surprise everyone by his smartness. Very likely this will

Preparing the food

cause him to be dubbed an uncertain animal, but the trainer will know to what his success is due, and will make a note of it for further use.

Cases of dogs winning important stakes when practically

untrained are common enough, and their connections immediately say, 'If Fly-by night could perform like that in such condition, what could he not do if thoroughly prepared?' So they proceed to trot and gallop him vigorously, stuff him with slices of mutton from prime joints, and bring him to the slips heavily backed for a big stake; and great is their dismay when he is upset in the first round, perhaps by a dog whom he easily beat when untrained.

As with racehorses so with greyhounds: many an under-trained one wins, and many an over-trained one goes down. Moral:—It is better to under-train than to over-train your horses and dogs.

Many trainers are in the habit of 'letting down' their charges immediately before running—that is to say, they give them a strong preparation to within four days of the meeting; they then dose with Epsom salts, and substitute a light farinaceous diet up to the day on which they are to run. The wisdom of this plan we take the liberty of doubting, believing that a too sudden reaction of the digestive organs would be induced, and a consequent relaxation of nerve and muscles ensue; and we have noted that greyhounds thus treated have perhaps shown speed and brilliance, but have failed to stay beyond a course or two, even when they have been lightly let off. With regard to general feeding, variety should be the watchword; for, however good the food may be, no dog will thrive without a change, not only in the ingredients used, but in the method of preparation and the consistency of the pudding. Taking a dog of ordinary constitution whose peculiarities are unknown to us, and given a month to prepare him for a stake, we should feed him as follows, having first administered opening medicine followed by alterative condition balls, and an external dressing of black sulphur and train oil.

*For the first week.*—Well-boiled and shredded horse-flesh with its broth, old hound-meal, mashed turnips and beetroots.

*Second week.*—Toasted horse-flesh cut into small squares, brown bread, trotter jelly, carrots or parsnips.

*Third week.*—Boiled sheep's heads, a very little meal, brown bread, Brand's Extract, a few potatoes and no tripe.

*Fourth week.*—Toasted mutton, no meal, brown bread, trotter jelly, and a few mashed turnips (every other day).

Pity the poor trainer and owner whose brightest hopes are centred on the female members of the kennel! When bitches are really brilliant there is no denying them, and it is almost impossible to refrain from hopes that may at any moment be dashed by the exigencies of Nature. All may go well till the night of the draw, and then the discovery is made which leads to despair.

Sometimes a bitch in use will run with even greater fire than usual; but the effort generally dies away after a course or two, and a collapse may be looked for at any moment; nor do we think it is fair for an owner to send a bitch to the slips in such a state. Should she meet a dog, the latter is sure to be upset and his attention will be distracted; nevertheless, it is a remarkable fact that on the appearance of the hare everything will give way to the ruling passion for the chase.

Where important issues are involved, owners and trainers often make great efforts to bring a bitch to the slips in the face of Nature's attack. Should she come in use, say, three weeks or a month prior to the date on which the stake is to open, a common practice is to put her to the dog, and it not infrequently happens that at the beginning of pregnancy she may quite retain her form.

If a bitch is allowed to pass (i.e. if she is withheld from the dog), it will be useless to dream of running her for at least three months from the first appearance of the symptoms. The reason of this is that Nature keeps on accumulating internal fat and tissue to fit the bitch for the duties that should have been hers, while toward the time when, in the natural course of things, her whelps would have been born, the lacteal glands secrete a certain amount of milk. To be on the safe side, fourteen weeks should elapse before the bitch is sent to the slips, though training may start three weeks earlier.

Having regard to this difficulty, the hopes of a courser's kennel should never be entirely centred in bitches; and so often does this exasperating disappointment occur, that there are many old and knowing hands who never train or run bitches, but keep them, if found in the kennel at all, solely for breeding purposes.

# CHAPTER VI

## ENCLOSED COURSING

THE idea of enclosing grounds for coursing purposes originated with Mr. T. H. Case, who, as is well known, showed marked acquaintance with the habits of the hare, and also considerable powers of organisation. Towards the end of December, 1876, the ground at Plumpton, which had been enclosed with wire-fencing at considerable expense, was ready for the first meeting to be held in the new style. A programme, consisting of a thirty-two, two sixteens, two eights, and a four, was considered large enough to start with, and the stakes filled without difficulty. The dinner and draw were held at the Gloucester Hotel, Brighton. The late General Goodlake, V.C., took an active part in the general arrangements, and also used his influence to have special trains run from London and Brighton at convenient hours each morning. The principal event was the Street Place Stakes, which was won by Mr. H. G. Miller's Master Banrigh, Mr. T. Quihampton's Quaver running up. The success which attended the first fixture induced Mr. Case to increase the entry fee, and in the following March we had the Southern Cup for thirty-two All-ages at 10*l.* 10*s.* each. This brought eight ex-Waterlooers to slips, namely: Dark Rustic, Kilkenny, Serapis, Huron, Sir Magnus, Conster, The Squatter, and High Gillerspie. The stake resulted in a division between Mr. G. Darlinson's Dark Rustic and Mr. H. Heywood's Early Morn. The following year more important stakes were run for, the entry for the Great Southern Cup (sixty-four subscribers) being increased to 12*l.* 10*s.* each, the winner to receive

250*l.* and a piece of plate value 50*l.* In the final course Mr. G. Darlinson's Deceit beat Mr. G. Woodward's Woodland King. The fame of the Plumpton ground had now spread far and wide, and we had amongst the Irish supporters Lord Lurgan, Captain Archdale, Mr. F. Watson, and Mr. J. Sands. Other patrons of the meeting were the Duke of Hamilton, Lord St. Vincent, Sir John D. Astley, and Colonel Goodlake.'

Enclosed coursing. Driving out a hare

It may be mentioned that, although the new style had become popular with a certain section of the coursing community, many of the old school opposed it strongly, and with the best reason, for it utterly lacked the elements of real sport. The Ground Game Act, however, which came into operation in September 1880, having naturally led to a lessening of the number of hares throughout the country, it was urged that, if coursing was to exist, the enclosed system became almost a necessity. From that time old-fashioned meetings dropped out one by one, owing to the scarcity of game.

The September fixture in 1884 was a very successful meeting at Plumpton, the Grand Produce Stakes of 6*l.* each, 1*l.* ft., securing no fewer than 128 runners, out of an original entry of 298. The prizes were 500*l.* the winner, 150*l.* the second, and 50*l.* each third and fourth. For the deciding course Mr. T. Graham's Glen Islay, by Glenlivet—Glengowan,

Starting the hare

and Mr. H. J. Norman's Newsboy, by Peter—Nellie, divided after an undecided. Mr. C. W. Lea's Latha and his Lara were third and fourth. The meeting was carried on for another five years, but despite the erection of a commodious stand, the outside public held aloof, and February 1889 saw the last of the Plumpton gatherings.

Gosforth followed Plumpton (the enclosure being made by Mr. Case), and was well supported, as might be expected from the number of greyhounds kept in the north of England, and the ardour with which coursing has always been pursued in this locality. The trials at Gosforth during Mr. Case's management were of the very best description. Coursing continued to flourish there until March 1889, when several of the directors who did not care for the sport called a special meeting of the company and it was resolved to discontinue it. The following return of the winners and runners-up in the Gold Cup shows that speed has well served at Gosforth, for we find that a greyhound like Cangaroo, whose only redeeming point was speed, carried off the prize from a brilliant performer like Greentick. Many greyhounds who distinguished themselves in the open ran at Gosforth, notably Mineral Water and Burnaby (both Waterloo Cup winners), Free Flag (Netherby Cup winner), Markham (Netherby Cup divider as a puppy), Waterford, Todlaw Dene, Nimrod, Glenkirk, and Plymouth Rock, whose names will all be found in the following list:—

1881

THE HIGH GOSFORTH PARK GOLD CUP, at 6*l.* 10*s* each; winner 150*l.* and gold cup, value 50 guineas, second 90*l.* 64 subs.

Mr. G. Darlinson ns (Mr. J. Hinks's) be d Marshal M'Mahon, by Master Sam—Death, beat Mr. W. J. Morrison's bk d Free Flag, by Freeman—British Flag.

1882

GOSFORTH GOLD CUP, at 10*l.* 10*s.* each; winner 500*l.* and gold cup, second 200*l.* and silver cup; 128 subs.

Mr. G. J. Alexander's w bd d Alec Halliday, by Fugitive—Free Trade, beat Mr. W. Osborne's r or f d Waterford, by Bothal Park—Curiosity.

1883

GOSFORTH GOLD CUP, at 10*l.* 10*s.* each; winner 500*l.* and cup, second 200*l.* and piece of plate; 128 subs.

Mr. L. Hall ns (Mr. A. Vines's) w f d Markham, by Banker—Pall Mall, beat Mr. O. Markham's bk w d Woodpecker, by Bedfellow—Agricola.

1884

GOSFORTH GOLD CUP, at 10*l.* 10*s.* each, cup value 50 guineas, with piece of plate, value 15 guineas to the second; winner 500*l.* and gold cup, second 200*l.* and piece of plate; 128 subs.

Mr. M. Spittle ns (Mr. W. Carver's) r or f d Britain Still, by Misterton—Arama, beat Mr. W. P. Greenall ns (Mr. H. J. Norman's) bk w d Nimrod, by Misterton—Fair Helen.

1885

GOSFORTH GOLD CUP, at 12*l.* 12*s.* each, with 500*l.* added; winner 1,000*l.*, second 250*l.*; 128 subs.

Mr. J. Mayer's w bk d Mineral Water, by Memento—Erzeroum, beat Mr. Postlethwaite ns (Mr. H. Thompson's) r d Todlaw Dene, by Herrera—Terrific.

1886

GOSFORTH GOLD CUP, at 12*l.* 12*s.* each, with 500*l.* added; winner 1,000*l.*, second 250*l.*; 128 subs.

Mr. H. Emmerson ns (Mr. J. Kellett's) bk d Cangaroo, by Bothal Park—Bundle and Go, beat Mr. R. F. Gladstone's bd d Greentick, by Bedfellow—Heartburn.

1887

GOSFORTH GOLD CUP, at 12*l.* 12*s.* each, with 500*l.* added; winner 1,000*l.*, second 250*l.*; 128 subs.

Mr. H. G. Miller's bk d Mullingar, by Misterton—Gulnare II., beat Mr. E. Dent's w bk d Huic Halloa, by Jester—Countess.

1888

GOSFORTH GOLD CUP, at 10*l.* 10*s.* each; winner 470*l.* and cup, value 50 guineas, second 190*l.*; 119 subs.

Mr. E. Dent's w bk d Huic Halloa, by Jester—Countess, and Mr. L. Pilkington's bk w d Burnaby, by Be Joyful—Baroness, divided.

1889

GOSFORTH GOLD CUP, at 10*l.* 10*s.* each; winner 350*l.*, second 125*l.*; 75 subs.

Mr. T. Edwards' r d Glenkirk, by Misterton—Glengowan; Col. J. T. North's bd b Kate Cuthbert, by Greentick—Bit of

Fashion; and Mr. W. Paterson's r w d Plymouth Rock, by Carratze—Process, divided, without the latter running his bye.

Kempton came next, and the fact of Mr. S. H. Hyde being at the head of affairs (coursing) was a guarantee for good management. It was over the Sunbury pastures that the first 1,000*l.* prize was run for, the ground, like Haydock, being a dead flat. Hares ran very weakly at first, and coursing was a comparative failure, but after a year trials were fairly good, and continued to improve subsequently. Coursing at Kempton took immensely at first with Londoners, but after a few meetings the attendance fell off, and the patronage of the general public became so scant that the directors resolved to cease holding meetings, and the champion fixture of January 1889 was abandoned.

The reason given was that during the last three years the directors had to fill several nominations the best way they could, so as to secure the requisite number of runners, and the meetings were carried on at a loss. The following return gives the winner and runner-up in the Great Champion Stakes:—

1883

CHAMPION STAKES, at 25 guineas each, with 500*l.* added; winner 1,000*l.*, second 500*l.*; 64 subs.

Mr. L. Nicholl's f d p Royal Stag, by Ptarmigan—Raby Lass, beat Dr. T. S. Hosford ns (Mr. W. Osborne's) r or f d Waterford, by Bothal Park—Curiosity.

1884

CHAMPION STAKES, at 25 guineas each, with 500*l.* added; winner 1,000*l.*, second 400*l.*; 64 subs.

Mr. G. Bell Irving ns (Mr. H. G. Miller's) r d Manager, by Misterton—Devotion, and Mr. T. Stone's r d Sea Pilot, by Haddo—Sea Beauty, divided.

1885

CHAMPION STAKES, at 25*l.* each, with 500*l.* added; winner 1,000*l.*, second 400*l.*; 64 subs.

Mr. S. H. Hyde's bd d Ballangeich, by Craighton Castle—Heathbird, beat Mr. W. Carver's r or f d Britain Still, by Misterton—Arama.

1886

CHAMPION STAKES, at 25*l.* each, with 500*l.* added ; winner 1,000*l.*, second 400*l.* ; 64 subs.

Mr. T. Stone ns (Mr. L. Pilkington's) bk d Phœbus, by Coleraine Diamond—sister to Lady Hester, beat Mr. C. Hibbert ns r d Gay City, by Paris—Lady Glendyne.

1887

CHAMPION STAKES, at 25*l.* each, with 500*l.* added ; winner 1,000*l.*, second 400*l.* ; 64 subs.

Mr. W. Reilly ns (Mr. E. Dent's) Huic Halloa, by Jester—Countess, beat Mr. R. F. Gladstone's bk d Greater Scot, by Macpherson—Madge.

1888

CHAMPION STAKES, at 10*l.* 10*s.* each ; winner 600*l.*, second 200*l.* ; 64 subs.

Mr. S. Handford ns (Mr. G. Hobbs's) bk d Holmby, by Clyto—High Opinion, beat Mr. H. G. Miller's bk d Mullingar, by Misterton—Gulnare II.

1889

CHAMPION STAKES, at 10*l.* 10*s.* each, with 400*l.* added ; winner 600*l.*, second 200*l.* ; 64 subs.

Major H. Holmes's bk w d Puddletown, by Domino—Bonniness, beat Mr. A. Sydney's bk w d p Pilate Black, by Northern Express—sister to Petrarch.

Haydock Park succeeded Gosforth Park, and with capital management some good sport of its kind has been witnessed here from time to time. Being in the midst of a coursing district, and adjacent to such populous centres as Liverpool, Manchester, Wigan, &c. &c., Haydock has hardly received that amount of patronage from the public one would naturally expect. Many stirring and striking associations attach to Haydock Park, and Greentick, Fullerton, Herschel, and Gay City have all tingled the blood of onlookers by their brilliant displays. Fullerton first came out in the Lancashire enclosure, and took people by storm in his succession of fine courses, though one hammering after another over the adamantine surface, the ground being very hard that week, entailed defeat in the final trial, the only one he has suffered. Herschel won his spurs at Haydock by dividing the Champion Produce Stake, and undoubtedly his very best performance was over this ground, in the Haydock Gold Cup, when he shot clean away from one speedy greyhound after another. Probably Gay City's best display was for the same cup upon another occasion. One of Greentick's Haydock victories will always be recollected from the sensational incident of his striking the escape hurdle with such force as to fall back apparently dead. The sympathy that existed for this gallant greyhound was shown by the cheer that greeted him when his trainer, John Coke, led him back shortly after the accident, and his own gameness was testified when he afterwards won the final course.

The Irish greyhound, Pinkerton, also upon one occasion made a succession of brilliant displays, winning course after course in one-sided fashion, though every hare took him to the top of the ground.

The Wye Racecourse being easily converted into an enclosure, Mr. G. Kennett started his first meeting in 1883. The trials generally are of indisputable excellence, and as the ground gradually rises to the escape, a capital view is obtained of the working-powers of a greyhound, which is often lost when running on the level. A few years since, Mr. Kennett started the East Kent Club, and has on his list sixty members. Wye, however, fares no better than Haydock Park as regards the support of the public, and it remains to be seen if either of these meetings[1]—now the only two enclosures in England—will be carried on after another season. Several good greyhounds have made their *début* over the Wye ground, viz. Holmby, Puddletown, Glenmahra, Winfarthing, Myra Ellen, and Janet's Pride.

The Four Oaks Park Company was started with a large capital to carry on racing and coursing, and, being situated close to Birmingham and other large Midland towns, everything

[1] Since the above was written, a new enclosure has been opened at Witham in Essex.

GREENTICE

looked promising for the shareholders. The coursing entailed a considerable loss from 1883 to the close of the season 1886; but as the enclosure never took with either the racing or coursing public, the autumn of 1890 saw the company go into liquidation, and the estate is now to be built over. Many good greyhounds were seen at Four Oaks Park, amongst

Counting the slain

others Marshal McMahon, Winchester, Witchery, Quicklime, Rosewater, Golden Star, Miss Staton, Fair Floraline, &c.

The Doncaster Coursing Company, Limited, with a capital of 5,000*l.* in 5*l.* shares, had a very brief existence. The first meeting was held December 1882, and the next and last the following year, when, owing to want of proper management, hares ran so badly that many sportsmen left the ground in disgust. The fixtures were soon afterwards sold off, and the ground is now under cultivation.

Mourne Park, the first of the Irish enclosures, was established by the Earl of Kilmorey in the autumn of 1879. The ground could hardly then, nor could it till a couple of years later, be strictly called an enclosure, as the hares were driven from a spinney; in fact, it was not an enclosure as the term is generally understood. A few years later the present coursing ground was designed by Mr. Case. Hares have never run stoutly at Mourne Park, but it was well adapted for trying puppies, and being generally the first meeting of the season was well patronised by English and Scotch coursers; the beauty of the surrounding scenery was also a great attraction to visitors. One meeting, sometimes two in the season, continued to be held until the year 1890.

Purdysburn has been established within the past year and a half in the North of Ireland. A club was formed in Belfast, and permission obtained from that good sportsman, the late Mr. R. N. Batt, to hold a couple of meetings during the season in his demesne. The ground is well adapted for coursing, and the management being in the hands of a most business-like and energetic committee, it may fairly be anticipated that Purdysburn will soon take high rank amongst the coursing fixtures of the season. As with Holestone, there is no lack of support in the shape of greyhounds, large numbers being bred every year in the surrounding country. A most successful gathering was held over the Purdysburn enclosure, November 1890.

Trabolgan, in the South of Ireland, if not so easy of access as the other three meetings just mentioned, is not inferior to any of them in the quality of the sport provided. Situated in Lord Fermoy's demesne overlooking Cork Harbour, in fine weather it is a delightfully wild and picturesque spot. Hares are reared on the ground, and are driven from two spinneys, one at each end of a large field, so that the running happily partakes of the character of open coursing. Few understand better than the noble owner of Trabolgan, Lord Fermoy, coursing and the management of hares, and hence sport of a high order may always be reckoned upon at the Southern Club meetings. Unfortunately, there is not the same keen ardour

Driving hares out of the wood

for coursing in the province of Munster as in Ulster, and a difficulty in filling stakes is often experienced.

Holestone followed Mourne Park, and from the very beginning was a decided success. The enclosure is situated on Mr. James Owen's property, and a better or more genial sportsman than the proprietor of Holestone does not exist. The running is rather severe, as it is all uphill, but the trials are of the very best kind. The running ground being in the midst of a district celebrated for the number of good greyhounds it has produced, it is almost needless to add that little difficulty is experienced in filling the stakes. Indeed, there is no part

True to their hares

of Ireland where so many greyhounds are bred and reared as in the district surrounding Holestone, nor in Her Majesty's wide dominions are there keener coursers to be found. Two, and sometimes three, meetings are annually held at Holestone.

In comparing the two styles, greyhounds repeatedly run at enclosed meetings very quickly acquire a dangerous knowledge and lose the better instincts of the animal, which we take to be a determination to regain possession when thrown out, jealousy of a rival in possession and anxiety to displace him, fearlessness in following the hare, no matter what the difficulty.

All these qualities in time become wanting in the 'enclosed

greyhound.' How often do we see him take the upper ground, and deliberately wait, showing no anxiety to regain possession! No doubt the enclosed system has caused a marked deterioration in greyhounds, and many of their good qualities have become extinct, the exception being speed. Very possibly the dangerous knowledge acquired at enclosures may be transmitted

The high jump

to the offspring: at all events greyhounds within the past decade have exhibited brain power of rather too high an order. A return to the old system, which now appears imminent, should be welcomed in the interests of true sport; for, attractive as were the 1,000*l.* prizes, the winners came from a few kennels, and pace in most instances carried the day.

# CHAPTER VII

## SOME CELEBRATED GREYHOUNDS OF THE PAST

In our *résumé* of the Waterloo Cup we touched on the winners in the early contests when the trophy was a thirty-two dog stake; and among the heroines of those days Cerito is worthy of a niche in the Temple of Fame: she won no fewer than three times—viz. as a puppy in 1850, in 1852 and 1853. She was by Lingo out of Wanton. The next greyhound of mark that comes under notice is Senate, for his victory of 1847 was repeated by his son Sackcloth in 1854; and here we append a table of Waterloo winners whose progeny have also been successful:—

Senate (1847) begat Sackcloth (1854)
Judge (1855) „ Clive[1] (1859)
„ „ Maid of the Mill (1860)
„ „ Chloe (1863)
Canaradzo (1861) begat King Death (1864)
Brigadier (1866) „ Honeymoon (1875)
Bit of Fashion (1885)[2] gave birth to Fullerton (1889-90)

It will be seen that this is a very limited list, and the old adage that 'like begets like' is not borne out to a remarkable extent; however, there are many examples of dogs who have run prominently in the Waterloo Cup shining as sires of absolute winners; such, for instance, as Fusilier (sire of Muriel), Greentick (sire of Fullerton and Troughend), and Macpherson (sire of Greater Scot and Herschel).

[1] Divided with Selby. [2] Divided with Miss Glendyne.

| | | | | | |
|---|---|---|---|---|---|
| JUDGE (red dog)<br>Born 1852—the property of Mr. Jefferson | JOHN BULL | Lodor | Briton (late Knight of the Garter) | Emperor | Helenus<br>Fly, by Blue Wart |
| | | | | Knavery | Bachelor<br>Nimble, by Lunardi |
| | | | Lady | Nathan | Levite<br>Milliner |
| | | | | Risk (late Lalage) | Luff<br>Minikin |
| | | Jane | Sandy | Bachelor | Bachelor<br>Nimble, by Lunardi |
| | | | | Venus (sister to Solomon) | Dart<br>Smut |
| | | | Smart | Streamer | Colwick<br>Sister to Herdsman |
| | | | | Bride | Baron<br>Verity |
| | FUDGE | Oliver Twist | Sadek | Kouli Khan | Topper<br>Hannah |
| | | | | Harriet | Spartacus<br>Fly, by Snowball |
| | | | Sanctity | Stradbroke | Mariner<br>Fly (Rev. R. Day) |
| | | | | Leanthe | Lifter<br>Leah |
| | | Fairy | Carronade | Carron | Viscount(late Bluebeard) |
| | | | | Sister to Fairy | |
| | | | Gaunt | Vagrant | Balloon<br>Violet |
| | | | | Garland | Mortimer<br>Sister to Mirth (missing) |

Above is the pedigree of Judge, who won in 1855, ran up the following year, and was, moreover, the sire of three subsequent winners—viz. Clive, Maid of the Mill, and Chloe. His pedigree, it will be observed, goes back on his dam's side to Lord Sefton's strain, her sire, Oliver Twist, being an own brother to his Lordship's winner, Senate.

| | | | | | |
|---|---|---|---|---|---|
| CANARADZO (white dog)<br>Born 1858—the property of Mr. Campbell | BEACON | Bluelight (late Seabreeze) | Monsoon | Colonel | Topper<br>Pearl |
| | | | | Smart | Streamer<br>Bride |
| | | | Stave | Bugle | Bachelor<br>Nimble |
| | | | | Strawberry | Stradbroke |
| | | Frolic | Waterloo | Dusty Miller | Tinto<br>Swan |
| | | | | Exotic | Nestor |
| | | | Clarinda | Cessnock | Chance<br>Meriten[1] |
| | | | | Young Hornet | Sport<br>Old Hornet |
| | SCOTLAND YET | Wigan | Drift | Driver | Monarch<br>Lassie[1] |
| | | | | Coquette | Tippoo<br>Bustle |
| | | | Cutty Sark | Kirkland | Old Sport<br>Purity |
| | | | | Cutty Sark | Claret[1]<br>Swallow[1] |
| | | Velo | Dux | Driver | Monarch<br>Lassie[1] |
| | | | | Duppy | Bred by Mr. Marshall of Neilsland |
| | | | Tillside Lass | Draffin | |
| | | | | Old Tillside Lass | Smoker<br>Bess |

[1] Doubtful.

Here is an example of the celebrated Beacon and Scotland Yet blood. Canaradzo won the Waterloo Cup in 1861, and was the sire of King Death, who was victorious in 1864. His breeder was the late Mr. Ivie Campbell, and in Scotland Yet's next litter there were three of great merit—viz. Sea Foam, Sea Pink, and Cioloja. The first-named distinguished himself as the sire of Lobelia, but Cioloja was considered to be far and away the smartest of the lot, and though Mr. Campbell sold Sea Foam and Sea Pink to Mr. Spinks for 220 guineas, nothing would induce him to part with the other. She subsequently became one of the hottest favourites for the Waterloo Cup on record, but unfortunately, after reaching the scene of action in safety, she broke her thigh in a spin a few days before the contest. She was afterwards purchased by Mr. Brocklebank for stud purposes, but she brought him no return for his outlay. Although Cioloja was a failure, Canaradzo has been a pillar of strength to the 'Stud Book,' especially through his son Boanerges, who sired that grand bitch Bab-at-the-Bowster.

We now append the pedigree of King Death, the Waterloo winner of 1864, who adds lustre to the same telling strain:—

| | | | | | |
|---|---|---|---|---|---|
| KING DEATH (white and black dog) Born 1862—the property of Dr. Richardson | CANARADZO | Beacon | Bluelight (late Seabreeze) | Monsoon | Colonel<br>Smart |
| | | | | Stave | Bugle<br>Strawberry |
| | | | Frolic | Waterloo | Dusty Miller<br>Exotic |
| | | | | Clarinda | Cessnock<br>Young Hornet |
| | | Scotland Yet | Wigan | Drift | Driver<br>Coquette |
| | | | | Cutty Sark | Kirkland<br>Cutty Sark |
| | | | Veto | Dux | Driver<br>Duppy |
| | | | | Tillside Lass | Draffin<br>Old Tillside Lass |
| | ANNOYANCE | Heart of Oak (late Felling Pet) | Game Chicken | Figaro[1] | King Cob<br>Frederica |
| | | | | Fancy | |
| | | | Seedling | Spring | King of the Links (late Dan O'Connell)<br>White Cockade |
| | | | | Marigold | Tout<br>Maudlin |
| | | Miss Johnson | Admiral | Miner | [illegible]<br>Witch |
| | | | | Count[illegible] | |
| | | | Miss Quack (bought from Mr. C. Jardine's kennel) | | |

[1] Doubtful.

The next pedigree is that of Brigadier, who won the Cup in 1866, and was the sire of Honeymoon, the 1875 winner. It is noticeable that his sire Boreas was closely inbred to King Cob, Figaro, who begat Boreas, being by that dog out of Frederica, whilst his dam was by King Cob—Lively.

A third cross of this strain is found on the dam's side, Wee Nell being out of Lady Watford, who was out of Consideration, who was out of Kentish Fire by King Cob.

| BRIGADIER | BOREAS | Figaro | King Cob | Ion | Stumps<br>Ida |
|---|---|---|---|---|---|
| | | | | Kate | Deptford<br>Sister to Fanny |
| | | | Frederica | Damon | |
| | | | | Daffodil | What Not<br>Non Pareil |
| | | Bessy Bedlam | King Cob | Smoker | |
| | | | | Lady | |
| | | | Lively | Brother to Brigand | Rubens<br>Eve |
| | | | | Lady | Tinker<br>Fan |
| | WEE NELL | Seacombe | Hermit | Weapon | Figaro<br>Ruby |
| | | | | Sister to New World | Columbus<br>Wilful |
| | | | Fly | Croton Oil | Case is Altered<br>Waterwitch |
| | | | | Lady Maria | Bang Up [1]<br>Tulip |
| | | Lady Watford | Larriston | Liddesdale | Bowhill<br>Lady Seymour |
| | | | | Hannah | Buff<br>Catlowdie |
| | | | Consideration | Kentish Fire | King Cob<br>Knab |
| | | | | Linnet | Emperor<br>Old Linnet |

[1] Lord Stradbroke's Mawworm has been given.

A sterling bitch was Lobelia, the 1867 winner. In our chapter on the Waterloo Cup will be found an account of her remarkable performances in that event. She lived in the days of giants, and, with the exception of Master McGrath and Bab-at-the-Bowster, she could hold her own gallantly against all comers. Twice she fell foul of the Irish wonder in the Cup, but she defeated Bab after an undecided on the first occasion of their meeting—viz. in the Waterloo Cup of 1868: but a month later the latter had her revenge in the Douglas Cup and administered a decisive beating.

| | | | | | |
|---|---|---|---|---|---|
| LOBELIA (white and blood bitch) The property of Mr. W. J. Legh | SEA FOAM | Beacon | Bluelight | Monsoon | Colonel<br>Smart |
| | | | | Stave | Bugle<br>Strawberry |
| | | | Frolic | Waterloo | Dusty Miller<br>Exotic |
| | | | | Clarinda | Cessnock<br>Young Hornet |
| | | Scotland Yet | Wigan | Drift | Driver<br>Coquette |
| | | | | Cutty Sark | Kirkland<br>Cutty Sark |
| | | | Veto | Dux | Driver<br>Duppy |
| | | | | Tillside Lass | Draffin<br>Old Tillside Lass |
| | LILAC | Liston | Skyrocket | Bluelight | Monsoon<br>Stave |
| | | | | Syncope | Worcester Marquis<br>Synecdoché |
| | | | Silkworm (Stone) | | |
| | | Snowdrop[1] | Barabbas | Egypt | Vraye Foy<br>Elf |
| | | | | Cobœa Scandens | Foremost<br>Cygnet |
| | | | Medora | Czar | Foremost<br>Catch'em |
| | | | | Wideawake | Grasshopper<br>Nell |

[1] The entire pedigree of Snowdrop is doubtful, and indeed some authorities give Limeflower as the dam of Lilac.

From what we have just written it will be seen that here is another example of the excellence of the Scotland Yet strain.

Next we append the pedigree of 'the mighty McGrath':—

| | | | | | |
|---|---|---|---|---|---|
| MASTER McGRATH 1868–9 and 71 | DERVOCK (Gardiner) | St. Clair | Figaro (Fyson) | King Cob (Daintree) | Ion<br>Kate |
| | | | | Frederica (Fyson) | Damon<br>Daffodil |
| | | | Black Fly (Pridmore) | Marquis (Webb) | Rocket<br>Stella |
| | | | | Kirtles (Webb) | Kouli Khan<br>Knavery |
| | | Erin (Douglas) | Lightfoot (Howie) | Sam (B. Robinson) | Hilcoolie<br>Old Whiskey |
| | | | | Empress (B. Robinson)[1] | Bennet's Rocket[1]<br>Easterby's Empress |
| | | | Jenny Lind (Jones) | Scythian (Edleston) | Fox<br>Warwick |
| | | | | Syren (Lord Sefton) | Sadek<br>Sanctity |
| | LADY SARAH (Lord Lurgan) | David (Long) | Motley (Jardine) | Sam (Gibson) | Traveller<br>Tippitywitchet |
| | | | | Tollwife (Jardine) | King Cob<br>Matilda Gillespie |
| | | | Wanton (Wadham) | Senate (Lord Sefton) | Sadek<br>Sanctity |
| | | | | Coquette (Webb)[2] | Kouli Khan<br>Knavery |
| | | Lady Watford (Willis) | Lariston (Sharpe) | Liddesdale (Sharpe) | Bowhill<br>Lady Seymour |
| | | | | Hannah (Saunders) | Buff<br>Cutlowdie |
| | | | Consideration (Willis) | Kentish Fire (Daintree) | King Cob<br>Knab |
| | | | | Linnet (Thomas) | Easterby's Emperor<br>Old Linnet |

[1] Doubtful. [2] Spelt 'Koker' in Thacker.

Reference to our chapter of reminiscences of the Waterloo Cup will give particulars of this incomparable dog's career, so that here we shall simply add his measurements and list of his performances, with amounts won by him during his

MASTER McGRATH

career. It will be noted that his dam, Lady Sarah, was, like Boreas (sire of Brigadier), inbred to King Cob, though in a more distant degree.

WINNINGS OF MASTER McGRATH

| Meeting | Courses Lost | Courses Won | Value |
|---|---|---|---|
| 1867–68 | | | £ |
| Won Visitors' Cup, Lurgan | — | 5 | 60 |
| Divided Moneyglass Purse, Creagh | — | 4 | 40 |
| Won Waterloo Cup | — | 6 | 500 |
| 1868–69 | | | |
| Divided Brownlow Cup, Lurgan | — | 4 | 50 |
| Won Waterloo Cup | — | 6 | 500 |
| 1869–70 | | | |
| Lost first course Waterloo Cup | 1 | - | — |
| 1870–71 | | | |
| Won Brownlow Cup, Lurgan | — | 5 | 100 |
| Won Waterloo Cup | | 6 | 500 |
| | 1 | 36 | 1,750 |

*Measurements of Master McGrath.*

(Taken from the 'Coursing Calendar,' vol. xxi.)

*Head.*—From tip of snout to joining on to neck, 9½ in.; girth of head between eyes and ears, 14 in.; girth of snout, 7½ in.; distance between eyes, 2¼ in.

*Neck.*—Length from joining on of head to shoulders, 9 in.; girth round neck, 13¾ in.

*Back.*—From neck to base of tail, 21 in.; length of tail, 17 in.

*Intermediate points.*—Length of loin from junction of last rib to hip-bone, 8 in.; length from hip-bone to socket of thigh-joint, 5 in.

*Fore leg.*—From base of two middle nails to fetlock-joint, 2 in.; from fetlock-joint to elbow-joint, 12¼ in.; from elbow-joint to top of shoulder-blade, 12¼ in.; thickness of fore leg below the elbow, 6 in.

*Hind leg.*—From hock to stifle-joint, 9¾ in.; from stifle-joint to top of hip-bone, 12 in.; girth of ham part of thigh, 14 in.; thickness of second thigh below stifle, 8¼.

*Body.*—Girth round depth of chest, 26½ in.; girth round loins, 17¾ in.; weight, 54 lbs.

A study of these particulars by those accustomed to greyhound measurement will show what a 'big little one' McGrath was. Unfortunately he did not survive his triumphs long enough to give him a really fair chance at the stud, for it is seldom that a dog sires anything of high class until he has been at least a year out of training, though there may be exceptions to the rule. In his two seasons he was sire of several minor winners, and his blood is to be found in the pedigrees of some of the smartest dogs of the present day.

| | | | | | |
|---|---|---|---|---|---|
| BAB-AT-THE-BOWSTER (red bitch) The property of Mr. G. Blanchard | BOANERGES | Canaradzo | Beacon | Bluelight | Monsoon<br>Slave |
| | | | | Frolic | Waterloo<br>Clarinda |
| | | | Scotland Yet | Wigan | Drift<br>Cutty Sark |
| | | | | Veto | Dux<br>Tillside Lass |
| | | Baffle | Hughie Graham | Liddesdale | Bowhill<br>Lady Seymour |
| | | | | Queen of the May | King Cob<br>Minerva |
| | | | Wild Duck | Sam (Gibson's) | Traveller<br>Tippitywitchet |
| | | | | Nimble | Douglas (Raine's)<br>Unit (Raine's) |
| | MISCHIEF (Gland's) | Priam (Ireland's) | Priam | | |
| | | | | | |
| | | | Virago | Cambridge[1] | Figaro<br>Bessy Bedlam |
| | | | | Mischief | |
| | | Mischief | Mynheer | Muley (Forster's) | Sportsman (Jolly)<br>Lucy |
| | | | | Alice Hawthorn (Hutchinson's) | |
| | | | Sister to Lass o' Gowrie | Mangonel | Figaro<br>Countess (Bartholomew) |
| | | | | Marionette (sister to Mocking Bird) | Figaro<br>Malvina |

[1] Said to be brother to Bedlamite.

As a companion picture we now give the pedigree of Bab-at-the-Bowster. There are many who consider this bitch the best greyhound of all time, though her actual achievements do not equal those of her great opponent. True she won more courses—viz. sixty-two—but five times the flag went against her; nevertheless she stands out from all others of her sex, and her gameness and stamina were wonderful. To have won such big events as the Scarisbrick Cup and the Douglas Cup two years in succession is a mighty record. Her merit in this respect is to be expected by students of running blood, as she is closely connected with the Scotland Yet strain through her sire Boanerges, son of Canaradzo, and through her paternal grandam Baffle. She goes back to King Cob, and is very much inbred to that pillar of the 'Stud Book' on her dam's side through Figaro, whose name occurs three times in five generations. That Bab would have had her name enrolled in the list of Waterloo Cup winners had she not chanced to live in the days of McGrath is a moral certainty.

We append a list of her winnings:—

| MEETING | COURSES LOST | COURSES WON | VALUE |
|---|---|---|---|
| *1867–8* | | | £ |
| Divided Scottish National St. Leger | — | 5 | 75 |
| Divided Croxteth Stake at Altcar | — | 5 | 65 |
| Won two Courses Waterloo Cup | 1 | 2 | 25 |
| Won Scarisbrick Cup at Southport | — | 7 | 350 |
| Won Douglas Cup at Scottish National | — | 6 | 180 |
| *1868–9* | | | |
| Won Altcar Club Cup | — | 3 | 60 |
| Divided Elsham Cup at Brigg | — | 4 | 105 |
| Second for Waterloo Cup | 1 | 5 | [illegible] |
| Won Scarisbrick Cup at Southport | — | 7 | [illegible] |
| Lost first Course Douglas Cup at Scottish National | 1 | | |
| Divided Biggar Stakes at Scottish National | | 1 | [illegible] |
| *1869–70* | | | |
| Won Douglas Cup at Scottish National | | [illegible] | [illegible] |
| Won one Course Brownlow Cup at Lurgan | 1 | 1 | |
| Won three Courses Waterloo Cup | 1 | 3 | [illegible] |
| Divided Clifton Cup at Altcar | | [illegible] | [illegible] |
| | [illegible] | [illegible] | [illegible] |

The next to come under notice is Sea Cove, the Waterloo winner of 1870, and we give her pedigree as another instance of a successful combination of the same blood, through Blackcloud (an own brother to Beacon) on her dam's side, and through Bugle (own brother to Canaradzo) on her sire's side, whilst several traces of King Cob are found through Figaro.

| | | | | | |
|---|---|---|---|---|---|
| SEA COVE 1870 | STRANGE IDEA (Hyslop) | Cardinal York (Dunlop) | Jacobite (Gibson) | Bedlamite (Brown) | Figaro<br>Bessy Bedlam |
| | | | | Flounce (Fox) | Carronade<br>Gaunt |
| | | | Forest Queen (Dunlop) | Ruthless King (Dunlop) | Merry Monarch<br>Ruby |
| | | | | Fornarina (Dunlop) | Dreadnought<br>Judy |
| | | High Idea (Hyslop) | Blackcloud (Borron) | Blue Light (Borron) | Monsoon<br>Stave |
| | | | | Frolic (Lord Eglinton) | Waterloo<br>Clarinda |
| | | | Eve (Hyslop) | Eden (Clemitson) | Winspiel<br>Brenda |
| | | | | Old Eve (Atkinson) | Tyrant<br>Hannah |
| | CURIOSITY (Clark) | Bugle | Beacon (Borron) | Blue Light (Borron) | Monsoon<br>Stave |
| | | | | Frolic (Lord Eglinton) | Waterloo<br>Clarinda |
| | | | Scotland Yet (Campbell) | Wigan (Hyslop) | Drift<br>Cutty Sark |
| | | | | Veto (Greenshields) | Dux<br>Tillside Lass |
| | | Banter (Black) | A Lambert) | Bedlamite (Brown) | Figaro<br>Bessy Bedlam |
| | | | | Calypso (Lambert) | Field Marshal<br>Effie Deans |
| | | | The Pullet (Black) | Gamechicken (Anderson) | Figaro<br>Fancy |
| | | | | Sultana (Surties) | Sultan<br>Alice Grey |

| | | | | | |
|---|---|---|---|---|---|
| BED OF STONE 1872 | PORTLAND | Effort | Lariston | Liddesdale | Bowhill<br>Lady Seymour |
| | | | | Hannah | Buff<br>Cathowdie |
| | | | Hopmarket | Bedlamite | Figaro<br>Bessie Bedlam |
| | | | | Cerito | Lingo<br>Wanton |
| | | Prairie Flower | Blackcloud | Blue Light | Monsoon<br>Slave |
| | | | | Frolic | Waterloo<br>Clarinda |
| | | | Prize Flower | Paramount | Idas<br>Pamela |
| | | | | Isis | Probity<br>Dam by Fantai |
| | IMPERATRICE | David | Motley | Sam | Traveller<br>Tippitywitchet |
| | | | | Tollwife | King Cob<br>Matilda Gillespie |
| | | | Wanton | Senate | Sadek<br>Sanctity |
| | | | | Coquette[1] | Kouli Khan<br>Knavery |
| | | Java | Judge | John Bull | Lodore<br>Jane |
| | | | | Fudge | Oliver Twist<br>Fairy |
| | | | Moll Troll | Young Champion | Champion (Atkinson)<br>Fly (Cuthbert) |
| | | | | Maid of the Mill (Slater) | |

[1] Spelt by Thacker 'Koket.'

Bed of Stone, who won the Waterloo Cup in 1872, was certainly a remarkable bitch, and showed to great advantage on the Altcar Flats. She gradually worked her way to the pinnacle of a greyhound's fame, for she won the Purse in 1870 and the Plate in 1871. Her pedigree is full of the blood of Waterloo winners, and that of King Cob crops up on both sides. Her dam, Imperatrice, is a granddaughter of Judge, and her sire, Portland, a great-grandson of the triple winner Cerito.

Appended is a short pedigree of King Cob, which we have taken from the appendix to 'Stonehenge's' well-known work on the Greyhound. Going beyond the dog himself we feel out of our depth, so refrain from any comment on his ancestry.

| | | | |
|---|---|---|---|
| KING COB, 1838, w and bd, Captain Daintree | ION bd '34 | Stumps '28 | Pilot<br>Bliss |
| | | Ida '29 | Pilot<br>Spring |
| | KATE r '33 | Deptford w '28 | Gunshot, late Webb's Whirlwind, according to Mr. Howard, and *not* Lane Fox's, as generally given; but Capt. Daintree gives it as Lord Rivers'; seventh from the bulldog |
| | | Sis. to Fanny '29 | |

Reverting to the time when the Waterloo Cup was a thirty-two dog stake, this list would certainly be incomplete without the addition of Cerito's pedigree, for this bitch won the stake three times, and although the feat was not to be compared with that of Master McGrath, when the nominations were doubled, the competition keener, and the *éclat* more coveted, yet it must be admitted that the performance was a most meritorious one.

| | | | |
|---|---|---|---|
| CERITO (fawn and white) 1848—Messrs. Cooke and Hinds | LINGO r '45 | Lark[1] b '43 | Leader<br>Tongue |
| | | Lady bk | Gunshot<br>Venus |
| | WANTON bd '41 | Emperor bk '35 | Helenus<br>Fly |
| | | Blossom | Hæmus<br>Hadiz a Higa |

[1] Mr. Goodlake gives Best's Turk 1822, who was by Lane Fox's Turk—Lord Rivers' Fly

Cerito in all won forty-five courses out of fifty-three, and just 1,000*l.* in stakes, exclusive of trophies.

In writing the name of Misterton as a celebrity of the past we almost seem guilty of an anachronism, for he has carried his powers as a stud dog to a comparatively recent date; his sons and daughters are still running, and he has left plenty of sterling greyhounds to carry on one of the most successful strains of modern times; and whilst such dogs as Mullingar, Aberbriant, &c., are advertised at stud (with them we shall deal in a subsequent chapter), there is little fear of its being neglected. A glance at the subjoined pedigree will show a profusion of the ever-telling Scotland Yet blood combined with the equally desirable Judge cross.

| | | | | | |
|---|---|---|---|---|---|
| MISTERTON (black dog) The property of Mr. H. G. Miller | CONTANGO | Cashier | Cardinal York | Jacobite | Bedlamite<br>Flounce |
| | | | | Forest Queen | Ruthless King<br>Fornarina |
| | | | Lady Stormont | Blue Ruin | Antipas<br>Carolina |
| | | | | Holiday (late Jubilee) | Skyrocket<br>Jailbird |
| | | Bab-at-the-Bowster | Boanerges | Canaradzo | Beacon<br>Scotland Yet |
| | | | | Baffle | Hughie Graham<br>Wild Duck |
| | | | Mischief (late Bessy Bedlam) | Priam | Priam<br>Virago |
| | | | | Dam | Mynheer (late Flying Dutchman)<br>Sister to Lass o' Gowrie |
| | LINA | Cock Robin | King Death | Canaradzo | Beacon<br>Scotland Yet |
| | | | | Annoyance | Heart of Oak (late Felling Pet)<br>Miss Johnson |
| | | | Chloe | Judge | John Bull<br>Fudge |
| | | | | Clam | Lopez<br>Mrs. Kitty Brown |
| | | Corinna | Freshman | Combat | Stanley<br>Money Taker (late Click 'em in) |
| | | | | Lively | Forerunner<br>Linda |
| | | | Consequence | David | Motley<br>Wanton |
| | | | | Remedy | Mechanic<br>Ratcatcher's Daughter |

Misterton on his first appearance showed great promise, and was very unluckily beaten in the Newmarket Champion Puppy Stakes; notwithstanding this he started at a good outside price for the Waterloo Cup. Having won it, his subsequent performances were very moderate, but he proved a gold mine to Mr. Miller, and a complete list of winners by him would fill several pages.

| | | | | | |
|---|---|---|---|---|---|
| HONEYWOOD (red and white dog) The property of the Earl of Haddington | CAVALIER | Cauld Kail | Union Jack | Bridegroom | Judge<br>Bartolozzi |
| | | | | Attermire | British Grenadier<br>Lady Neville |
| | | | Scotia's Thistle | Selby | Barrator<br>Ladylike |
| | | | | Meg | Bonnie Prince Charlie<br>Fanny |
| | | Princess Royal | Cardinal York | Jacobite | Bedlamite<br>Flounce |
| | | | | Forest Queen | Ruthless King<br>The Fornarina |
| | | | Meg o' the Mill | Bonnie Prince Charlie | Cardinal Wiseman<br>The Widow |
| | | | | Fanny | John o' Badenyon<br>Repentance |
| | HUMMING BIRD | Bendimere | Cauld Kail | Union Jack | Bridegroom<br>Attermire |
| | | | | Scotia's Thistle | Selby<br>Meg |
| | | | Bergamot | Sackcloth | Senate<br>Cinderella |
| | | | | Darkness | Jacobite<br>Queen of Hearts |
| | | Baby Blake | Strange Idea | Cardinal York | Jacobite<br>Forest Queen |
| | | | | High Idea | Blackcloud<br>Eve (late Jane's my Darling) |
| | | | Curiosity | Bugle | Beacon<br>Scotland Yet |
| | | | | Bahter | A bk<br>The Pullet or Emily Deans or Miami |

Honeywood, the winner of the Waterloo Cup, 1880, was inbred to Cauld Kail, and possessed an infusion of the Beacon-Scotland Yet blood, his dam, Humming Bird, being out of Baby Blake, out of Curiosity by Bugle.

There seems to be a general impression that the pedigree

of Coomassie is not absolutely authenticated. With this doubt, which we are not in a position to traverse, we shall not give a tabulated pedigree, but shall reprint the following particulars of this 'pocket edition' from vol. 41 of the 'Coursing Calendar.' Coomassie, a light fawn bitch, by Celebrated out of Queen (whelped March 10, 1875), was bred by Mr. J. Cafley, of Runham, near Yarmouth. The dam of Queen was Cottage Girl by Monarch out of Nell, the property of Mr. Bulwer; she ran years ago at a local meeting near Yarmouth. Magic was the property of Mr. Pollard, of Burgh St. Peter. The sire of Celebrated was Mr. Allen's f. w. d. Albatross by Tullochgorum (own brother to King Death) out of Cygnet by Brewer out of Glimpse at Glory (an own sister to Gaudy Poll), and through this Coomassie has the same excellent strain of blood as Bed of Stone had. Gilderoy had this strain, as he was by Crossfell out of Gaudy Poll. Queen was by Captain Dod's r.w.d. Lord Derby by May Morning out of Lady Bathilde. The dam of Celebrated was Mr. Cafley's Caribella by Magic out of Regalia, Magic by Joe out of Topsy.

The measurements of Coomassie, corrected by Mr. J. T. Shaw, Northallerton, are appended.

COOMASSIE

*Head.*—From tip of snout to joining on to neck, 9 in.: girth of head between eyes and ears, 13 in.; girth of snout, 7 in.; distance between the eyes, 2 in.

*Neck.*—Length of joining on from head to shoulders 7¾ in.; girth round neck, 13 in.

*Back.*—From neck to base of tail, 22½ in.; length of tail, 16½ in.

*Hips.*—Length of loin from junction of last rib to hipbone, 8½ in.; length from hipbone to socket of thigh-joint, 7¼ in.

*Fore leg.*—From base of two middle nails to fetlock-joint, 2½ in.; from fetlock-joint to elbow-joint, 10½ in.; from elbow-joint to shoulder-blade, 11½ in.; thickness of the fore leg before the elbow, 6 in.

*Hind leg.*—From hock to stifle-joint, 10 in.: from stifle to top of hipbone, 10½ in.; girth of ham part of thigh, 15¼ in.; thickness of second thigh below stifle, 7½ in.

*Body.*—Girth round depth of chest, 27 in.; girth round the loins, 19¼ in.

Weight the day before starting for the Cup, 44 lbs.

As a marked contrast to this little creature we give the measurements of the 1881 Waterloo Cup winner, Princess Dagmar, who was a remarkably fine slashing bitch. She was bred on the same lines as Misterton :—

| | | | | | |
|---|---|---|---|---|---|
| PRINCESS DAGMAR 1881 | PTARMIGAN | Contango | Cashier | Cardinal York | Jacobite<br>Forest Queen |
| | | | | Lady Stormont | Blue Ruin<br>Holiday |
| | | | Bab-at-the Bow-ster | Boanerges | Canaradzo<br>Baffle |
| | | | | Mischief (late Bessy Bedlam) | Priam<br>Dam by Mynheer (late Flying Dutchman) |
| | | Petronella (late Graceful) | Waywarden (late Leek Kail) | Cauld Kail | Union Jack<br>Scotia's Thistle |
| | | | | Charmer | Canaradzo<br>Speculation |
| | | | Bocca Chica | Strange Idea | Cardinal York<br>High Idea |
| | | | | Witchery | Canaradzo<br>Speculation |
| | GALLANT FOE | Don Antonio | Elsecar | Patent | David<br>Lady Clara |
| | | | | Jessica | Regan<br>Cordelia |
| | | | Peggy Taft | Gallant Graham | Nimrod<br>Princess Royal |
| | | | | Emily | Harold[1]<br>Benton Belle |
| | | Meggie Smith | Engineer | Canaradzo | Beacon<br>Scotland Yet |
| | | | | Benton Belle | Fyson<br>The Pullet |
| | | | Snow | Gaspard | Beacon<br>Miss Nightingale |
| | | | | Nellie | Grasper<br>Moonlight |

[1] A stolen service

PRINCESS DAGMAR

*Head.*—From tip of snout to joining on to head, 8½ in.; girth of head between eyes and ears, 13¼ in.; girth of snout, 8¼ in.; distance between the eyes, 2 in.

*Neck.*—Length of joining on from head to shoulders, 9¼ in.; girth round neck, 13¾ in.

*Back.*—From neck to base of tail, 24 in.; length of tail, 19 in.

*Hips.*—Length of loin from junction of last rib to hipbone, 8¼ in.; length of hipbone to socket of thigh-joint, 5½ in.

*Fore leg.*—From base of two middle nails to knee-joint, 6 in.; from knee-joint to elbow-joint, 9¼ in.; from elbow-joint to shoulder-blade, 12 in.; girth (thickness of the fore leg below the elbow), 6 in.

*Hind leg.*—From hock to stifle-joint, 11¾ in.; from stifle to top of hipbone, 12¼ in.; girth of ham part of thigh, 16¼ in.; thickness of second thigh below stifle, 9½ in.

*Body.*—Girth round depth of chest, 27 in.; girth round the loins, 23 in.

Weight the day before starting for the Cup, 58 lbs.

A comparison of measurements is very interesting, for it will be noticed that in several points the little bitch exceeds the other, and, despite the disparity in size, she equals her in chest measurements.

Another sterling bitch that now claims our attention is Snowflight, who won the Waterloo Cup in 1882 and ran up the following year. She was the first of Bothal Park's progeny to show up conspicuously, but since her victory he has produced a long list of winners and added to the lustre of Scotland Yet, to whom Snowflight traces back on both sides.

| | | | | | |
|---|---|---|---|---|---|
| SNOWFLIGHT (black bitch) The property of Mr. T. Hall | BOTHAL PARK | The Admirable Crichton | Cashier | Cardinal York | Jacobite<br>Forest Queen |
| | | | | Lady Stormont | Blue Ruin<br>Holiday |
| | | | Bab at the Bowster | Boanerges | Canaradzo<br>Baffle |
| | | | | Mischief (late Bessy Bedlam) | Priam<br>Dam to Mynheer (late Flying Dutchman) |
| | | Elsass | Black Boyd | Cardinal York | Jacobite<br>Forest Queen |
| | | | | Hurrara (late Blossom) | Sackcloth<br>Winifred |
| | | | Gang-a-wee | Clansman (late Nana Sahib) | Acrobat<br>Tela |
| | | | | Bergamot | Sackcloth<br>Darkness |
| | CURIOSITY | Criterion | Linnæus | St. George | Seagull (late Reveller)<br>Seaweed |
| | | | | Luxury (late Convent Chime) | Monk of Thorney (late Seth)<br>Mazourka |
| | | | Spendthrift | Canaradzo | Beacon<br>Scotland Yet |
| | | | | Speculation | Judge<br>Banter |
| | | Fly | Kingwater | Jacobite | Bedlamite<br>Flounce |
| | | | | Meg | Bonnie Prince Charlie<br>Fanny |
| | | | Widow Machree | The Bounding Elk | Baron<br>Fairy Queen |
| | | | | Old Grannie | Captain<br>Lady |

Herrera was one of the most successful sires of modern times, and when his pedigree is carefully examined the reason of this success is easily perceived.

| | | | | | |
|---|---|---|---|---|---|
| **HERRERA** (white and fawn) Bred by Lord Haddington 1878. Property of Mr. N. Dunn | FUGITIVE | Cock Robin | King Death | Canaradzo | Beacon<br>Scotland Yet |
| | | | | Annoyance | Heart of Oak<br>Miss Johnson |
| | | | Chloe | Judge | John Bull<br>Fudge |
| | | | | Clara | Lopez<br>Mrs. Kitty Brown |
| | | Fortuna | Cardinal York | Jacobite | Bedlamite<br>Flounce |
| | | | | Forest Queen | Ruthless King<br>The Fornarina |
| | | | Meg | Bonnie Prince Charlie | Cardinal Wiseman<br>The Widow |
| | | | | Fanny | John o' Badenyon<br>Repentance |
| | HONEYDEW | Cashier | Cardinal York | Jacobite | Bedlamite<br>Flounce |
| | | | | Forest Queen | Ruthless King<br>The Fornarina |
| | | | Lady Stormont | Blue Ruin | Antipas<br>Carolina |
| | | | | Holiday (late Jubilee) | Skyrocket<br>Jailbird |
| | | Bright Eyes | Cauld Kail | Union Jack | Bridegroom<br>Attermire |
| | | | | Scotia's Thistle | Selby<br>Meg |
| | | | Bergamot | Sackcloth | Senate<br>Cinderella |
| | | | | Darkness | Jacobite<br>Queen of Hearts |

Herrera won nine courses out of ten as a puppy, but met with an accident, and although he ran again he never recovered his form.

The last pedigree we publish in this chapter is that of Macpherson, who may be placed in the same category as Misterton, as he has passed away recently, and seems to belong more to the present than the past. Macpherson was a good greyhound, and won the Waterloo purse in Snowflight's year (1882), but it is as a sire that his name will live, and the names of Herschel, Greater Scot, Happy Rondelle, Rhoda Macpherson, Jock Macpherson, Lance Macpherson, and a host of others are a credit to any dog. In the chapter on theoretical breeding we have taken occasion to allude to him as one of the greatest pillars of the 'Stud Book,' and the representative of a strain that must never be lost sight of. His sire, Master Sam, was a son of Contango and one of the speediest greyhounds ever slipped, but a bad killer. The descendants of Macpherson are usually very fast, but they likewise display sterling cleverness, a fact borne out by the running of Happy Rondelle—who when at her best was a gem of the first water—Herschel, one of the best greyhounds of all time, and Greater Scot.

In siring the two last named Macpherson shares with Greentick the honour of having begotten co-dividers of the Waterloo Cup.

By glancing at the appended pedigree it will be seen that the excellence of the strain is the combination of the Contango and Judge blood, the latter derived through Fusilier, sire of Annie Macpherson.

| MACPHERSON | MASTER SAM | Contango | Cashier | Cardinal York<br>Lady Stormont |
|---|---|---|---|---|
| | | | Bab-at-the-Bowster | Boanerges<br>Mischief (late Bessy Bedlam) |
| | | Carlton | Samuel | David<br>Patch |
| | | | Lucy (late Rachel) | Pugilist<br>Cinderella |
| | ANNIE McPHERSON | Fusilier | Picton | Jacobite<br>Forest Queen |
| | | | Blooming Daisy | Judge<br>Fanny Fern |
| | | Maid of Powhillon | Black Tom | Wellington<br>Bessie |
| | | | Miller's Maid | Merry Miller<br>Alice |

# CHAPTER VIII

## OPINIONS OF NOTED COURSERS

WHEN chatting with the coursing fraternity on subjects connected with their favourite sport, one is often asked, 'Which do you consider the best greyhound of all time?' 'Who is the most successful courser?' 'What is the best-looking greyhound you ever saw?' and so on. When engaged in the writing of this work of love, it struck us that a consensus of opinions on these leading questions, gleaned from those whose knowledge and experience of coursing matters are undeniable, would prove of interest to our readers. With a view to this we sent circulars to a large number of the leading owners, trainers, and breeders, the result being that most interesting matter was returned, furnishing tables that must prove of the greatest value to all those who have made a hobby of this ancient and fascinating sport.

The questions put were as follows :—

1. Give in your opinion the twelve greatest greyhounds of the century.

2. Name absolutely the best you have ever seen run.

3. Give in your opinion the twelve most successful stud dogs of the last thirty years.

4. Name the most successful living one.

5. Describe the best contested and most exciting course you ever saw.

6. Name the six best-looking dogs or bitches you remember to have seen.

7. In your opinion, have greyhounds improved or de-

teriorated of late years; and to what do you attribute such improvement or deterioration?

8. State whom you consider

(a) The most successful Courser
(b) " " Breeder
(c) " " Trainer
(d) " " Judge
(e) " " Slipper

9. Relate any anecdotes or incidents relating to greyhounds or coursing that may prove of interest to readers of this volume.

10. What do you consider the best coursing ground,

(a) In England and Wales;
(b) In Scotland;
(c) In Ireland?

11. Do you think it prejudicial to the welfare of a sapling to run him

(a) At an enclosed meeting when the shield is moved half-way up the ground;
(b) In the open?

12. Your opinion on any other matters connected with coursing will be highly esteemed.

Now, in the first place, let us analyse the returns as relating to the 'greyhounds of the century.' As might be expected, Master McGrath heads the poll with 32 votes, and Bab-at-the-Bowster follows with two fewer, whilst Fullerton comes third with 26, a reversal of the order we had expected; the fact being that there are a few old coursers who took exception to the latter's style on the occasion of his winning (or rather dividing) his first Waterloo Cup, a prejudice that time and most brilliant achievements have not altogether effaced. But we confess it does seem strange that any of those answering the questions—even though they considered the claims of one or two other dogs and bitches to surpass those of Fullerton—should go so far as to omit his name altogether from the list of the *twelve best* dogs of the century. Let these remarks suffice for the present; elsewhere we have entered more closely into the merits of this remarkable dog. To proceed, Coomassie and Miss Glendyne tie with 25 votes, then there is a drop to 18—a number obtained by Bed of Stone. Herschel is two behind with 16, Greentick and Cerito tie with 13 each, Patent has 10, and Honeymoon and Lobelia tie for last place with 8; the honoured twelve reading as follows:—

| | | Votes |
|---|---|---|
| 1. | Master McGrath | 32 |
| 2. | Bab-at-the-Bowster | 28 |
| 3. | Fullerton | 27 |
| 4. | Coomassie / Miss Glendyne | 25 |
| 6. | Bed of Stone | 18 |
| 7. | Herschel | 16 |
| 8. | Greentick / Cerito | 13 |
| 10. | Patent | 10 |
| 12. | Honeymoon / Lobelia | 8 |

Others that have received a fair share of notice are Mocking Bird, Princess Dagmar, Honeywood, Chloe, David, Canaradzo, Rebe, Gay City, Misterton, and Riot; whilst a whole host have received one or two votes each. Even Simonian is included in the list by one enthusiast, which shows that in some cases the form has been filled up without due consideration; for surely this promising *fin de siècle* puppy (1891) had hardly, when the question was put, done sufficient to ensure himself a niche in the temple of fame.

With regard to the second question—viz: 'Name the best greyhound you have ever seen run'—Fullerton, being fresh in everyone's memory, gets a good majority. The older coursers go for Master McGrath, with the exception of three, two of whom name Bab-at-the-Bowster and the remaining one Patent.

The following is the return for the twelve most successful stud dogs of the past thirty years:—

| | | Votes |
|---|---|---|
| 1. | Greentick | 30 |
| 2. | Misterton | 28 |
| 3. | Contango | 27 |
| 4. | Macpherson | 26 |
| 5. | Patent | 18 |
| 6. | Canaradzo | 17 |
| 7. | Ptarmigan<br>Judge | 14 |
| 9. | David<br>Cardinal York | 12 |
| 11. | Countryman<br>Paris<br>Brigadier | 11 |

whilst Beacon, Clyto, Fusilier, Master Sam, Bothal Park, Bedlamite, King Death, Jester, and Cashier have all gained more than six votes.

Of course Greentick's name at the head of the poll was a foregone conclusion, and well he deserves the honour; so also was it certain that breeders would not forget Misterton, Contango, and Macpherson; but we must confess to a feeling of considerable surprise at not finding Beacon's name higher up, though the compliments to his descendants are a sufficient testimony to his own merits.

Clyto, again, is one who might have received more substantial recognition, and we fancy that his blood will be very highly prized in the near future.

For the best stud dog of the day Greentick 'walks in,' as they say in racing parlance.

Of course there is an immense diversity of opinion when it comes to electing the six best-looking dogs and bitches within the memory of voters. The results gave :—

| | | Votes |
|---|---|---|
| 1. | Fullerton | 18 |
| 2. | Miss Glendyne | 16 |
| 3. | Bit of Fashion | 9 |
| 4. | Lauderdale | 8 |
| 5. | Honeymoon<br>Princess Dagmar | 6 |

with Canaradzo, Shepherdess, Jester, Chloe, Mespilus, London, and Greater Scot, close up. It will be seen from the reduction of the poll that the question has been altogether shirked by quite a third of those who have answered others; and we frankly admit the difficulty that lies in making a satisfactory selection. We were pleased to find that Lauderdale, who was a shining light on the show bench, had not escaped notice; undoubtedly he was a grand specimen of the greyhound to look at, and we believe, unlike most show dogs of the breed, was a useful performer in his day and secured a fair share of stakes.

Fullerton could hold his own in any show ring, as also could his dam and her peerless half-sister, whilst a really grand-looking dog is Colonel North's Not Out by Greentick—Miss Glendyne, consequently own brother to Cagliostro. Handsome is as handsome does, and though Master McGrath was, we are told, by no means the sort to take a prize at a beauty show, the sons and daughters of Greentick from Paris bitches are pleasing both to the eye and the pocket.

Beauty may only be skin deep, but that skin often covers a conformation calculated to realise a courser's fondest hopes, and long may it be so.

The accounts of the most exciting and best contested courses are somewhat meagre; for instance, a man of such experience as Mr. William Ellis names that between Master McGrath and Bab-at-the-Bowster in the deciding course for the Waterloo Cup, but omits to favour us with particulars from his own point of view, which would surely be interesting: but another writer, choosing the same course, thus describes it:—

The bitch was going the faster, until the hare bearing to the dog's side crossed the drain by a hare-bridge. In taking the drain the bitch had to go round by a post at the end of the bridge, or she would have made the turn—a point just achieved by the dog: the course continued in three wide circles in which 'six of one and half a dozen of the other' was the cry; at last the dog, on the inside, wrenched and killed, thus winning a grandly contested course.

Mr. Edward Dent, whose remarkable success as a breeder, trainer, and courser is almost unprecedented, speaks as follows :—

I have many times stood alone at Altcar, placed where I thought it best to be to pick up my dog, with none near me, but I shall never forget the roar from the crowd when Fullerton drew out for the finest kill I ever saw made in my life, and he also made a point during this course [1] which for quickness and sagacity I never saw equalled. The following were remarkably fine performances, and all intensely exciting :—

Phœbus beating Gay City
Gay City beating Greater Scot
Greater Scot beating Gay City
Miss Glendyne beating Greater Scot
" " beating Penelope II.

The greatest race I ever saw to the hare was at Haydock, between Greentick and Nolan ; they ran neck and neck for at least 300 yards, and the former just shot out for the turn. Nolan never got over it.

When Princess Dagmar ran her first course at Newmarket, the hare dropped dead inside the Jerusalem Covert, and her opponent (Haford) died half a mile before reaching it. The bitch lay down just outside, but notwithstanding this terrific gruelling, she came out and won two more courses, and in the interval of three months divided at Plumpton and won the Waterloo Cup. When she ran at Newmarket she must have been very well and trained to the hour.

The longest course ever run in my time was between England Yet and Bishop Juxton, this being the 'decider' for the Uffington Cup at Ashdown.

We have already spoken of the course between Master McGrath and Bab-at-the-Bowster in the Waterloo Cup of 1869.

[1] Mr. Dent omits to say which of Fullerton's numerous Waterloo courses he refers to, but we presume it was the final for the Waterloo Cup, 1891. Whatever the great dog lacked in killing power as a puppy, there is no doubt that this weak spot in his performance was quite remedied subsequently; for during the campaigns of 1890–91 he was handy enough with his teeth and made some remarkably fine kills.

AN EVEN SLIP

This is selected by no fewer than five coursers as by far the best contested and most exciting they had ever witnessed; and of these three are strongly of opinion that, had the bitch been better placed, the remarkable record of the little Irishman would have been somewhat tarnished. It was obviously owing to a close and skilful observance of this course that Bab-at-the Bowster is, on several papers, pronounced *the* greyhound of the century.

It will be observed that one of the courses named by Mr. Dent was that between Gay City and Greater Scot at Kempton; and Mr. G. M. Williams, a courser of considerable experience, refers to this, remarking that, though the son of Paris fell, he was quite under the impression that he finished a winner. We were ourselves a witness of this course, which was undoubtedly a most exciting one, and our opinion as to the result quite tallies with that of Mr. Williams.

The following courses are named once:—

Between Bed of Stone and Lurline
„ Honeymoon and Corby Castle
„ Fullerton and Real Lace
„ Burnaby and Duke Macpherson

It will be noticed that nearly all have been fought out on classic Altcar, and there are several reasons why such records live in the minds of spectators. In the first place, excitement runs higher on these occasions, and the impressions are therefore calculated to be more lasting; secondly, the high class of dog competing tends to well-contested and exciting trials; and, finally, the nature of the ground lends itself to the highest tests of a greyhound's merit.

Before closing our remarks on the answers to this question, it will be interesting to note the opinion of no less an authority than Mr. James Hedley. During the intervals of coursing on the occasion of a recent Waterloo Cup contest, in conversation with the judge we asked him what was the best contested, cleverest, and most exciting course he had ever seen. He paused, but only for a second or two, and then replied decidedly, 'That between Miss Glendyne and Penelope II. in the final for the Cup.' It will be seen that Mr. Dent has made particular mention of this trial, and we fancy that there are very many skilled coursers who will readily endorse the verdict of our leading judge. The course is thus described by 'Robin Hood':—

> From a splendid slip Penelope II. quickly began to show in front, and held the lead for quite two-thirds of the run up, then Miss Glendyne, who was certainly slow in getting into her stride, began to get on terms, and, after drawing level, made a great effort on nearing the hare, and eventually made the turn just over a length in front; the hare went to Penelope II.'s. side, and she swept round with it for two short points before Miss Glendyne resumed possession, and then a couple of exchanges followed, after which the brindled drew out for a wrench and a fine kill, thus winning a very exciting trial.

When we consider what a pigmy Penelope II. was, her performance in this spin was really marvellous, and she must have been made of the best stuff.

The question relating to the improvement or deterioration of greyhounds we will leave for subsequent discussion, and will pass on to the ballot for pride of place as courser, breeder, trainer, judge and slipper respectively.

Taking the first named, we find Colonel North at the head of the poll with 21 votes; Mr. E. Dent, 11; Mr. H. G. Miller, 9; the Earl of Haddington, 1; Mr. Hornby, 1; Mr. Gladstone, 1.

Undoubtedly the success of Colonel North as an owner of greyhounds has been phenomenal as far as it has gone, and it is hardly to be wondered at that those who have filled in the forms should pronounce him the most successful courser of modern times. We believe it was Mr. W. J. Hope-Johnstone who recruited him to our ranks, and who acted as guide, philosopher, and friend during his novitiate. His first important purchases were, if we remember rightly, Jock Scot and Mickleton, both good second-rate dogs, with which he took a stake or two; but in the Waterloo Cup of his first year (1888) he was represented by a real good one in Duke Macpherson, and when this puppy met an older and more seasoned opponent in Burnaby in the finale, we were treated to a most exciting tussle, and the old one only just pulled through. Shortly after, Colonel North had the misfortune to lose this most promising youngster; but he was not to be denied, and, in the face of this disaster, he outstayed all opposition when Fullerton was placed before Mr. Rymill's rostrum at the memorable sale of Messrs. Dent and Hibbert's greyhounds. The price (860*l.*) was a long one, but the purchase has proved most profitable, and the young dog's first essay under the new ownership quite recouped the purchaser, who was also rewarded when he gave a good round sum for the beautiful half-sisters and co-dividers of the Waterloo Cup, Bit of Fashion and Miss Glendyne; and it is somewhat remarkable that, when mated with the same dog, the bitch who was doubtless of inferior class has produced the best runners. At present Miss Glendyne's reputation as a matron rests upon decent performers such as Cagliostro and Not Out; but how can she compare in the stud-book with Bit of Fashion, the dam of Fullerton, Simonian, Young Fullerton, Jupon Vert, Kate Cuthbert, and others?

From Messrs. Thomson, Colonel North purchased Troughend, who soon made a capital beginning to his career; and when this dog, somewhat luckily be it confessed, divided the Cup with his kennel companion, also lucky in having met the mighty Herschel when that dog was quite spun out, the Colonel had good reason to shake hands heartily with himself, and to glow with gratitude towards those friends who had counselled him when making selections for his kennel, and choosing a trainer. Nor did his success stop here; for, as everyone interested in coursing knows, Fullerton stalled off all opposition, and easily secured the coveted blue ribbon of the leash the three following years. When we say *easily* we must pause to remark that the overthrow of the big dog was very nearly being brought about by his younger brother and kennel companion Simonian, in the first round of the Cup, 1891; and we may mention in parenthesis that when the names of Colonel North's two cracks were drawn together from the classic jug, there was a good deal of commiseration showered on the owner; but the sequel proved that nothing could have been more fortunate. When these two went to the slips there was much curiosity and excitement, as Mr. Dent had not hesitated to state his opinion that the younger dog was the faster, though he would not hear of the elder being beaten. To a bad hare the black came at a great pace from the slips, and soon showed in front. We were luckily placed for the run up, which was not a long one, and we should say the puppy finished a good length in front, Fullerton never having fairly got into his stride. After making the turn, however, Simonian went wide and let in the brindle, who put in two or three dashing points in his own inimitable style before letting in the other, who wrenched twice and then just failed to kill, when Fullerton took possession, and using puss smartly for a couple of minor points, picked her up and just won. This was a scrambling course with a weak hare, and till the flag went up there was some uncertainty as to the result. Later on the brindle improved on this form and wound up with another brilliant victory, whilst his early opponent and younger brother ran through the Purse in grand style. Here is Colonel North's record for his four essays in the classic event of the coursing year:—

| | | |
|---|---|---|
| 1888 | Duke Macpherson . . | Ran up for Cup |
| 1889 | Fullerton . . . . . / Troughend . . . . . | Divided Cup |
| 1890 | Fullerton . . . . . | Won Cup |
| 1891 | Fullerton . . . . . | Won Cup |
| 1891 | Simonian . . . . . | Won Purse |
| 1892 | Fullerton . . . . . | Won Cup |

Besides these wonderful achievements, the Colonel has won a number of good stakes with such dogs as Mickleton, Tarset, Blue Green, Huic Holloa, Nuneaton, Not Out, Netheravon, Kate Cuthbert, &c.; and as long as he sticks to the strain of which he is the fortunate possessor, nothing but a complete reversal of the luck that has followed him can prevent him from appropriating a good share of the plums of the season.

The brilliant career of this meteor on the coursing firmament has thrown into shade the consistent shining of such stars as Mr. Dent and Mr. Miller. The former is so closely identified with the success of Colonel North that the honour is due to him even in a greater degree than to the owner; not only did he breed Fullerton and his progenitors on the dam's side, but he also trained them for all their engagements, and certainly no trainer of modern times can show such a record as regards the special preparation requisite for success at Altcar. The eleven voters who named Mr. Dent as the most successful *courser* must have borne these facts in mind, and in *the highest sense of the word* theirs is a happy selection; for we take it that there is a distinction to be drawn between a *courser* and an *owner*, and in the former capacity there is no doubt that Mr. Dent easily bears off the palm.

Mr. Miller, who comes third, has very great claims; in fact, in all-round coursing his successes, if totted up, would, we fancy, exceed those of the master of Shortt Flatt, though as regards the Waterloo contest his record is not so brilliant. Misterton's victory came as a pleasant surprise, judging by the price at which he started; and from this mighty sire sprang a host of winners to do honour to the Dorsetshire courser. Mullingar, Millington, Middleton, Madeleine, Mickleton, Match Girl are but a few from a long list, and a reference to the table of winners got by the Waterloo Cup winner of 1879 will reveal many a winner that credited Mr. Miller with good stakes. Of late years Mr. Gladstone, by the aid of Greentick and his descendants, can show a brilliant list of triumphs; while the Messrs. Fawcett, who stick religiously to their own particular strain, can be quoted as coursers whose success has been conspicuous of late — a remark that also applies to Mr. Hornby and the Messrs. Thomson.

Mr. Dent, of course, heads the list of breeders with 27

votes, and what we have already said renders further comment needless. Mr. Miller can, on the same grounds, be dismissed with the remark that he takes second place with 13 votes, whilst Mr. Hayward is the only other breeder who has gained suffrage. This gentleman, who bred, amongst a host of other good ones, that sterling little bitch Happy Rondelle (whose litter brothers and sisters, Have-a-Care, Iulus, and Rotula, were all good winners) by Macpherson—Rota, has a wide knowledge and experience and a fine faculty for pedigrees, only equalled by that of Mr. Ellis and Mr. N. Dunn. Once more Mr. Dent heads the poll as a trainer with 23 votes, the late Archie Coke coming second with 11 and J. Coke following with 9; but as this vote is practically identical, the mass brings this kennel to 21 votes, which is a strong testimony to the esteem in which it is held and to the success that has attended its efforts. Many an owner can bear witness to the integrity and energy of the late veteran, and the establishment now presided over by his son is patronised by some of the most influential and enthusiastic followers of the greyhound.

We now come to an opinion on the merits of the judges of the day. Two stand out conspicuously, and these are Mr. James Hedley and Mr. Brice. It is easy to see what the opinion of the coursing world is; for the former gains 31 votes to 7 scored by Mr. Brice, and the election of the former as judge of the Waterloo meeting year after year by a large majority speaks volumes for the confidence which nominators repose in him. We take it that, with Mr. Hedley put out of the question, Mr. Brice would distance all other opponents quite as markedly, as there is no doubt that he is held in very high esteem by all classes of coursing men and also by the public. He is always steady, careful, and entirely impartial in his decisons, and his services, especially in the South, are in great request. The advent of Judge Hedley marked a new era in the sport; for we are informed by the most competent authorities that the earlier systems and methods of deciding trials were far from satisfactory, and he (Mr. Hedley) was the first to mitigate the nuisance of undecideds—an evil that had previously flourished to an irritating and dangerous extent; one courser of long experience informing us that in the old days he had seen the judge's hat come off *no fewer than five times* for one trial, which shows how the practice was used as a foil to the confusion and vacillation of judges.

Tom Wilkinson scores as easily in the list of slippers as Mr. Hedley did in that of judges, receiving as many as 27 votes. Some of the older generation of coursers 'go for' Tom Raper, so that he is second with 11. This slipper is beyond our memory, but the fathers of the sport speak of him in terms of the highest praise. Jeffery and Bootiman get 1 vote each, and they are undoubtedly painstaking and skilful men.

Opinions differ considerably as to the merits of the various coursing grounds, but with regard to the English venues Amesbury is held in highest esteem, and is voted for by fifteen of those who filled up the forms. Altcar and Border Union are next with seven. Other grounds that are thought well of are Ashdown, Newmarket and Brigg. Carmichael is, *par excellence,* the pick of the Scotch meetings, whilst Upper Nithsdale and Kelso Border Ground are also noticed. With one voice Lurgan is pronounced the ideal of Irish coursing, and we have been told that this ground will bear comparison with any in the United Kingdom.

With reference to the question, Which have been the most successful sires within the last thirty years? we will go somewhat further back, and give a rough sketch of the best strains as far as we have any information which can be relied upon: and that, as all breeders know, at the cost of much time and temper, is most meagre.

The average generation of a greyhound is about five years; by which is meant, that from Topham's Snowball, who was pupped about 1796, to the present time we shall find in any pedigree about nineteen or twenty generations. And the usual age of successful breeding seems to tally with this period. But there are very great exceptions. We have not been able to go further back than Lord Orford's Czarina, who was pupped about 1778. She was the grandmother of Snowball. It is recorded of her that she won forty-seven matches, and never was beaten. A melancholy interest attaches to her last appearance, as her owner, Lord Orford, was so excited at seeing his favourite win that he fell off his pony and died.

This bitch is the progenitor of all our best greyhounds, we might almost say of all greyhounds of the present day. She was exceptional in every way. Not only was she an exceptionally good performer, but she was exceptional in breeding: we are told that she did not breed till she was thirteen years old, and then she bred Claret and Vengeance, two very good greyhounds, of which Claret was the sire of Snowball and Major. This is more exceptional than it would seem at first sight; for very few bitches have bred at that age, and none that we know of have produced winners, even if they had litters. Mr. G. Carruthers's Meg, by Terrona, the winner of the Waterloo Cup, is the only instance we have come across at all like that of Czarina. She bred Bellini when she was twelve years old, and he in his turn has got some winners. We believe she had a litter when she was fourteen years old, but do not think any of the produce could be called successful. It is rare for greyhounds to produce anything good at the age of ten years. Out of a list of about 2,400 successful breeders, there are only about 110 of that age or more. Those of the age of eleven and twelve are very few indeed, certainly not twenty; while not one has attained the age of Czarina—thirteen years. It is to be understood that the point dwelt upon is success in *breeding*, not in running. It is possible that Misterton may have winners to represent him begotten when he was thirteen years old; but we cannot tell if they will, in their turn, be successful as breeders. That is the point. David and Meg are the only two we know who have produced successful breeders at the age of twelve years.

It will now be clear that Czarina must have been truly an extraordinary greyhound; and from her must date an improvement in the quality of the breed. Her sons, Claret and Vengeance, were famous; but still more was Topham's Snowball, the Eclipse of the leash, and his brother, Thornton's Major, who were her grandsons. Snowball never was beaten, and his fame was so great that Sir Walter Scott immortalised him in verse. From him and from his brother Major come all our successful runners, through Senate and Oliver Twist. Most probably King Cob, who might be compared to Touchstone, was of the same blood. He was of what would be called in those days the Newmarket breed. Gunshot, one of his ancestors, is said to be of Lord Rivers's breed; and Lord Rivers's Rhoda, a favourite brood bitch, was a granddaughter of Snowball. Other breeders about Newmarket, such as Inskip and Hassall, would value the strain as highly as he did. There is probably not a greyhound now running who has not King Cob as his progenitor.

Lidderdale's Champion, Best's Streamer, and later on Hassall's Hercules and Longden's Old Derbyshire Grasper, were all of this breed.

It is difficult for us at the present time to say which were the successful breeders among greyhounds in the early years of this century; there was so much more private breeding then, and with it so much jealousy in keeping successful strains to their own kennel, and a dislike to give information on the subject. Unfortunately for us, Thacker was aware of this feeling, and excused some of his mistakes in his 'Annual' on the ground that it would have been an impertinence in him to have written to a breeder of greyhounds for information on the subject. As a consequence, the records of pedigrees are faulty in detail.

When we come to Hill's Bachelor in 1828, and to Daintree's King Cob in 1838, we find ourselves on somewhat firmer ground. Captain Daintree was one of the first to put his dog at the service of the public, and from that time we find more pedigrees advertised.

From these two greyhounds come the modern breed. Bachelor was the ancestor of Bugle, who through Borron's Bluelight founded what might be called the Canaradzo breed; including in this title the progeny of Lady Stormont, and that of Blackcloud. Bugle is also represented in the pedigree of David. Bachelor is likewise the ancestor of that other famous line of Senate and Oliver Twist. Oliver Twist, who was said to be by no means a good dog himself, though he was second to Harlequin for the Waterloo Cup, was the sire of Judge at a year old, and died two years afterwards. He was the grandsire of Judge and Sunbeam. The family of Judge was, and is, one of the most successful. Sunbeam, we think, still lives in Sir Thomas Brocklebank's strain, which is ever astonishing us by exhibitions of its stoutness.

Oliver Twist's brother, Senate, has a larger and an equally successful family to represent him. The descendants of his sons, Junta and Sackcloth, still take high rank among the best. He is also the ancestor of Long's David. In this great sire the two branches are united, for he has also a double strain of King Cob.

This other great branch in modern pedigrees, i.e. King Cob, was the sire of Figaro and The Tollwife, and grandsire of Sam. Through Figaro we have Bedlamite and the four sisters Mocking Bird, Marionette, and Humming Bird, and one without a name, which has made a name for herself, as the ancestor of Bab-at-the-Bowster, the most worthy descendant of Czarina.

Bedlamite was the grandsire of Cardinal York, his brother Picton, and that great family. Mocking Bird, through Mansoor and Mechanic, has a large family to keep her name alive. Humming Bird lives in the progeny of Lady Stormont and her son Cashier, and joins her unnamed sister in Contango.

Again, Sam was the progenitor of Bab-at-the-Bowster, and the union of Sam and The Tollwife produced Motley, and Mrs. Kitty Brown, the ancestors respectively of David and Chloe.

Roughly speaking, here are the lines of the great sires of that time: Canaradzo, Judge, Cardinal York, David.

Contango represents the lines of Canaradzo and Cardinal York; the dams of Misterton and Greentick (his son and grandson) furnish those of Judge and David. These two, the great sires of modern days, will be seen to be of almost the same blood; and are worthy of the greatest sires in their several generations.

Several strains of Mocking Bird and her sisters are to be found in both; Greentick boasts also the names of Cerito, Racketty Hoppicker, Riot and Prizeflower in his ancestry. Some hold that the excellence of the greyhound comes more from the dam, and some believe that he will prove the greatest sire of all time. With these great names in addition to the others, 'Is it folly that we hope it may be so?'

In some sort of way, the above account, as it may well be termed, of these two champion sires furnishes us with an answer as to the most successful sires of the last thirty years.

Bugle, Bluelight, Beacon, Canaradzo, King Death, Judge, Senate, David, Sam, Figaro, Bedlamite, Cardinal York, have made their mark among the sires of old; while Cashier, his son Contango, his grandson Ptarmigan, and the produce of the last from Gallant Foe, Jester, Peter, and Paris are among the best of later days. Bedfellow, a son, and Macpherson, a grandson, of Contango have much the same blood.

Cauld Kail has the addition of some very good lines, notably of Barrator, by many thought to have been the very best, certainly the most wonderful dog of his day; of Jardine's Ladylike, and of Lord Eglinton's Waterloo, the champion of his day.

Patent was of the same blood as the great-granddam of Greentick, and was great-grandsire of Gallant Foe; but with these exceptions, neither he nor Clyto, who shares most of his lines with Greentick, will be found in the pedigrees of the day as often as their success in the first generation seemed to promise.

It should be remarked that Beacon owes his chief, if not sole, representation in these days to his union with Scotland Yet, as Ptarmigan does to that with Gallant Foe. The family of the last couple, Ptarmigan and Gallant Foe, is probably the most distinguished in the annals of coursing. Princess Dagmar, Miss Glendyne, Bit of Fashion, Fullerton, all winners, two of them more than once, of the Waterloo Cup, and in 1891 the winner and runner-up for the Cup, as well as the winners of the Purse and Plate, may be said to have established a record.

Strange Idea should not be passed over. He was one of the successful sires of his day; and furnished the winner of the Cup in Sea Cove. Brigadier was another favourite sire; and he claims Honeymoon among the Waterloo roll. Bothal Park should also be named, being the sire of the winner of the Waterloo Cup and of the Gosforth Gold Cup; these stakes requiring very different styles of running. And Fusilier should not be left out, as in his short career he was the sire of one of the Waterloo Cup winners in Muriel, and laid the foundation of the success of Mr. Thomas Graham's kennel with Annie Macpherson and Mary Hill. His strain is undoubtedly much valued by breeders.

But, after all, it is difficult to say which sires are the most distinguished for their success. The grounds on which to found the distinction are so various. The number of winners of all kinds may be one standard: the numbers of winners of the first class may be the recommendation to others; the power of perpetuating its good qualities, as breeders would term it its prepotency, would be valued by another class.

Then, again, the length of stud life would greatly modify any statistics. We have Oliver Twist, a sire at a year old, and dead in three years; Fusilier, with a stud life of about three years; Macpherson, with four years, compared with David and Misterton, who lived till they were thirteen years old.

Once more; the means of popularising the dog or the fame of the kennel would have an effect. Bothal Park, for instance, was allowed to run loose in a pit village till Snowflight had made a name for him; while Misterton was carefully managed, the best of mates were found for him, and a word was never wanted to illustrate the excellence of his produce.

We add, as a sort of rough guide, the number of times in which each of the sires named appears in a collection of pedigrees of the winning strains of modern days. It must be noted that it cannot be accepted as a criterion of the success of each dog, for the above reasons; besides which, the latest sires are credited with winners whose excellence in breeding has not yet been proved. The older sires occur only as the parents of those who preserved their names in the annals of breeding, not of running. Still, some interest may attach itself to the list:—

| | | | |
|---|---|---|---|
| Misterton | 168 | Ptarmigan | 40 |
| Greentick | 87 | Jester | 39 |
| Canaradzo | 68 | Brigadier | 36 |
| Macpherson | 59 | Cardinal York | 35 |
| Patent | 52 | Cashier | 33 |
| Bedfellow | 50 | Pinkerton | 31 |
| Clyto | 49 | Strange Idea | 27 |
| Cauld Kail | 45 | Bothal Park | 27 |
| Contango | 40 | King Death | 22 |

The following are rather before 1860:—

| | |
|---|---|
| David | 45 |
| Judge | 35 |
| Bedlamite | 32 |

We now come to those questions which relate to coursing in general, and first we will go over the answers received to question No. 5, viz. 'In your opinion have greyhounds improved or deteriorated of late years? To what do you attribute such improvement or deterioration?'

There is a strong balance of opinion that pace has improved, but that pluck and determination have deteriorated, and many prominent coursers have attributed this state of things to the run on enclosed coursing, which lasted till the obvious evils arising therefrom, and the great danger that threatened the sport, as it had hitherto been conducted, fairly frightened the better class of coursers into a steady opposition. A valuable opinion in this direction is given by Mr. J. Porter Porter, who says:

Now that enclosed coursing is losing popularity, all must see the ruin that has arisen from it; good greyhounds spoiled; fluky, flashy ones benefited: stamina and determination lost sight of; encouragement to every public-house landlord to keep a dog of

Unsighted

sorts; encouragement to small bookmakers and welshers; and deterioration of all long-odds betting before a meeting, and consequent prejudice to *good* books; strong incentive to run for money value only, and not for sport's sake. It now lies with the real sportsmen of Great Britain and Ireland, who course for the love of the thing only, to raise the standard of coursing, which has sunk far below its proper level. The thanks of all may thus be ensured, no matter how a few may be annoyed for a year or two.

Mr. Frank Richardson, a northern courser who took to the sport as far back as 1850, but who for the past four or five years has ceased to maintain a kennel of greyhounds, declares himself *Laudator temporis acti*, and proceeds thus :—'The enclosed meetings have spoiled the all-round characteristics of the greyhound ; for since these meetings were established he has been bred for speed alone. There is also much more in-breeding than in the olden time, which tends to deterioration.' The latter part of this opinion is well worthy of notice, and induces speculation as to whether or no in-breeding tends to lower the general standard of merit, and if so in what direction. Is it prejudicial to stamina? and does it promote speed? In our chapter on breeding this will be found fully discussed, and with it attention is called to the evils arising from the overstrained procreative powers of the fashionable sires of the day, a reason assigned by J. T. Shaw for what he holds to be a slight deterioration in our present running dogs. The opinion as to the evils arising from enclosed coursing and the consequent 'flashiness' and lack of stamina given by Messrs. Porter Porter and Frank Richardson is shared by Messrs. W. Ellis, J. L. Reed, J. Taylor, Horace Ledger, and A. J. Humphery, who all express themselves more or less strongly on the subject.

Some there are who stoutly maintain that the greyhound is a decidedly improved animal, and they mostly attribute this desirable state of things to the greater care and attention bestowed by coursers on breeding, rearing, kennelling and training, as compared with the slipshod procedure of the days of yore. Amongst this number are Messrs. Dent, F. Graves, F. Dobson, G. M. Williams ; several others hold that the average of merit has been maintained.

Now, to sum up this question, we are inclined to agree with those who point to flashy and roguish greyhounds as the product of the enclosed meetings, to admit a great improvement in average speed, and a corresponding falling off in stamina and courage ; and moreover we would point to a quality that may bear good fruit, but which, if abused, may be disastrous in its consequences, viz. intelligence, which, if unduly developed, is prone to induce cunning and trickery. We have already traversed the opinions of the old writers who held as an axiom that 'the greater the fool the better the greyhound,' for we do not believe that crass stupidity is calculated to fit the individual, human or animal, for any work that he may be set to do; and many a noted greyhound has been well developed in the intellectual faculties without ever having run otherwise than bravely and honestly.

Doubtless the enclosed meetings are responsible for the increase of this roguish propensity in far greater degree than the development of the intellect; though in such cases a clever dog is far more likely to fall a victim to undesirable habits than if his efforts had been confined to the open country. A dog of average intelligence, running time after time at the same enclosure, cannot fail to notice the run of the hares; and his deductions, though they may lead to his picking up puss before the escape is reached, will probably have lost him the verdict and possibly cost him a fatal knock on the head; whereas this identical greyhound, if relegated to the open, would have sufficient intelligence to see that his old style of running did not lead to like results, and in the interests of his teeth he would find that honesty was the best policy.

Still, although we agree as to the evil induced by a too free patronage of the enclosures, we cannot subscribe to the dictum that the alleged deterioration affects either the average or the aggregate, and we feel convinced that, though there may be more rogues than in bygone eras, there are undoubtedly more good greyhounds and fewer bad ones running than ever there were; and we join those who attribute the improvement to the care, trouble, and expense that are nowadays bestowed in breeding, training, and running greyhounds capable of holding their own in the important stakes of the year. The fact of the matter is that in olden times the few good dogs stood out as Gullivers in Lilliput; but now, unless a dog is quite phenomenal—a Fullerton, in fact—his merits are applauded when he wins; then he is forgotten until the occasion of his next success, and he is continually meeting opponents of equal calibre and class. A parallel may be found in the case of the Turf; for we opine that during the past decade we have been richer in the aggregate of *good* horses than we ever were previously, while the average of merit far surpasses that of the earlier portions of the century.

Therefore our verdict on all counts is as follows :—

1. The average speed has increased.
2. Stamina and courage have decreased.
3. Both average and aggregate merit have improved.
4. Flashiness and roguishness are far more frequently met with.

*Rider.*—The causes that have led to the unsatisfactory portion of this verdict are :—

(*a*) The attention that has been bestowed on *pace* at the sacrifice of stamina and courage, consequent on breeding for the rostrum and the demand for 'speedy ones.'

(*b*) The evils resulting from the system adoped at enclosures.

(*c*) The breeding on lines which, however good, are too closely identified : whereby we do not mean in-breeding ; but rather the too free use of 'fashionable' sires to the exclusion of a host of hardy, useful customers whose merits at the stud are never fairly tested, yet whose blood is of the bluest, and whose performances have been full of merit. A reference to the list of greyhounds running through the season will reveal the fact that there are not above half-a-dozen sires who have as many runners to represent them—which is remarkable, considering the large number of sterling dogs advertised as at the service of the public. Before quitting this subject we must not forget to point out that, as every dark cloud has a silver lining, it would be unfair in the extreme to heap nothing but unqualified abuse on all enclosed meetings. They have their uses and abuses, and in the former capacity should receive recognition from even the most bigoted of the old school. A large produce stake such as is run at Haydock is a most interesting event. For a puppy competing it is likely to be more beneficial than the reverse, and may prove an excellent initiation, whereas the ordeal of the open with so large an entry might very well settle all future hope for those that got to the end of the stake.

We now approach the much-vexed sapling question, viz.: --

Do you think it prejudicial to the welfare of a sapling to run him—

(*a*) At an enclosed meeting, where the shield is moved half-way up the ground?

(*b*) In the open?

The answers we have received to this query are so diverse and diametrically opposed to one another that it is almost impossible to arrive at a real consensus of opinion. For instance, Mr. Dent boldly declares that he would not hesitate to run saplings, and that in so doing their career would not be in any way prejudiced, bar accidents; while Mr. J. L. Reed and others are strongly opposed to running saplings under any circumstances. Some see no harm in running them at enclosures, but condemn open coursing: whilst others—a more limited band—hold that to run a youngster in the open, where he has a fair chance of killing his hare, is preferable to the first proposition, where they may use their hare to the escape, and then be disappointed—which they are apt to remember, to their owners' cost, when their legitimate running career commences—an argument in which there is some sound common sense, albeit the risks and dangers of over-exertion and heart-breaking trials are so great under such circumstances that the disadvantages must inevitably outweigh the advantages.

Some hold that sapling-running is only detrimental when training is involved, whilst others declare that it must be injurious unless the youngster is well trained. Here we should certainly fall in with the views of the latter section. To run a sapling soft and quite untrained would surely be to court disaster. On the other hand, be it understood, we should not advocate a course of training such as would be given a mature greyhound. In foregoing pages the method of a semi-preparation has been carefully set forth, and it would be out of place to discuss the matter any further in the present chapter.

To revert to the opinion of Mr. Dent and his followers, who pooh-pooh the idea of harm accruing to the sapling through running, that astute breeder, owner, and trainer points triumphantly to the fact that both Miss Glendyne and Bit of

Ready for action

Fashion won sapling stakes, which is a fair clincher to his argument. But, notwithstanding this, we fancy that statistics would go far to prove that winners of these affairs very seldom distinguish themselves subsequently, and that the exceptions might be quoted to prove the rule. To dig to the root of the matter and unravel the problem satisfactorily would be a hard task, for it is difficult to ascribe a feasible reason why a trial of moderate length should be prejudicial to a young greyhound. Take, for instance, one which is born, say, in January. He does well, gets over a mild attack of distemper, and by March of the following year is, as far as the eye and the hand can tell, a well-developed and mature youngster, as well fitted for the task as a two-year old racehorse or a University athlete. His speed may be at its prime; his stamina should be sufficient to carry him through the apparently by no means trying ordeal of working his hare up half the space of an ordinary coursing enclosure. Without being trained to the hour, he is yet in a state of excitement, health, and fitness, carrying no superfluous flesh or fat within or without. He does what is asked, and shows no outward or visible signs of temporary distress or lasting deterioration; he has seen a hare, and enjoyed the fiery joy of the chase; henceforth he is on the alert, he has a degree of confidence lacking in the green novice, and he despises opposition. When the forthcoming campaign looms in the near future you have no reason to doubt his prowess. His performance as a sapling was unexceptionable, his physique and breeding all that could be desired; but what is the result? In nine cases out of ten he proves to be practically useless, and his retirement from public running rather than 'the Blue Ribbon of the Leash' is the goal to which he is inevitably drifting.

Hence, in summing up, we are reluctantly compelled to record our opinion that, though in theory there is no discernible reason why a mature sapling of fifteen months, in a state of physical well-being, is unfit to compete against one of his own age in a trial of limited length, practice, on the other hand, holds up a warning finger, and, despite the mighty achievements of Miss Glendyne and her half-sister, the peerless matron Bit of Fashion, warns us that, if we have a sapling of exceptional promise, his public efforts should be delayed until he enters upon the season of his legitimate puppyhood. With these remarks we bring to a close our analysis of the answers received to our circular. Such an expression of opinion from

those whose experience in coursing matters carries immense weight must prove both interesting and instructive to all who follow the fortunes of the leash, and our most grateful thanks are tendered to them for having given so much time and thought to our appeal.

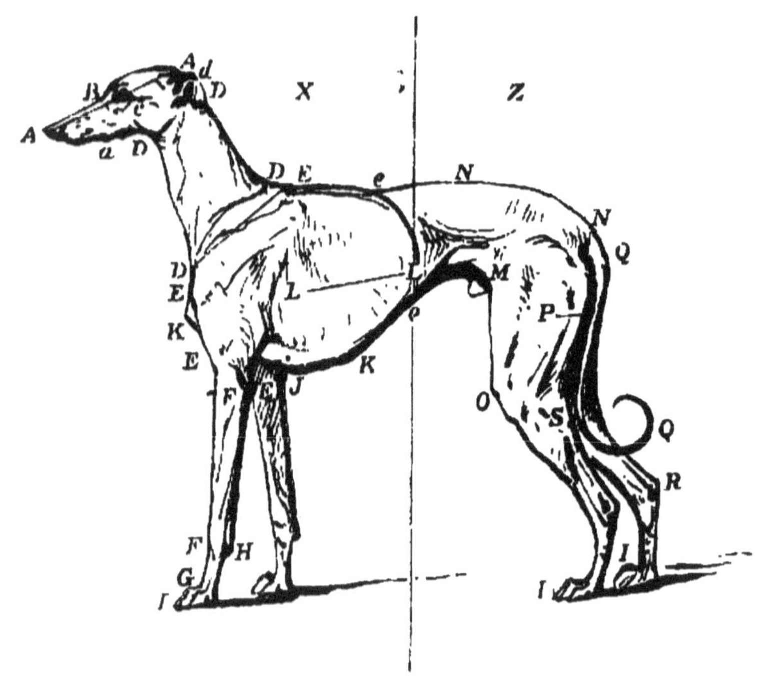


# CHAPTER IX

## DESCRIPTION AND POINTS OF THE GREYHOUND

'Handsome is as handsome does' is an old and trite adage; but all who have had any intimate experience of the various species or breeds of dogs will agree with us that, as a rule, the best looking are the best. That exceptions are frequently met with cannot be gainsaid. Many a plain-looking greyhound has proved of sterling merit; but then, if his points be carefully scanned, it will be found that they are well balanced, and that what is deficient in striking beauty is made up for by some remarkable development conducive to speed, stamina, or activity, or else that all points are so evenly balanced that no great merit or defect stands out prominently. Master McGrath was by no means an imposing specimen; but he was compactly built, and had a phenomenal development of quarter that lent him remarkable propelling power which enabled him to put in that wonderful 'extra bit' when he was apparently fully extended, a power shared by every *great* greyhound or racehorse.

The sketch at the head of this chapter represents the outline of a greyhound of well-balanced physique. The letters indicate the points familiar to all cynophilists, but useful as references when studying the description which ensues :—

A A Head
A B Muzzle
A *a* Jaws
C Eye
D D } Neck
D D }
*d* Ear
E E Shoulder
E E *e e* K K Chest
F Elbow
F F Forearm
F G Pastern
H Pastern-joint
I Foot
J Brisket
D N N Back
L L Ribs
L M Couplings
N O Stifle
P Thighs
Q Q Whip or tail
R Hock
S Second thighs

The vertical line cutting the diagram divides the dog into :

X Fore quarters
Z Hind quarters.

The term *forehand* is generally taken to include chest, shoulders, brisket, and forearm ; whilst *quarters* signifies back, couplings, stifle, thighs, second thighs, and gaskins ; but each term is elastic, and is often applied to the whole of the fore and hind quarters respectively.

## DESCRIPTION OF THE SHOW POINTS OF A GREYHOUND

An old writer has summed up the description of the greyhound in the following rhyme :—

Heade lyke a snayke
Necke lyke a drayke
Backe lyke a beame
Cheste lyke a breame
Foote lyke a catte
Tayle lyke a ratte.

With regard to the head of the greyhound it is somewhat far-fetched to liken it to that of a snake, although the term is very frequently met with in modern journalism; 'a long snake-like head' being quite a cant phrase with advertisers of fox-terriers and other such dogs.

'Neck like a drake' is fair, for in this particular no dog can vie with the greyhound and his cousins-german as regards the acme of grace and symmetry. If novelists would only describe their heroines as being possessed of greyhound-like necks instead of swan-like ones, the simile would be more acceptable. It is madness to allow the mind to dwell on a vision of female loveliness attached to a swan-like neck!

'Back like a beam' would seem to imply a broad, flat back, the same width from end to end, which would, of course, be wrong; but we must only take it as applying to its strength and breadth.

'Chest like a bream' is sufficiently descriptive, and quite applicable.

'Foot like a cat' will not quite do, as the foot of a greyhound is not as round as that of grimalkin, nor are the toes of the latter as arched as those of the former, though in closeness and compactness they resemble one another.

'Tail like a rat' will do, except that we do not often see rats with the terminal pot-hook, characteristic of the greyhound.

The following is a categorical description:—

*Head (including nose, muzzle, jaws, eyes, ears, and skull).*—'That head is the best which is most often in front,' was the answer given by a well-known M.F.H. when asked which he considered the best type of foxhound head. This applies with almost equal force to the greyhound. We say 'almost' advisedly, for the latter has more work to do with his head (physically speaking) than the former. The head itself should be long and tapering, the skull slightly domed, but flat at the junction with the neck; the muzzle long and powerful, and the nose pointed; the jaws strong, muscular, and level; pig-jaws or overshot teeth are very objectionable, and prevent a dog from holding his hare when he has floored her. Undershot greyhounds are seldom met with, and should not be encouraged.

*The eyes* are of moderate size, neither deep-set nor pedunculated, and of varying colour; generally speaking, a light eye in a dog of dark colour is to be avoided. The usual measurement of the head round the ears would be from $14\frac{1}{2}$ to $15\frac{1}{2}$ inches according to sex and size, but a tape run round the eyes should show a considerably reduced measurement.

*The cheek* should be very muscular, so as to lend additional strength to the striking and holding power of the jaw.

*The neck* of the greyhound is peculiarly graceful, and its length, symmetry, and set on are of vital importance. It must be of sufficient length and flexibility to enable him to strike his hare without losing stride. A ewe neck—i.e. one that is concave above and convex beneath instead of the reverse—is a terrible fault, and one seldom met with, for the simple reason that all puppies thus afflicted are as a rule promptly destroyed. If the tape is run from the point of the nose to that of the shoulder, the junction of the head with the neck will, in a well-formed dog, be found to be midway. This fact is mentioned by 'Stonehenge,' and is well worth remembering, for where the test fails it will be found that either the head or the neck is too short for well-balanced symmetry. A long, graceful, and well-set neck adds greatly to that vague—but to experts well-understood—term, quality.

*Chest and shoulders.*—The chest of the greyhound is somewhat flat, but deep and roomy, giving plenty of space for lungs and heart to bear the extra strain so often put on them. The shoulders are long, oblique, and laid well back, working smoothly on the flat surface of the ribs, the latter being well separated and more convex as they approach the quarters. It is of great importance that in none of these details excess should be noticeable, for unless a happy medium is maintained the effect of the whole is neutralised.

*The back* is arched and very powerful and supple: it is broad, and shows enormous muscular development. These muscles should lie forward, setting the back well into the shoulder-blades, and rising prominently on each side of the spine, which lies, as it were, in a trough between the ridges.

*The quarters.*—The general impression is one of great power, and in following a good and well-trained dog, it will strike the observer that the balance of power is uneven, and that the development of the hind quarters somewhat dwarfs that of the fore: such an impression as is produced in inverse ratio when *meeting* a bulldog. This is not really the case, the fact being that the functions of the hind quarters are more obvious to the eye than those of the fore.

*The thighs* are well breeched, and full of muscle.

*The stifle* long and well bent.

*The second thighs and gaskins* exceedingly muscular, and far more developed than in any other animal. This is one of the first points to which a practised courser will direct his eye.

The hocks let down, strong, and well separated from the leg bone.

*The tail* long and slightly curled at the extremity—a fine whip tail is sometimes insisted on, but some of the hardest and speediest strains show a considerable coarseness in the stern. This peculiarity is very noticeable in the dogs inbred to Contango.

*The fore legs* should be straight, and the bone carried well down, muscular on the outer surface, but flat on the inner.

*The pasterns* long, but very strong and springy.

*The feet* of moderate size; the middle toes, being slightly longer, make them appear more oval or pointed than round, but the impress will show that such is not the case. A flat foot is very bad, and a splay one horrible. The knuckles should be strong, close, and well-arched; but it is a bad sign to see a dog too much 'on his toes.'

*Quality.*—It is difficult to define this point; but, as we previously hinted, it is easily discerned and appreciated by all 'doggy' critics. It consists in a *coup d'œil*, which precludes analysis, but which embraces symmetry, blood, life, grace, movement, condition, and freedom from all coarseness.

*Colour.*—There is really no rule in this respect, and no allowance should be made in a scale of points. 'A good horse cannot be a bad colour,' is a saying as true when applied to a greyhound. A long chapter—and interesting to boot—could be written on the cause and effect of colour-production: for a good deal remains to be learnt by breeders in this direction. One fact is worth mentioning, however, which may only

The right sort and the wrong

be due to the accident of chance. It is that, until Fullerton appeared, no *brindled dog* had ever gained any marked distinction, though numerous *brindled bitches* had had their names enrolled as classic winners.

SCALE OF POINTS OF THE GREYHOUND

| | |
|---|---|
| General symmetry and quality | 10 |
| Head and neck | 20 |
| Chest and shoulders | 20 |
| Back | 10 |
| Quarters | 20 |
| Legs and feet | 20 |
| Total | 100 |

This is a simple and compact scale, and would be convenient for judging a dog roughly; but each of these items could be subdivided; for instance, the quarters, for which we have allowed 20 points, could be made up as follows:—

| | |
|---|---|
| Rump | 3 |
| Tail | 2 |
| Stifle | 3 |
| Thighs | 3 |
| Second thighs | 5 |
| Hocks | 4 |
| Total | 20 |

And so on, with regard to the other divisions.

In the Hunting volume of the Badminton Library the Duke of Beaufort gives a specimen of a good and a bad foxhound. The latter is of course presented in the guise of such a monstrosity that no master or K.H. would ever have sent him out to walk; but he serves as an example in every way of what a foxhound should *not* be.

Following his Grace's example, we give (p.159) the counterfeit presentments of two greyhounds. One, 'The right sort,' the other, 'The wrong.' The one a model of symmetry and power, the other a nightmare. Observe his ewe neck, his straight shoulder, his tucked-up chest, weak ribs, straight back, long couplings, straight stifles, muscleless thighs, upright hocks, long (and presumably splay) feet; and you will at a glance perceive what a greyhound should *not* be.

[illegible]

# CHAPTER X

## SOME ENGLISH COURSING CLUBS

By Charles Richardson ('King Cob').

Clubs have at all times played an important part in the history of coursing, and the earliest records of the sport show that for many years the public meetings were all promoted by one or other of the existing clubs, which, according to historians of the leash, differed very widely in their rules, constitution, and method of conducting their fixtures. The early history of the clubs is so much mixed up with the early history of coursing, and so many once important associations have so long ceased to exist, that I shall pass over the historical part of the subject as quickly as possible, and shall deal almost exclusively with the clubs which are in existence to-day, as in writing of these I am able to trust my own experience instead of searching the badly kept records of bygone generations. I have made some attempts to obtain particulars of the early doings of existing clubs: but, except in a few instances, so little record has been kept, and so little is really known, that a successful issue of the investigations was quite out of the question, and with secretaries in office who had had innumerable predecessors, I was referred from one to another, and then back again, until I found the utter impossibility of getting correct information.

To revert, however, for a moment to earlier times, the Swaffham Club in Norfolk, founded by Lord Orford in 1776, was the first association of coursers of which there is any record, and four years later the Ashdown Park Club was brought into existence. Swaffham and Ashdown were both very powerful associations in bygone days, and among the rules of the former it is stated that the number of members was confined to the letters of the alphabet, each member taking a letter and also a colour. What the colour was used for is not shown, but each member was bound to use the particular letter allotted to him in naming his dogs. The running consisted almost entirely of matches, and, curiously enough, everyone chose his own judge, the two judges for each match appointing an arbiter, who was to decide when they disagreed. At Swaffham, a 50*l.* cup was run for by sixteen greyhounds once a year, but stakes were the exception and matches the rule. Malton Club was founded in 1781, one year after Ashdown, with a membership limited to twenty, and two meetings annually, in November and February. The immortal Snowball won the cup twice, and in 1828 the list of members embraced such well-known names as those of the Duke of Gordon, Lord Macdonald, Sir John V. B. Johnstone, Sir Bellingham Graham, Messrs. Lowther, Best, Vansittart, and Bower.

A coursing club was founded at Louth, in Lincolnshire, in 1806, and in the same year the association at Ilsley, in Berkshire, was established by Lord Rivers, one of the leading figures in early public coursing. About this time, too, the Newmarket Coursing Society sprang into existence, and in 1812 Berkshire was again to the fore, with an association at Newbury, under the patronage of Lord Carnarvon. In 1814, Mr. Goodlake formed a club to course on his estate of Letcombe Bowers, in Dorset, and one year later the Morfe Club was established by Mr. Davenport, already a member of the Swaffham, Ilsley, and Ashdown. This last sentence may not seem of much importance at first glance, but it shows that gentlemen were in the habit of taking their dogs long distances by road, years before railways had come into existence, and thus we find Mr. Davenport a member of clubs which are more than 150 miles apart. The next few years witnessed the establishment of several other coursing associations or clubs, but all, without a single exception, have ceased to exist; although there is coursing at Ashdown to this day, the meetings of late years have been entirely open, and therefore quite out of my province. In 1825, Altcar Club was founded, and from that date a gradual change came over the spirit of public coursing, with the result that the Lancashire association in the course of a few years came to be looked upon as the most influential of all the clubs, and was soon recognised as the leader in all matters relating to innovation or reform.

Since the foundation of Altcar, dozens of other clubs have had their day and have died out, and it is with regard to these chiefly that the information obtainable is so meagre. In the Midlands, the Derbyshire, the Chester, the Sheffield, and the Burton-on-Trent were all important institutions for many years, whilst in the South, the Rock (Epsom), the Everley (Amesbury), the Spelthorne, and the Amicable had long and interesting careers. Of late years large open meetings have taken the place of club gatherings, and to-day Altcar and Ridgway in Lancashire, the Scottish National, and the South of England are the only important associations of coursing men where the hard-and-fast rule is complied with to the effect that no dog is allowed to run which is not absolutely the sole property of a member. Other flourishing clubs there are, of the hybrid order, where certain stakes are 'club,' and certain others are open, or where all the stakes are open to the public after the members have taken what nominations they require, and in dealing with the associations now in existence I shall make mention of these half-and-half affairs, as they are just now so much in fashion. It may be observed that Altcar still takes the lead, whilst Ridgway comes in a good second. The North of England affords its members far the most meetings, and the Yorkshire has taken a much higher place of late; the South of England is still comfortable and exclusive, and the Cliffe and Hundred of Hoo has come to the front with extraordinary rapidity. The new institution at Sleaford also bids fair to attain prestige.

## ALTCAR COURSING CLUB

Although it would seem that at the beginning of the present century some of the southern and eastern counties stood first in the coursing world, it has long been a recognised fact that Lancashire holds the pride of place, and at the present time we find the two most important clubs of the kingdom—Altcar and Ridgway—with their coursing grounds only twenty miles apart, and both situated near the coast-line of Southern Lancashire. The former club 'was established in the year 1825 by Viscount Molyneux, on his father's property near Liverpool,' and from that date to the present time the association has continually gained in importance, whilst 'its influence upon coursing has been an ever-increasing quantity.' The last sentence describes in a few words the position of the Altcar Club with regard to the rest of the coursing world, and although the words quoted are Mr. Harold Brocklebank's (the Honourable Secretary of the Altcar Club) and not mine, I can testify that they exactly bear out the general feeling with regard to Altcar which is held by coursing men who are not fortunate enough to be members of the premier association.

Writing of Altcar historically, I must dip into Mr. Brocklebank's interesting volume on the doings of his club, and, following the sentence about Viscount Molyneux, I must note his remarks that :—

> At the first meeting of the club the members acted as umpires for each other, but last season (probably *1827*) when a cup was run for, a regular tryer was employed. The members dine together on the first day of the meeting at the Waterloo Hotel, Liverpool, when the matches for the cup and other sports are arranged. The hares are abundant, and the noble Earl of Sefton appears gratified when the sport is good. There are two meetings each season, the first in the early part of November and the last in the early part of February. The club consists of twenty members, and four honorary members.

It will be seen from the above that in some particulars there has been little change, for the members still dine together on the first day of the meetings, and annually hold their first fixture in the early part of November. Their second gathering has, however, been moved forward about a month, to make way for the Waterloo Cup, which is run for over the same ground; and whereas the membership was twenty strong some sixty years ago, it is now of nearly three times the strength, whilst honorary members have almost disappeared from the list. This membership of Altcar is an honour which is eagerly coveted by all good coursers, and perhaps no higher evidence as to the prestige of the club can be afforded than the fact that the greatest care has always been maintained whenever the ballot box has been in requisition. A courser who is elected a member of the Altcar Club has been thereby embossed with the hallmark of the leash, and it is satisfactory to note that the first great essentials for membership are a liberal patronage of the sport, and a line of conduct in public coursing which must be altogether above suspicion. Social position, too, is justly made something of a *sine quâ non*, but it is not the case (as has been sometimes alleged) that the club is a peculiarly exclusive one. Although it recognises the fact that a long purse in coursing has as much power as elsewhere, it insists that an applicant shall have served a proper apprenticeship, and shall have proved himself (as far as can be judged) a stayer at the game.

As may be easily understood, Lancashire men are numerically stronger in the club than sportsmen from any other county; but this is perfectly natural, for coursing is the sport of the County Palatine, and where the nature of the land will not admit of riding across country, it can easily be understood that greyhounds are to the Lancashire man what foxhounds and harriers are to the denizens of more accommodating counties. Then, again, the South Lancashire seaboard probably carries a greater head of hares than any other portion of the Kingdom, and go to whatever public coursing you will, nowhere else are to be seen the droves of hares which come down the ground at Altcar when beating operations have begun.

Reverting again for a moment to the history of the Altcar Club, it should be noted that the far-famed Altcar Cup has been in existence almost from its first year. Produce Stakes were first introduced at the November meeting of 1852, since which time they have always figured at the earlier of the two annual gatherings. From that date up to 1887 the entries for this class of stake had been 5,486, of which number 2,620 started. The club matches at Ashdown and Amesbury in 1860 and 1864 are perhaps the most important landmark in the Altcar history, and of these Mr. Brocklebank has furnished us with a complete history.

## Altcar Club Matches at Ashdown and Amesbury, 1860 and 1864

In commenting on the club's meetings during the several seasons, I have made no reference to the matches in which it took part in the years 1860 and 1864 respectively, considering that they could best be treated in a separate notice.

The first and least important of the matches took place over the Ashdown country, in the March of 1860. It resulted from a challenge issued by the club to the World, to match sixteen greyhounds in the Craven Challenge Cup against sixteen to be drawn by the members of the Ashdown Club from any source. Great interest centred in the contest, and when at the close of the first round the World stood with ten winners against six, it seemed as if the challengers were to have the worst of it; but this unfortunate start was retrieved as the struggle progressed, and when Rosy Morn beat Little Wonder and Lord Sefton's Sweetbriar overthrew Veronica, the club was left with first and second, Mr. Randell being the ultimate winner with Rosy Morn. In addition to this important stake there were a number of others in which North of the Trent was pitted against South, and much wrangling ensued on the point of guarding. At this distance of time it would serve no good purpose to enter into details of the arguments advanced on both sides: certainly the visitors considered themselves aggrieved, and the conditions appear to have been so loosely drawn as to leave some justification for the feeling they manifested.

It sounds somewhat un-English, but there does not appear to have been any anxiety manifested on the part of 'the World' to try conclusions again with the club, and the next proposal for a renewal of the contest appears to have come from the club itself; for we read in vol. xii. of 'Stonehenge's' Calendar, p. 59, that at the Wiltshire Champion Meeting in October, 1863, 'The Earl of Sefton, Lord Grey de Wilton, Viscount Uffington, Mr. Jefferson, Mr. Brocklebank, Mr. Jebb, and Mr. Randell represented the Altcar Club (Mr. Hornby being absent from ill health), and broached the subject of a match between that flourishing institution and the World at the next Amesbury Meeting, they taking sixteen nominations in the Ladies' Plate and Challenge Cup.'

What brought about this proposal on the part of the club was, I understand, a suggestion made by Mr. Brocklebank to Mr. W. Long, the Secretary of the Wiltshire Club, that the dogs of the members of the Altcar Club, who had come so far should be guarded, as they had plenty of opportunities of competing against each other over their own ground. Finding his suggestion could not be met, Mr. Brocklebank hinted that the best way out of the difficulty would be to make a match, the club taking the one half of the nominations in the plate and cup. The subject having been favourably discussed, the Earl of Sefton on behalf of the club at once took sixteen nominations in each stake for the following season, on condition of being guarded throughout.

With a view to carrying the match to a successful issue I find that the Hon. Secretary of the club promptly issued the following circular, and the details it gives confirms the particulars above related.

'Dear Sir,—It has been arranged that sixteen nominations in the Challenge Cup for thirty-two greyhounds of all ages, and sixteen in the Ladies' Plate for thirty-two bitch puppies at the Wiltshire Champion Meeting in October 1864, are to be taken by members of the Altcar Club. Dogs belonging to members of the club will be guarded throughout in the above-named stakes, and also in two open Produce Stakes which will be run for at the same time.

'I beg you will be so good as to let me know whether you wish to take any, and if so, what part in this engagement, before the Club Meeting in January at which the allotment of the nominations will be settled.—I am, Dear Sir,—yours truly,

'T. D. Hornby, *Hon. Sec.*

'Druids' Cross, Liverpool, December, 1863.'

During the end of 1863 and early part of 1864 steps were taken on the part of the club and the world to perfect their arrangements, and it was agreed that, instead of two stakes in which the club and the World should compete there should be three, and I find that in March 1864 the following circular was issued by the committee of the Amesbury Match, and as it gives the corrected programme and illustrates the vigour with which the contest was taken up, I think it is well to give it in full :—

*(For Private Circulation only.)*

WILTSHIRE CHAMPION COURSING MEETING will take place at Amesbury, on Monday, October 17, and following days, when the following stakes will be run for.

THE GREAT WESTERN CUP, for an unlimited number of bitch puppies of 1863; entrance 5*l.* each, 2*l.* forfeit. To be named and close on August 1. The Altcar Club to be guarded as long as possible.

THE DRUID CUP, for dog puppies of 1863. The conditions the same as above. The Altcar Club to be guarded as long as possible.

THE LADIES' CHALLENGE PLATE (No. 1), for thirty-two bitch puppies of 1863; entrance 6*l.* 10*s.* each, 1*l.* from each nomination to be applied to the purchase of a bracelet for the winner, and 10*s.* from each nomination for a brooch for the second. To close and name on the evening of the draw, October 17. Sixteen nominations in this stake have been taken by the Altcar Club, to contend against the World; both parties to be guarded as long as possible.

THE LADIES' CHALLENGE PLATE (No. 2), for thirty-two dog puppies of 1863; entry and conditions the same as in Ladies' Challenge Plate (No. 1).

THE CHALLENGE CUP, for thirty-two dogs and bitches of all ages; entrance 6*l.* 10*s.* each. To close and name on the evening of the draw, October 17. Sixteen nominations have been taken by the Altcar Club, to contend against the World; both parties to be guarded as long as possible.

The rules of the National Club will be strictly enforced.

No dog will be allowed to start on any account unless the stake be paid.

Application to be made to the Hon. Secretary, Red House, Amesbury, Wilts.

| | | |
|---|---|---|
| THE EARL OF SEFTON, | T. D. HORNBY, Esq. | *Committee of Management.* |
| C. RANDELL, Esq. | W. LONG, Esq. | |
| J. S. BOWLES, Esq. | JOSHUA EAST, Esq. | |

MR. W. LONG, *Hon Sec.*
MR. WARWICK, *Judge.*
T. RAPER, *Slipper.*

It has been decided by the committee, who are engaged in collecting greyhounds which shall be best qualified to represent the World in the match with the Altcar Club at Amesbury, next October, that, as the honour of the World is at stake, the only principle to be adopted is that of 'Selection,' and that this must be left entirely to the committee, or to those to whom they may depute the management of the matter.

It is indispensable, therefore, that all applications which may have been already made to the Hon. Secretary, and entered by him, as well as future applications, shall be considered simply as Provisional, and not at all as entitling the applicant to the right of a nomination hereafter, in any of the Challenge Stakes.

A memorandum has been made of the names of those who have applied to the Hon. Secretary; but, with the view of facilitating the eventual selection, it will be very obliging, if all those who may be desirous to compete in a match, which promises to be one of unusual interest, should at once communicate with the committee.

It is recommended, wherever it may be possible, that the owners of greyhounds shall endeavour at once to ascertain which are the most promising puppies, and forward full particulars to the committee, with names, ages, pedigrees, &c. The specification of their size and weight would also be useful.

It is taken for granted that parties who may be anxious to compete in the match will also enter their puppies in the unlimited Open Produce Stakes, so as not to be without the opportunity of running their greyhounds in a good stake, should they ultimately not be selected for the Challenge Stakes, such entry for the Produce Stakes to be made in due course to the Hon. Secretary, in pursuance of the advertisment.

The present intention (should time and opportunity admit of its being carried out) is to appoint some day, of which notice will be given in the Autumn, previous to the Amesbury Meeting on which preliminary trials shall be arranged in the presence of a selected body of competent public coursers, to determine who shall be the champion representatives in the Challenge Stakes: and it is expected that owners of greyhounds engaged in this competition will cheerfully agree to abide by the selection which shall be thus made.

All communications on the part of the world, in regard to the Challenge Stakes, should be addressed to

THE COMMITTEE FOR THE AMESBURY MATCH,
15, *Great Stanhope Street, May Fair, W., London.*[1]

London, March 19, 1864.

[1] The address given at the end of this circular was that of Mr. Marjoribanks (of Messrs. Coutts and Co.), who undertook the chief direction of the arrangements on the part of the World.

It will be noticed that, in addition to the three Challenge Stakes, there were two Open Stakes for puppies in which the club was to be guarded as long as possible. It is also worthy of note that, while the draw is announced for the 17th, it really took place on Saturday the 15th, and the running beginning on Monday extended over the whole week, the final tie for the Druid Cup not being run off till the Monday following.

The Committee of the Altcar Club were not behind in their anxiety to be worthily represented, as the following circular shows :-

'March 31, 1864.

'All the members of the Altcar Club will be anxious that it should be represented as strongly as possible in the match-stakes, at Amesbury, in October next: and in the meantime there may be some desirous either to give up a nomination, on finding the want of a dog of sufficient quality, or to acquire one in the expectation of being able to fill it with a good greyhound. As the committee appointed to act for the club at the Amesbury meeting, we beg leave to offer to be the medium of communication and arrangement in such cases, and shall be glad to hear from any member who may wish either to drop a nomination or to take one up. Letters to be addressed to the Secretary.

'SEFTON,
C. RANDELL.
T. D. HORNBY.

'In case of any transfer of a nomination by private arrangement, it is requested that the secretary may be informed of it.'

There probably was on both sides some difficulty in getting together the most reliable representatives, and the anxiety of the club to be fully prepared is strikingly exemplified in the annexed circular :—

ALTCAR CLUB

'DEAR SIR,—I beg to draw the attention of those members who think of attending the Amesbury Meeting to the advertisement in last Saturday's papers of the Great Western and Druid Cups (the entry for which closes on August 1), and especially to the condition of a very small forfeit for puppies entered, if subsequently chosen to run in the Challenge Stakes, while they retain the option of starting again in the former stakes, if in the latter they are unluckily put out in the first round.

'I take this opportunity of expressing the hope that all the members will co-operate as far as possible towards success in the Challenge Stakes by promoting the entry of the best greyhounds that the club possesses. This can only be done by comparing notes as to the results of trials and by trials between the kennels of those members who are neighbours. If this view is adopted, I hope I may receive by-and-by from the members reports of the opinion they entertain of the form of their kennels, and of the trials on which the opinion is founded. If information can thus be brought together, it will not, I think, be difficult (without interfering with the rights of any gentleman who holds a nomination) to make arrangements, by common consent, which will ensure (at any rate pretty nearly) the representation of the club in the three Challenge Stakes by the greyhounds most likely to do it credit.

'Yours faithfully,

'T. D. HORNBY, *Hon. Sec.*

'July 25, 1864.

Of course between this time and the date of the meeting many details had to be adjusted, both as to competitors, quarters, &c.; but at last all was arranged, and the meeting began on October 17, the draw for the three Challenge Stakes having taken place on the Saturday after dinner, at which Mr. Hornby, Mr. B. H. Jones, Mr. Rundell, and Mr. Brocklebank represented the interests of the club.

At the close of the first day it was found that the club were winners of eleven courses out of sixteen in the Bitch Puppy Stake, nine in the Dog Puppy Stake, and eleven in the All-Aged. This was a great triumph for the club, and it is satisfactory to note from the comments on the day in the 'Calendar' that 'the members mustered in great force on the downs and bore their honours with a proper amount of modesty.' After the dinner in the evening the Open Stakes were drawn, and it was found that in the five stakes 208 different dogs had been engaged, probably a larger number than had ever been brought together at a meeting before.

At the dinner on the evening of the second day's running a discussion took place as to guarding, and I give the comments upon the subject as given in the 'Calendar':—'Some little discussion took place among the subscribers as to the method to be adopted in drawing up the pairs in the Challenge Stakes, for which both sides were guarded; but fortunately Mr. Rundell had seen the necessity of providing against the chance of any dispute like that which occurred at Ashdown some years ago, and had set down his ideas in writing, which were agreed to by all the other stewards present, and thus all discussion was avoided. The rule is clear enough, viz.: that the draw once made shall only be disturbed for the purpose of guarding. The programme set forth that both sides should be guarded as far as possible and the general practice in the north, where Scotch and English are usually guarded, is that the first brace of either side coming together shall be split and each shall take the next two of the opposite side. This was proposed by Mr. Randell and adopted, and I cannot see how it can be objected to, though next morning there were several influential coursers who thought the plan wrong.'

The result of the third day's running was still in favour of the club, and after a full week's coursing the match ended in success attending them in the first and second events, while the World took the third. For the All-Aged Challenge Cup, Mr. T. T. C. Lister's Cheer Boys beat Mr. Borron's Bit of Fashion in the final, and it is rather remarkable that while the World had five representatives that survived the first round, all of these went down in the second. In the Challenge Bracelet for bitch puppies the same proportion stood in the first round, and Mr. Bartholomew's Mock Modesty managed to get into the fourth, but the final was fought out between Mr. Randell and Mr. G. A. Thompson, both members of the club, the former with Rising Star, by Beacon—Gregson's Polly, defeating Theatre Royal, by Cardinal York—Meg of the Mill. In the Challenge Bracelet for dog puppies, the fortune of war was completely reversed, the World having three of the last four left in, and running first and second with Mr. Strachan's St. George by Seagull—Seaweed, and Mr. J. Jardine's Jacob by David—Goneril. In addition to these three thirty-twos, wherein the club dogs were guarded as far as practicable, there were two open stakes for bitch and dog puppies, seventy-four of the former and forty-six of the latter putting in an appearance. In these stakes the final positions were reversed, for while the club, in the person of Mr. Randell, won the Druid Cup for dogs with Revolving Light (beaten in the first round of the Challenge Bracelet, No. 2 for dog puppies by Jacob, one of the dividers), a brother of Rising Star, the World was first and second in the Great Western Cup for bitch puppies with Mr. Purser's Pastime by Seacombe—Peony, and Mr. S. Smith's Sultana by Sea Foam—Editha. The triumph of the club was very marked, especially as in the Open Stakes they were to a large extent overmatched in numbers by the representatives of the World. Mr. Warwick, of Shrewsbury, who judged the meeting, declared to me long afterwards that the second day's coursing over Tanner's Down was the grandest he ever witnessed, course after course going right away from the slips for quite a couple of miles. On a moderate computation he calculated that he rode over 120 miles that day.

For any further comments on the actual running I cannot do better than refer to the account of the meeting as it appears in vol. xiv. of the 'Coursing Calendar,' from which much interesting information may be gathered, and in conclusion I quote from the remarks prefacing the report of the Saturday's running :—

'By two o'clock all but the deciding course of the Druid Cup were run and the party separated with a vivid impression of the charms of Salisbury Plain as a coursing ground, and a strong impression that we shall never see the like of the late meeting, which has gone off without a single *contretemps*. Of course, one side must lose ; but as the managers of the World have the consolation of knowing that no pains have been spared to bring the contest to an issue successful to themselves, and as after the first round the contest has been a very close one, they have no reason to feel in any way disgraced. The trouble of carrying through the management of the World in a meeting of this kind is so enormous, that I do not believe there is the slightest chance of a return match, especially as, with the prestige gained by the Altcar Club, it would be considerably increased.'

The following is the return of the matches detailed in the foregoing article :—

## ASHDOWN PARK CHAMPION MEETING. MARCH 1860

*Stewards*—LORD SEFTON, LORD UFFINGTON, MR. T. D. HORNBY, MR. RANDELL. *Field Stewards*—MR. ETWALL AND MR. BOWLES. *Flag Steward*—MR. MALLABEY. *Judge*—MR. J. H. M'George. *Slipper*—H. SPRINGALL.

### CRAVEN CHALLENGE CUP

1

| | | |
|---|---|---|
| (W) Mr. King's bk d *Kate*, by Rutland—Redwing................. | beat | (C) Mr. B. H. Jones's bk b *Jay's Bird*, by Junta—Humming Bird (1) |
| (C) Capt. Bathurst's r b *Bapta*, by Skyrocket—Shame ................. | " | (W) Lady B. Craven's bk d *Comet of '58*, by Ld. Mayor—The Cure (1) |
| (W) Mr. Oates's bk w d *Glengarry*, by Blackcap—Black Bess .......... | " | (C) Mr. W. G. Borron's r d *Bloody Heart*, by Beacon—Judy |

## ASHDOWN PARK CHAMPION MEETING—*Continued.*

| | | |
|---|---|---|
| (c) Mr. C. Randell's f d *Rosy Morn*, by Black Cloud—Riot.............. | beat | (w) Mr. G. Gregson's bk w d *Rate Recruit*, by Harpoon—Cat-o'-nine tails |
| (w) Mr. W. Long's bk d *Little Wonder*, by David—Lexanna.... | " | (c) Mr. Jebb's bk b *Sharps*, by Powdermaker—Blooming Heather |
| (c) Lord Grey de Wilton's f d *Greek Fire*, by Weapon—Pearl... | " | (w) Mr. Hill's bk b *Hobby Bird*, by Black Cloud—Lady |
| (w) Mr. Hole's bk b *Opal*, by Barrator—Integrity.................... | " | (c) Mr. Hornby's bk b *Hammer*, by Junta—Jael |
| (c) Lord Sefton's r b *Sweetbriar*, by Skyrocket—Shame.............. | " | (w) Lady E. Craven's f w d *Hackman*, by Larriston—Lively (1) |
| (w) Mr. Minton's r d *Sailor Prince*, by Euclid—Minerva.............. | " | (c) Mr. E. Haywood's f d *Hardy*, by Bloodstone—Humming Top |
| (w) Mr. Price's bk b *Patience*, by Black Cloud—Riot.................. | " | (c) Lord Uffington's bk w b *Trip-the-Daisy*, by Jacobite—Forest Queen |
| (w) Mr. Allison's bk d *Hyena*, by Black Cloud—Young Eva.......... | " | (c) Mr. Spinks's bk w b *Seashell*, by Weapon—Japonica |
| (c) Mr. Blundell's bk w b *Barbelle*, by Weapon—Japonica.............. | " | (w) Mr. Loder's bk d *Snap*, by Lovus—Vanity |
| (c) Mr. Randell's bk b *Refulgent*, by Black Cloud—Riot.............. | " | (w) Mr. T. L. Hoole's f b *Wild Wave*, by Larriston—Fly |
| (w) Mr. Marfleet's bk b *Monolo*, by Ranter—Highland Home........ | " | (c) Capt. Spencer's bk b *Skittles*, by Black Cloud—Southport |
| (w) Mr. G. Gregson's bk w d *Ravensworth*, by Conqueror—Campfollower...................... | " | (c) Mr. T. T. C. Lister's bk w d *Corporal*, by Corporal—Clara |
| (w) Mr. Etwall's bk w b *Veronica*, by Vauban—Valinda.............. | " | (c) Mr. W. G. Borron's bk d *Bold Enterprise*, by Beacon—Judy |

II

| | |
|---|---|
| Bapta beat Ruler (1) | Barbelle beat Sailor Prince |
| Rosy Morn beat Glengarry | Patience beat Refulgent (1) |
| Little Wonder beat Greek Fire | Monolo beat Hyena |
| Sweetbriar beat Opal | Veronica beat Ravensworth |

III

| | |
|---|---|
| Little Wonder beat Bapta | Sweetbriar beat Monolo |
| Rosy Morn beat Patience | Veronica beat Barbelle |

IV

| | |
|---|---|
| Rosy Morn beat Little Wonder | Sweetbriar beat Veronica |

V

Mr. C. Randell's ROSY MORN (C) beat Lord Sefton's SWEETBRIAR (C) and won the Cup

## WILTSHIRE CHAMPION (AMESBURY) MEETING. OCTOBER, 1864

*Stewards*—Lord Sefton, Messrs T. D. Hornby, C. Randell, Bowles, and Strachan. *Field Stewards*—Messrs. F. Long, C. Rendall, R. Loder, W. Long, and East. *Hon. Sec.*—Mr. W. Long. *Judge*—Mr. Warwick. *Slipper*—T. Raper.

### The Challenge Bracelet, No. 1—Bitch Puppies

I

| | | |
|---|---|---|
| (c) Mr. C. Randell's bk w *Rising Star*, by Beacon—Gregson's Polly | beat | (w) Mr Price's be *Pride of Bishton*, by Seacombe—Patience |
| (w) Mr. Saxton's be w *Skylark*, by David—Patch | .. | (c) Mr. Borron's r *Bright Star*, by Skyrocket—Tritonia |
| (c) Mr. Brocklebank's w *Bowness*, by Cannaradzo—Bowfell | .. | (w) Mr. Ellis's bk w *Evening Bell*, by Seacombe—Patience (1) |
| (c) Mr. J. Brundrit's bk *Birdseed*, by Dunmwell—Bird of Passage | .. | (w) Mr. East's f *Entertainment*, by Effort—Columbine |
| (c) Lord Sefton's f *Soubrette*, by Skyrocket—Susannah | .. | (w) Mr Purser's w bd *Purity*, by Seacombe—Peony |
| (c) Mr T. T. C. Lister's r w *Cora*, by Red Lion—Kitty | .. | (w) Mr Morgan's bk *Melody*, by David—Brunette |
| (w) Mr. W. Long's w bk *Lulu*, by Sea Foam—Editha | .. | (c) Mr. Spinks's w be *Sea Fair*, by Seacombe—sister to Blue Hat |
| (w) Mr. R. Jardine's f w *Annabelle*, by David—Goneril | .. | (c) Lord Uffington's be w *Rob-keena*, by David—Trip the Daisy |
| (w) Mr. Bartholomew's be w *Mock Modesty*, by David—Bonnie Lassie | .. | (c) Mr. Jefferson's bd *Ida*, by Sea Foam or Derry—Java |
| (c) Mr. Blanshard's r *Brownie*, by Cardinal York—Baffle | .. | (w) Lord Craven's bk t *Country Dance*, by Monk of Thorney—Mazourka |
| (c) Mr. G. A. Thompson's w f *Theatre Royal*, by Cardinal York—Meg of the Mill | .. | (w) Mr. J. C. Russell's bk *Roseleaf*, by Regan—Gambol |
| (c) Mr. Jebb's bk *Regan*, by Regan—Judge Bitch | .. | (w) Mr. Davy's bk t *Convent Chime*, by Monk of Thorney—Mazourka |
| (c) Lord Grey de Wilton's bk *Guillemot*, by Seagull—Golconda | .. | (w) Mr Deighton's bk *Donna Diana*, by Errand boy—Early Blossom |
| (c) Mr. B. H. Jones's bk *Joke*, by Seagull—Jollity | .. | (w) Mr. F. Long's bd *Celeste*, by Bigwig—Columbine |
| (c) Mr Hornby's r w *Her Majesty*, by Balmoral—Martha | .. | (w) Mr. Hole's bk *Yes*, by Silversides—Quiver |
| (w) Mr Cunningham's bd *Belle of Eden*, by Mongoose—Maid of the Vale | .. | (c) Mr. S. C. Lister's bk *Lace*, by Liverpool—Lovely |

II

| | |
|---|---|
| Rising Star beat Skylark | Cora beat Belle of Eden |
| Lulu beat Bowness | Theatre Royal beat Brownie |
| Birdseed beat Annabelle | Regan beat Guillemot |
| Mock Modesty beat Soubrette | Her Majesty beat Joke |

## WILTSHIRE CHAMPION MEETING—*Continued.*

III

| | |
|---|---|
| Rising Star beat Lulu | Theatre Royal beat Cora |
| Mock Modesty beat Birdseed | Regan beat Her Majesty |

IV

| | |
|---|---|
| Rising Star beat Mock Modesty | Theatre Royal beat Regan |

V

Mr. C. Randell's RISING STAR (C) beat Mr. G. A. Thompson's THEATRE ROYAL (C) and won.

### CHALLENGE BRACELET, No. 2—DOG PUPPIES

I

| | | |
|---|---|---|
| (W) Mr. Strachan's f *St. George*, by Seagull—Seaweed | beat | (C) Lord Grey de Wilton's bk *Glamour* (late Lanchester), by The Wizard—Rosley |
| (C) Lord Lurgan's f *Master Mark*, by Seagull—Lady Norah | " | (W) Mr Bland's f w *Bishop of St. David's*, by David—Rip |
| (C) Mr. G. A. Thompson's r *Teddy the Tiler* by Cardinal York—Meg of the Mill | " | (W) Mr. R. Jardine's r *Aimsfield*, by David—Goneril |
| (C) Mr. Borron's r *Bright Bell*, by Black Flag—Isabelle | " | (W) Mr. Fuggle's f *Farmer Foster*, by Woodman—Finesse |
| (C) Col. Bathurst's f *Ace of Trumps*, by Bosphorus—Bapta | " | (W) Mr. Purser's be *Pleader* by Seacombe—Peony (1) |
| (C) Lord Sefton's bd *Signal*, by Skyrocket—Susannah | " | (W) Mr. F. Long's r *Chief Justice* by Bigwig—Columbine. |
| (C) Mr. Blanshard's r *Bubwith*, by Baffler—Burning Shame | " | (W) Mr. Trinder's w bk *Triad*, Seacombe—Lola (2) |
| (C) Lord Uffington's f *King Cole*, by Effort—Enjoyment | " | (W) Mr. Esdaile's bk *Sunbeam*, by Shakespeare—Sister to Silverside |
| (W) Mr. T. L. Reed's f *Rambler*, by Flashman—Risk | " | (C) Lord Sefton's bk *Stingo*, by The Brewer—Sylphide |
| (C) Mr. J. Brundrit's bk *Bulrush*, by Sister of Jacobite—Sister to Wild Wave | " | (W) Mr. Dunlop's be *The Blue Boy*, by Canaradzo—Diana Vernon |
| (W) Mr. Saxton's bk *Samuel*, by David—Patch | " | (C) Mr. J. Johnston's bd *Joint Stock*, by the Brewer—Sr. to Streamer |
| (C) Mr. W. W. Brundrit's r *Accident*, by Joshua—sister to Gauzewing | " | (W) Mr. Loder's f *Light-Train* (l. Long-train), by Railroad—Lustre |
| (W) Mr J. Jardine's r *Jacob*, by David—Goneril | " | (C) Mr. C. Randell's r *Revolving Light*, by Beacon-Gregson's Polly |
| (W) Mr. East's f *Evident*, by Effort—Enjoyment | " | (C) Mr. Hornby's r *Highland Chief*, by Balmoral—Martha |
| (W) Mr. Davy's bk t *Consternation*, by David—Doubt | " | (C) Mr. Brocklebank's w *Broadwater*, by Canaradzo—Bowfell (1) |
| (W) Lord Craven's bk t *Sir Roger de Coverley*, by Monk of Thorney—Mazourka | " | (C) Mr. H. B. Jones's bk *Jemshid*, by Shooting Star—Jenny Caxon |

II

| | |
|---|---|
| St. George beat Master Mark | Signal beat Evident |
| Teddy the Tiler beat Rambler | Bubwith beat Consternation |
| Samuel beat Bright Belt | K. Cole beat Sir Roger de Coverley |
| Jacob beat Ace of Trumps | Accident (a bye), Bulrush (dr. 1.) |

## WILTSHIRE CHAMPION MEETING—*Continued.*

III

| | |
|---|---|
| St. George beat Teddy the Tiler | Jacob beat Bubwith |
| Samuel beat Signal | King Cole beat Accident |

IV

| | |
|---|---|
| St. George beat King Cole | Jacob beat Samuel |

V

Mr. Strachan's St. George (W) and Mr. J. Jardine's Jacob (W) divided.

### The All-Aged Challenge Cup

I

| | | |
|---|---|---|
| (c) Mr. B. H. Jones's be w d *Jem Mace*, by Pugilist—Happy Lass and | beat | (w) Mr. Gregson's bk w b *Torpedo*, by Canaradzo—Sealed Orders |
| (c) Mr. T. T. C. Lister's bk d *Cheer Boys*, by Skyrocket—Clara | " | (w) Mr. Cunningham's w bk b *Belle of the Campbells*, by Canaradzo—Sister to Black Fly (1) |
| (c) Lord Sefton's r b *Syringa*, by David—Sweetbriar | " | (w) Mr. Bland's be w d *Beadle of the Parish*, by The Brewer—Haidee |
| (c) Mr. G. A. Thompson's bk w b *Tirzah*, by Mariner—Titmouse | " | (w) Mr. Green's r b *Gipsy Queen*, by Twixt—Thanks |
| (w) Mr. S. Smith's w b *Snowflake*, by Cantab—Enna | " | (c) Mr. Borron's f w b *Bonâ Fide*, by Flashman—Elfin |
| (c) Mr. B. H. Jones's f d *Justice*, by Vengeance—Swiss | " | (w) Mr W. Long's f d *Loud Timbrel*, by Lapidist—Kissing Crust (1) |
| (w) Mr. [illegible] bk b *Coronella*, by Blackadder—Luck's All | " | (c) Lord Lurgan's bd w b *Lady Java*, by David—Java |
| (c) Mr. Borron's bk w b *Bit of Fashion*, by Black Flag—Bit of Fancy | " | (w) Mr. J. Jardine's bk d *Owersby*, by Selby—Mazourka |
| (c) Mr. Jebb's w f b *Dog-sick*, by Skew—Desdemona | " | (w) Mr. Boote ns bk b *Trip the Daisy*, by Brandy—Polly |
| (c) Mr. Spinks's r b *Sea Girl*, by Seacombe—Sea Flower | " | (w) Mr. Marshall's bk b *Riotous Hoppicker*, by Buckshorn—Racketty Hoppicker |
| (w) Lord Craven's f w d *Commercial Traveller*, by Wrangler—Welfare | " | (c) Lord Uffington's f b *Evangeline*, by Effort—Just Decision |
| (w) Mr. Price's bd w d *Patent*, by David—Lady Clara | " | (c) Mr. Brocklebank's r b *Bindweed*, by David—Sweetbriar |
| (c) Lord Sefton's r d *Sackbut*, by David—Sweetbriar (a bye) | " | (w) Mr. Loder's r b *Lyra*, by David—Czar Bitch (dr.) |
| (w) Mr. Dunlop's bk d *Marshal Forward*, by Picton—Coquette | " | (c) Mr. C. Randell's bd w b *Rhodanthe*, by Dalgig—Myrtle |
| (c) Mr. Blanshard's f d *Boanerges*, by Canaradzo—Baffle | " | (w) Mr. Saxton's be b *Sea Nymph*, by Seacombe—Prairie Flower |
| (c) Mr. Brocklebank's bk d *Baron Lyndhurst*, by Nestor—Blengdale | " | (w) Mr. Ellis's bk b *Evening Star*, by Baronet—Muslin |

II

| | |
|---|---|
| Jem Mace beat Snowflake | Justice beat Marshal Forward |
| Cheer Boys beat Coronella | Bit of Fashion beat Dog-sick (1, dr.) |
| Syringa beat Commercial Traveller | Sea Girl beat Sackbut |
| Tirzah beat Patent | Baron Lyndhurst beat Boanerges (1) |

WILTSHIRE CHAMPION MEETING *Continued.*

III

| | |
|---|---|
| Cheer Boys beat Jem Mace | Bit of Fashion beat Justice |
| Tirzah beat Syringa | Baron Lyndhurst beat Sea Girl |

IV

| | |
|---|---|
| Cheer Boys beat Tirzah | Bit of Fashion beat B. Lyndhurst |

V

Mr. T. T. C. Lister's CHEER BOYS (C) beat Mr. Borron's BIT OF FASHION (C) and won

The Altcar meetings of to-day are among the most popular coursing fixtures of the year, and are attended by coursers from all parts of the kingdom as well as by the club members ; indeed, the January meeting is now-a-days a huge gathering, and probably more interest is attached to the Members' Cup than to any other stake of the year, the Waterloo Cup alone excepted. When the enclosures were at their zenith some few years ago, their influence had an effect upon nearly all open country meetings ; but at Altcar, in January, this was less noticable than elsewhere, and during the time I have just referred to the stake filled as well as ever, such celebrities as Stitch in Time, Hornpipe, Greentick, Penelope II. and Herschel having either won or divided the coveted trophy. The ground coursed over is the same estate which is used for the Waterloo Cup, but the beats are varied, and while the Withins was a few years ago the best going and productive of the strongest hares, there has lately been a leaning to North End, Monks Carr, and the meadows below Lydiate Station. Hares, as I have just stated, are exceedingly numerous on all portions of Lord Sefton's estate, but wet weather has an adverse effect upon their well being, and during the last two or three seasons it has unfortunately been the case that the sport has sadly suffered from their weakness. A few days of frost and hard weather before a meeting generally insure the strength of the game ; but the fact is that there are no dry hillsides of which hares can avail themselves in long-continued rain, and the moisture hangs so much about the flats that poor puss's food becomes far too soft, and she suffers accordingly.

Occasionally a third meeting is held in March, but for the reason just stated this has not taken place for the last two or three seasons. Luckily for spectators of Altcar coursing, there are plenty of high mud banks on which the crowd can be placed, and although it is sometimes necessary to take up one's position on the dead level and in sloppy ground, this is the exception and not the rule.

### THE BOTHAL CLUB

Although little is now heard of this once celebrated club, it is still in existence, and, thanks to three of its chief patrons, the Hon. W. C. Ellis, Dr. Richardson of Harbottle, and Mr. Nathaniel Dunn of Newcastle-on-Tyne, the coursing world was placed in possession, some four or five years ago, of the 'Bothal Club Stud Book,' an amusing and interesting work, which dealt with north-country coursing generally, and the Bothal Club in particular. The writer was luckily fortunate enough to visit Bothal when the meetings were at their zenith, some twenty years since, and in his opinion the place was then quite unique as regards the amount of enthusiasm shown by the natives. Even now, at the revived meetings, 'the crowd' is wonderfully large; but the pernicious Ground Game Act has done its deadly work here as elsewhere, and, in spite of the efforts of Mr. Ellis and Mr. John Stott of Coneygarth, only comparatively small programmes are now possible.

Dealing with the history of the club, it must be mentioned that the present society only came into existence in 1866, but as the ground was simply first-rate, coursing had long been a favourite sport of the district, and other clubs had previously availed themselves of the permission granted by the Lord of the Manor. Thus, we find in 'Thacker' that the Morpeth Club held a meeting over the Bothal Barony in 1841, by permission of the Rev. Mr. Parry, the rector, when Mr. Jobling won a fifteen-dog stake, value eighty guineas. The Morpeth Club at this period was a very powerful association of coursers, who had 'leave' over all the best ground in South Northumberland, and whose meetings were numerous and largely patronised. There must, however, have been something wrong with the customs in existence at their gatherings, for about 1850 the club died out, and, as far as Bothal is concerned, the Newcastle, Northumberland, and Durham Union took its place. The newcomer did not last long, but was soon merged into the North of England Club, and then, after a short interval, the Bothal Club, well supported by the tenants on the estate, sprang into existence. The promoters of the new venture were Mr. Ellis, the rector of the parish, a relation of the then Duke of Portland, whose property Bothal was, and Mr. Angus of Whitfield, one of the largest tenants on the estate. These gentlemen actually succeeded in organising fortnightly private meetings, which at once 'caught on' with the inhabitants of the district. In 1866 the first public meeting was held, fifty-four greyhounds taking part in the puppy stakes, and victory going to Mr. Ellis's El Soudan, among the defeated lot being such a first-rate after-performer as Hyslop's Strange Idea, a subsequent winner of the Waterloo Plate, and the sire of a Waterloo Cup hero, in Sea Cove, two years later. The succeeding years saw an enormous increase in the Bothal entries, and as the place became more widely known, so much the more did it grow fashionable as a trial ground for puppies; indeed, such produce stakes in the open were never equalled elsewhere, the entry in 1870, when Cottage Girl and Charming Belle divided, reaching 345 for one of them. This enormous number of subscribers caused a division of dogs and bitches, with the result that in 1871 the former numbered 209, the bitches reaching the gigantic total of 242. The big entries were found to be quite unworkable, and, consequently, the next year the stake was limited to members only. Even then 259 names were set down. At this period there were five members' meetings in a year. With the victory of Gallant Foe in 1875 the early history of the club ceases, as for some years afterwards the meetings were in abeyance.

I need hardly remind my readers that Gallant Foe was the mother of that wonderful litter which included, amongst others, Princess Dagmar, a winner of the Waterloo Cup; Paris, the sire of Miss Glendyne and Bit of Fashion, and therefore the grandsire of Fullerton, Palm Bloom, Prenez Garde, and Pathfinder. Gallant Foe, as Mr. Ellis tells us, was altogether a Bothal Club greyhound, for her sire was Mr. Nathaniel Dunn's Don Antonio, by Mr. Ellis's Elsecar, from Coxon's Peggy Taft, and her mother Wilson's Meggie Smith; all four owners mentioned being members of the club.

During the ten years which followed the victory of Gallant Foe only one public meeting took place over the Bothal ground, but in 1884 a revival was brought about, and with Mr. Ellis showing all his old energy in the interests of the Northumberland coursers, the club gatherings soon began to be of importance again. It was, however, never intended that any more large stakes should be attempted, and thus the revived meetings have been kept within limits. For all that, the number of members of the Bothal Club is still very considerable, and as long as the supply of hares holds out, the fixtures will be quite as important as any held in Northumberland. During the last two or three years the meetings have been run off as joint affairs of the Bothal and North of England Clubs, and as this arrangement allows of the services of Mr. Thomas Snowdon as secretary, the prosperity of the gatherings has been increased.

And now, for the benefit of south-country coursers, I may add that the ground is, most of it, quite first-rate. There is a mixture of arable and grass, with hedges between; but the grass predominates, and the large field between two small coverts, which is called 'Abyssinia,' is as grand a trial ground as any to be found in England. From the Cooper's shop at Ashington, on either side of the lane, right down to Longhirst, the coursing is always unexceptionable, and it is only when the few rough fields, directly east of Longhirst station, are used, that the fluky element is ever likely to enter into the trials.

The venue is on the main line of the North-Eastern Railway from Newcastle to Edinburgh, and a morning train from the first-named place (about twenty miles) brings visitors to Longhirst exactly at the right time. Those who come from a distance with greyhounds can stay at Morpeth, five miles away, or at the little watering-place of Newbiggin-on-the-Sea, four miles off, on the eastern side of the ground.

The North Seaton estate, which adjoins Bothal on the east side, has also been a favourite Northumbrian coursing-ground for a long period. Since Mr. I. Lowthian Bell went to reside at North Seaton Hall, some half-dozen years ago, the revival, which I mentioned in connection with Bothal just now, has extended to the sister estate, and for the last two or three seasons the meetings have been joint affairs, under the auspices of the North of England Club, the coursing taking place one day on North Seaton and the other day on the Bothal estate. Mr. Bell has been most generous in his numerous presentations of tenants' prizes, and no Northern courser has worked harder in the interests of the sport, or has had more difficulties to contend with, he having essayed—with success—the task of getting back a head of game where, owing to the Ground Game Act, it had almost ceased to exist. The North Seaton ground is very similar to that of Bothal, and between the line of railway and the village first-rate coursing is always obtained, the big pastures round the 'ten acre plantation' being particularly good. Nearer the sea a high ridge and furrow, even on the grass, slightly spoils the view, and causes occasional flukes, but on the whole the place ranks high among coursing fields. The hares are always strong and never affected by wet as in some parts of Lancashire.

### CLIFFE AND HUNDRED OF HOO CLUB

Of late years the Cliffe and Hundred of Hoo Association for the Preservation of Hares and Wildfowl, to give it its proper title, has become a very important factor in south-country coursing; indeed, the club is now the most influential within hail of London. Its rise has been of a very rapid description, whilst its ever-increasing popularity is a sure sign that coursing still has a great hold upon the Kentish sportsmen, who assemble in great numbers whenever it is announced that the hare will be publicly coursed upon the

A Cliffe meeting

marshes which lie between the chalk cliffs and the river wall of the Thames in Northern Kent.

The meetings are well worthy of more than passing mention; for the venue, now that the North Woolwich and Amicable clubs, whose meetings used to be held on Plumstead Marshes and about Bushey Park and Hampton respectively, have ceased to exist, lies nearer to London than any other coursing-ground, and the sport enjoyed is of the good old-fashioned type, where hares are walked up and slipped at as they leave their 'form.' The headquarters of the Cliffe Club are at the Bull Hotel, Rochester, and this old-fashioned inn, with its museum of curiosities and countless relics of the late Charles Dickens, is well worth a visit. Here it was that Mr. Jingle abstracted Mr. Winkle's dress coat while that worthy was enjoying a post-prandial nap, and in the long room, where the club members now dine, was celebrated the famous ball, whereat the extraordinary strolling player cut out Dr. Slammer of the 99th with the widow of Rochester.

It appears that Dickens had actual foundation for this particular story, for much the same thing had *really* occurred at the Bull some years before 'Pickwick' was written, and to this day one is shown the two bedrooms, one within the other, where the two Pickwickians slept, and from the inside one of which the garment was taken. Be that, however, as it may be, the Bull is full of interest to a lover of Dickens's works, and apart from the coursing attraction at Cliffe there is much to be seen in Rochester and Chatham which will repay the stranger from a distance.

At the December meeting of the Cliffe Club, which is the most important fixture of their season, an annual dinner is given at the Bull Hotel to the landholders on the Cliffe Marshes, which function is generally attended by nearly one hundred members and friends, and where, with the popular and versatile Dr. Swayne in the chair, the fun generally grows fast and (almost) furious as the evening wears on. I have, however, heard at this dinner better speeches on coursing than I have ever listened to elsewhere, and the visitor who is not identified with the neighbourhood of Cliffe cannot fail to be impressed with the good feeling which exists between the club and the tenants of the land coursed over.

The drive from Rochester to the marshes is through about seven miles of pretty country, and the hotel need not be left before 9 A.M., the 'meet' being usually fixed for one hour later. This reminds me, too, that Gravesend is also well within reach, either by road or rail, so that anyone preferring the

IN THE MARSHES

well-known hostelries overlooking the river in the last-mentioned town have their choice of quarters. I myself have tried both Rochester and Gravesend, and find that the only advantage in the former place lies in the fact that the express trains to Chatham are available.

With meetings recurring every two or three weeks during the season, the stakes at Cliffe are made to suit all comers, and, ranging from 30*s.* to 4*l.* 10*s.* and 5*l.* 10*s.*, the average is probably about 3*l.* 3*s.* The one-day fixtures are entirely confined to members of the club, but at the larger meetings the more important stakes are of the hybrid character so often met with nowadays, i.e. open to the public after the members have taken what subscriptions they may require. Thus we have seen here, at a December meeting, dogs from Lincolnshire, Yorkshire, Derbyshire, and South Wales, in addition to the usual supply from the Southern Counties, and curiously enough many owners have sent animals in order that they may get something approaching a Waterloo trial. I shall refer to this subject again directly, but first it may be as well to mention that the coursing ground is of enormous extent, and *almost* entirely composed of what are called 'Marshes' in the local vernacular, but they really are the soundest old pasture, enclosures intersected and divided by dykes or ditches. The country lies on the south side of the river Thames, and, beginning at a point half-a-dozen miles east of Gravesend, it extends to Port Victoria, five-and-twenty miles away. Readers who are acquainted with the lower reaches of the Thames will know that the cliffs lie back some four miles from the river between Gravesend and Sheerness, and the tract between the sea-wall and the higher land—25 × 4 miles—forms the happy hunting ground of the Cliffe Club. Oxen and sheep are grazed on the marshes, and one has only to glance once at the live stock to be able to form an opinion as to the enormous feeding properties of the grass, which necessarily must be also the regular diet of the hares. Down on the 'Isle of Grain' close to Port Victoria there is some arable land, but as it lies fifteen miles from Cliffe, and is not very plentifully populated by hares, it is seldom resorted to, and indeed is mostly used for trials. I have occasionally seen rare good coursing here, and once remember to have witnessed the driving of a few acres of Brussels sprouts, with the result that half a dozen capital spins were obtained.

The first meeting of the club's season is usually held in the same week as that of the South of England Club at Stockbridge, and sometimes at this fixture long grass is a sad deterrent to the sport. Indeed, the 'marshes' have to be very carefully chosen early in the autumn, or else the mortality among the hares is out of proportion, and the trials too short and fluky. As soon as there has been half a dozen degrees of frost in the night, the grass is laid, and the going of the very best. The hares are on the whole very strong indeed, so much so that 'homes' are scattered about the marshes, and if this was not the case there would be any amount of distress amongst the puppies, who, as it is, sometimes get courses of abnormal length.

The run up is perhaps the least satisfactory part of the business, the lead being often of very little value at Cliffe, owing to the fact that a majority of the hares lie close to the drain-side, and that in consequence the slipper is obliged to give them very short law, or else miss them altogether. The drains are very much wider than those at Altcar, and hares rarely jump them when coursed, but usually make for the gateway and bridge leading on to the next marsh. There are, generally speaking, an entrance and exit to each enclosure, and great pains are taken to prevent the crowd getting in the way of these modes of egress; the result is that the drains are seldom used by puss unless she is very hard pressed, and then she generally tries to swim, and is often seized in the water. From the above it will be noticed that Cliffe and Altcar are really quite dissimilar, and I have frequently met disappointed individuals who have taken dogs into Kent with a view to a Waterloo trial, and who, when considering the matter afterwards, have recollected that no drain jumping was brought into play.

No beaters are engaged at Cliffe, but the farmers and others generally ride in line up and down the marshes with the Slipper and Judge together in the centre. The progress is a steady three miles and a half per hour, the crowd following behind the horses and never getting a rest for a moment, unless it happens that a marsh is walked over to which there is only one entrance. There is absolutely no galloping when a course is going on, and as at Altcar it is often impossible for the judge to leave the marsh in which the dogs were slipped. I have seen Mr. Brice ride a long way occasionally, but this has always occurred when he has been able to follow his dogs through an open gate. Coursing generally ranges over a period of from six to seven hours--according to the time of year—with half an hour's interval for lunch. The spectator, therefore, gets a fair day's walking in addition to the sport, and I have often wondered how the Lancashire men, who stand still whilst all their hares are driven for them, would like the change to the primitive style of the Kentish marshes. An intending visitor should write to Rochester for a hack if he does not care about pedestrian exercise, and I may mention that once, when suffering from a sprained ankle, I borrowed a pony from the shepherd, upon whose back (the pony's) I was able to write the full report of a three days' meeting.

Although visitors generally choose Rochester or Gravesend for their temporary quarters when running dogs at Cliffe, I must not omit to state that there is a station only a mile from the village—on the single branch line from Gravesend to Port Victoria—and this brings to my mind a somewhat amusing recollection in connection with the splendid time kept by the railway which serves the district. The incident took place two or three years ago, when the Company referred to used to run a special to Cliffe, and was as follows. The special had come down fairly well filled in the morning, and as the day was the last of the meeting we, who had been stopping in Kent, were very anxious to know what time it returned, as by availing ourselves of it the journey to London *ought* to have been shortened by two or three hours. We were informed that 4.45 P.M. was the appointed hour, and when four o'clock arrived we were just finishing close to the Sea Wall, nearly four miles from the station. I was very anxious to get to town, as my 'copy' was required as soon as possible, and bearing this in mind I made the best of my way across the marshes, almost at a run. When I reached the village the church clock showed that it was already a quarter to five, but I jumped into a tradesman's trap that was standing about, and was at the railway in another five minutes. I need not have hurried, for the waiting-room was full of coursers who had come on before, and they all reported that not only had the special not started, but that it had been sent down to Port Victoria, instead of being shunted into the Cliffe siding. The officials, however, told us they expected it back every moment, and so we waited, an impromptu concert taking place in the waiting-room. Meanwhile half an hour passed, and still no train—an hour, and then another quarter, when (at six o'clock) a porter began to ring a bell furiously. We all rushed on to the platform, only to be told that 'the bell meant six o'clock, time to change hands in the Signal Cabin.' Another quarter was passed, and then someone suddenly fancied that a green light, a long way down the line, was moving towards us. The porter could give no information, but the betting fraternity began to gamble over the apparition, and in about ten minutes it was placed beyond doubt that the lamp was moving towards us. Everyone waited anxiously, wondering whether this was the special, and when lighted compartments were discerned our fears were set at rest. On came the train, the pace increasing as it neared the platform, and as it steamed slowly *past* the crowd, someone shouted out to the functionary whose head was seen looking out of the van, 'Is that the special, guard?' 'Oh no, sir,' was the reply. 'This is a yesterday's train that was lost in the fog; we're now taking it back to Charing Cross.'

The day before had been extremely foggy—indeed, coursing had been interrupted for some hours—and the official, like many others on the line referred to, was so accustomed to getting chaffed, that he had his little bolt ready for us the moment he was tackled.

### THE ESSEX CLUB

This club in itself is of such minor importance that, were I to place it upon its own merits, half a dozen lines would suffice to describe its doings; but as it is mixed up with one of the most important southern fixtures, I may treat of the combined affair at rather greater length. The Essex Club is, in fact, affiliated to the Southminster meeting, and although that gathering is nominally celebrated under the wing of the club, the open stakes are of far larger dimensions than those confined to members, the support of the public being absolutely necessary to maintain the present standard.

How matters would be, supposing the Essex Club was properly worked up—like its neighbour on the south side of the Thames at Cliffe—I do not pretend to know, but certain it is that Southminster coursing has an exceptional popularity among south-country followers of the sport, whilst the running witnessed there is usually of the very best type. Southminster used to be a most unapproachable place when the nearest railway station was at Maldon, twelve miles off, but now, with a new line right up to the village itself, there is little to complain of in this respect, and London is brought within about two and a half hours of the place. The meeting is generally run off in the first week of December, and all the arrangements are in the hands of Dr. Salter, a rare type of sportsman, who acts for both the club and the open stakes, and who has brought about, and thoroughly maintained, a feeling of extreme cordiality with the Marsh farmers.

The programme consists of a Produce Stake for dogs and bitches, for club members, and the D'Arcy Cup for all ages, also confined to members, but beside these there are the Southminster Derby and Oaks, open to the public, and the Cowley Cup (also open), a really important All-aged Stake at

5*l.* 10*s.*, to which is added a handsome cup, given conjointly by Mr. E. R. Lightfoot of Cowley and Messrs. Elkington of Regent Street, London. This stake usually produces a very good class of greyhound, and is a most coveted trophy amongst southern coursers.

The meeting extends over three, and sometimes four days, and headquarters are at the King's Arms Hotel, Southminster, where there is a largely attended dinner each evening. Most of the regular habitués of the fixture go to the same lodgings each year, for the hotel can only accommodate a very small portion of the visitors, and so the cottagers have to make provisions for strangers. I can safely affirm that the accommodation set forth, though primitive in appearance, is spotlessly clean and extraordinarily cheap; there is none of the 'fleecing' existent at other places, and it is a well-known fact that coursers who have once been to Southminster always want to go back when the meeting comes round.

Whilst I am on this subject of quarters I may mention, too, that the change in diet is very welcome; for it is the fashion during the sojourn in the village to live upon oysters and widgeon, both of which are procured in their *native* excellence on the spot. Indeed, the oyster carts follow the coursing all day long, and wonderful are the stories as to the vast quantities of Burnham natives which have been swallowed by some of the midland division, who have come from a country where the bivalve is an unaccustomed luxury. The widgeon are brought from the decoy close at hand, and no one is thought to have done his Southminster meeting properly unless he gets through at least one each evening at dinner. As a rule, the widgeon is a bird that is not much esteemed, but cooked in Southminster fashion he becomes a veritable tit-bit, as witness hundreds of attesting coursers.

The system was thus explained to me:—'You wring the bird's neck, then cut an incision in the skin (of the neck) and lay a piece back all round. With one quick stroke you then chop the head off, and sew the skin over, without allowing a drop of the blood to escape. The bird must then be "drawn" very quickly, and the place instantly sewn up also. Ten minutes before a hot fire, and the trick is done.'' When dissected, the flesh is apparently quite blue, but it literally melts in one's mouth, and no one who has eaten widgeon cooked as I have described will ever care for them done in any other way.

The ground coursed over is very similar to that at Cliffe; grass covers by far the larger portion of it, but there is

An oyster cart

some arable, which latter affords rather heavy going. The land is, however, quite free from stones or flints, and as the enclosures are mostly large, very genuine trials are seen. Wide dykes intersect the various fields, and I think that hares jump more than they do at Cliffe, but still there are 'homes,' and the short 'breaking back' from the bank often occurs. The hares are uniformly stout, and by the end of the meeting the dogs which are left in the various stakes have all had enough of it. Coursers go to Southminster from all parts of the South of England. A year or two ago over a hundred greyhounds competed, the number being about the third largest seen out at any open gathering in that particular season. I omitted to mention that a third very valuable cup (the Essex Cup) is given to be run for by the winners of the Derby and Oaks, and as this is subscribed for by a deduction of 10s. each from the stake, the amount is generally over 20*l*.

Carried over a dyke after a course

Before the railway was opened to Southminster, the reports of the coursing had to be sent by road to Maldon, whence they were telegraphed to town, and on one occasion I recollect that when the London papers reached the village next morning not a word was to be found about the meeting, except a footnote in each to the effect, 'our correspondent's message had not reached the office in time for publication.'

Great was the consternation amongst the scribes, for sport had finished early, and the man entrusted with the messages had had ample time at his disposal. Enquiries were at once made for this functionary—a well-known *follower* of coursing, and he, being run to ground in a beer-shop, at once confessed that he had posted the reports in the hollow of a tree as he left the marshes. There surely enough they were found; the general laugh that followed—in which no one joined more heartily than the unabashed offender—was small consolation to the discomforted writers, who had to witness their handiwork drawn out of a puddle of water, which had entirely obliterated the account of the day's doings.

## LICHFIELD COURSING CLUB

Since the passing of the Ground Game Act, many coursing meetings have altogether died out in the Midlands, and now Lichfield and Wappenbury, the latter an open meeting, have to do duty for a large tract of country, wherein there are still, luckily, plenty of greyhounds kept. The Shropshire and Worcestershire one-day country fixtures are still in existence, but in Derbyshire and Notts public coursing has almost entirely disappeared, so that the dwellers in those counties have no really good meeting nearer than Lichfield, where, however, there are always two, and sometimes three, lengthy programmes during the winter months.

The club at Lichfield is well established and of good position, but of itself is not strong enough to attract outside attention, and therefore its meetings are worked off with valuable open stakes, the latter being really the most important events on the card. All the land coursed over now is the property of the Marquis of Anglesey, but at one time other estates were requisitioned besides Beaudesert, and King's Bromley in particular used to afford good sport.

The first meeting is usually held in the early days of October, the second about eight weeks later, and the third six or eight weeks beyond that date, the running generally extending into a third day. The programme mostly consists of two thirty-twos, one for puppies and one for all ages, the Anglesey Cup (club) for all ages at 5*l.* 10*s.*, and at least three supplementary eights. If the first day has proved very successful, made-up stakes are quite the rule, and matches are also often added to the card. The fixtures are attended by coursers from all parts of the kingdom, Scotland, Ireland, and at least a dozen English counties, being sometimes represented at the same meeting.

The draw dinner at Lichfield is a great institution, and Mr. Trevor, the secretary (at whose Swan Hotel headquarters are), is so popular in the district that some of the neighbouring gentry always put in an appearance, prepared to support the host and welcome the visitors from a distance.'

The first day's coursing usually takes place at Cooper's Coppice, about six miles from the city, and on high land in the immediate vicinity of Cannock Chase. On this part of the ground there are some first-rate trial fields, but the stubbles are not quite free from stones, and the venue, good though it is, is not to be compared with Flaxley Green, which is the alternate meet. This place is quite ten miles away from headquarters, but the drive, either by way of Longdon and Rugeley or through Beaudesert Park, is exceedingly pretty, and though the train to Rugeley does the distance in a quarter of an hour, it is little used except in wet weather. The courses at Flaxley Green are now run entirely upon grass, and the forty-acre meadow at the bottom of the hill is undoubtedly one of the finest trial grounds in England. There is a give and take about it which causes an infinite variety in the coursing; the view to the crowd is, from the conformation of the ground, simply perfect, and it can safely be said that the courses average at least forty points before puss comes to grief or makes good her escape at the boundary fence.

A characteristic of the coursing on Beaudesert estate is to be found in the fact that speed is hardly so much served as elsewhere, and though dogs are sometimes slipped to demon hares who take a vast deal of reaching, it is nevertheless the fact that clever—and sometimes little—bitches always show their best form over this ground, quick turning and general sharpness being an important factor in the result of many of the trials. Reference to the Calendar will show that clever bitches, who would be outpaced in an open stake at Haydock or Wye, are often returned winners at Lichfield, and writing from memory of what has occurred in the last few seasons, I can instance such as Daisy of the Green, Rheda Macpherson, Jenny Jones, Flowering Fern, and Dear Sal, all of which were successful in the more important stakes.

## NORTH OF ENGLAND CLUB

Since Mr. Snowdon became secretary of the North of England Club, that association has rapidly increased its operations, and now is virtually the controlling power of all the open public coursing in the county of Durham, and a very great part of that which takes place in Northumberland and the North Riding of Yorkshire. No other coursing club has ever assumed the dimensions of the North of England, and in proof of what it can do, let me state that in the season 1890-91, thirteen meetings with eighteen days' coursing were satisfactorily accomplished, while no fewer than eighteen different postponements took place. This is a tremendous record for such a severe winter as that just mentioned, and it may further be added that, had the season been an open one, second meetings would have been held over several of the estates where leave is granted.

Begun in a very humble way by a few Newcastle-on-Tyne innkeepers, the North of England dates back to 1835; but early accounts are altogether wanting, and I can only learn that the draws were held at the houses of each of the licensed victualling members in rotation, and that he whose turn it was engaged his own judge and slipper. Tradition further adds that the choosing landlord generally won; but I will not insult the good people of Newcastle by asserting that I believe this. Joking apart, however, the club under discussion was never exclusive as regards membership, and although respectability and integrity in running were, of course, rigidly insisted upon, social status was not an important factor when the ballot was in requisition; thus we find at the present moment a membership of 215, ranging from all the most prominent northern coursers to small village tradesmen and even sporting colliers. This liberality with regard to election has really been of enormous benefit, for it has made the club exceedingly popular with all classes of northern coursing-men, and now its hold upon the affections of the districts where it flourishes is so strong that nothing is ever likely to interfere with its well-being. The present patrons are the Duke of Portland, the Marquis of Londonderry, the Marquis of Ripon, the Earl of Ravensworth, Sir William Eden, Sir John Lawson, Hon. W. C. Ellis, Admiral Carpenter, Mr. W. D. Russell, and Mr. V. W. Corbett, all of whom grant leave for meetings. There are in addition several shooting lessees, who occasionally allow small meetings to be held on their ground, and between Eslington in Northumberland, the most northerly fixture of the club, and Rainton, near Boroughbridge, the most southerly gathering, there are at least a dozen estates where the North of England is received. The two places just named are more than one hundred miles apart, and this fact alone will convey to the uninitiated some idea of the magnitude of the club's operations. Of late years quite the most important fixture has been the three days' meeting held over the Marquis of Ripon's estate at Rainton, which usually takes place in the week following Waterloo, and always brings out a fair class of greyhound, with, generally, several of the previous week's Waterlooers in the principal stake. The Rainton meeting has been in existence some sixteen or seventeen years, and from a very humble beginning it has risen to exceedingly large dimensions, the programme now consisting of a sixty-four, a thirty-two, three sixteens, and some minor stakes. The ground lies on the east side of the town of Ripon, and consists for the most part of large enclosures, of an average of from thirty to forty acres, which are divided by small fences, and are almost alternately grass and arable land. The best of the coursing takes place on either side of Leeming Lane, that famous old North Road which has for more than a hundred years served as the trotting ground for North Riding matches, and hares are generally driven off the ploughing on to grass. The 'crowd' have to move pretty often, but a fair view of the sport is always obtainable, and the going is for the most part first-rate, flints and stones being almost entirely absent. The breed of hares, too, is far above the average, and the courses are, in nineteen cases out of twenty, sufficiently long to thoroughly test the greyhounds' merits. I may here recount an incident which occurred some half-dozen years ago, and of which I myself was a witness.

We were coursing in the low ground close to Rainton village, where the inclosures are rather smaller than on 'the Moor,' and where also the hedges are very much thicker and higher. Hares were being driven into a grass field, Bootiman the slipper being hidden behind the fence, Mr. Hedley standing some fifty yards out. A brace of greyhounds were slipped, the hare was reached about the centre of the field, and a pretty course followed, puss finally taking her pursuers through the further hedge. Some twenty points at least were scored in the slipping field, and Mr. Hedley rode over to the other side as his dogs worked their hare across. He (Mr. H.) could, however, see nothing more of the course after he reached the hedge, and so the decision was given, and a second brace put in the slips. Another hare was quickly sent through, slipped at, coursed, and killed, without having left the field, and then a third brace of greyhounds were taken to Bootiman, who still remained in the same place. We had not long to wait for the third hare, and she, being of the short running, jerking type, went round and round the centre of the field, affording a pretty course of the sort, and really standing up well. This trial had been in progress for some considerable time, when hare number one, with her attendant followers, struggled back into the original arena, and there we had the spectacle of the two courses going on close together. The greyhounds who were running number one were, of course, dead beat, and neither was any use afterwards, but it was clearly established at the time that the *same* hare was always before them, several of the stragglers having been able—in different positions—to watch the performance from start to finish. I may mention that the hare was fresher than her opponents at the end, and, if my memory serves me right, she actually escaped.

Of course, with such an enormous programme set forth every year, it can easily be understood that game is very plentiful over the Rainton estate, but for all that the card often takes a lot of working off, and to my mind the dimensions thereof are sadly in want of a shortening process, which would allow of a somewhat later start in the morning. As it is, Mr. Snowdon marshals his forces long before the February sun has struggled through, and on the first and second days headquarters at Ripon have to be left very shortly after seven o'clock, it being nothing unusual to find the sport in full swing an hour later; indeed, I once saw the sixth brace handed over to the slipper just as the Ripon Cathedral clock tolled out the half after eight, and I recollect perfectly that there had been no waiting for late dogs, and that the crowd was even then almost as big as at any portion of the day.

Another very important fixture of the Club is the two days' gathering held over Lord Ravensworth's Eslington estate in North Northumberland, and here again the early rising movement is strongly practised. The country is of a wild and roughish type, but the scenes amid which the courser's day is spent are exceedingly picturesque, and the air which blows off the Cheviots is of the purest and keenest character. The getting to and from Eslington was once a very serious matter. Hundreds of enthusiastic coursers used (before the railway was made) to make Alnwick their headquarters, and, rising in the middle of the night, drive in December darkness over the fourteen miles of hilly ground which lie between the ducal domain of the house of Percy and the battle-ground of the club. The meeting generally takes place early in December, and is therefore often postponed; but when the weather *is* right, no more enjoyable fixture exists for those who are stimulated by the air of the Cheviot Hills, and who do not mind roughing it to a certain extent.

Dealing with the other grounds in vogue with the North of England Club, Bothal and North Seaton have been treated of in the account of the Bothal Club. West Rainton, near Leamside, in Durham, is another very favourite spot for one-day meetings. The ground lies so handy for all the big northern towns that it is easily reached from Newcastle, &c., on the morning of coursing, and the programmes usually consist of a sixteen and two eights, with sometimes a supplementary stake. Hares are very numerous, despite the fact that the neighbourhood is a densely populated one, and good coursing generally ensues. The class of greyhound competing here is not, however, so good as at Ripon or Eslington, and the meeting may be said to be of local interest only. The same remark applies to the fixture held over Sir William Eden's Windlestone estate, but at Catterick and Scorton, in Yorkshire, larger programmes and of better class are to be found. At both the last-named fixtures two-day meetings are held, but the enclosures are smaller than those coursed over at the Rainton (Ripon) gathering, and the meetings, generally speaking, of a less important character. New ground, too, is being constantly requisitioned by Mr. Snowdon, and, in addition to the places I have mentioned, there were last season meetings at Rusheyford, Lumley and Washington, in the county of Durham, and at Londonderry in the North Riding. Good ground has been used by the club where coursing no longer takes place, and I may mention Minsteracres in South Northumberland, where a large and important meeting was held for many years, and Flotterton in Coquetdale, where the coursing—in the time of the late Mr. Weallans—was exceptionally good. It happens sometimes at the larger meetings of the club, that there are nominations to spare, and if that is the case, non-members are allowed to take them up. Should any south-country coursers wish to witness the doings of the most successful club in the north-east district, they should arrange to visit Ripon, where they could hardly fail to be delighted with the entertainment provided.

## THE RIDGWAY CLUB

I have before stated that the Ridgway Club ranks second only in importance to Altcar among the coursing institutions of the country, and this opinion I actually find to be the opening line of Mr. David Brown's account of the club, which—probably before these lines are in print—will have been given to the coursing public in the tenth volume of the Stud Book, the proof sheets of which have been most kindly placed at my disposal by a gentleman who has done much for coursing literature, and whose indefatigability in research has gained him the warm approval of all coursing men. I attempted some months ago to get at the history of the Ridgway Club, but at the outset I found that Mr. Brown had taken up the matter some time before, and therefore I gladly avail myself of his permission to use his information. As regards the early doings of the association, I cannot do better than quote his own words, remarking at the same time that such obscurity about an institution not more than sixty or seventy years old seems most remarkable. Mr. Brown's account will, however, show the trouble he has been at in his research, and, although it is probable that the earlier history of Ridgway is still far from perfect, it is also pretty certain that no further light will be forthcoming about the early doings of the Club.

Mr. Brown writes:—

Long ago I began to institute enquiries about its (the Ridgway Club's) early history, but found upon application to Mr Mugliston, its present courteous secretary, that he could afford me not the slightest assistance. When he took over the books from his predecessor, Mr. Percival, he found that these went no further back than Mr. P.'s appointment in 1879. Prior to this Mr. James Bake, of Bird's Cliff, Cheetham Hill, had been in office from the March Meeting of 1854, exactly a quarter of a century, and doubtless his books contained a carefully kept record of the club's transactions, possibly from its start. By some strange carelessness it would

The game

appear that no effort was made at his death to recover the books and documents belonging to the club, and possibly it is too late to make any effective attempt now. This is greatly to be deplored, as the most contradictory reports exist as to its inception. Goodlake, whose history of coursing was published in 1828, makes no mention of the club, and as he appears to have taken great pains to elaborate a complete list of all the existing clubs, going so far as to supply the names of the members in most cases, I should have been tempted to believe that it did not exist in his day were it not for the testimony of a living member to the contrary. During the winter of 1889 two letters appeared in the 'Field' from 'A Sportsman of the Olden School,' appealing to the younger members to take the trouble of supplying a history of the club, such as had been published in connection with Altcar. There being no response to his appeal, I opened up a private correspondence with this gentleman, which has ever since been maintained with much pleasure on both sides. He supplied me with many details of coursing as conducted in his early days, and specially of his connection with the Ridgway Club. Contrary to my belief, he affirms that when he joined the club in 1828 it had been in existence some years, and was at this date a flourishing institution, to be connected with which was accounted no small honour. He was barely twenty years of age when he found admittance to the Select Circle, and the circumstances were impressed upon his mind, as well by the fatherly interest which the president took in him, as by the sound advice he gave him 'to drink little wine or spirits, avoid cards and gambling, and go early to bed.' Mr. W. G. Borron, the gentleman referred to, has been at great pains in corresponding with the descendants of Mr. Ridgway in the hope of being able to throw light upon his connection with the club, but except a remark contained in a letter from Mr. Ridgway's daughter, there is nothing to help us materially. The note is to the following effect; 'I cannot tell when the Ridgway Coursing Club was founded, certainly some years before my marriage in 1832.'

Mr. Brown then goes on to tell us how he visited the British Museum, and overhauled *Bell's Life* in search of what he wanted, but that he could find no trace of the club earlier than 1839; he, however, also discovered that at the Southport meetings there had been a 'Ridgway Stakes' as far back as 1833, which stake continued to be run until the meeting disappeared in 1839, and the Ridgway took its place. This appears to have raised a doubt in Mr. Brown's mind as to whether Mr. Borron was right in his dates, but, on being interviewed, the latter gentleman stuck to his story, detailing incidents which had made a firm impression upon him at the time, and recounting how the field costume of the club in 1831-2 was a green-cloth frock-coat, drab vest, corduroy breeches, and long leather boots coming well up on the leg. Mr. Brown next consulted the files of several local papers, but his investigations led to little or no result, and therefore he fell back upon the conclusion that the Ridgway Club grew out of the Southport Club, and that the latter was merged into the former through the growing popularity of its president, Mr. Thomas Ridgway, in whose honour a stake had been named some ten years before the actual change of title took place.

I believe that local testimony goes to favour the idea just promulgated as to the Ridgway Club having sprung out of the Southport, and it is certain that the meetings of the former were held over the ground of the latter at no very far away date; indeed, the present ground at Lytham was not used until 1845, and for twenty years after that date the meetings were divided between the two places. Since 1865, the club has been wholly indebted to the Clifton family for its leave, and no better *locale* for the sport is to be found in all that part of Lancashire, where, by the way, there is a meeting of some sort at nearly every village.

Leaving the historical epitome and treating of the association of the present day, Ridgway holds quite a unique place amongst coursing clubs. The membership is almost as select as Altcar, and there is a certain spirit of *bonhomie* and good-fellowship in the Lytham gatherings, which is altogether wanting in some more sedate and dignified institutions.

The present membership of the club is fifty strong, and the meetings held are two annually, one in the early days of October, and the other in the first week of February. At the first-named there are separate dog and bitch Produce Stakes, Clifton Cup, Tenant Farmers' Cup, and sundry supplementary stakes of minor importance; and at the latter the United Produce (North and South Lancashire) Stakes, Clifton Cup, Lytham Cup, and Peel Stakes, a goodly programme, which causes the running to extend over a third day. The ground coursed over is a mixture of grass and arable land, but there are some nice sloping hillsides, which, though not high in themselves, are sufficient to afford dry lying for the hares, and, as a consequence, there is none of the 'weakness' referred to in the account of Altcar. The hares, indeed, are veritable demons in point of staying powers, and the particular breed to be found on one portion of the ground has earned great notoriety by the name of 'Jock o' Pods.' These specimens of the furry tribe have the reputation of being the stoutest hares in the kingdom, and although I, personally, have seen game go stronger at Stockbridge than anywhere else, I must say that a 'Jock o' Pods' hare takes a great deal of killing, even when he has a pair of the fastest greyhounds of the day at his scut.

As mentioned before, the coursing takes place on the Clifton property, and although the present owner, Mr. Talbot Clifton, has not yet joined the ranks of public coursers, he takes great interest in the sport, and certainly shows a wonderful head of game. On the first day of the meetings Birk's Farm is generally the meeting-place, and operations are begun with the driving of a large tract of arable land on to a grass flat. The sport is generally very fair here, but if puss once reaches the hillside, she generally gives her pursuers leg-bail in the plantation. The 'crowd' have a first rate view of this beat, which generally takes a couple of hours to get through. A move of half a mile is then made to another large flat, and sometimes the card is worked off here: if, however, this cannot be managed, a second move of another half-mile has to be undertaken, the ground reached this time being generally arable. On the second day the coursing is somewhat further afield, and the ground sometimes rather deeper, but 'Little Plumpton' now serves for all the finals, and the field so nicknamed affords a grand stretch of galloping, where, so long as hares do not attempt the 'wired' fence, the trials are most legitimate. I have seen some gruelling courses on Little Plumpton at the end of a meeting, but the going is always delightfully sound and springy, and after running on such stuff dogs naturally recover much more quickly than on really hard ground.

## SLEAFORD CLUB

The club which has been recently formed in connection with the Sleaford Open Coursing Meetings is hardly more than a year old, and has, as yet, done little to establish its claims to be reckoned as of first-class importance amongst coursing institutions. The sport, however, with which it is associated is so good that I imagine there should be a great future before the meetings, and in the face of the support accorded them during the last few seasons, I feel tempted to put on record (for the benefit of those who do not know) what manner of coursing Sleaford provides.

At present, all the stakes are offered to members of the club first, and after they (the members) have taken what nominations they require, the balance is submitted to the public. Whether in the future the club or the outsiders will play the chief part it is impossible to say just now, but about the quality of the sport there is 'no possible probable shadow of doubt whatever'; and, given good management and a strong committee, I see no cause why Sleaford should not take high rank amongst the hybrid associations which seem to suit the coursing public of to-day better than really enclosed clubs where no one but members can run greyhounds.

Public coursing at Sleaford is only about half-a-dozen years old, but Lincolnshire has always been a great greyhound county, and when several old fixtures, such as Brigg, disappeared [by the way, Brigg has been resuscitated again as an open meeting], it was only natural that new ground should be sought for. This was forthcoming on the Marquis of Bristol's estate at Sleaford, and as the shooting was, and is, mostly in the hands of the tenants, that sporting body are mainly responsible for the new departure. Mr. Fred Ward of Quarrington has in particular bestirred himself in the matter, and I may also mention the names of Mr. G. H. W. Hervey, agent to the Marquis of Bristol, and the Messrs. Sumner, as gentlemen who have lent able and willing hands, and who, with Mr. Charles Smith, landlord of the Bristol Arms Hotel at Sleaford and secretary of the club, are possibly the leading spirits in the movement.

The meetings, two in number, are held about the end of October and in the middle of January, and the programme generally consists of four thirty-twos, two of which are for all ages—one at 6*l.* 10*s.* and the other at 2*l.* 10*s.*—and two for dog and bitch puppies respectively, both these latter being at 4*l.* 10*s.*, non-members in every case paying 5*s.* per nomination more than those who have joined the club. As may be imagined, with such valuable stakes on the programme the class of greyhounds competing is very good all round, and now the meetings, like Lichfield, are attended by coursers from all parts of the kingdom. On the evening of the draw a large public dinner is held in the Corn Exchange, and some two years ago, when I was last present, the company numbered over one hundred, tenant farmers turning up in great force, and by their presence entirely disproving the idea that they wish the hare to be exterminated.

The show of game is first-rate everywhere, and each time I have visited the meeting the question of a close time for hares has been vigorously discussed, the farmers hereabouts being particularly keen on the Bill, and most desirous that a restriction should be placed upon the wholesale slaughter which occurs elsewhere.

A peculiar feature of Sleaford coursing lies in the fact that there is no long walk or drive to the scene of action, for the meet on two days is just outside the little town, and a five minutes' stroll from the Bristol Arms down the old-fashioned street brings one to the first stand. The land coursed over is a mixture of grass and arable, but at the earlier meeting hares are nearly all driven out of turnips on to grass and slipped at in large enclosures where a good view can be obtained and where the trials are of a most legitimate character. This turnip driving is worked in small beats, the village schoolboys being employed to the number of about sixty, each boy carrying a small yellow flag. The little army is 'dressed' up in close rank, and with the noise they make, and the waving of the flags, it is 100 to 1 on *all* the hares going forward. The moment game is on foot the captain calls a halt, the flanking horsemen ride forward, and generally succeed in sending puss where she is wanted. Mr. Ward is particularly clever at this riding hares out, and as a natural consequence of the pains he takes with the beating arrangements, it is always possible to run off about sixty courses or more between ten and five o'clock—really good work for the open! The fences are mostly small, and on the Quarrington Side I have seen Mr Hedley jump at least half a dozen when following a course of exceptional length.

## THE SOUTH OF ENGLAND CLUB

Coursers on the south-western side of the metropolis used to be cared for some thirty years ago by a couple of clubs--the Amicable and the Spelthorne—both of which used the same ground, viz. the home park at Hampton Court. It was, however, found that the members of one mostly belonged to the other club, and therefore the two were joined together under the title of South of England. The membership of the joint venture some few years ago was sixty-four strong, but the numbers have fallen off of late, and now the list is only of half the strength it used to be. It is exceedingly probable that the Ground Game Act is responsible for the decline, for now the club has to go much further a-field for its sport, and last year the meetings were held at Stockbridge in Hampshire and Amesbury in Wiltshire, both first-rate coursing grounds but by no means so easy of access as Hampton Court had been a few years before. Newmarket, too, has been frequently visited by the South of England, but hares are woefully short on

Chippenham field to what they used to be, and I do not know that the club ever used the Six Mile Bottom or Lord Gerard's ground where the Newmarket open meetings now take place.

The Stockbridge Meeting is usually held in the early days of October, and if the weather is fine (which by the way it generally is) no more enjoyable *small* fixture occurs in the year's Calendar. The stakes consist of a Produce Stakes for dogs and bitches, the Stockbridge Cup for all ages, and the Longstock, Andover, and Danebury Stakes of lesser importance. Headquarters are at the Grosvenor Arms Hotel at Stockbridge, where the club use the same room which has served for the Bibury racing club three months before, and where the party is always jovial and pleasant, if not of very large dimensions. The ground coursed over belongs to Mr. Joshua East, of Longstock House, himself an old courser of note, and a most enthusiastic sportsman, who, despite the fact that he is an octogenarian, still rides with the beat all day and continues to direct all the arrangements. The meet is usually at Vicar's Cross, hard by the pretty Danebury racecourse, and operations are conducted in a circle round the copse-crowned hill of Money Bunt, so well known as a landmark in the Tedworth Hunt, which serves so efficiently as shelter for the Longstock hares.

The drive—or walk—up to Vicar's Cross on a pleasant autumnal morning is a thing to be enjoyed by London sportsmen, and a stranger coming upon the scene, and accustomed to other coursing grounds, could hardly fail to note the striking difference between this and the usual state of affairs at a coursing meet. No cardsellers are here, no itinerant vendors of 'Ormskirk gingerbread,' or other well-known coursing viands, no loud-voiced bookmakers vociferating the odds on the coming event, no miscellaneous crowd of 'hangers-on' or 'pickers-up,' but, instead, a group of gentlemen, gaitered and knickerbockered to their hearts' content, some mounted and some on foot, and attended only by their servants with the dogs in charge.

Veritably a private day it seems, and yet by the time the

ON THE DOWNS

low ground is reached on the other side of Money Bunt, a goodly array of carriages, bearing their freights of Hampshire ladies, will have put in an appearance, and when the good things, which are spread out on a table in the stack-yard of the farm where the luncheon halt is made, are tackled, it will be found that the scene savours more of a picnic than anything else. As the afternoon wears on the 'crowd' is also increased by numerous horsemen from adjacent Danebury, but the attendance is never large, and the rowdy element at all times conspicuous by its absence.

The best of the sport is generally forthcoming from a beat along the valley, where turnips are driven on to grass in most systematic and clever fashion. The beat is not very wide, but is flanked on either side with horsemen, and the boys employed carry a long rope, which they keep dropping on to the tops of the turnips in order to prevent hares breaking back. The effect is first-rate, and though it is a difficult matter to conceal the slipper hereabouts, the quarry is easily sent where he can reach it. Hare after hare is 'used' in the low ground, and hare after hare clears her pursuers as the hill-side is reached, only to go right away on the steep ascent and gain the covert far in advance of the greyhounds. I have seen course after course from this low ground when the points scored would tot up to seventy or eighty, could anyone keep count, and not many years ago two stakes had to be divided after having been once run down, not a single hound being fit to go to slips again!

The stock of hares, too, is large enough for a meeting of four times the dimensions, and some three or four years ago Mr. East told me that 300 had been shot in one drive, in the preceding year, and after the coursing had taken place.

The second meeting of the club is generally held about a month after the first, and now Amesbury is the venue, the old place having been once more requisitioned after a spell of Newmarket. Another Produce Stake is run off at this fixture, but the chief event is the Craven Cup for all ages, and the first day's sport is usually on Tanners' Down, the finals being run off hard by the weird pile of Stonehenge. Headquarters are at Amesbury, but Salisbury is of course available also, and if only the weather is right the meeting is sure to be enjoyable. Some old coursers think Amesbury Downs the finest coursing ground in England, and certainly the 'going' is better for greyhounds' feet than the flinty downs at Stockbridge; but on a wet day there is no escape from the downpour, and late in the year the wind makes itself very strongly felt in the elevated positions. Down coursing is essentially a fine-weather pastime, for rain and wind which would hardly inconvenience the crowd on Cliffe Marshes, or on the Lancashire coast, seem to come in the form of hurricanes here, and the severest wetting I ever got when watching the long-tails was in a twenty minutes' storm on Tanners' Down. The force of it was quite strong enough to 'unsight' the only pair of greyhounds slipped during the time of its continuance.

## WEST CUMBERLAND CLUB

Coursing meetings have been held in the Whitehaven district for many generations, and, indeed, love of the leash is so inherent in Cumberland men that it is really difficult to say in what part of the country there has not been coursing, out of the mountain district. There is, however, no doubt that the Ground Game Act had a severe effect here for some years after it had been passed, and it was only when that ardent courser, Mr. Anthony Dixon, took matters into his own hands, that the sport began to look up again. Mr. Dixon began very young as a public courser, almost his first purchase being the brother and sister Record and Requisite by Hector from Netley Burn, which pair he afterwards renamed Dunmail and Disguise. Both were fast greyhounds, a fact that was clearly proved when they got to the end of Gosforth Derby and Oaks respectively, and while the former won some good stakes for his new owner, the last-named—a beautiful bitch of the seldom-seen colour of white, black, and fawn—has been invaluable as a matron. At one West Cumberland meeting lately, nearly all the winners were greyhounds bred by Mr. Dixon, of whom it can certainly be said that his energy, determination, *bonhomie*, and popularity have worked wonders with regard to the coursing revival on the west coast of Cumberland.

The Rheda estate of Mr. Thomas Dixon—elder brother of the gentleman just mentioned—furnishes the ground for the West Cumberland Club, which was founded in 1887 by Mr. Anthony Dixon, and which, supported by coursers like Sir Thomas Brocklebank, Mr. E. M. Cross, the Messrs. Hyslop of Denton, Mr. Lowingham Hall and Mr. H. B. Boardman is certain to increase in popularity and importance. The stakes range from *2l.* to *4l.* *10s.*, and the Club and Rheda Cups, of twenty-four dogs each, are limited exclusively to members, the minor stakes being generally open. The membership shows a steady increase every year, and the meetings, two or three in number, are nearly always of two days' duration. The ground coursed over lies principally in a circle round Rheda Hall, and it may be mentioned that the estate is situated between two large mining centres, Frizington and Cleator; but the stock of game is simply enormous. At no open meeting of to-day do courses follow each other more quickly than at Rheda, and this, occurring with an attendance of 5,000 miners looking on, speaks volumes for the hare-preserving qualities of the delvers for coal and iron. The crowd at a West Cumberland meeting is certainly most remarkable, and even more wonderful still is the manner in which they are held in check. Mr. Thomas Snowdon of the North of England Club is almost *facile princeps* in the management of a *chance* crowd, but Mr. Anthony Dixon is absolutely not to be beaten in this line, and as a rule he has a much more cramped country in which to manœuvre his forces. The first time I visited the meeting I found the system was worked thus: Mr. Dixon and his friend Mr. Robert Jefferson (master of the Whitehaven Harriers) were mounted, and when a change of beat took place they simply drove the vast herd of miners before them like a pack of hounds, the effect being perfect in its result, but exceedingly laughable to watch. Hares run very strongly on all parts of the estate, but there is too much covert near the Hall for the coursing to be quite first-rate there, and my experience inclines to the belief that Weddicar Hill is the best trial ground used.

Headquarters of the club used to be in the village of Frizington, but lately they have been moved to the Grand

At a North-country meeting

Hotel at Whitehaven, and at that hostelry the stranger can be thoroughly comfortable. I could tell many stories of the social part of a modern West Cumberland meeting, but I do not care to tell tales out of school, and therefore will content myself with saying that the Whitehaven people give a ready welcome to coursing visitors—only they would rather they did not come on a ball night. The drive out to the ground is about five miles, up and down hill.

One little story and I have done with the West Cumberland Club. Many years ago, not quite at Whitehaven, but somewhere else in the north of England, I was lugging a greyhound along the road, being then a youth of tender years with a strong partiality for the long-tails. My canine friend was being sent under my charge to a field half a mile off in order that he might be tried, and as usual when there were trials in the neighbourhood, some of the miners were hanging about to witness the sport. On my journey to the field one of these worthies rose from under the wall where he had been sitting, and, taking his pipe out of his mouth, addressed me as follows very solemnly: 'Master C——, if ivvor ye want to make yer fortun at cooours-ing, ye mun get a grand bitch and put her to a grand dog, and keep on breedin, till yer get five pups, arle (all) of one colour. They needn't be mair (more) than five, but mind ye, they mun be arle of one colour.'

The last words were spoken with great emphasis, and thus having got rid of what he had to impart, my mining friend resumed his pipe and his seat. I was most anxious to know what he meant, but he only kept repeating his last words, 'they mun be arle of one colour,' and it was some years before I understood the gist of the remark. This story was a great one for Mr. Dixon to tell the miners at a Frizington draw, and coursing men—especially those of the North county—will instantly understand the old miner's implication.

Dr. Lace of Frizington is the secretary of the West Cumberland Club.

# FALCONRY

BY THE

HON. GERALD LASCELLES

## CHAPTER I

### INTRODUCTORY—THE MODERN FALCONER—IMPLEMENTS USED—GLOSSARY OF TERMS

A WORK upon falconry, the most ancient of all the field sports which men follow at the present day, needs no apology for its introduction to the public, especially when, as is the case with the following chapters, it forms part of the series of volumes which deal comprehensively with all our English sports. That falconry is not better known or more commonly practised is due to the great alteration in the character of the country since the days when it was the pursuit chiefest in the estimation of the sporting public. The almost universal enclosure of the land, accompanied in many cases by the planting of hedgerow timber, the introduction of the art of shooting flying, which at once supplanted hawking as a means of providing game for the table, the adoption of the system of forming plantations which came so much into vogue about one hundred and fifty years ago—all these things contributed to make falconry less possible and therefore less popular than it had been up to the time of the Commonwealth, when men's minds were occupied with greater concerns than those of sport, and when falconry, the chief amusement of the upper classes, received its rudest shock. So now in the present day the parts of the country where hawking can be successfully carried on are comparatively few and far between, and though there are a goodly band of devotees to the sport (and there is no pursuit with the love of which its votaries become more deeply imbued), yet it is not possible for them to respond to the innumerable invitations which they receive to show their friends something of their favourite diversion, because the country where their host would seek to fix the venue is not merely bad, but *impossible* for the sport. This is rarely understood. In other sports the best can be made of a bad country: foxes can be hunted over plough lands, if not with the same success as attends the sport in the wide pastures of the Midlands, yet with satisfaction to those who are enterprising enough to carry on the pursuit under grave difficulties. In the absence of covert birds may be driven, and so on. But in a country unfavourable to that sport falconry cannot be carried on *at all*, and any crude attempts to do so must result in the disappointment of all concerned and in the depreciation of what is, under more favourable circumstances, one of the wildest and noblest of all the field sports in which man has ever indulged.

Hawking can only be carried on in a perfectly open country, that is to say, open enough for the particular flight that is to be followed. Thus partridge hawking can be pursued wherever the fields are large and the fences small without much hedgerow timber. Magpies require a rather more open country and entire absence of trees of any kind, while rook hawking can only be practised successfully in a perfectly open country, such as the downs of Wilts or Berks, or Newmarket Heath. It is therefore clear that only the residents in certain favoured localities can follow this amusement with the same facilities as are ready to hand in the case of most other field sports, and on the other hand a man must be really deeply 'bitten' who is willing to leave his home and his ordinary avocations in order to follow his favourite amusement in suitable yet distant localities. Yet there are many such enthusiasts left even in these degenerate days. Falconry has never for a single hour been extinct in Great Britain; and there are probably at the present time more hawks in training, well and ably trained too, both by amateurs and professionals, than ever there were since the beginning of the century.

In this work we propose to treat of modern falconry alone. That it is the most ancient of sports none can doubt. That it was the popular sport in the East centuries before it travelled to Europe is well known. Sir A. Layard records in his work on 'Nineveh and Babylon' that in the ruins of Khorsabad he found a bas-relief representing a falconer bearing a hawk on his wrist. In this case we may start our history of the sport from 1200 B.C. But we have no intention of following its course from that date to the present. As from the time of Alfred to that of James I. falconry was the chief sport of the aristocracy, so there were published more works on that subject than perhaps on any other. To these we would refer those who are curious in the history of the sport. First and foremost is the old 'Boke of St. Albans,' printed in 1486, purporting to be written by Dame Juliana Berners, Abbess of Sopwell, Herts, containing treatises on 'Hawking, Hunting, and Cote Armour.' Next the 'Booke of Falconrie,' by George Turberville, Gentleman, a most excellent and quaint work abounding in good advice. In 1615 was printed 'The Faulcon's Lure and Cure,' by Symon Latham, a thoroughly good, practical work on hawking, full of good sense. In the various editions of Blome's 'Gentleman's Recreations' (1670) are to be found many hints on training hawks, although most of the letterpress is copied from the older works quoted above. But a very good and original work, now very scarce, treating chiefly of the management of the short-winged hawks, is 'A Treatise on Hawks and Hawking, by Edmund Bert, 1619.'[1] In these books, with various other treatises, can be found many interesting details of this sport, which probably was at the height of its popularity about the time of Elizabeth. Her chief falconer was Sir Ralph Sadler (who was for some time the custodian of Mary Queen of Scots), and the abode which he selected in order to follow his favourite sport and for the better training of her Majesty's falcons was Everley in Wiltshire, now the seat of Sir J. D. Astley. In the old manor

[1] A reprint of this work was published in 1891 by Mr Quaritch, limited to 100 copies.

house there is a portrait of Sir Ralph in the Court costume of the period, with a falcon on his hand bearing a jewelled hood. Not far from the manor house is the old chalk pit, to this day known as 'Sadler's Pit,' where tradition says that a member of the chief falconer's family met his death by unwarily galloping over its precipitous edge while eagerly following a flight. There is an ancient hostelry hard by the spot which has now for many years been selected as the headquarters of the Old Hawking Club, showing how little the character of the country has changed since Sir Ralph Sadler selected it as the best he could find for the sport he loved so well.

That hawking was intensely popular in the days of Shakespeare can be proved by a hundred trite quotations, which we spare our reader, with the exception of one which shows so perfect a knowledge of the falconer's practice, and is expressed so exactly in the technical language of a falconer, that it is hard to believe it was written by anyone who was not a perfect adept in the art. It is in 'The Taming of the Shrew,' where Petruchio says of Katherine—

> My falcon now is *sharp*, and passing empty ;
> And, till she *stoop*, she must not be full *gorged*,
> For then she never looks upon her *lure*.
> Another way I have to *man* my *haggard*,
> To make her *come*, and know her keeper's call ;
> That is, to *watch* her, as we *watch* these kites
> That *bate*, and beat, and will not be obedient.
> She ate no meat to-day, nor none shall eat ;
> Last night she slept not, nor to-night she shall not.

Had Petruchio been a falconer describing exactly the management of a real falcon of unruly temper he could not have done it in more accurate language.

But to pass by the ancient practice and to come to modern falconry. There, again, we find the art fully described in many a work. Campbell's treatise, dated 1773, though full of extravagant nonsense, contains many a useful hint. The brief treatise of Sir John Sebright (1828) is most excellent, and has but one fault, viz. that there is too little of it. 'Belany on Falconry,' 1848, is a useful work, and in 1855 was published 'Falconry in the British Isles,' which has ever since been recognised as a standard work on the subject, excellent for its letterpress, but beyond all praise for the admirable engravings from the drawings of the late Mr. W. Brodrick, with which the book is so copiously adorned. This book was followed by 'Falconry: its History, Claims, and Practice,' by Messrs. Freeman and Salvin, and by various other smaller treatises which bring the history of the sport down to the present day.

These works are all in the English tongue. There are in French, German, Italian, in Swedish, Russian, Japanese, and Hindustani, nay in every tongue that has existed since the days of the Tower of Babel, works on falconry. Of all these, manifold and curious as they are, we will commend but one to the notice of the student on falconry; that is the magnificent work of Messrs. Schlegel and Wulverhorst, published at Leyden in 1841. The illustrations, from the pencil of Wolff, are in themselves an education in falconry, while the letterpress (in the French language) comprises as good a treatise upon the art as it is possible to write. Especially interesting to English readers are the graphic accounts of the heron hawking at the Loo, which was chiefly carried on by the Hawking Club, a full history of which is appended to the work.

The student of falconry who desires to perfect himself in the art need only possess himself of all the lore to be found in these books. To their instructions we can add nothing. With the knowledge contained in them we cannot presume to vie; but we will endeavour to describe the pursuit of falconry precisely as it is carried on at the present day, with all the advantages of modern science, with the disadvantages of modern agriculture, and the modern manner of life. This is an age of progress, and hawking, like other sciences, has not altogether stood still. Facilities for travelling, modern education, and the more rapid mode of thought have left their mark upon this ancient art, just as they have upon other matters. Clever as our ancestors were in the training of hawks, much as we have learnt by following closely in their footsteps, yet, as we live faster ourselves in these days, so we expect more to be got out of our hawks than would have contented the falconers of an hundred years ago. At that period the training of falcons was entrusted either to a man well taught in the practice of the Scottish school, and, therefore, well versed (and probably very clever) at hacking and training hawks taken from the nest; but the mysteries of catching and taming the wild-bred hawks were a sealed book to a man of this stamp, and the higher forms of falconry to be followed by the aid of hawks of this class were unknown to his employers. Or, again, where the master of the hawks was of more ambitious temperament, a Dutch falconer was imported, whose patience, skill, and delicate handling of the 'passage' or wild-caught peregrine were incomparably superior to the arts of the rougher professional, who was only familiar with the easily tamed, because never wild, nestling. But such a man as this was, as a rule, entirely ignorant of game or of game hawking, and, good as might be the sport which he showed, a great deal of the fun which, on an English manor, can be got out of a team of hawks, was lost to his followers.

The falconer of the present day is a different personage altogether. Met, perhaps, in the spring on the breezy downs, with a first-rate team of wild-caught hawks, where he is showing sport every day—ay! and *all* day—to a large party at rooks, magpies, &c., you next encounter him on the platform at Perth on his way north to fly grouse with a combined team of eyesses and passage hawks which he has educated on totally different principles for a totally different flight. Some, perchance, are the very same rook hawks as were flown in the spring, but so altered in education and habit as hardly to seem the same birds. Next he will be seen at Holyhead, returning from a successful trip to Ireland, where he has been pursuing the flight of the magpie, just in time to cross over to Holland to help the Dutchmen in capturing the hawks for the following year, and to render no little assistance in the early breaking and training of these captious pupils. Naturally he must be a man of experience, versatile, intelligent, and of some education, so as to be able to study and master the different forms of the science. No rule-of-thumb education will do here, for at a few weeks' notice he is called upon to train different kinds of hawks, in an entirely different manner, for flights which differ one from another almost as much as it is possible for sports to do.

As is the modern falconer, so is the modern sport. We travel faster, we get over more ground, and our hawks do more work. Only a year or two ago the score of quarry killed by our principal hawking club reached 600 head of winged game taken in England, Scotland, and Ireland by different kinds of hawk, all differently trained, entered, and managed. In ancient days where one system was pursued such scores were impossible, and though, perhaps, we are not nowadays superior to the best of the old Scotch falconers as regards game hawking, nor are we able to beat the best Dutch falconers as to their management of the wild-caught hawk, yet in the combination of both systems, with perhaps a few wrinkles from the Oriental falconers, whose practice has been a good deal followed of late years, we believe that modern falconers can lay claim to a distinct superiority in their science over those of any one school in ancient days.

In one respect, certainly, English falconry has made a great stride during the last twenty-five years—that is, in the general management of passage hawks. A great deal has been learnt here from the Indian falconers, to whom nestlings are unknown, but who are able to do as much in every respect with their wild-caught birds as European falconers can with their eyesses.

At any rate, in these later years, passage hawks are tamed and trained, and that early in their career, to an extent which was unknown to those masters of the art who, forty years ago, achieved great results with them in certain flights, where clever management and good entering were essential, but where very high training was not required.

In the 'Encyclopædia Britannica' Col. Delmé Ratcliffe, a falconer second to none, states it as his opinion that eyesses or nestling hawks, have been far better managed in the nineteenth century than they were in the middle ages. Whether this be so or not we cannot tell; certainly if backing such hawks was not formerly practised, this would be the case, but we are disposed to think that this practice was generally followed by the old falconers in Scotland and the north of England, where falcons could easily be procured from the nest, and that the good sport which they appear to have enjoyed was shown by eyess falcons which can hardly have been without hack. At any rate, he has placed upon record his opinion that the falconers of the present time have learnt to manage their hawks better than their ancestors were able to do, and we believe that he is perfectly correct in this view.

The hawks which are used in falconry in the present day are of various kinds, and are divided into two great varieties. First, the true falcons, or long-winged hawks; secondly, the short-winged, or true hawks.

In 'Falconry in the British Isles' we find the following excellent definition of the two varieties :—

> The falcons or long-winged hawks are distinguished from the true or short-winged hawks by three never-failing characteristics, viz. by the tooth on the upper mandible (this in some of the foreign species is doubled), by the second feather of the wing being either the longest or equal in length to the third,[1] and by the colour of the irides, dark in the case of the falcons, yellow in that of the hawks.

Falconers will, however, find many more differences between the two species than are here described; for their whole nature is different, and so, consequently, is their mode of flight.

[1] In the short-winged hawks the fourth is the longest feather in the wing. The tail and also the legs are far longer than in the falcon, and the foot more powerful.

Whilst the falcons are fine-tempered, generous birds, whose home is in the open country, and whose dashing style of flight is only adapted to wide plains or hills, the hawks are shifting, lurching fliers, deadly enough in their own country, which is the close woodland through which they can thread their way like a woodcock or an owl, and that with extreme rapidity, for a short distance.

Of the first-named variety the species which are commonly used in modern falconry are, first and foremost, the peregrine, which is to be found in every quarter of the globe, and wherever it has been trained, east or west, has always proved itself to be the hawk which is by far the best suited to the service of man; next the gyr-falcons and the merlin. These have been regularly made use of from time immemorial. Besides these we sometimes find the Barbary falcon, the sacre, the lanner, and the hobby; but though, no doubt, these birds are very capable of showing sport, they have been treated more as pets in this country, and trained as an experiment rather than with any serious intention to kill game with them. In the East both sacre and lanner are trained with success, as well as various other species of falcon.

Of the short-winged hawks the goshawk and the sparrow-hawk are the only varieties in use.

Of the implements which are in use for the confining and training of hawks, the first and the most important is the HOOD. This is a cap of stiff leather, so contrived as to blindfold the hawk, while at the same time it fits easily to her head and does not press upon her eyes, and yet is so well fitted that she cannot get it off. Two patterns are in ordinary use, Dutch and Indian. The Dutch hood is the old European form, and is made of three pieces, one body-piece and two eyepieces. These latter are usually covered with cloth or velvet, not only for appearance' sake, but also because the cloth being drawn into the seams of the leather makes a close joint and does not allow a glimmer of light to come through the hood just above the hawk's eye, and just where it should not.

Many a fine falcon has been made into an incurable 'jumper' or a 'restless brute' by straining to get at a ray of light which fell through an ill-made hood, and was just enough to do away with all the effect of hooding her, while at the same time it gave her no comfort or sense of freedom.

A good pattern of hood, nearly akin to the Indian pattern, made out of one piece, is given in 'Falconry in the British Isles,' Plate XVI., but we have never seen this hood in actual use. The Indian hoods are excellent, easily made, and most comfortable to the hawk. In fact, they are perfection so long as the hawk is on hand ; but hawks can readily get them off if left hooded by themselves, and therefore there are many occasions on which they are useless.

FIG. 1.—Dutch hood

Rufter hoods are light caps of leather which blindfold the hawk, but are open at the back, and securely tied with a strap and button round the neck. Hawks can readily feed through them, but they cannot be taken on and off, and are only used for the controlling of hawks that are just caught.

What the bridle is to the horse, that the hood is to the falcon; it is the only means by which she is controlled; without it, so nervous and excitable is her temperament that she would, even if trained and fairly tame, dash herself from the

FIG. 2.—Indian hood

perch at every strange sound or sight, and after an exhausting struggle would not, perhaps, recover her equanimity for a whole day. To take her to the field on the hand, or to travel with her from place to place, among sights and people most strange

FIG. 3.—Rufter hood

and alarming to her, would be an impossibility. With the hood on her head she sits like a stuffed bird; she can be handled, passed from one person to another, carried for hundreds of miles, and taken through streets, railway stations, or where you will, without the slightest trouble and without feeling any alarm or inconvenience herself.

Sir John Sebright very aptly remarks:—'It may, perhaps, appear paradoxical to assert that hawks, by being kept hooded, are brought nearer to their natural habits; but this is undoubtedly the case, for, by this treatment, they are induced to remain at rest when they are not feeding or in pursuit of game, and such are their habits in a wild state when left undisturbed.'

JESSES are two short strips of leather (see fig. 4) by which the hawk is held at all times. They are about one quarter of an inch wide for the greater part of their length, and half an inch wide at the part where they encircle the hawk's legs. Two slits are made about oné and a half inch apart,

Jesses

and the jess being placed round the hawk's leg, the shorter end is passed through the slit nearest the middle of the jess, and the longer end passed through both slits, which makes a neat knot around the leg. (See fig. 5.)

At the end of the jess furthest from the hawk's leg is a long slit which is passed over a swivel (see fig. 7), through the lower end of which is run the leash. This is a strap or thong of leather about three feet in length, with a button at the end, formed by folding the leather several times, then punching a hole through the folds and drawing the end of the thong through the hole. By this leash the hawk is tied to her block or perch. Dog-skin well tanned is the best leather that can possibly be used for jesses, and out of the centre part of the back, in very large skins, can be cut the best leashes. When skins of sufficient size cannot be got, calf leather or 'kip' is very good.

Once we saw some capital leashes cut out of lion's skin, but this leather is not often found in the tanyard. White horse-skin is very tough and very good for hawks that are prone to gnaw and tear their jesses, but it is apt to grow very hard with wear and requires constant greasing and attention, and nothing is better for leashes than 'porpoise' hide or the leather of the white whale. In India a leather is used that is very light and good, and also soft: it is usually dyed some bright colour on one side and appears to be goatskin. Swivels should be made of brass in all cases; iron or steel rust with bathing and then do not act well. In old days 'varvels' or rings of brass, silver, or even gold (often engraved with the owner's name) were attached

FIG. 6.—Leash

FIG. 7.—Swivel

to the jesses, and the leash run through them. But this more clumsy arrangement has for a long time been superseded by the swivel.

BELLS should be very good ones or they are not worth putting on to a hawk. By far the best and most durable are the Indian bells, of which the shape is peculiar (see fig. 8, p. 230). They are easily procured through any friends who may have taken up falconry in India, and they are largely made in Lahore. Of rough manufacture and cheap in price, they are perfect for the purpose for which they are intended and few falconers use any others. They are light, of good tone in general, and marvellously durable. We have used some for many years, even until a hole was worn through the metal of the bell by the clapper within it, and yet the tone was unimpaired. Many attempts have been made to get these bells exactly copied in Europe, but the result has always been utter failure : probably the metal used in India is a different alloy to that in use in Europe. Bells are made in Holland and are fairly good when new, but nearly always crack and lose their tone after a season's use. Bells are fastened to the hawk's legs by short straps called 'bewits,' which are attached in the same manner as the jess.

FIG. 8.—Indian bell

The CADGE is a frame or perch on which hawks are carried to the field. It should be made of light deal, and the edges well stuffed and covered with stout canvas. It is supported by four legs, which can be made to fold up for convenience sake, and it is hung over the shoulders of the bearer, who stands in the midst of the frame, by two cross belts. The box cadge is simply a light box, without a lid, and with padded edges, on which hawks are placed for railway travelling, &c. To induce hawks to sit quietly on the cadge they must frequently be brailed. The BRAIL is a strip of leather similar to a jess, about ten inches long, with a slit in the middle about two inches long. This slit is passed over the shoulder, and one end of the brail is passed round the wing and tied on the outside. The wing is thus lightly confined in its natural position, and the hawk, being unable to use it, will sit perfectly still as long as she is allowed to do so.

The Lure is a most important instrument in the training of hawks. The chief requirements are: that it should be attractive in form to the hawk, too heavy for it to carry, and convenient for the falconer to carry and use. A very good lure is made of a horseshoe, well padded with tow, and bound and covered with leather. It should be covered over with two pairs of wings, of which wild duck's will be found to be the best, and strings are attached by which food may be fastened to the lure, on which the hawk may feed. A lure is figured below.

A good lure is formed of two or four fresh pairs of pigeon's or fowl's wings laid face to face, and bound together. The hawks can pull enough at it to be rewarded after a flight, and it more closely resembles a bird, dead or alive. But, as hawks can carry such lures as these, they must be held by a long string, and are usually thrown up to the returning hawk to be taken in the air, instead of being thrown out on to the ground.

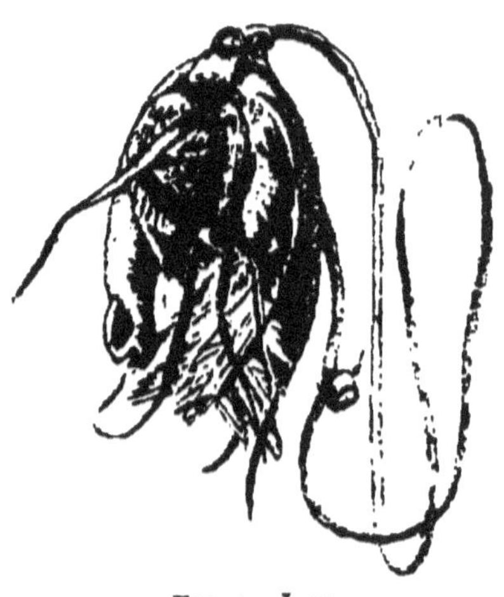

Fig. 9.—Lure

The falconer's left hand[1] on which hawks are carried must be protected by a stout glove. Buckskin is the proper material for this, roughly tanned, and it should be sewn double over the thumb, fore-finger, and upper part of the hand, or sharp claws will penetrate.

A Falconer's Bag, with different compartments for live and dead lures, snaring lines, &c., is most useful. A pattern is

[1] European falconers always carry the hawk on the left hand, but Indian, Persian, Arabian, and other Oriental falconers invariably on the right. Japanese falconers, however, use the left hand, like Europeans.

shown below. It is usually worn round the waist on horseback, or, if used on foot, over the shoulder.

Many falconers use the voice freely when training or exercising their hawks. Tradition is in favour of the practice, and it seems to have been in use in Shakespeare's time, or he would not have made Juliet exclaim :—

> Hist! Romeo, hist! O! for a falconer's voice
> To lure this tassel-gentle back again.
>
> *Romeo and Juliet*, Act II. Sc. ii.

Yet we have our doubts as to the efficacy of the practice. A short sharp cry as game rises is certainly of use, as it may attract the attention of a hawk that is waiting on so wide that her eyes may be turned for the moment in another direction. An old hawk, too, may become so used to her trainer's voice that she may not, however wilful she be, stray beyond sound of it. But, as a rule, hawks are birds that work solely by the eye. They will generally detect game the instant it rises from the covert, many seconds ere the sound of the falconer's voice reaches them. So, too, they will see the lure the moment it is shown to them, and if they will not come to it when well in their view, no strains of the human voice, however melodious, will attract them. If the falconer has a fine sonorous voice and he likes to exercise it either in calling or in cheering on his hawks, he can do so with eyesses without doing the slightest

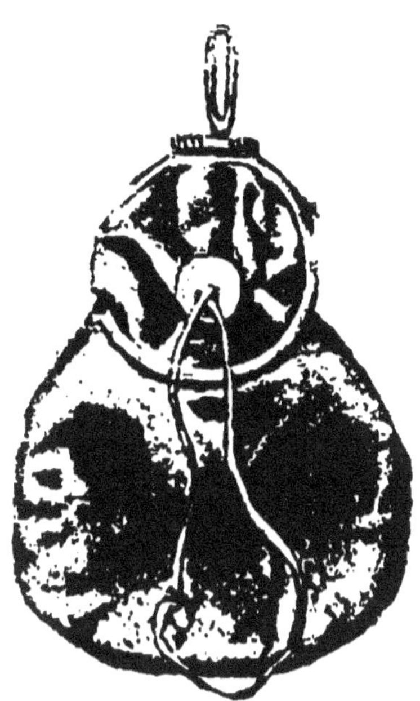

FIG. 10.—Falconer's bag

harm; but many passage hawks do not like a noise, and, as a rule, in hawking, as in all other sports, the quieter you are about it the more successful are you likely to be.

In ancient times the number of technical expressions used in falconry were almost innumerable; hardly a motion could be made by the hawk, hardly a feather shaken, but a special term was applied. We in modern times have much reduced the number of these terms, and in describing our hawks are content to make use of the ordinary expressions of everyday life; but in a sport so peculiar there are necessarily many technicalities and many terms which must be used and understood when falconry is the topic. We here append a glossary of terms now used in hawking, and, while we have endeavoured to include all those that are in daily use, we have excluded all that are unnecessary or obsolete.

## Glossary of Terms used in Hawking

Bate.—To flutter off the perch or fist through wildness or from temper.

Bewits.—The strips of leather by which the bells are fastened to the legs.

Bind.—To seize and hold on to quarry in the air.

Brail.—A strip of leather with which one wing of a hawk is secured so as to prevent her from moving it.

Cadge.—A frame of wood with padded edges upon which hawks sit when carried to the field. Cadges for travelling are made in the form of a box without a lid, and the edges of the box are padded as in an ordinary cadge.

Calling off.—To call the hawk to the lure from the fist of an assistant.

Carry.—To fly off with the quarry which has been taken, on the approach of the falconer: a fault hawks are very liable to contract.

Cast.—A couple of hawks.

Castings.—Fur or feathers given to a hawk, together with its food, to promote digestion.

Cere.—The waxlike skin above or round the beak.

Check to.—To leave the bird flown at for another.

COPING.—Trimming and paring the beak and talons.
CRABBING.—Hawks fighting with one another.
DECK FEATHERS.—The two centre feathers of the tail.
ENTER.—To train a hawk to a particular quarry.
EYESS, or EYAS.—A hawk taken from the nest.
FALCON.—Means the female of any hawk as opposed to the male, when used by falconers. Naturalists use the word to signify a long-winged as opposed to a short-winged hawk.
FALCON GENTLE.—Another name for a peregrine.
FROUNCE.—A disease in the mouth and throat of a hawk.
GORGE.—To give a hawk as much as she will eat.
HACK.—A state of liberty in which young eyesses are kept for some weeks to enable them to gain power of wing.
HACK-BOARD.—A board or table upon which the hawks at hack are daily fed.
HAGGARD.—A hawk captured after she has assumed the mature plumage—*i.e.* is two years old at the least.
HOOD.—A cap of leather used for blinding a hawk, so as to bring her under proper control.
IMP.—To repair broken feathers.
INTERMEWED.—A hawk that has been moulted in confinement.
JESSES.—Leather straps about six inches long permanently secured to the legs of a hawk.
LEASH.—A leathern thong fastened by a swivel to the jesses in order to secure the hawk to a perch or block.
MAKE-HAWK.—An old hawk flown with a young one to assist and encourage her.
MANNED.—A hawk that is tame enough to endure the company of strangers.
MANTLE.—To sit on the perch with wings and tail fully spread—a sign of an ill-tempered hawk.
MEWS.—The place where hawks are kept.
MUTES.—Hawks' droppings.
NARES.—Hawks' nostrils.
NESTLING.—The same as an eyess.
PANNEL.—The gut of a hawk.
PASSAGE.—The regular flight of any quarry to or from its feeding-ground; also the annual migration of hawks.
PASSAGE HAWKS.—Hawks which are caught when fully grown, as they migrate.
PERCH.—The pole or rail on which hawks are usually kept within doors.

PITCH.—The highest point to which a hawk rises when waiting on.

POINT, TO MAKE.—The perpendicular shoot up of a hawk over the exact spot where quarry has put in.

PUT IN.—The quarry is 'put in' when driven to take refuge in some covert.

PUT OVER.—To digest food.

QUARRY.—The game flown at.

RAMAGE.—Wild and stubborn.

RANGLE.—Small stones which hawks take with their food to aid digestion.

RECLAIM.—To tame a hawk, or bring her from her wild condition to such a point that she is fit to enter at quarry.

RED HAWK.—A hawk of the first year—*i.e.* in the 'red' or immature plumage (sometimes also termed a 'soar' hawk).

RING.—To rise in wide circles, or spirally.

ROUSING.—Shaking all the feathers.

RUFTER HOOD.—A hood of peculiar construction used for freshly-caught hawks.

SERVING A HAWK.—Driving out the quarry which has 'put in' to the hawk as she waits overhead.

SLIGHT FALCON.—A peregrine.

STOOP.—The rapid descent from a height upon the quarry.

SWIVEL.—Used as a link to attach the jesses to the leash, and to prevent entanglement.

TIERCEL, TERCEL, or TASSEL.—The male hawk as opposed to the female; he being a 'tierce' or third smaller in size.

TRUSS.—To clutch or hold on to the quarry in the air.

VARVELS.—Small rings of brass or silver which used to be attached to the end of the jesses. Now disused and a swivel adopted, being less likely to become entangled in trees, &c.

WAITING ON.—To soar steadily above the head of the falconer or his dog, in expectation of the springing of game.

WATCHING OR WAKING.—Sitting up at night with a newly caught hawk, so as to tire out and tame her.

WEATHERING.—Is placing hawks unhooded upon their blocks in the open air.

YARAK.—An Indian term to signify good flying condition.

## CHAPTER II

THE PEREGRINE—EYESSES—HACKING HAWKS—TRAINING—GAME HAWKING—RECORDS OF SPORT—MAGPIE HAWKING

THE peregrine falcon breeds in most parts of the United Kingdom where a suitable situation can be found for its eyrie and where it is allowed to remain unmolested. Wild sea-cliffs or lofty scaurs on inland hills are the most common situations; but the sea-cliffs are generally preferred because of the abundant food which is provided, both for the parent birds and the young, by the dense flocks of sea-birds and rock-pigeons which have also resorted to the same range of cliffs for breeding purposes. The chalk cliffs of the South Coast; rocky islands, such as Lundy or Handa; the headlands on the Welsh coast; the north and west of Ireland; and almost the whole of the coast of Scotland, are dotted with the breeding-places of the peregrine. Only one nest is found within a considerable circle, for the pair which have taken possession of an established eyrie will brook no intruder on their hunting-grounds. Taking the young from the nest is an operation attended with considerable difficulty and danger, and, if possible, experienced cliff-men, who are in the habit of descending the cliffs by means of ropes in order to take sea-birds' eggs or to gather samphire, should be employed. It is absolutely essential that the right moment should be selected for taking the young birds, and that moment arrives when the birds are nearly fledged, but have not yet left the nest. If taken too young the nestlings are very difficult to rear; are very liable to be taken with cramp, which is incurable, and, even if they survive, are almost certain to contract

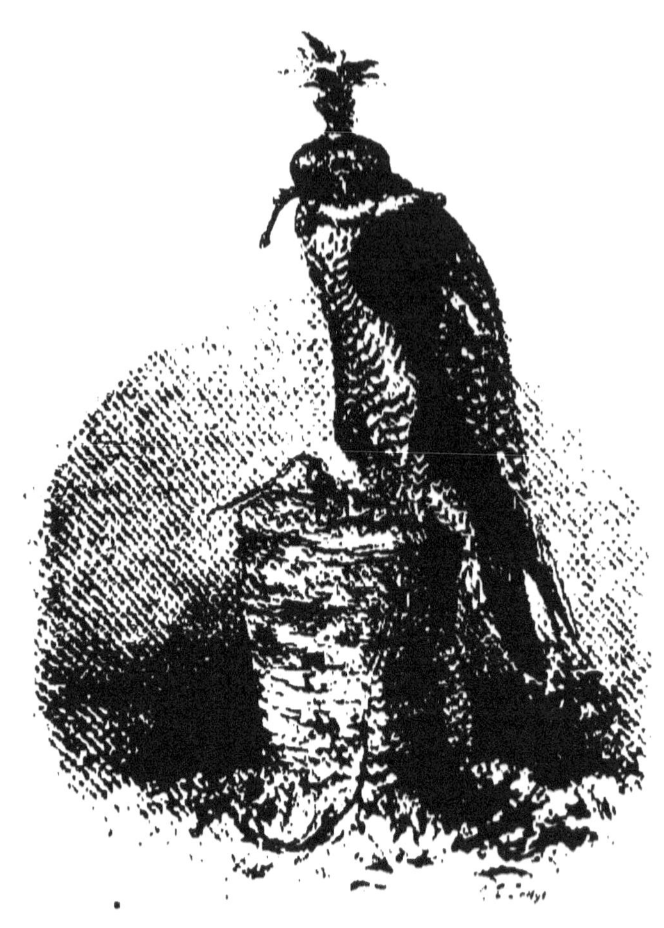

the vile habit of incessant screaming, and to be hot, bad tempered birds. The nest should be carefully watched with a glass from some coign of vantage until all the down which at first clothes the nestlings is seen to be replaced by brown feathers, and, when this is the case, the birds may be taken.

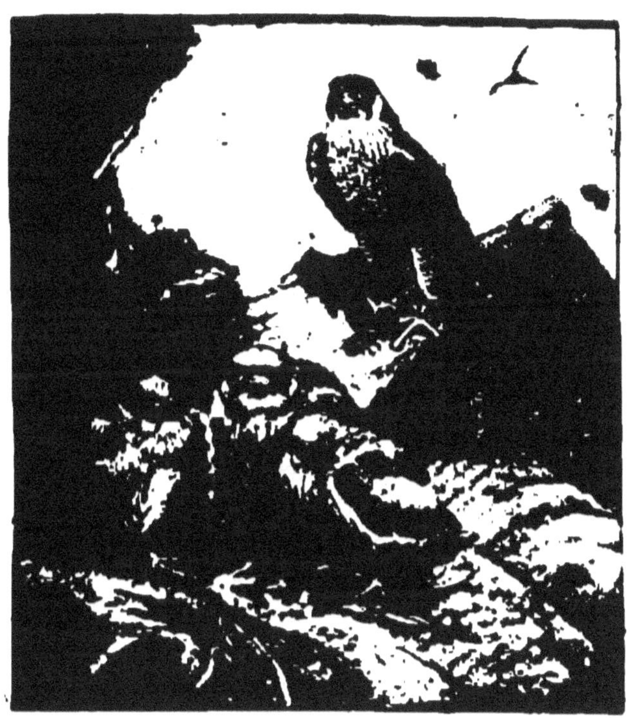

A peregrine's nest

This should be done if possible, towards evening. They should be placed upon long straw (not upon hay), in a hamper well lined with canvas, and sent off at once to the falconer, so that they may accomplish as much of their journey as possible during the night. No food should be placed in the hamper unless the journey is likely to be a very long one, and great care must be taken that no hay, grass, or woollen material be placed at the bottom of the hamper, or else the young birds will very probably pick up and swallow pieces thereof. Many a young hawk has been destroyed in this way. Young hawks well taken and well sent off are worth about 1*l.* to 1*l.* 10*s.* each. Those taken too young are literally not worth one shilling. Unless the falconer can thoroughly rely upon the cliff-men who are to take the nest for him, it is well worth his while to go himself or to send a man to see the nest taken. Not unfrequently there is some competition as to which man or set of men shall secure the nest, and in such cases birds are often taken young, and kept, generally in a bad place and on bad food, until they are fledged, and then sent to the falconer as freshly taken birds. Such nestlings as these are the most worthless of all; their weakly nature, tame disposition, and screaming will betray them at once, and the best and cheapest plan is to send them straight back again to wherever they came from, if, as should always be the case, proper directions have been sent for taking them, and a stipulation made that they are carried out. As soon as they are received, they should be taken from the hamper and placed in a roughly-made nest on the floor of a large loft, or even a shed or coach-house, in the vicinity of which they are intended to fly at hack; jesses and a couple of large bells should be put upon them at once, and, after that, the less they see of any human presence the better. The object of flying at hack is to get the young hawks wild and powerful on the wing. All training should be left until this part of their rearing is past and done with; the wilder they get the better, so long as they feed regularly. Food should consist of fresh beef finely chopped, with every other day a new-laid egg mixed with it; a change of diet should also be resorted to as the birds get older, and freshly-killed birds, rabbits, and even squirrels and rats, form good diet for hawks at hack. All food should be tied on a piece of board (which should be kept scrupulously clean) and placed within sight of the young birds by the falconer, who should show himself as little as possible and retire as quickly as he can. If the young hawks learn to associate his presence with a supply of food, they will at once begin to scream at the sight of a human being, and, if this habit is contracted, it will never be lost, and the hawks will become a positive nuisance to their owner. The method of rearing hawks which was adopted by Peter Ballantyne, one of the most successful of Scotch falconers, was to place them in an open loft or old pigeon-house, along the front of which was nailed a wide board or shelf at such a height that a man standing underneath it could just reach up high enough to place food on the shelf. On this board the young hawks spent most of their time in fine weather, their food being placed before them twice or three times a day without their catching sight of a living creature near enough to alarm them. Gradually they extended their flight to the roof of the house and the adjoining trees, and soon were on the wing and taking long trips into the adjoining country, regularly returning when hungry to the board, where they never failed to find their food at regular intervals. This was an excellent method of rearing nestlings, and its principle should be followed as nearly as possible. Where the hawks are reared in an ordinary loft, the window should be set open as the hawks get stronger, and they should be allowed gradually to come out, care being taken to set their food, when they have done so, on a large board called the hack-board, in a conspicuous place just outside the loft: for, when once in the open air, they will not re-enter the house.

In some places the contiguity of a village or some other circumstance renders it undesirable to let the hawks out until they are strong enough on the wing to extend their first flight to the tops of high trees well out of harm's way. In the first short flights of the very young birds they are, of course, very liable to be knocked over by a stone from some mischievous boy, or picked up and injured by some ignorant but well-meaning person. In such a case as this the hawks must be reared in a good large loft or loose box until they are quite strong on the wing. They must then be taken out and tied down to blocks close to the hack-board for two or three days until they get thoroughly familiar with the surroundings.

At the end of that time the falconer should quietly, and without frightening the hawk, cut its jesses off close to the swivel and leave it on the block loose. At night, after the hawk has fed, is the best time to do this. In the morning it will, after looking about it, quietly take wing, though its first flight will probably not take it out of sight of the hack-board, to which it will come down and feed, as it has been accustomed, at the usual time.

As soon as the young hawks have each spent the day on the wing and returned to feed at evening on the hack-board, they may be considered safe, and may be kept in this state of liberty until they learn to prey for themselves, which will not be for some weeks. It is a beautiful sight to see them playing together, coursing each other through the air, stooping and dodging, till at last, hot and weary, they ring up in wide circles into the cooler currents high overhead till they are out of sight and you see them no more till the feeding-time draws near.[1] Possibly as the time approaches, none, or at most but one or two, are to be seen about the hack-board; but before the hour strikes, a little dot will be seen in the far distance, which in a few seconds resolves itself into a falcon, hastening like 'a bolt from the blue,' to take her place at the dinner-table; in a minute more another speck is visible in another direction, then two or three together, and in a few minutes the whole vicinity of the hack-board will be alive with hawks, racing and chasing each other, till at last they drop down

[1] In the summer of 1881, an old wild tiercel came daily to play with the young hawks which we were flying at hack, and so lost his natural fear of mankind, through associating with them, that he would at times stoop within a few yards of the windows of the house, and even took to roosting on the adjoining church-steeple with the young hawks. When some of the nestlings were caught up, he disappeared, but, unhappily, carried off with him his favourite playmate, an exceedingly promising young falcon, which he kept so well provided with food that she ceased to feed at the hack-board and so never could be taken up.

one by one to the ground, and soberly settle down to the serious business of the evening meal.

Strict punctuality must be observed in feeding young hawks: six o'clock morning and evening are good hours to appoint.[1] They will not go far away at so late an hour, and will drop down from their roosting-places for their morning feed before they attempt to leave the place for the day; consequently every hawk goes away with its crop full, safe from getting into mischief for the present. Care must be taken to fasten the meat securely to the hack-board, so that it cannot be carried off by any hawk, and for feeding at this stage very tough beef, alternated with rabbits, skinned partially and cut into four quarters, is as good as anything.

As long as each young hawk appears regularly at the morning and evening feed, it is in no danger of being lost by its own fault, however far it may roam from home, and a careful watch must be kept to see that all have attended. But directly a hawk absents itself at feeding-time it is a sign that it is killing for itself, and, should it be missing a second time, it should be caught at once. Probably, however, this will not happen until the hawks have been at large for a fortnight or three weeks.

In order to secure them the bow-net must be used. This is a plain, circular, or oval net about three feet in diameter; for half of its circumference it is fastened to a light hazel-rod, bent into a semicircular or 'bow' shape. To the centre of the bow is attached one end of a line fifty yards long. To set the

[1] Hawks that are irregularly fed, or are allowed to go for any protracted length of time while their feathers are growing, are apt to develop a serious defect in their plumage known as 'hunger traces.' Sir John Seibright in his work on falconry describes it thus:—'The defect when strongly marked may be seen in some degree on every feather of the body, but it is especially observable on the expanded wing or tail, in a line crossing all the feathers. On the shaft of each feather the mark may not only be seen but felt as a ridge slightly projecting. It may also be seen as a line of imperfection across the web of every feather neatly marked as if a razor had been lightly passed across the wing. The injury from this cause is sometimes such as to occasion the feathers to break off at the hunger-trace, and it is not improbable that the razor-mark seen on the web is in fact owing to the breaking off of all the fine fibres of the web in the line of the trace.'

net, spread it open on the ground near the hack-board, and peg down that half of it to which the bow is not fastened with half a dozen pegs set round its outer edge. Then fold the bow back over the pegged-down portion, tuck away all the loose part of the net under the bow itself, till but little is seen except the hazel stick lying on the ground. In the very centre of the net place the food of the hawk, firmly pegged down, draw the long line tight, and the net is ready. Care must be taken not to allow the hawk which is wanted to feed with the others, and, as it will probably be the shyest and wildest of them, it will be easy enough to move it off till all the others have fed. Then remove all food except the piece which is in the net, and ere long the hawk will come to it. One pull of the line brings the bow flying over the hawk's head ; the net is spread out to its original shape of a circle, in the centre of which, under the net, is the hawk. It must be secured as quickly and as quietly as possible—a hood put on its head, a swivel and leash attached to the jesses, and then it should be tied down upon soft grass with a block to sit upon, and so left to itself for an hour or two to settle down.

No unnecessary delay must intervene before training must be seriously taken in hand. At first the young falcon must be carried on hand for two or three hours at a time, being continually stroked with a feather and otherwise gently handled. She will show great impatience at every touch and every strange sound, but she will gradually settle down to her unaccustomed perch and its concomitant disagreeables. As soon as she does this she will pull at a piece of meat laid across her feet, and will shortly take a fair meal through the hood. The next stage is quietly to remove the hood, by candle-light, while the hawk is feeding and hungry. Probably she will continue her meal without taking much notice, but the hood must be replaced ere the meal is at an end, and a few mouthfuls given after it is put on ; for the appearance of the hood must never be associated with the abrupt termination of dinner in the hawk's mind. If, however, she will feed well and fearlessly by candle-light, she should be tried by daylight on the following day, and, if she has been carefully handled, no doubt she will feed well enough on hand in a short time in the open air, with strange people about her. She should now be carried as much as possible among strange dogs, children, &c., and her idle moments may be spent bareheaded on a block in some place where she will see many strangers of all sorts, and in this way she will tame herself in a few days, and will eagerly jump to the fist for the evening meal, which she has become accustomed to take there. The next step in her training is to break her to the hood, and this is a most important one, for to be shy of the hood is one of the most serious vices with which a hawk can be cursed. It is hardly too much to say that there is no fault that a hawk can possess which may not be induced by a dislike to the hood in the first instance. It lies with the falconer himself whether his hawk shall be perfect in this respect, and there is no greater test of the skill and patience of the trainer than the way in which his hawks stand to the hood. Not on his own fist. He may be an exceedingly skilful hooder, and his hawks may know him perfectly, and let him hood them easily enough; but a well-broken hawk should stand well to the hood on the hand of any and every man who knows how to use his hood with ordinary skill. To do this well requires much practice and some dexterity: it is hardly possible to describe the process on paper. It should be done firmly, quickly and gently; no shots or dabs taken at the hawk's head, nor should the middle finger of the hand which holds the hood by the plume be used to thrust the hawk's head into the hood; but it must be gently placed on her head and a quick movement made of the hand on which she perches, so as to cant her forward, as it were, and let her hood herself. Any person who aspires to become a successful trainer of hawks must practise this branch of his art under good tuition, and should he master it he may be assured that the rest of the business will give him no great trouble.

But suppose the young eyess to feed well on the hand, to

jump readily to the fist for food, and to stand well to the hood, the next step is to introduce the lure—an instrument which has been described at page 231, but which is really any convenient piece of food which may be offered to a hawk, and which she cannot readily carry away. A dead pigeon or a fowl will do very well. Let your hawk take a bite or two from it and then fling it to the ground; she will follow it with a little encouragement, and, after you have helped her to feed upon it, she will again fly a few yards to it when thrown from her. During this part of her education she must be confined by a long string. Let her finish her meal upon the lure with your assistance; and the next day if she will fly keenly at it directly it is thrown at a little distance from her, and not offer to leave it at your approach, she is fit to fly loose with due care. She should be called from the block a few times at increasing distances, but before this lesson has been often repeated, the falconer will find that he cannot walk far away from his hawk with the lure in his hand without her following him.

She should be now placed on an assistant's hand and 'hooded off' to the falconer, who will swing the lure at a distance of about 200 yards. The hawk will be well on the wing when she reaches him, and when she stoops at the lure he will twitch it from her, and keep it from her sight for a while. She is sure to mount and circle round his head for a few moments, when the lure will be thrown out to her, and she should be fed on it. In a few lessons she will follow her master, circling round his head at a greater or less height, according to her natural inclination, for five or six minutes at a time, and then the rest of her education is a mere question of practice.

This hawk has never killed for itself, so it will be necessary to arouse the instinct within it by offering her a pigeon at the block. She will almost surely seize and kill it, and the next time she is flying round the falconer may be offered an easy pigeon, which also she will take and instantly kill. If the falconer has thoroughly won the confidence of his hawk he will have no fear of her carrying, but if it be otherwise the

[illegible]

pigeon must have a short line attached to it. When the hawk has taken two or three pigeons from the hand thus, let her have a real good old blue-rock fresh taken from the dovecote. If she should catch him, you may hug yourself on having got a 'wonder,' but in nine cases out of ten he will either beat her to some covert, if she presses him hard, or will fairly defeat her in the air.[1] In either case (if the country be open, and none other should be selected for such a trial) the hawk will return *high in the air* in consequence of the distance from which she comes. Then the moment she is well overhead throw out to her a pigeon which she can easily catch, feed and reward her well, and the lesson is learnt—viz. that to catch quarry she must be *high* and well placed over her master's head. Another lesson or two of this sort and the hawk is fit to fly at game. The less work that is done at pigeons the better—it is but a paltry amusement not fit to be called sport—and if hawks are kept very long at bagged quarry, they will soon fly at none other, and become useless, half-hearted brutes. This remark applies to all kinds of hawks and all varieties of quarry.

The first essay at wild game should be attempted with great care, and, if possible, in private, so that the hawk may be given every chance, and nothing sacrificed in an endeavour to show sport to an admiring circle. The weather must be fine—not necessarily a dead calm. A steady, good dog, well used to hawks, must be put down on favourable ground—the most favourable that can be selected—and should he get a point at birds in a good place, let the young falcon be flown. Plenty of time must be given her to attain her highest pitch, which the falconer will employ in getting round the birds so as to head the dog. The hawk must be exactly 'placed' when

[1] For three years we tried all our hawks, to the number of six or seven, annually with the same old Belgian homing pigeon that was the pride of a very fair loft. He stood the test well and sailed home in triumph year by year, when his feebler mates were defeated, although some very high-class hawks were tested by him. At last '*Buccaneer*' fairly caught him, and, though we were fortunately up in time to save the old bird's life, we never used him as a 'trial horse' again.

the birds are sprung—that is to say, she must be as high as she is likely to mount, exactly over the birds, but a little up wind of them. If, then, the falconer springs the birds at the right moment, and turns them down wind, a good stoop will be made, which will probably result in a kill.* *O fortunati nimium!* if such be the result, for, with future care and caution, the hawk is made. Let then the falconer go carefully in to her as she sits with the game in her foot; if he has trained her carefully he need have no fear of her carrying, for she will but regard his approach as an extra assistance by which she may the more rapidly obtain the tit-bits of her meal. She should be given a fair good three-quarter crop with plenty of casting, hooded up and taken home, and flown again the afternoon of the next day. Should she kill her bird again, treat her in the same manner, and then fly her twice or thrice a day as long as she kills well, and get all the sport you can out of her. After being flown for a while at game the hawk will (if it is ever to become a good one at all) begin to mount higher and higher. Unless it does so, it will be of no use at all later in the season, and, indeed, it is surprising how few hawks can kill grouse regularly and well after September 15, or partridges (especially in the case of tiercels) after November 1. The higher a hawk mounts the more ground it will cover, and where the pitch is good game will be killed that has sprung very wide of the hawk; but, as a rule, the hawk should be high, and directly over the game, which should be sprung down wind, so as to ensure a down-wind stoop. To ensure success these three points must ever be strictly observed, and for grouse late in the season, or even December partridges, the falconer will find that he can afford to give very few points away.

Should the quarry be driven into a fence or other covert, a good spaniel is useful either to retrieve or to drive him out. Old hawks are thoroughly alive to this part of the sport, and will recover their pitch with extraordinary rapidity after having driven a bird headlong into covert, so as to be ready should he emerge from it.

Game hawking, contrary to what might be expected, has

not the effect of banishing the game flown at from its haunts. A single afternoon at the sport will prove to any man of experience that it is not likely to have this effect. Immediately a covey is flushed, the hawk being overhead, its members hurry with the utmost speed they can command to the nearest covert. One bird only is killed, and the rest find a refuge within a few hundred yards of the place where they were

Falconer 'making-in' to a hawk

found. Directly they discover that they are not pursued they will be out on the feed again, for there is nothing unnatural or unusual to them in being frightened by a hawk. Probably on any ground open enough for hawking, they see a wild one every other day, and merely consider the trained bird to be one of their natural enemies, which they readily avoid by their natural powers and instinct.

We have not unfrequently, in countries where there were but few spaces open enough for hawking, flown almost daily at the same coveys, both of grouse and partridges, and found them without fail on the same feeding grounds, though in diminished numbers, as they were one by one taken ; nor did flying hawks at them regularly appear to make them nearly so wild as even a day or two of shooting over the same ground. On moors where, for convenience, a separate beat is devoted to the use of the hawks, it has been found that, towards the end of the season, birds lie better to dogs and are considerably more numerous than they are upon the beats where they have been shot regularly. This has been proved most conclusively upon the Achinduich moors in Sutherlandshire in 1882 and 1883, and upon the Langwell moors in Caithness in the seasons of 1885, 1886, and 1887.

A good flight at game is one of the prettiest sights hawking can afford, especially when grouse is the quarry. The moor should be rather a flat one, and the less broken the ground is, and the fewer burns intersect it, the better the hawk's chance of success. Grouse will 'put in' to a burn with steep sides, like a partridge into a fence, and get right underground where the banks are hollow. Good dogs are essential : they must be wide rangers, very steady, and thoroughly understand the sport, into which they will enter most keenly. As soon as the dog stands the falconer should unhood his hawk and throw her off. If she is an old hand at the game she will not be long mounting. Possibly, if a dashing flier, she will do so in very wide circles, ranging, it may be, a mile or more from her master. Especially will she do this when flying hard daily, and being fully fed upon the game she is killing, she becomes full of flesh, muscle, and vitality, and at the same time what is called 'a little above herself.' Should she stray too far away the swinging of the lure, or in extreme cases, one flutter of the wing of a pigeon, will bring her back ; but, as a rule, all exhibition of lures while a hawk is mounting high on the wing should be condemned. Directly she returns, and has shown by a few short turns

that she is steady, the birds may be flushed. The hawk ought now to be hanging steadily, with her head to the wind, at least three gunshots high. She looks no bigger than a butterfly, and here and there bits of scud may be seen drifting between the earth and her; yet she is under command, and, should the point prove a false one, will follow her master at that lofty pitch while, say, fifty acres of heather are beaten below her. But at the right moment the falconer, who has moved quietly round so as to head his dog while the hawk gains her pitch, dashes down upon the point; the birds are sprung, and the hawk, turning on her side, flies downward for a few strokes as hard as she can, and then with wings closed she falls like a stone slung from a mighty catapult, almost like a flash of light, right on to the very top of the bird she has from the first moment selected. Should she hit him fair and square, there will be a little cloud of feathers in the air, and the grouse will bound on to the heather as dead as though he had received the contents of a choke-bore at forty yards; but if the quarry pursued be an old cock grouse, perchance at the critical moment he will give three or four abrupt side shifts like those of a newly-sprung snipe, and the baffled hawk will shoot up after her stoop to a height half as high as that which she came from, ready to drive at the grouse again as he scuds off to the shelter of the nearest burn. It then becomes a trial of speed between the two, the result of which depends on the distance of the flight, the lay of the ground, and similar circumstances; but the falconer will only occasionally be able to see the actual finish, and following on the line of flight will either find his falcon beneath the lee of some great boulder surrounded by a mass of feathers, about to begin her feast on the body of her victim, or else hears the tinkle of her bell as the defeated hawk, having recovered her wind, takes flight again to search for her master.

It is a great advantage when the dog can be trained to dash in towards his master and flush the birds at a given signal, instead of the man having to run down and spring them himself. The dog's nose tells him exactly where the birds are.

They may be at a little distance from him, and will lie like stones with the hawk overhead, so that the falconer may be unable to light upon them instantly, and the delay of a few moments may be fatal. We have seen two or three dogs of the breed of lemon and white setters, belonging to Mr. St. Quintin, that would dash in 'as keen as mustard' at the signal and flush the nearest grouse of the covey, dropping instantaneously as they did so. There they would remain during the time the hawk was flown, was taken up, and a fresh hawk taken from the cadge and hooded off, and after she had got to her pitch would again dash in and flush, at the exact moment, the remaining bird or birds of the covey. In this way we have seen, especially with one magnificent setter called 'Prince,' who worked for many seasons solely with hawks, three and four flights obtained from the same point at one covey, the dog lying immovable during the long time—perhaps twenty minutes—that elapsed during the flight and taking up of the hawk in each case. Yet these dogs were no potterers, but were dashing, high-ranging dogs of the highest class, thoroughly acquainted with the work they had to do, and fond of it. They were seldom used with the gun, and seemed to work with more intelligence and sense of responsibility than dogs which are shot over usually display. As a rule we have found setters more suited to hawking, and more capable of understanding the peculiar work that is required of them than pointers. This appears to have been the experience of falconers at all times, and is placed on record in various books.

Partridge hawking is very similar to grouse hawking, but is, from the nature of the country, more circumscribed. Hence very dashing fliers that have done well at grouse cannot always be flown in the low country. Tiercels, which, as a rule, cannot kill grouse regularly after the first fortnight or so, are best suited to this flight, and if only they will go high enough, and wait on steadily, they will show perfect sport wherever the fields are large enough to give a fair chance of a flight. A good spaniel or two that is used to the hawks should be taken out in order to put out or retrieve a bird driven into a hedge.

It is, of course, not possible to kill very large bags with hawks, nor is the sport of such a nature that the number of head killed can be always taken as a fair criterion of the amusement which has been afforded. In 1830 the hawks belonging to the Duke of Leeds[1] are recorded to have killed 317 head of game, and in 1832 one tiercel of his, 'The General,' killed 129 head out of 134 flights. Most of this work was done at partridges.

In the season of 1870 that excellent falconer Peter Ballantine killed 269 head of game in Ayrshire, being then in the service of Mr. Ewen, and in 1871 he killed no less than 346 head with six hawks, which is, we believe, the highest score (if ground game killed by goshawks be excluded) that a team of game hawks has yet made. The greater number were, however, partridges, with a few grouse and young blackgame in the early part of the season.

In 1882 the hawks belonging to the Old Hawking Club achieved what may be termed a 'record' in the annals of game hawking, killing between August 12 and September 14 exactly one hundred brace of grouse upon the Achinduich moors, in Sutherlandshire, which were taken by Mr. St. Quintin and Colonel Brooksbank for the purpose. The score for this season is sufficiently remarkable to be appended here, and is as follows:—

| Hawks | Grouse | Partridge | Pheasant | Hares | Sundries | Total |
|---|---|---|---|---|---|---|
| Parachute, eyess falcon, 2 years old | 57 | 76 | 5 | 3 | 5 | 146 |
| Vesta ,, ,, 1 year ,, | 43 | 18 | — | — | 1 | 62 |
| Angela, passage falcon, 2 years ,, | 36 | — | — | — | — | 36 |
| Creole ,, ,, | 10 | — | — | — | — | 10 |
| A.-D.-C., eyess tiercel, 1 year old | 16 | 9 | — | — | 1 | 26 |
| Amesbury, passage falcon, 3 years old | 32 | — | — | — | — | 32 |
| Virginia, eyess falcon, 1 year old | 3 | 1 | — | — | — | 4 |
| Belfry, eyess tiercel, 1 year old | 3 | — | — | — | — | 3 |
| | 200 | 104 | 5 | 3 | 7 | 319 |

[1] See *Falconry in the British Isles*, p. 64.

In 1883 the Club hawks, under the same management, killed:—

| | |
|---|---|
| Grouse | 85 |
| Blackgame | 7 |
| Partridges | 87 |
| Pheasants | 3 |
| Sundries | 21 |
| | 203 |

But considering how bad a partridge year this was, and that no hawking was done after November 1, it can hardly be called a fair average year. About six hawks were flown during the season. In 1886 ninety-six grouse and one woodcock were killed at Langwell, Caithness, in August and September, and in 1887 ninety-three grouse on the same moors, two blackcock, and two pheasants.

Where grouse are so wild that they cannot possibly be induced to lie to the dog, flights may be obtained by putting up the hawk to wait on as soon as likely ground is reached, and forming a good wide line of beaters across the moor. If the hawk is steady and goes high, a good many grouse may be killed in this way; but it is, of course, an inferior sport to the legitimate practice of working the highly trained dog in conjunction with the highly trained hawk, which has been described in the preceding pages.

The method of putting the hawk up beforehand has been regularly followed by Major Hawkins Fisher, a falconer of thirty years' experience, who has met with success of no mean order. In 1887 Major Fisher made the excellent bag of 111 grouse, nine partridges, one snipe, and a woodcock owl, and in 1886 he also met with excellent sport, of which we have not a record. Major Fisher also gives an account of an extraordinary flight which one of his eyess falcons made at a woodcock on the shores of Loch Eil, when both cock and hawk mounted into the air over the loch to such a height that even powerful glasses failed to discern them. At last a speck was seen coming out of the sky, and the woodcock dropped like a stone towards the very patch of bracken from which he had originally been sprung. His pursuer, however, was close behind him, and long ere he could reach his haven of refuge he was cut over stone-dead in mid-air and fell at the falconer's feet. In another

Tiercel and teal

moment the hawk was upon him, and received the full crop she had so well earned.

Wild ducks and teal afford the best of sport, provided the water is not too large and they can be driven out of it. Most hawks will fly them readily, but ducks shift quickly from the stoop, and will then take the air, when a fine high flight is sometimes obtained, the duck when outflown generally making straight for the pond whence he was sprung. Few tiercels will take mallard, but for teal they are excellent.

Woodcocks afford the finest kind of game hawking, but can rarely be found in sufficiently open ground to be flown at. Should the cock avoid the first stoop, as it probably will do, even when a high-mounting hawk is waiting on, he will certainly ring up into the air, and a beautiful flight, akin to heron hawking, may be witnessed after the usual description of game flight is over. Falcons are the best for this quarry, and though it taxes the powers of the hawk, yet with a really good falcon the woodcock is not an exceptionally difficult bird to kill. Snipe are occasionally cut down by a good tiercel, and sometimes the hawk will ring up over them, but they are not easy to kill except in August. Pheasants, if found in the open, are easily caught, but not many tiercels care to tackle an old cock, which buffets them sadly when on the ground.

Blackgame when young are very readily taken, and are useful for entering young hawks, but when fully fledged, say after October 1, the blackcock can take care of himself. A high-mounting hawk, well placed, may cut him down at the first stoop, but should he shift from it he will almost certainly outfly the hawk.

We have never known hares to be successfully taken with the peregrine except in one season. This was in 1883, on the Achinduich moors, when a particularly fine, high-mounting grouse-falcon, called 'Parachute,' was waiting on at a great pitch over a point, which turned out to be at a blue hare instead of a grouse. To the surprise of all, the moment the hare moved the falcon came down like a flash, and striking it behind the ears rolled it over and over. Shooting up, she repeated the blow again and again, and finally binding to the exhausted hare would no doubt have very shortly killed it, even if an officious spaniel had not come to her assistance. The case seemed so remarkable that the experiment was tried again the next day, and the hawk purposely allowed to gain her pitch over a blue hare that had been espied in its seat. Precisely the same thing happened, the hawk flying her game with the greatest courage and determination, and a third essay produced the same result. Without a doubt, then, if a little pains were taken to enter peregrines

Tiercel and woodcock

to this quarry, they could be trained to take it, and perhaps might, with the help of a dog, tackle even an English brown hare; but it seems a pity to use the noble long-winged hawks for a flight at ground game which is far better suited to the goshawk.

Magpie hawking, though not one of the higher branches of falconry, is nevertheless most excellent sport, and possesses this charm, that the field, one and all, may take an active part in the chase, for their assistance is necessary to bring about a kill. It is a flight well within the powers of either eyess tiercels or falcons that do not mount high enough to kill game well. Passage tiercels are also very good, and if they become well entered to the quarry are, from their superior dash and style, rather more deadly than eyesses. Two tiercels should be flown together, as the magpie shifts so rapidly from the stoop, and avails himself so cleverly of every possible covert that might protect him, that a single hawk has not much chance with him, and the whole beauty of the flight consists in the pretty double stooping in which the one tiercel takes up the chance that the other has missed.

A partially open country devoid of trees is the best for the purpose. The best sport we have seen is in Ireland, where the sport was ever heartily welcomed and cordially joined in. Great sport has been seen in co. Kildare in the neighbourhood of Sallins and of Kildare, and in Wexford, near Enniscorthy. In Tipperary, near Fermoy, Captain Salvin[1] records that in 1857 he killed in four months 184 magpies, killing as many as eight in one day with his excellent tiercels 'The O'Donoghue' and 'Dhuleep Singh.' In 1873 the same gentleman, together with the author of this volume, took twenty-eight magpies, three sparrow-hawks, and about the same number of rooks and other quarry in one month's tour in Ireland; and in 1879 certain other members of the Old Hawking Club had a most successful trip of three weeks in Kildare and Tipperary, killing fifty-eight head. Of this number 'Buccaneer' and 'Meteor,' two excellent eyess tiercels, killed in thirteen days forty-four magpies.

The great object in flying the magpie is to cut him off from his point, and to drive him into the open at the moment when the hawks are well placed for a stoop. Cunning to the last

[1] See *Falconry in the British Isles*, p. 68.

degree, however he may be pressed, a magpie never loses his head, or ceases to make for the point on which he has set his mind from the first. Unless he is headed by horsemen or active runners, he will sneak from bush to bush, from tuft to tuft, nay, even within a deep rut or a furrow, never moving

Magpie hawking

except when the hawks are a little wide of him, and shifting rapidly into covert the instant he is stooped at. No hawk can kill him without assistance, except in the most open ground. As soon as a magpie is seen a high-mounting hawk should be thrown off; his presence in the air will keep the magpie quiet in the bush or hedge in which he may be. This will give the field time to get well round him and cut him off from any strong covert there may be in sight. The quarry may now be moved, and as soon as the first hawk comes at him, a second may be flown. It will all depend upon the ability of the field to keep the magpie out of covert, and move him often enough for the hawks to stoop at him, whether the issue will be successful or not; but in favourable ground we have often known a magpie hunt, with an active field, and two good hawks, to last thirty minutes, and not always result in a kill then.

Good sport may be obtained on open downs where many scattered bushes exist if there are magpies breeding in any plantations bordering such ground. The woods must be beaten systematically, down wind, by a line of beaters, and the hawks concealed to the leeward of the covert. The magpies usually pass out very high, and it requires a good and experienced hawk to go straight and well at them, and fetch them down into the scattered bushes. As soon, however, as they see the tiercel coming hard at them, they will drop, and if he waits on well and steadily, they will remain in their hiding place till the field comes up and the hunt begins. But they are exceedingly clever, artful birds, and on ground of this kind a great deal of manœuvring is necessary to obtain a flight at all.

## CHAPTER III

THE PEREGRINE—PASSAGE HAWKS—ADVANTAGES OF—HOW CAUGHT—MODE OF TRAINING—HERON HAWKING—ROOK HAWKING—GULL HAWKING—PASSAGE HAWKS FOR GAME—LOST HAWKS

WHAT the professional is to the amateur, or rather, perhaps, what the thoroughbred horse is to all other varieties of the equine race, the passage hawk is, according to species, to every other hawk which is trained, inasmuch as she is swifter, more active, more hardy, and more powerful than the nestling. That this should be so is no matter for surprise when it is recollected that the passage, or wild-caught, hawk has spent days and weeks on the wing in every kind of weather, and has killed dozens, or perhaps hundreds, of wild birds in fair flight, while the nestling has only gained what power of wing she possesses from some three or four weeks of flying at hack, and since that time has been flown at from two to three birds a day, and that only when the weather was fine. Moreover, though we cannot definitely account for this, the temper of the wild-caught hawk is, as a rule, far gentler and more amiable, when once she is tamed, than is that of a hawk taken from the nest; and, while the latter are rarely free from the horrible trick of screaming, that vice is almost unknown among passage hawks.

These differences in temper were well understood by Symon Latham, who published in 1615 his book called 'The Faulcon's Lure and Cure' (which is to this day the best English work on falconry ever written), and who says in conclusion of a chapter on eyess falcons: 'But leaving to speak any more of these kinde of scratching hawks, that I did never love should come too neere my fingers, and to returne unto the curteous and faire conditioned haggard faulcon whose gallant disposition I know not how to extoll or praise so sufficiently as she deserves.'

What the falconers of ancient days thus recorded is abundantly confirmed by the practice of their successors in modern times. The passage hawk, as every wild-caught peregrine is termed, with the distinction of 'haggard' when she is captured in the mature plumage—perhaps aged several years—has proved herself, in our own experience, the superior to the eyess in every kind of flight to which the peregrine can be put. But, moreover, there are many flights such as those at the heron and the rook, for which the passage hawk alone is well adapted, and of which the eyess, as a rule, is not capable. It is true that there have been many eyesses which have been fairly good rook hawks—in one or two instances they have even taken the heron 'on the passage,' but such hawks were exceptional ones.

To obtain a team of, say, six good hawks that would take the heron, or even the rook, in the rough winds of March as he passes to and from his feeding-grounds, it would be necessary to train and test at least twenty eyesses; but a better result would be obtained from the training, in experienced hands, of ten well-caught passage falcons. And, again, even if the trainer of the eyesses were to succeed in producing hawks that took rooks or herons fairly well, he could never hope that they would emulate the style and dash with which their wild-bred congeners accomplished the feat; nor, above all, would he be as independent of weather as are those who use the hardy passage hawk, which seems to glory in a gale and laugh at the bitterness of the north-east wind.

For game hawking the passage hawk requires both time and careful training, and here, perhaps because of the difficulty of managing the wild-caught hawk, the eyess holds her own. Yet even when the best possible eyesses are being flown—

hawks that may be trusted to kill three and four head of game every day if there be in the stud a passage falcon that will wait on high and steadily, she will so eclipse the eyess for style and pace, and above all in 'footing qualities,' i.e. accuracy of striking her quarry, that there is no comparison between the

Tiercel on partridge

pleasure which is afforded by the flights shown by the two hawks. Probably no game hawk has beaten the record of 'Parachute,' as shown on page 251, of 146 head of game in five months, or of 'Vesta,' also the property of the Old Hawking Club, who has killed 297 grouse (besides other game in numbers) during her nine years. Yet in nearly every season that such hawks have flown they have had to take the second place, as regards brilliancy of execution and deadliness of stoop and style, to some one or two of the passage hawks which have accompanied them to their hawking ground, and this will ever be the case when both varieties are given a fair trial.

Naturally, the hawk which has spent so long a period in a wild state, during which she has imbibed a holy horror of man and all his works, regarding him as her natural foe, is very much more difficult to train at first than the nestling, which requires at any rate little or no taming, and whose idea of man is that he is a being created in order to bring food to hawks. First, however, how are passage hawks to be obtained? They may be caught doubtless in many parts of the United Kingdom, where, every autumn about the middle of October, peregrines appear, for a day or two, on ground where they certainly do not breed, and where they are very seldom seen at other times. Thus falcons have been taken, at huts specially put out for the purpose, both in Northamptonshire and on the downs of Wiltshire. These no doubt were stragglers from the great army of birds of all kinds and descriptions which annually migrates from north to south at the commencement of winter. Upon the outskirts of this army hang the falcons and other raptorial birds; whether they are themselves following the same migratory instinct that urges onward the other innumerable varieties of birds, or whether they are simply following their food as it changes its quarters, it is impossible to say.

In North Brabant in Holland, near to Eindhoven, there is a vast wild plain or heath, and this plain appears to lie in the very centre of the track which the great concourse of migratory birds follows. Wild fowl of every kind, cranes, larks, linnets, all varieties of birds may be seen, during October and November, passing over this plain and steadily pursuing their route southwards. Here, too, come the falcons, first the haggards and tiercels, after them the young falcons of the year, and here from time immemorial have they been captured for hawking purposes. On the edge of the heath lies the little town of Valkenswaard, which takes its very name from the falcons, that in old days were its staple article of trade. Therein reside certain families of men who from generation to generation, as far back as history goes, have been falconers and catchers of falcons. Some hundred years ago, even, there were from twenty to thirty huts put out at Valkenswaard for the capture of hawks during the autumn passage, and the little town could boast of the like number of men skilled in training hawks. In those days a sort of fair was held after the migration was over, which was attended by the chief falconers of various noblemen and princes from every country in Europe. The hawks that had been caught were sold by auction, and rare prices were occasionally paid for very choice specimens, with such a competition as took place under the circumstances described. Ichabod! The glory has departed. Some three huts now supply all the wants of the hawking world. They are under the management of one family, the Mollens, the head of which, Adrian Mollen, was formerly head falconer to the King of Holland, and his customers average annually some half-a-dozen only, mostly Englishmen, with a Frenchman or two added to them. The actual instrument which is used in taking the hawks is the bow-net, which has been fully described in the chapter on hacking and training eyesses at page 241. Two or perhaps three of these nets are set out at about a hundred yards each from the falconer's hut, into which lead the strong lines by which they are worked.

The hut itself is a very simple affair, partly sunk in the ground and partly built of turfs and sods covered with heather. The roof is very often made of an old cartwheel, which is well covered over with heath and turf, so that the hut itself looks exactly like a small natural mound on the surface of the plain, and perfectly conceals the falconer even from the sharp eyes of a bird of prey.

The bait for each of the bow-nets is a live pigeon, which is kept in a cleverly constructed little house built of turves, with a hanging curtain over the door, made of a heather sod, so that when the long line, which is attached to the pigeon by soft buckskin jesses, is pulled by the falconer the curtain gives way and allows the bird to be drawn out. This line passes through an eye in the head of an iron pin, which is driven into the ground exactly in the centre of the bow-net, so that the falconer knows, whether he can see it or not, that when the pigeon's line is pulled taut and checks, the bird itself is on the ground exactly in the middle of the net.

A fourth pigeon inhabits a similar little house immediately in front of the hut, and about fifty yards from it. The line from this pigeon passes over the top of a light pole about twenty feet high, so that when this line is pulled the pigeon is raised to that height and flies well out so as to be easily seen. This pigeon is intended to serve as a lure and attract a hawk from a distance.

Sometimes it happens that the falconer will catch, early in the season, an old or a bad plumaged falcon that he does not think highly of for hawking purposes. Such a falcon he will set out, hooded, with a line attached to her, passing over a pole just as in the case of the lure pigeon. A few feet in front of the hawk is fastened to the line a bunch of feathers, so that when the line is pulled tight the hawk is lifted to the top of the pole and flies round with the bunch of feathers in front of her, looking from a distance exactly like a hawk in full pursuit of, and on the point of catching, some quarry. This forms a most attractive lure to a wild hawk, which is almost certain to pause in her flight and lower her pitch to join in the fray.

Last of all comes the most important adjunct to the apparatus, in the shape of a butcher bird, or grey shrike, which is used as a watch-dog or sentinel to give notice of the approach of a hawk. These curious little birds are always on the alert and on the look-out for birds of prey; their power of vision is most marvellous, far beyond the reach of any human eye. They can detect a falcon, which minutes afterwards will come into sight as a tiny black speck, high in the heavens. Two of these shrikes are generally used, tethered upon mounds near the hut, with a little house, like those in which the pigeons are kept, to shelter them. As soon as they see a hawk they will chatter and scream, pointing steadily in the direction of the bird's approach. An experienced falconer can tell fairly well from the action of his butcher bird what species of hawk is in view. More alarm will be shown at the approach of a goshawk than of any other variety, while at tiercels or merlins his gestures are those of absurd indignation and defiance.

Everything being then prepared, the falconer will arrive at his hut and have all in readiness by daybreak. Early morning is the best time for catching hawks, and the passage for the day is over by three o'clock as a rule. With a good stock of tobacco and some occupation such as net-making or cobbling, to while away the many weary hours of waiting, he establishes himself inside his hut; presently, if all goes well, his butcher birds will chatter, point, and warn him to be on the look-out. Far away, it may be, he sees a tiny speck, which he believes to be a peregrine. At any rate he pulls the line attached to the pole hawk, and soon brings up the wild bird to rather closer quarters. Should it be a peregrine such as he desires to capture, he drops the line attached to the pole hawk, which at once subsides to the ground, and draws that which lifts the pigeon to the top of the pole, and lets it fly well out. At this pigeon the wild hawk most likely 'comes with a rattle,' but at the nick of time the falconer drops the line, and the frightened bird will bolt into its little hut for safety. Angry and disappointed, the wild hawk will shoot into the air and give a circle round to see what has become of her prey. At this juncture the falconer pulls out the pigeon attached to one or other end (according to the direction of wind and position of the hawk) of his bow-net. The wild falcon's blood is up: she has been disappointed once, and she dashes like lightning on to the pigeon, which she imagines to be the one that just escaped her. Of course she has no difficulty in taking it, and as she is killing it the falconer steadily draws the line till it checks at the head of the iron pin in the centre of the net. One pull of the net line and the hawk is safely caught. As rapidly as possible she is taken out of the net, a rufter hood is placed on her head—that is to say, a light, comfortable hood, open at the back, and easy for a hawk to feed through—she is then placed in a 'sock,' which is simply the leg of an old stocking, which pins her wings to her sides and acts as a strait-waistcoat, making it impossible for her to move or to struggle. Jesses are placed on her legs, the points are taken off her beak and claws, and she is left to lie quiet until the time arrives for leaving the hut and going home.

Two hawks in one day is unusually good fortune. More often the falconer sits day after day without any luck at all. Sometimes it happens that from something going wrong with his tackle, or from some such cause, he misses the hawk. This is a serious reverse, for he will not easily get the chance to catch the same bird again. Such a mishap occurred to Mollen, senior, in 1872. He had just caught a falcon, and was taking her out of the net when there came up, attracted by the pigeon, an exceedingly fine dark falcon. It was too late to hide; but when, an hour or so afterwards, she again appeared on the scene, and he pulled out the lure pigeon, all that resulted was, that after a shy stoop the falcon followed the line at the height of a yard or two right from the net to the hut, spread her wings, and sailed away. There were many wild fowl on the heath at the time, and he could see this grand hawk day after day chasing and killing them in the finest style, till his mouth fairly watered to catch her. In vain did he try all his arts; every time he showed his lure the crafty bird would sail along the extended string, as if to show how well she understood the game, and then would bid him good-bye. Worst of all, she would brook no intruder on her hunting grounds, and day after day as other falcons passed and began to stoop to the pigeon, she would descend upon them from the clouds, and after a buffeting match would drive them away. Mollen was in despair, the season was slipping away, and his business being lost.

At last he took his gun to the hut, having made up his mind to shoot the hawk as a last resource and free himself from the incubus. Hour after hour he sat with gun in readiness—a strange position, indeed, for a falconer. But that day she came

Passage hawk under bow-net

not, nor the next, and at last the gun was laid aside and the hawk catching went on as before.

At the end of the week one of Mollen's sons who was working a hut many miles away returned home with his catch. He had not much to boast of, except one, 'a real beauty.' Hardly had the old man set eyes on her than he recognised his tormentor—unmistakable from her size, dark plumage, and beauty. She had gone straight to the other but after plaguing him the last day he saw her, but never having been frightened at that place was less suspicious and so was caught. This hawk came into the possession of the Old Hawking Club, where she was known as 'the Duck-killer,' and was one of the grandest hawks for temper, flying qualities, and steadiness that the Club have ever owned, killing over forty rooks her first season. She was eventually lost when flying rooks at Feltwell in Norfolk, and it is to be hoped became the mother of falcons as good as herself on some wild cliff in North Britain, or Scandinavia.

But to return to the freshly caught falcon. Her captor will have little difficulty in carrying her home on his fist; so dazed and terrified will she be by her novel situation that she will sit like a hawk of stone. On arrival the hawk may be temporarily set on the perch with any others that have been lately caught, or, better still, fastened securely to a soft grass mound (which sometimes takes the place of the sock); but the sooner she is taken in hand, the better. The directions which have been already given for the training of the freshly taken-up eyess will apply in this case also, but it must never be forgotten that the passage hawk has hitherto spent her days in avoiding men as her natural enemies, and that it will take much time, care, and gentleness ere this terror and aversion can be overcome. A single impatient action or hasty gesture may undo the work of days, and the man who tries to tame a wild-caught hawk should possess a temper which is under perfect command and a patience which is 'above proof.'

The first step is to take the hawk on hand and to handle her gently, stroking her with a feather or some such thing, to accustom her to being taken hold of and handled. Hawks differ marvellously at this stage of their education. Some will display the most passionate temper, will fight, bite, even scream, and dash themselves about like passionate children. Such as these are usually the easiest to deal with; their passion soon abates and generally develops into a fine, generous temper.

Some sit like statues—immovable, indifferent, resenting no handling, noticing no food—such are difficult hawks to train, and only time and patience, added to experience, will train these, though it can be, and annually is, done. Gradually the hawk will become reconciled to the touch, to the sound of the human voice, and will in a few days comport herself more like a tame bird and less like a wild beast. Most of this work is done at night; and the best method of training wild-caught, or indeed any other birds, is to deal with them at night and to tame, them by depriving them of their natural rest and by handling them by lamplight, which dazes them and takes away half their power of resistance. Where time is an object, hawks are kept awake for the whole night for three or four nights together, and by such treatment a hawk may be tamed in about four days. Such haste is rarely needed, and in ordinary cases any hawk may be got into good order in reasonable time by taking her on hand, say, from seven in the evening until eleven at night; and, indeed, a man may have two or three hawks on the perch by his side, and by taking them in hand alternately bring them all on together at the same rate.

It is very important, if the most is to be made of passage hawks, that each one should be taken in hand as soon as she is caught, and tamed at once. This is not always easily managed, and sometimes several birds are left to stand idle for many days while others are being caught. This leads to many faults, always causes delay (sometimes very great delay) in the training and entering of such hawks, and not unfrequently ruins them altogether.

The great secret in successful training of passage hawks is *to get food into them* by fair means. This is by no means so easy as it appears to be, and requires no little skill in the way of handling the hawk so as to get her to bite at the food which is held on to her feet, and to continue feeding after she has once begun. The room must be perfectly quiet, there must be no changes of light or distant sounds heard, or the hawk's attention will at once be arrested and she will leave off feeding.

There is also great knack in getting her to pull at the meat without being frightened. Adrian Mollen boasts, not without reason, that he can get a quarter of a crop more into any hawk after any other man has done his best with her. It is very important that hawks shall be well fed; they will lose their wild condition quite fast enough from the change of food, the numerous shocks to their nervous system, and the loss of exercise; but if they are allowed to get down too low they will never recover their power or their courage. If all goes well, however, in a few days the hawk will feed well and boldly through the rufter hood, will allow herself to be handled, and will feel more at home on the fist. The rufter hood should now be removed by candle-light, and the hawk induced to feed bare-headed. A hood of ordinary make can also be placed on her, and she can be frequently hooded and unhooded and broken carefully to the hood in the same way as eyesses are treated. When she sits quiet and bare-headed by candle-light, the same lesson may be repeated by daylight, and ere its close the hawk will jump to the hand for her food—at first a short distance only, afterwards the full length of the leash—and will do so promptly and briskly as soon as the meat is shown her. All this takes a good deal of time and patience, but anything like hurry is to be avoided, or the hawk will probably go back rapidly as soon as she is taken out into the open air. So long as a little progress, be it ever so little, is made every day, the falconer should be content, and not endeavour to hurry his more backward, shy-tempered birds in order to keep pace with one or two good-tempered ones that 'never look behind them,' and almost train themselves.

As soon as the hawk will feed fearlessly on the hand bare-headed she should be entered to the lure: this at the first outset must, in the case of wild-caught hawks, consist of a live pigeon. The moment the hawk seizes it the falconer should twist its neck, so as to kill it instantaneously and painlessly, and the hawk should be allowed to break into and eat it while still warm.

Many passage falcons are very stupid and troublesome to enter to the lure just at first. The process of taming and training them seems to have completely transformed their nature and driven all recollection of their past life out of their minds. It is very curious to notice how the young eyess, which has no fear at all of man or nervousness at its surroundings, will, almost to a certainty, seize and kill instinctively the first live pigeon shown to it, though it has never killed a bird before; while the passage hawk, which has, perhaps, chased and killed hundreds of wild birds during its life, and has subsisted on nothing else, will sometimes sit and blink stupidly at a pigeon within a few feet of it, as though it had never seen such a creature before. A little patience will overcome this difficulty also, and as soon as the hawk will seize and kill a pigeon within doors, and feed quietly upon it without fear of the falconer, she may be tried out of doors on a long string with the pigeon similarly confined. Should she behave equally well this time also she may be trusted to fly loose. A good deal of care must be exercised the first few times she is flown, for if any little thing should go wrong and upset the hawk's equanimity it may become a difficult matter to take her up at once; and if she is at large, even for an hour or two, out of control, her wild ways will at this stage return to her with great rapidity. She should be very sharp-set, and for the first trial it will be quite enough to call her from the fist of an assistant (who must not be a perfect stranger to her) about a hundred yards to the falconer. One or two stoops will be enough, and she should then be allowed to feed on the lure. As soon as the hawk behaves well and flies keenly, the use of live pigeons should be abandoned, and the hawk trained to the dead lure. In former days it was supposed that passage hawks could not be trained to dead lures until they had been in work for a long time, but we have proved this to be a fallacy, and that it is, with care and good management, quite as possible to get passage hawks to come to the dead lure as it is to train eyesses to it. The early education cannot in either case be carried on without the sacrifice of two or three pigeons. These should be killed instantaneously the moment the hawk touches them, and all unnecessary cruelty avoided. But as soon as these first stages of the falcon's education are completed the 'live lure' should become a thing unknown, except in cases of emergency, such as a lost hawk.

As soon as the passage falcon flies well and steadily to the lure, stooping at it for seven or eight minutes at a time, she should be entered to the quarry at which she is to be flown. It is a very bad plan to keep hawks that are fit to be entered flying on at the lure day after day, for weeks together. Such hawks will become very tame and very handy, but they will lose all that dash which is the special charm of the passage hawk, and will become so wedded to the lure that they will fly at nothing else.[1]

The quarry which, as a rule, the passage hawk alone is capable of taking, is the heron 'on the passage'; to enter her to this quarry she should first be allowed to take and kill a few large-sized fowls. If she should seize and tackle these powerful birds with determination, she will have no hesitation in binding to a heron if ever she shall get to close quarters enough to do so. After this education she must be flown at a bagged heron, first in a string and afterwards loose and at some distance from her. During these lessons her beak and talons must be cut very short and well rounded off, so that beyond seizing the heron she can do him no injury before the falconer runs to save him. Having once 'bound to him' the falcon must be fed upon some food which she relishes, and after a lesson or two of this kind she should be fit to fly at a wild heron. .

Heron hawking, however—sad as it is to record it—must be written down as a sport almost extinct in England. To catch

[1] But it is necessary to observe that the passage hawk must at first only be entered to quarry which she cannot easily carry (unless, indeed, extraordinary pains are taken to tame her). Otherwise she is very likely to lift any light bird (such as a pigeon), and, though not actually wild at first, she becomes so frightened at being followed with a bird in her foot, which she repeatedly carries, that she becomes unapproachable.

a heron with a hawk as it rises from the stream where it may be feeding is easy enough; any nestling that has been well entered, even the short-winged goshawk, can do this to an absolute certainty every time that it is brought near enough to the quarry; but this is not heron hawking. To arrive at this sport the following conditions are necessary. A heronry of large size, situated far from any river or feeding-ground, so that the herons pass continually to and from the nearest river to the heronry, and pass also over some vast open space of ground suitable to be ridden over and wide enough to afford a flight of at least two miles ere the heron could reach either a sheltering wood or a piece of water into which he will dive like a duck. Nay, we have known a heron to put in even to a sheepfold when hard pressed on an open field!

Such conditions as these were well fulfilled at Didlington in Norfolk, which was for many years the scene of the sport of the High Ash Club. But here, even so long ago as 1838, the draining of the fenland and breaking up and cultivation of the open heaths so limited the area in which it was possible to pursue the sport that blank days became more and more common, and eventually the club was broken up. Better still were the conditions under which the sport was pursued at the Loo in Holland, where the heronry was of vast size, and the country surrounding it even better than at Didlington. Here heron hawking was pursued on a princely scale, the joint establishments of the King of Holland and of the English Club being equal to any emergency, and some idea can be obtained of the sport which they obtained when it is recorded that in one year (1852) the hawks took no fewer than 292 herons, while for eight years in succession they actually averaged 178 herons annually.[1]

Of course so large a number of herons taken in the breeding season would very soon ruin the finest heronry in the world, but it was the practice to save and liberate every heron that was taken, and it was a point of honour with the members of the Club to

[1] See Schlegel's *Traité de Fauconnerie*, 1844.

ride hard enough to be handy at the finish, so as to make sure that the heron should not be injured. When liberated a small copper ring was fixed to his leg with the date of his capture written on it, and herons have been taken with as many as three and four of these rings on their legs.[1]

The method of conducting the sport is as follows. The falconers with their hawks are placed at intervals of half a mile, in two or three parties, down wind of the heronry, and at some considerable distance from it. As the heron passes homewards with his crop full of fish, he must pass within sufficiently close distance of one or the other of these parties. As soon as he is well past, and up wind of the hawks, they are hooded off. Probably the heron is two hundred yards away, and at least a hundred yards high, and with such a start as this he can set to work to ring into the air with confidence. It is useless for him to attempt to reach the heronry, which is dead up wind, while he has such pursuers as these behind him. Below him is no protecting covert, and therefore his only resources are the clouds above him. Ring after ring he makes, mounting into the air in long spiral curves. Ring after ring do the hawks make after him, tearing into the wind for perhaps half a mile without a turn, and then swinging round in a great circle that sends them higher and higher. At last one hawk is over him, though at such a height we cannot distinguish the distances between them ; but we can see her shut her wings and drive like a bullet at the heron. A rapid shift, and the hawk has fallen many hundreds of feet below her quarry, but, shooting up with the same impetus, at once sets to work to ring into the wind, so as to regain her lost advantage. During this time the second falcon has climbed almost out of sight above her mate and her quarry, and can be just distinguished poising herself for a terrific stoop. The good heron can just, but only just, avoid it, and that with the loss of a few feathers and a downward sweep that sacrifices some minutes of the hard ringing by which the height he is now at was attained. This sweep gives

[1] See *Falconry in the British Isles*, p. 81.

a chance to the first hawk and down she comes, pressing the heron hard—so hard that as her mate follows her at an interval of a second or two he is hit heavily. In another moment one hawk has bound to him, and ere the struggle can commence the other has joined in the fray, and all three birds steadily descend to the ground. The wind has carried them for at least a mile from where they were hooded off, and that, too, at a pace as good as a horseman cares to gallop over fairly rough ground with his eyes in the air.

Old hawks will always let go the heron as they approach the ground, so as to avoid the concussion, and will renew the attack the instant that they are safely landed. Some falcons are a little slow in 'making in' to a heron on the ground, and in this way have been badly stabbed. If the heron has time afforded to him to collect himself and get into a fighting attitude he is a dangerous opponent, but the fables of hawks spitting themselves as they stoop upon beaks upturned in the air are myths which have no foundation in fact. A heron on the ground is, however, a formidable enemy, and when hawks are flown at a bagman it is essential that his beak be muzzled by being cased in a double piece of soft elder, one for each mandible, or mischief is sure to ensue.

It is absolutely necessary that hawks should be well entered to herons and should be kept to this flight alone. So far as we know, there is hardly any place left in England where a heronry exists with suitable country round it so that one or even two flights could be obtained daily. It is not, therefore, worth the while of any falconer to set aside a cast or two of his best hawks for a flight which, noble as it is, he could not obtain with any certainty. Probably at the Loo—although even there much of the country is enclosed and cultivated—very good sport could be obtained, but it is thirty-six years since the cry of 'A la vol' echoed in the domain of 'Het Loo,' and it is doubtful if there are more than two or three falconers now alive who have seen the heron taken 'à la haute volée.' Heron hawking must, for the present, be looked upon as a thing of the past;

but hawks are still trained annually that are as capable of this noble flight as any that ever have been reclaimed by man, and it needs only a little enterprise to reinstate this, the most magnificent form of falconry, if it could meet with the same cordial support, and be organised under those Royal auspices that were extended to it forty years ago.

Perhaps even superior to heron hawking was the flight at the kite, for which passage falcons combined with gerfalcons were used. It is many years since kites were common enough in England to be an object of sport, and the method of flying them is more particularly described in a subsequent chapter on the gyrfalcon.

The modern substitute for heron hawking is the flight at the rook, and it is by no means a bad one. Rook hawking is the finest form of the sport that is nowadays readily available, provided that it is carried out in a proper manner, in a good country, and with the best of hawks. Rooks, just like herons, may be caught in a bad country by very inferior hawks. In the autumn, in a country where the fields are large, the fences small, and the hedgerow timber scarce, rooks may be driven into covert and (possibly) caught, after a chase partaking of the nature of a rat hunt, by almost any hawk that has courage enough to go straight and hard at her quarry. But this is not rook hawking. The falcons that have beaten down rook after rook into fences or covert in enclosed country in November would find themselves at a sad nonplus if they were hooded off at an old cock rook travelling away over the wide downs of Wilts or Berks in the teeth of a March north-easter. The proper time for this sport is the month of March or early April when the hen birds are in the rookery and the cocks are travelling great distances in search of food. A very open country is requisite. The chalk downs of the south of England are, generally speaking, the best. Parts of Salisbury Plain, the downs near Lambourne and Ashdown, and near Brighton, at Royston, and other parts of Cambridgeshire are capital country, and in fact, wherever a clear open space of a mile can be found rooks may be flown with success. The difficulty is to find any country where flights can be obtained day after day; for this quarry becomes very crafty, and the appearance of the well-known hawking party over the sky-line is enough to send every rook in the plain below scurrying to his home if the visits have been too frequent to the same portion of country.

A flight may be obtained wherever the quarry is found far enough from covert, whether following the plough, feeding on new-sown corn, or on open downs. After rain with a south-west wind they will be found on the turf downs, but in dry, cold weather they will haunt sheepfolds or villages, and flights are not so easily obtained. The best flights are obtained at rooks 'upon the passage'—that is to say, passing regularly from the rookery to some favourite feeding ground across an open stretch of ground. Such a slip is generally a pretty long one; the rook at any rate is well on the wing, and a fine flight is almost a certainty. It is most essential that the hawks should be slipped dead up wind at the rook. This is a cardinal rule, and must never be transgressed, although with a very good hawk liberties may be taken now and then. If the slip is down wind, or so nearly on a side wind that by a swerve right or left the rook can get to leeward of the hawk, he will dash away down wind at a pace that will leave all riders far behind. Although the hawk will follow him just as fast, it will be a stern chase and a long one, and in no country that we are aware of is there room for a flight of this kind to end successfully; the result *must* be a long uninteresting chase without a stoop, with the rook safely ensconced in covert at the end, some miles from the falconer. The hawk is there with no one to take her down to the lure, and is left to dash after any fresh quarry as soon as she gets her wind, and thus is lost.

If the slip be dead in wind, the rook cannot go straight away from the falcon, who is better at flying into the wind than he is; but he will at first do his best to escape her by flying up wind, rising all the time to keep above her; thus ere she can reach him both birds will have attained a considerable height.

But as soon as the hawk gains her pitch fairly over the rook, he can no longer carry on in the teeth of the gale, but must turn down wind, thus passing under the falcon and giving her the chance of her stoop, and also passing by all the horsemen, who, up to this point, have been following the flight up wind. Although the rest of the flight will be down the wind, the hawk will have so far got the advantage that she will put in stoop after stoop, and thus the horsemen will be able to keep up fairly well, and, at any rate, to see a pretty flight with many stoops, far different from a long down-wind stern chase, and should, moreover, be near enough at the finish (if their horses can gallop, and they can ride them) to secure the hawk, if, perchance, she is, after all, beaten to some covert. Let it then be considered an inviolable rule in rook hawking and all similar flights that the hawk be flown dead in the wind at the quarry, just as in game hawking the birds should be flushed dead down wind under the hawk.

It is not always an easy matter to enter falcons at rooks. The quarry is distasteful to them because it is difficult to catch, difficult to master when on the ground, and disagreeable to eat. Many hawks can only be brought to fly them by very skilful management, and at first all must be extra sharp set when first entered to them. No hawk, however, can be made to show any sport by the process of starvation, and, though she may be so reduced by hunger as to dash keenly at anything alive, yet her strength will fail her directly she is asked to climb into the wind over a rapidly mounting rook. The famous hawk 'Bois-le-Duc' was a striking instance of this unwillingness to fly rooks. Throughout her training she had shown such power, speed, and dash that it was clear she was a hawk of no mean order. When entered at bagged rooks she would dash at them and take them out of sheer devilry; and when first flown at wild rooks she would tear away over them, in spite of wind, snow, or any disadvantages, but having them once at her mercy would disdain to stoop and finish her work. To have starved her into flying would have been to sacrifice her great powers or to lower her to the level of an ordinary falcon. Instead of this she was flown in a string at bagged rooks, and the moment she seized them a fresh-killed pigeon was thrust under the wing of the rook, and the falcon fed upon it. After a time or two she began to think that rooks were not such bad eating after all, and, being slipped at a wild one, brought it down in splendid style. The same process was repeated, and the lesson was learnt. After that day Bois-le-duc was slipped at sixty consecutive rooks, which she killed with but a single miss during that whole season, a feat which has never been rivalled by any other hawk. For some time the greatest care was paid to her condition and to her feeding, but ere long she became so wedded to her quarry that no slip was too far, no chance too bad for her, and she became, perhaps, the best rook hawk that has ever been trained.

Eyesses will sometimes take rooks very well, and there have been many good rook hawks of this kind. As a rule, they lack the dash and drive requisite for work of this kind. They will kill on fine days and in nice places, but cannot take the long slips in wild weather, and under all circumstances, that passage hawks will attempt, even if they cannot succeed, nor are they clever enough at footing to be deadly at a quarry so active in shifting as the rook. It would be almost impossible to produce a team of eyesses that would show sport to a large party, day after day, in all weathers during March and April; but with passage hawks this can annually be done.

Tiercels will fly rooks well enough, but are naturally rather more difficult to enter than falcons; for the rook is, on the ground, almost as powerful a bird as the tiercel, and knocks him about sadly. As a rule tiercels are not entered to this quarry, but are kept for game and for magpies, &c. One of the best that ever was flown was an eyess called 'Druid,' belonging to the Hon. Cecil Duncombe, which for three years held his own and flew in his turn with a first-class team of passage falcons—no small feat indeed when the difference in size, power, and training are considered. There have been many good passage tiercels trained to rooks, of which the last was, perhaps, 'Plenipotentiary,' in 1878. Rook hawking must needs take place in very open and exposed country. It is also pursued during a very bleak stormy time of year. To insure sport it is advisable to use a light covered van in which to carry the hawks, built after the fashion of a carrier's cart, or light game waggon; the interior is fitted with perches, on which the hawks sit as well protected from weather as if they were in their mews at home. Far different is it when they are dragged over the downs on an open cadge, straining themselves to the utmost to retain their footing against the bitter breeze, and, if feeding time be delayed for an hour or two, starved by the cold till they develop many diseases of different kinds. Without warmth and protection no man can keep his hawks in the high, yet keen, condition that is essential to sport, and without the 'van,' or some such contrivance, rook hawking could not be brought to the perfection to which it has attained of late years. In their comfortable carriage the hawks are readily conveyed from place to place over a large tract of country. If rooks cannot be found in one place, the party can easily shift to another, taking the hawks with them, and in this way can cover a great deal of country.

A good horse that can gallop, but that is quiet enough to carry a hawk, is indispensable. At the end of a flight, when the falconer must needs dismount to take up his hawk, he should be tethered by a leaden weight, which is carried in a socket at the pommel of the saddle and attached to the bit by a rein. To stand well with this weight, which can be dragged if the horse bolts (i.e. do not break the bridle), and to carry a hawk well, requires a little education, and we have always found thoroughbred horses (especially young ones) more fearless and better suited to this work than any others. A good deal may be done with a very nervous horse by keeping him in a loose box with three or four live pigeons till he is thoroughly used to them, and to stand with the weight is best learned by long hacking rides with the frequent use thereof among fresh spring grass, when the horse will rapidly appreciate the luxury of being left to himself with only a slight check upon his movements, and will be only too glad to remain near the spot where his master dismounts as long as he pleases to leave him.

The following description of a flight at rooks appeared in print some years ago, but as it gives a fair idea of the sport we venture to reproduce it with slight alteration :—

Let us suppose that we are out for a day's rook hawking, and that we have arrived at our ground. All around, as far as the eye can reach, are wide rolling downs, partly cultivated, but still in a great measure clothed by the smooth virgin turf that has never known the touch of ploughshare or harrow. It is a lovely spring day; there is a mild gentle wind from the south, with a warm sun, tempered by great fleecy clouds, throwing upon the turf huge shadows which seem to race one another from slope to slope of the downs.

We take up our position behind a stack to wait for a rook passing on his way from the rookery in the valley to the sheepfold on the hill. Presently we see one coming, toiling slowly over the shoulder of the down. Shall we fly one of the young falcons lately entered and coming on so well? Or shall it be the old heroine of a hundred flights, victress over more than double that number of rooks, that flies now in her fourth season with all the vigour and dash she displayed in the blinding snowstorms and heavy gales of her first year? A hundred or two of yards is far enough for a slip with a young hawk, but with a real good one a quarter of mile is not too far, while many and many a time, if the wind be right for her, the old hawk has been slipped at rooks a fair half-mile away. It looks as if this slip would be too far for a young hawk, so the handsome old falcon is taken on hand, to the delight of the whole field, not one of whom, however large it may be, but will stay out 'just one half-hour more' when it is announced that it is the turn of old 'Bois-le-duc' to fly at the next chance that occurs.

All is hushed as the rook, a single bird, presumably a strong old cock, comes slowly up. He passes us and is going nicely on up wind when something about the party awakens his suspicions, and he gives a sudden swerve that in one second takes him about 150 yards off on a side wind. We are not to be done in this way though, and in a moment the head of our party, with the falcon on hand, dashes out at a brisk gallop down wind of the rook, which hastens on up wind. But a hundred yards or so is no matter to us with this hawk, and the moment we are fairly down wind of him the old hawk is unhooded and flung off; and the falcon is in hot pursuit of her quarry, rising with each stroke of her powerful wings till she seems to shoot upwards like an arrow from the bow. The rook has seen her, and is making his way upwards at no mean rate, but the pace of the falcon is too much for him, and ere long she is above him; poising herself for a moment she comes, with one terrible perpendicular stoop, straight at him. It would seem as though nothing could escape; but our rook is equal to the occasion, and with a clever shift he has dodged her attack by a good yard or more. Well done, rook! but there is clearly now no safety for him in the air, for the falcon has shot up again with the impetus of her stoop to a height scarcely inferior to that from which she descended; so, turning his tail to the wind, he makes all possible haste to a small patch of thorns and whins that promises a temporary shelter, having, however, on the way to evade two similar stoops from the hawk, almost as fine as the first. Alas for friend rook! On reaching the covert he finds it already occupied by the enemy, in the shape of the excited field, who soon drive him with halloo and crack of whip from his shelter, and compel him to again seek the open. The falcon has, however, strayed a little away, so he starts with might and main to ring in spiral curves into the very clouds. After him starts the hawk, but soon finds that a really good rook, such as this is, can mount nearly as fast as she can. Up, up they go, gradually becoming smaller and smaller. Ring above ring does the falcon make, yet without getting above him, till, apparently determined to gain the victory, she starts off into the wind to make one tremendous circle that shall attain her object. Steadily into the wind she goes, the rook striving to follow her example, and appearing from below to be flying after the hawk. At length, as she almost completes the outer circumference of her circle, the rook, perhaps feeling his powers exhausted, turns down wind, and, at a great height, makes off as fast as he can go. Surely the flight is over, for the falcon is still working away, head to the wind, as hard as she can—in fact, the two birds are flying in opposite directions, half a mile apart. 'Not a bit of it!' say the initiated, who are off down wind as fast as they can ride. In another moment you see the falcon come round, and though at such a height she looks no bigger than a swallow, you can see that she is far above the rook, whilst her pace, slightly descending as she is, is almost that of a bullet. So thinks her quarry apparently, for, shutting his wings, he tries to drop like a stone into a clump of trees now nearly beneath him. Swiftly as he drops there is a swifter behind him, and down from that terrific height comes the falcon like a thunderbolt. Lord! what a stoop! By the powers, she has missed! And now surely he must escape. But no! shooting

Falcon flying rook

upwards like a rocket, the old falcon puts in one more straight swift stoop, and the rook is taken just as he enters the sanctuary which he has had his eyes on from the first. Whoo-who-op! A grand ring! a magnificent stoop! a splendid flight!--Bravo, 'Bois-le-duc!'

All flights are not of course so long or so good as this one, but generally afford some sport. As many as nine and ten have been killed in one day, while the total score of rooks and crows taken in the spring of 1887 by the Old Hawking Club reached 209. One year with another some 150, for the last fifteen seasons, have generally been killed, which represents many a ringing flight, and many a brisk gallop over the breezy downs.

Another flight which taxes to the full the powers of the best passage hawks, but which is capable of affording the finest of sport, is the flight of the seagull. In many places herring and other gulls are found far inland, and in open places following the plough or feeding on the land. In 1877 the Rev. W. Willimott, a thoroughly practical falconer residing in Cornwall, trained a passage falcon, that had been entered at rooks, to this quarry with no little success. The hawk took so keenly to the gulls that she would fly them well even with flocks of rooks or other birds around her, and several very fine flights were the result. In fact, on the only occasions when the falcon was defeated the gull made good its point to the sea, but in the air the falcon had the mastery. More recently considerable success has been achieved in flying gulls upon the Yorkshire Wolds by Mr. St. Quintin. This gentleman has chiefly used tiercels for the sport, and principally passage tiercels. With these he has succeeded, on one or two occasions, in taking even the big herring gull, and, perhaps, from their greater activity, they are even better suited than falcons to the small, black-headed gull. Still, upon the whole, we think falcons are most likely to achieve success with seagulls. In the year 1890 Mr. St. Quintin succeeded in killing no fewer than forty-three gulls during winter and early spring, using both tiercels and falcons, and many of the flights were of the finest possible description. As gulls will put in to no sort of covert except water, this flight can be obtained in a country where any other kind of ringing flight would be impracticable. It is not an easy quarry to enter hawks to, and considerable knowledge of the condition and management of hawks is necessary. As a rule, care must be taken to avoid letting the hawks break into and eat the flesh of the gull, which is very distasteful to them, and likely to sicken them of the flight. A freshly-killed pigeon should be substituted for the gull the moment it is dead, and the hawk fed upon it, on the body of the gull where it has killed. Hawks require to be very 'fit' for this flight, as the gull's power of shifting from the stoop is marvellous, while he can also ring into the clouds very rapidly, and both hawks will need to work hard and to stoop straight and often before they can master him. Moreover the gull, especially the herring gull, bites very sharply, and the falconer must make every effort to be near enough at the close of the flight to assist his hawk, as, should a hawk be injured at first entering, it is not likely to take well to the quarry ever afterwards. It is, however, placed upon record that the seagull is perfectly within the powers of hawks of the best class, and we are of opinion that it is a flight well worthy the attention of falconers, and likely, if well managed, to afford sport of the highest kind.

The lapwing or green plover is an exceedingly difficult bird to take, so much so that it may be termed outside the category of 'quarry.' We have, however, taken a few in the spring, when they are strongest, with a very first-rate cast of passage tiercels specially trained to the flight. In August or July, when the old birds are moulting and the young have hardly arrived at their full power, they could perhaps be taken readily, but at any period of the year their powers of high-mounting and of swiftly dashing from the stoop must make them a very difficult bird to catch.

The Norfolk plover, stone curlew, or thicknee, is comparatively easy to take, but is very powerful and fights hard on the ground. It is a good quarry at which to fly hawks that are intended to fly the heron later on. It may be flown either out of the hood, or it may be marked down, and a hawk trained for game-hawking may be put up to wait on overhead and to capture it as it rises. In this way they are more easily caught. Yet occasionally a bird is met with that will shift from the first stoop, and fairly ring away into the clouds, beating, as we have sometimes seen, hawks of the very highest class that were doing their best to catch them.

The marked excellence of passage hawks at game hawking was proved for the first time in recent years in the season of 1869, when the two falconers John and Robert Barr, the one in the service of the Champagne Hawking Club and the other in that of the Marquis of Bute, met at Grandtully Castle by the invitation of the Maharajah Dhuleep Singh. The team of hawks was a very strong one, both of eyesses and of passage hawks, the latter having been caught and trained for other purposes, but soon in the skilful hands of John Barr well entered to game. The report of this clever falconer to the author of these lines was as follows:—'We are having the finest grouse hawking here that has ever been seen, killing three or four brace of grouse a day, but our hawks are *too good*—they kill every time they are flown, very often far out of sight, and are not found the same day, and often are difficult to take up after they have been left out one night.' This, no doubt, is the fault of wild-caught hawks, if they are used for any kind of hawking in which they cannot be ridden up to; but for swiftness, style, and deadly stooping, eyesses have no chance with them. Haggards especially seem to take to waiting on very well as soon as they are thoroughly well tamed, and naturally they are most deadly at their stoop. In 1869—the year referred to above—John Barr had a very old haggard falcon named 'Granny,' that was a splendid game hawk and also very good at the heron. But the best of all his passage hawks was a falcon called 'Aurora,' so small that 'all the talent' assembled at Valkenswaard voted her to be a tiercel when first she was caught, until the veteran Adrian Mollen pointed out sundry points of distinction and proved them all to be wrong, and that she really was a tiny falcon.

Of late years 'Sibyl,' 'Bacchante' (an old haggard), and 'Elsa,' all the property of the Old Hawking Club, have proved on the Caithness moors that, however trustworthy and good eyesses may be, they cannot hold their own when tried against wild-caught hawks in an open wild country with a strong swift quarry like the grouse. The fatal word 'lost,' entered against the name of many a good passage hawk in the game book, has prevented her score from reaching that of the steady-going eyess, who is rarely lost, or if lost is very easily recovered after an extra day or so at hack; but even if the score of killed be not as great in the one case as in the other, the fine style in which the smaller number has been taken will fully balance the account between the two hawks.

In former years it was supposed that passage hawks were not fit to fly at game till after they had been for a long time in training. As long ago, however, as 1869 we saw passage tiercels waiting on perfectly in February that had been caught in the previous October and had been trained by John Barr. Since that time we have had several hawks that were perfectly steady for magpie hawking in the spring succeeding the autumn in which they were caught, and so lately as 1887 we took a magpie in April with a haggard falcon of the previous November. As a rule any passage hawk that has had a good spring season of work at rooks, &c. may be got up in condition, and after a few pigeons from the hand will wait on as well as any eyess.

Peregrines differ both in size, colour, and general appearance to an extent so great that it is sometimes almost impossible to believe that they are the same species of hawk. Some falcons of the first year are of a bright reddish cinnamon on the back, the breast being almost all of one rufous shade, blotched with dirty cream-coloured markings. Next to such a bird on the same perch will be perhaps a falcon nearly a third taller, with a rich dark brown back and wing coverts, and her breast and thighs of a bright cream colour regularly marked with very dark brown markings; the head of such a bird will be nearly black, her thighs very evenly marked, and not a trace of red or cinnamon in her whole body. Other hawks will perhaps be there, all caught on the same passage, of every intermediate shade between these two, some nearly black, others almost the colour of a kestrel. So, too, with the adult birds. One will moult out with a beautiful pale blue back, a crop and breast almost white, with a few regular bars across the lower part. Another will have a back of the darkest blue, with head and cheeks very nearly jet black and a breast of rich salmon colour, almost rose, so strongly marked with black that, excepting that the markings run horizontally and not perpendicularly, they are almost as thick as they were in the young plumage. In old hawks pale cinnamon feathers are not uncommon about the nape of the neck, so that the hawk has somewhat the appearance of *F. Babylonicus*.

We are satisfied from close observation that it is not possible to tell from the plumage of hawks in the immature stage whether, when fully moulted out, they will be of the darker or lighter variety. As a rule those falcons which are very black in the young stage will be of a dark variety when moulted out, but we have known very light red young hawks moult to a dark variety, and *vice versâ*.

A disagreeable but a common phase of falconry is the loss of a hawk, and her recovery taxes oftentimes both the patience and the skill of the falconer. Usually the first cause of the loss is that the flight has carried both hawk and quarry far beyond the ken of their followers. In such case the falconer will follow on down wind as fast as he can to the spot where he last saw the birds, or beyond that to any point where he thinks the flight likely to have terminated. Here he will search all covert into which the quarry may have been driven and killed, from time to time showing his lure, in case the hawk may be either soaring to cool herself after a hard flight or be sitting sulky and disappointed close to where she lost her prey. If he has with him any of the field on horseback, they must be sent on straight down wind to look over all likely places, and especially to the neighbouring rookeries. If the hawk is near these or within them there will be a most unmistakable commotion, and a signal will show the falconer either that she is there or has passed that way. If the latter prove to be the case, the hawk is probably to be sought for still farther down wind of this spot. Flying another hawk to the lure will often bring up a sulky hawk, if done in an exposed place where it can be seen from all sides.

Should all these devices fail, it may be taken as certain that the hawk has killed and has gorged herself upon her quarry. In that case she will not be recovered the same day. The falconer will therefore make his arrangements to be upon the spot where the hawk was last seen or heard of before daylight the following morning. He will, with a pair of good glasses, watch the motion of every bird that moves at dawn, and these will act as his scouts, especially in the case of rooks and crows. If he is able to reach a point where he can command a rookery from which the birds are travelling in all directions for their food, he can, sitting quietly glasses in hand, make good an immense extent of country. Should the hawk be sitting in a tree, or on her kill—nay, should she have recently killed any bird—no rook or crow will pass over it without 'mobbing,' i.e. circling round and cawing. If the rooks pass to and fro in all directions peacefully, the falconer may rely upon it that his hawk is not and has not lately been in that neighbourhood; but if he sees one or two consecutively 'mobbing' in one place he may be sure it is worth his while to inspect it. Possibly it is only the kill of the day before, but it is an assurance that the hawk is not far off. Later in the morning he may see a lot of rooks and plovers 'sky up' in a cluster as if alarmed, and if lucky he will, near that spot, find his hawk, perhaps half gorged.

If very tame, she may even in that state come to a live pigeon, and allow him to take her up. She will almost certainly come to the pigeon, but perhaps, with a full crop and a day (or may be more) of liberty, will not allow him to take her up. He should try every plan he can think of to do so, but if he fail, then he must snare her.

If she will, as is often the case, allow him to come within twenty or thirty yards without notice, he will produce from his bag a long light line of about 100 yards (a salmon line is very good) with a peg at one end. Driving the peg into the ground, at forty yards from the hawk, as she sits plucking the pigeon, he will walk round and round, never approaching her, but thus winding the line round her legs, above the bells. As long as he keeps moving and not coming towards her the hawk will not notice him. So soon as he sees that the string is well lapped round her legs he will make quietly in towards the hawk; but even now, if he can, let him try to take her up, so that she may not find out she is snared. If once a hawk realises this, she is always difficult to manage, very shy of a string and of all tackle, and half spoilt. But if she attempts to leave the pigeon and fly off, the falconer must needs pull his string tight, march in upon her, and the quicker the hood is on her head the better.

Possibly, if she is a wild-natured hawk and has been out for a few days, she will not allow any man even within gun-shot. The best plan in such a case is to throw out a live pigeon with a long string attached to it which it can carry away pretty well. If the hawk takes this and kills it, go right in upon her, seizing the string, and frighten her off it. She will not go far. The long line must then be set with an ordinary slip-knot round the pigeon, which must be *firmly* pegged down just as the hawk left it; a few wing feathers should be stuck round the noose so as to guide the line upwards and round the hawk's legs. The falconer must retire to the end thereof, conceal himself, and play the game of patience. Sooner or later the hawk is sure to return to her kill, and if she does so, one pull secures her.

This snare can be set with a long spring of india-rubber and a trigger, so that the lighting of the hawk on the pigeon will liberate it and tighten the noose. If the falconer finds more kills than one, a snare or two of this kind will aid him much.

A very good device for catching a half-hungry hawk that will stoop at a pigeon, half in play, half in earnest, is as follows. A short strap of stout leather is cut, about three inches long by three-quarters of an inch broad; to this there are attached four or five little snares of catgut, or of gimp, so arranged that, when open, they stand like a series of little wings on a salmon fly, upright, all along the strap, about an inch high. The whole apparatus is next fastened to a pigeon's back by means of double strings round the shoulder of each wing and one round the root of the tail. The strap then fits close along his back among his feathers without impeding his flight in the least, and the snares stand up the whole length of his back and well above it. The pigeon is now thrown out with a long line attached, and should the hawk make but a half-hearted stoop, it is ten to one she will catch her claws in one or other of the snares and be fast. With a pigeon, and a long string attached to her toe, she is readily taken, and we have known even wild hawks to be caught in this way in England. In the East, where they are far tamer, it is almost a certainty.[1]

[1] Should a hawk persistently carry any light quarry, the best plan to adopt is to fly another—a very tame hawk—at her. Both hawks will then hold on to the prey, and the falconer can easily approach. Failing this device, the hawk must either be snared, or else frightened off her quarry, and then taken down in the usual way.

## CHAPTER IV

GERFALCONS—KITE HAWKING—HARE HAWKING—MERLINS—HOW MANAGED—LARK HAWKING—THE HOBBY—THE SACRE—THE LANNER—SHAHINS—SPORT IN INDIA—OTHER VARIETIES OF HAWKS USED IN FALCONRY.

THE noblest kind of hawk that is, or ever has been, used in falconry is certainly the ger-, or gyrfalcon, as the three varieties of the great Northern falcons are each called indiscriminately by falconers. These varieties are. first, the Greenland Falcon, the handsomest of the three, almost (in its adult plumage) snow-white, with handsome, regular markings. This variety is more widely distributed than the other two, but the only specimens which have been trained have been either ship-caught birds or stray hawks that have been taken by some chance. Secondly, the Iceland Falcon. Very many hawks of this variety have been trained, some being birds taken from the nest in Iceland (to which country it is almost entirely confined) and others birds caught when fully grown, besides chance specimens. Thirdly, the Norwegian variety, which has been taken both adult and from the nest by expeditions of falconers sent expressly to procure them. Three specimens also have, during the last fifty years, been taken on the passage at Valkenswaard, all of which were trained with varying success.

Just as big yachts sail faster than little ones, so the gerfalcons, being nearly twice the size of peregrines, can fly far faster even than those swift birds. Moreover, in their style of flying they excel all other hawks. No gerfalcon that has the full use of her wings ever makes a bad stoop or flies in bad

G. E. Lodge.

form. Whether at the lure or at wild quarry their style is perfection. But yet, in spite of this, they cannot altogether be termed a success in falconry. Their tempers are generally very violent and stubborn, making them difficult to train in the early stages; they are always troublesome to break to the hood, and it requires an infinity of pains to get them to stand to it at all. From their great size and wild disposition they are very prone to carry, and altogether it requires a very experienced hand to do any good with them.

Worst of all, it is extremely difficult to keep them in health until they become thoroughly acclimatised. The Iceland variety especially is afflicted with a form of asthma that is almost universal among those hawks which are caught wild in the island, and which are in other respects the most likely to succeed. Few of those which are seized with this disease ever recover; it is closely allied to that lung disease which in ancient books is described as the 'pantas.' In the Norwegian falcons, within our experience, this disease has not been so prevalent, but they have been very liable to a virulent, and generally fatal, form of frounce, resulting in a tumour in the throat, which generally kills them. Both varieties, when flying well, have been apt to lose all form and to become useless when a change has occurred from cold to warm weather, and they seem especially sensitive to a damp, muggy climate. Of the constitution of the Greenland Falcon we cannot speak from actual experience, but from its wider distribution it may possibly be more hardy. One in the possession of Lord Lilford was a fine-tempered hawk and a good flier, keen at rooks.

When once, however, the first moult is past, these birds seem to thrive well in England. The Maharajah Dhuleep Singh possessed a beautiful Icelander which was moulted for many years, and there have been many instances of these hawks living to a considerable age. Symon Latham, writing in 1615, says: 'I have known a gerfalcon an excellent heronor, and to continue her goodnesse very neare twenty years, or full out the time.' In 1845, John Pells, the falconer, brought over several

Icelanders for the Duke of Leeds, and these were trained at the Loo and entered to herons. One or two were pretty good birds, but upon the whole they did not turn out well. Some of the falcons were entered to hares and took them fairly well.

In 1839, Mr. E. C. Newcome visited Norway in search of gerfalcons, of which he always had had a high opinion—so much so that, several years before that date, he had systematically issued hand-bills to the captains of whalers sailing in the North Seas, requesting them to take every opportunity of procuring for him birds of that species. Having selected the place most suited to the purpose, he caused huts to be built the following year for the taking of the falcons in the Dutch method, and in digging the foundations for these the men came upon those of the ancient huts which had been used by falconers in bygone days, all knowledge of which, except as an ancient tradition, had perished. In this place he took three gerfalcons, and in the succeeding year the Dutch falconers caught ten or a dozen. All of these birds were trained at the Loo, but out of all the lot only two—a falcon and a tiercel—turned out to be good ones, one being trained by James Bots and one by Adrian Mollen.

The great fault of gerfalcons, even when they could be induced to persevere at this flight, was that their stoop was so hard that they would either kill or cripple the heron, and this, in the breeding season, when it was important to save every heron, was a serious drawback. Their nature is ever to stoop repeatedly at their quarry, and after they have so knocked it about as to cripple it, then to seize or bind to it. In 1869, John Barr and James Barr, his nephew, were sent to Iceland by the Maharajah Dhuleep Singh for the purpose of procuring gerfalcons. In this they were exceedingly successful, bringing back no less than thirty-three of these magnificent birds.[1] In the spring of 1870 we had the pleasure of inspect-

[1] Naturally great difficulty was experienced in bringing these hawks home. The greater part of one steamer had to be specially retained for them, and for

ing this stud of hawks, together with Mr. E. C. Newcome. They were then established at Elveden, and all, or nearly all, were trained, and many entered. Probably, since the earliest days of falconry, a stud of hawks has never been seen of

Iceland falcon

so magnificent an appearance as this collection presented at that time. Besides the thirty-three gerfalcons, there was a fair team of peregrines, a sacre in full work, a goshawk or two, and

some half-dozen *ponies* which were purchased in order to be slaughtered during the voyage to provide the hawks with food, no other flesh being obtainable.

other varieties. Several of the gerfalcons were flying at the lure in the finest conceivable style. In fact, three of them were, in our opinion, and in that of Mr. Newcome, whose judgment could hardly be called in question, among the best, if not absolutely the finest, fliers that have been trained during the memory of any living man. The falcons were being, some of them, regularly flown at hares, and we saw a curious flight or two of this nature. Alas! Even at this early stage the asthma, to which we have referred above, was rife among these noble hawks, and by the close of the year almost the whole team were defunct or useless, with hardly a record to their names of wild quarry killed!

In 1876 John Barr, who was then employed by the Falconry Club, was sent to Norway in order to obtain gerfalcons of the variety of that country, which it was hoped would be more free from the fatal disease which was so destructive to the Icelanders. He succeeded in taking ten, all of which but one were females, and all young birds. Out of those which landed, six were dead by the end of December of the fatal 'pantas'; of the two which fell to the portion of the Old Hawking Club, one died in a few weeks, and the other was successfully, but with great trouble, trained and entered. She was in no respect a good hawk, and died the following August of a fatal form of frounce. Of the others, one only took wild quarry, viz. rooks, at which she was flown on Epsom Downs by Mr. J. E. Harting. Three gerfalcons have been caught at Valkenswaard. Of the first we have no record, save that it was trained at the Loo, and was no great success; the second was for some time in England, in the possession of Lord Lilford; the third was a noble tiercel caught in 1878 in the adult plumage, and, so far as we know, is the only haggard gerfalcon (of that species) that ever was trained. He fell into the hands of the Old Hawking Club, and was very carefully trained by their falconer, John Frost. Although a haggard, he had a finer temper than most gerfalcons, and was trained without a great deal of trouble. He was entered to rooks on Salisbury Plain, and turned out a most splendid hawk, one of the grandest fliers the club has ever possessed. Yet when hot weather set in he fell off in style, and refused to fly, being very untrustworthy, and was lost, owing to an unfortunate accident during his first moult.

Upon the whole, then, gerfalcons must be termed unsatisfactory hawks to train, and though no falconer likes to miss giving a fair chance to one of these noble birds, yet if sport alone be the object aimed at, it is not worth while to waste time upon them while the peregrine is readily obtainable.

In old times the gerfalcon was especially valued for the purpose of flying the kite, then a common bird, and probably that flight was the finest that has ever been followed in this country, not even excepting the 'heron on passage.' It is still a common flight in India, where the sacre, a bird of almost equal power to the gerfalcon, is used for it; but the difficulty of training and entering hawks to this quarry, and the courage and perseverance needed to overtake so swift and high-mounting a bird, show us how skilfully our ancestors must have managed their hawks in order to succeed in the undertaking.

The method by which the kite was flown was somewhat peculiar. As soon as the bird was descried soaring in mid air, generally at a height so great that it could hardly be distinguished, a live owl was let fly by the falconers, to whose legs was attached a fox's brush. This both impeded the owl's flight to such an extent that it could not escape, and also presented to the kite the spectacle of a bird of prey, such as could easily be robbed, carrying off some quarry. Immediately then he would descend from his lofty pitch to attack the poor owl, when the falcons, generally three in number, would be slipped at him.

In the Appendix to Mr. Southwell's edition of Lubbock's 'Fauna of Norfolk,' written by Professor Newton, it is stated, speaking of the practice of falconry in Norfolk, that --

Lord Orford's chief quarry seems to have been the kite, which was then very common throughout England, and apparently especially abundant in this district so rich in rabbits. Years ago

I well remember having heard from several old men in the neighbourhood of the excellent flights which this species afforded, and especially of one flight, which, beginning on Eriswell or on the adjoining part of Elveden, ended in Lord Bristol's park at Ickworth, near Bury St. Edmunds, a distance in a straight line of some ten or twelve miles.

The famous Colonel Thornton, who succeeded Lord Orford as the manager of the Falconers' Club (or, as the Colonel describes it in his 'Northern Tour,' 'The Confederate Hawks of England'), seems to have been very successful at this flight with the gerfalcon, as also at hares. Whence he got his hawks we are not able to trace, but as it is certain that the falconers of that day were in frequent communication with those of the Continent, we are inclined to suspect that the ancient huts for hawk-catching which Mr. Newcome discovered on the Dovrefjeld had some connection with the gerfalcons trained by Lord Orford and Colonel Thornton, and with the princely establishments of hawks which they maintained.

In Colonel Thornton's 'Northern Tour' is described an episode which bears so strongly upon the subject of this chapter that we venture to reproduce it verbatim. He says :—

A Mr. A——, attended by a little humpbacked servant with a large portmanteau, joined our party ranging for kite near Elden Gap. At length one was seen in the air, and I ordered the owl to be flown. He came as we wished, at a proper distance. The day was fine, and the hawks, particularly 'Javelin' and 'Icelanderkin,' in the highest order, and with them '*Crocus,' a famous slight falcon.* Never was there a finer day, a keener company, or for six miles a finer flight. When he was taken, in an ecstasy I asked Mr. A—— how he liked kite hawking. He replied with a sort of hesitation that expressed but small pleasure, 'Why, pretty well!' We then tried for hare with a famous hawk called 'Sans Quartier.' After ranging a little we found one, and in about two miles killed it. Mr. A——, coming up again slowly, unwilling or unable to leave his portmanteau, I repeated my former question, and though the flight of a hare is fine, yet being in no way equal to that of a kite, was surprised to see his countenance brighten up and to hear him express himself with uncommon pleasure. 'Ay, that,' he said, 'was a nobler kind of hawking; the hare would be of use—a good *roast*—the kite of none.' Desirous to gratify his wishes, and to get quit on easy terms of the trouble the servants would have to carry an old jack hare in the month of May, I begged his acceptance of it, to which he very readily consented; and his servant was ordered to add this trophy to the top of the enormous portmanteau. I leave every sportsman to guess the observations that were made by a set of lively young men on the occasion.

Apart from the humour of this anecdote, it is clear that the Colonel had in his service at least three good well-trained gerfalcons, and probably others. It is, we believe, on record that 'Sans Quartier,' the falcon that was flown single-handed at an old jack hare, was a gerfalcon. Clearly 'Icelanderkin' was one of that species, while the express allusion to 'Crocus' as a 'slight' or peregrine falcon seems to show that both the other two which were flown with her were of another species.

The kite, however, is no longer to be flown in this country, and with its disappearance the necessity for the gerfalcon as a bird of sport has also vanished. That they can be trained and used has been well proved in these modern times, but they now have to be flown at quarry for which the peregrine is better suited, and therefore it is not to be wondered at if they are beaten out of the field by that most serviceable of all falcons. Their chief excellence is at quarry that mounts high in the air, and we have never known one used successfully at game as yet.

Merlins are a very beautiful variety of hawk, tiny in size, but full of dash and courage. They are always great favourites with young falconers and with amateurs, because of their docile, even affectionate, nature, and of the ease with which they may be managed. Unfortunately their constitution is so delicate that they require the greatest care to keep them alive, and only few falconers have succeeded in keeping them through the winter, fewer still after the first moult.

They are not uncommon hawks in this country, breeding

on the moors of Yorkshire and the northern counties. Their nest is placed on the ground among the heather, and they are late breeders, the young being rarely fit to take before the third week in July. Wild merlins are also caught at Valkenswaard on the autumn migration, in the same manner as peregrines, special nets and lures being arranged for them. Those taken from the nest are easily reared with sufficient care. They should be fed three times a day on the tenderest possible beef, with all fat and gristle cut away ; an occasional change to pigeon, chicken or rabbit is desirable. When merlins are full-grown they must be kept as much as possible upon birds, trapped ones in preference to those that are shot ; but if a shot bird be given, an abundance of casting must be given with it in case any shot corns should be swallowed. They can be flown at hack, and if they are likely to be flown when trained near the place where they were hacked, it is a great advantage to rear them thus, as a lost hawk will then return home of herself very often. But it is impossible to fly them at hack together with peregrines, for the latter, being much more forward than the merlins, are easily able to take them when first put out, and would be very likely to kill them. Care must also be taken not to have peregrines sitting out on blocks near where merlins are hacked ; they are bold, confiding little hawks, and are very likely to drop down by the side of the peregrine, attracted perchance by some food, or else for company, and in that way are likely to be killed.

A very good way both to keep and rear merlins is to bring them up altogether in a good large room or a loft ; there must be a perch or two for them, and all corners should be rounded off as much as possible to prevent injury to the feathers. The bars to the windows must be fixed perpendicularly and not horizontally, so that the hawks cannot fly at the windows and cling to them. A very little carrying will soon accustom the merlins to fly to the hand of anyone they know well in order to be fed, and this with a little calling to the lure is really all the training they require. We have brought up birds in this way many times, and have also hacked them, and we have found those reared in a room prove just as good fliers as those that had been hacked. It was also the method employed by Mr. Newcome, who was very successful with these little hawks. Whether hacked or not, merlins will do better loose in a room than on blocks or perches. On days when they are to be

Lark hawking

flown they can be taken up, and after being given a few mouthfuls in the morning, set down on small-sized blocks or on the bow-perch (see description in Chapter VII.); the latter is the best perch for merlins. When in the house they can be secured on the 'screen.' The flight for which merlins are most esteemed is that of the skylark, and an exceedingly beautiful flight it is, closely resembling that of the heron in miniature. The lark as a rule mounts straight into the air, and that very rapidly. The little hawks must ring again and again to get above him, and even then will sometimes fail. It is a common thing to lose sight of the lark in the clouds, even on a clear day, and not unfrequently both the hawks flying with him will also disappear fairly overhead in the air. Presently the two larger specks reappear, and then in front of them you may see the smaller dot, falling like a bullet from the clouds into a fence below, with the little falcons stooping right and left at him till he is taken just as he gains his sanctuary. It is better to fly two merlins together at larks, and the females will be found more persevering and harder fliers as a rule than the males. During August the larks which are moulting can be readily taken, but after September I they are very much stronger, and it is not easy to get the merlins, which are easily discouraged by a few defeats, to persevere in flying them, unless a plentiful supply of bagged larks be kept wherewith to encourage them, after failure, by affording an easy flight. As the season grows later the larks get stronger, and generally the merlins give up the flight altogether, though we have known larks taken in the winter occasionally. Therefore in the North of England, where the corn remains on the fields, either standing or in stooks (into which the larks will drop instantly), until very late in August, it is no easy matter to get merlins entered in time to show any sport before the season is practically over.

The first falconer who took up this branch of hawking on any large scale, in modern times, was Mr. Newcome. He used merlins for several years, and killed a great number of larks, but we have no precise record of his doings. Like other falconers, he found merlins inveterate 'carriers,' tame as they are, and a small hook on the end of a long stick, by which he could lay hold of the body of the lark when killed, was often of great assistance. We have found a similar hook, at the end of a Japanese fishing-rod which folds into the butt, very useful, especially when the merlin has been so unfeeling as to carry her quarry into a tree. As larks, when put in, will often lie like stories, a good terrier, that will nose them out, is of considerable service. In more recent times the Rev. G. E. Freeman, author of 'Falconry: its History, Claims, and Practice,' has been successful with merlins at various different flights; his doings are well recorded in Chapter XIII. of that work, and he appears to have had considerable sport in flying the ring ousel as well as the skylark.

More recently Mr. E. B. Michell, an amateur falconer of some experience, met with great success with merlins. In 1881 he succeeded in taking, up to September 15, fifty larks with two male merlins; but in 1883, with three merlins, two of them females, he killed (on very first-rate ground on Salisbury Plain) no less than 136 larks. Whether this surpasses Mr. Newcome's scores of former years or not we do not know, but it is certainly very good work, and deserves to be placed on record. For ourselves, flying in bad country, we have found from thirty to forty larks killed between August 20th to September 20th to be fairly successful work, and our practice for some years was to allow our merlins to fly loose after the autumn migration began, and to procure fresh ones the following year, by which we avoided the probability of losing our little pets during the winter, and yet had fresh ones ready for the only time of year when much can be done with these hawks.

Any varieties of small birds can be flown with merlins, where the fields are large enough and the birds to be found; they are very quick and active, even among trees and bushes, partaking a good deal of the character of the true hawks, such as the sparrow-hawk and goshawk, as well as of the falcons, to which they properly belong.

The more courageous females can be trained to fly pigeons well, and so great is their activity that it requires a good pigeon to escape them; and if the quarry seeks refuge in a bush or a hedge the merlin is almost sure to follow and seize him. Their method of killing birds of this large size is peculiar, being by strangulation, a method not usually adopted by any other hawk; in fact, a full-grown pigeon is as strong as a merlin, and therefore the hawk cannot master its prey so as to put it to a speedy death as the peregrine does, by breaking its neck.

It requires some trouble, as a rule, to enter a merlin to pigeons, just as in the case of any other quarry that is somewhat beyond the strength of the hawk which is to fly it; but, although it is rather interesting to see these little falcons tackle a bird with powers fully equal to their own, yet as it can only lead to flights at bagged quarry, we do not propose to enter further into a description of this flight.

We cannot, from personal experience, say that snipe can be killed with trained merlins, but it seems very possible that hawks accustomed to ring after larks would be able to take this quarry also.

On the whole merlins, though, if compared with the falcons treated of in the preceding chapters, they must be ranked as toys, are well worthy the consideration of falconers, especially of the tyro in that art. They require but little training, or trouble to manage. They are not easily broken to the hood, nor is much education necessary, for so tame are these little birds that they will sit quietly enough bareheaded until the bird springs near them. The hood should only be used when travelling, and should be removed as soon as the field is reached, for it will be found that merlins will not fly readily 'out of the hood' as peregrines do, especially on bright sunny days.

They must always be fed twice a day, kept very warm, and especially free from damp; either a loft with a stove in it, or a condition of entire liberty at hack with liberal feeding, affords the best chance of keeping them alive after summer is past.

Of hobbies we can say but little from personal experience, except that they are, of all falcons, the most elegant, whether on the wing or on the block. Partly insectivorous in habits, they lack the dash and courage requisite for a bird of sport. Many have been trained of late years, but with no success as far as sport is concerned, although the hawks themselves were found perfectly docile, very fine-tempered, admirable at waiting on, and very fine fliers to the lure. Here their good qualities ceased; when tried at wild quarry of any kind they failed, and though, perhaps, with perseverance, individual birds might turn out well, this variety can hardly be included

Merlin 'feeding up'

among the birds used in sport at the present day. Mr. E. Michell did, we believe, succeed in training one to fly larks as well as the best merlins, but it is the only case we know of.[1]

[1] In the spring of 1885, a pair of hobbies took up their quarters for breeding purposes in an old wood in the country of the Old Hawking Club. It was a common practice to let fly an eyess tiercel near this wood for the purpose of 'drawing the hobbies,' which would rally out to mob and drive away the intruder with the greatest vigour. Never have we seen so fine an exhibition of flying and stooping as was shown by these beautiful little falcons, and deeply did we regret that it was not possible to make use of such splendid powers as they possessed for the service of man.

The sacre is a falcon almost equal in size and power to the gerfalcon, but belongs to a different species, now termed the 'Desert falcons.' They are fine fliers, but slack mettled, soft feathered birds, unable to face rough weather, and, therefore, unsuited to this climate. It is many years since sacres were used in this country. We have ourselves seen but one in regular use, which had been imported from Egypt, and in England was only flown at pigeons. They are mentioned in most of the old books on hawks, but seem to have been imported as passage hawks, taken in the Levant, Egypt, &c. But when Adrian Mollen was in the service of Prince Trautsmansdorff, near Vienna, about the year 1838, he trained three young sacres which were taken from the nest in Hungary. We know of no more recent instances of the training of European sacres, and we give this fact on the authority of Professor Schlegel, and of Mollen himself.[1] In ancient times the sacre was valued for her kite-flying qualities. Blome, in the 'Gentleman's Recreation,' treats of her thus:—

> This hawk will make excellent sport with a kite, who, as soon as she sees the saker (the male whereof is called a sakaret) cast off, immediately betakes herself to, and trusts in the goodness of her wings, and getteth to her pitch as high as possibly she may by making many turns and wrenches in the air, which, well if observed, together with the variety of contests and bickerings there are between them, it cannot but be very pleasant and delightful to the beholder. I have known in a clear day and little wind stirring that both the saker and the kite have soared so high that the sharpest eye could not discern them, yet hath the saker in the encounter conquered the kite, and I have seen her come tumbling down to the ground with a strange precipitancy.

Sacres are much used in India for flying at the kite, ravine-deer, bustard, and other quarry. They are difficult to manage, and are usually induced to fly by the free use of drugs; these can only be administered safely where the

[1] We have been offered nestling sacres through a falconer resident in Moscow, but we do not know where the eyrie is situated. They appear however, to be easily obtained.

climate can be relied on, and if for no other reason than this, sacres would be unsuitable for use in variable weather such as British falconers have to contend with. They are trained for gazelle hawking in Persia and Arabia, in conjunction with greyhounds. See also Burton's 'Falconry in the Valley of the Indus' for a description of this sport.

The lanner is a falcon of type similar to the foregoing, but considerably smaller in size, being somewhat less than the peregrine. In former years it bred freely in Europe, but recently we do not find a record of a single nest; in Egypt and Nubia it breeds freely on rocks and ancient ruins. Many specimens have been tamed in this country and kept without any difficulty; they are easily tamed, but like the species last described are too slack mettled to be of real service at European quarry, and nearly akin to the kestrel in their habits. The Barbary falcon is an extremely beautiful hawk very like the peregrine, but about one-third less in size. Several have been imported and trained in England of late years, and two nestling birds were hacked at Lyndhurst for a member of the Old Hawking Club in 1885. They are dashing little flyers, and take pigeons in fine form; they might make good partridge or even magpie hawks, but are not very well suited to English quarry. They have perhaps hardly had a sufficiently good trial in recent times, and we should certainly advise any falconer to try one if he has an opportunity to procure a specimen in good plumage.

There are besides these several varieties of hawks used in Oriental falconry, of which perhaps the chief are the black shahîn (*F. peregrinator*) and the red-naped shahîn (*F. Babylonicus*), both excellent hawks, nearly akin to the peregrine, but, though of smaller size, better built and equally good fliers; they are specially used for wild fowl, partridge, and the endless varieties of wader that India affords. The sacre and the luggur are also used, but in India, as in Europe, the best hawk that can be trained is the ubiquitous peregrine. Goshawks, merlins, and sparrow-hawks are all used with great success at various quarries. The East is the home of falconry, and in countries where for many centuries it has formed 'the sport of kings' it is only natural to find hawking carried to great perfection and exceedingly well understood. So great is the variety of quarry at which hawks may be flown, and so certain the climate, that the sport may be carried on under advantages such as the European falconer sighs for in vain. In India hawks are easily obtained and cheaply kept. Whatever species is trained, it is not difficult to get flights to use it at. From the highest art of training the sacre to the flight at the kite, down to the use of the sparrow-hawk, every branch has its votaries. Indian falconry would need a volume to itself, and it might be one far more comprehensive than the Western sport will admit of, but space does not allow of our dealing with the subject here. We would recommend any man, who is sufficiently enthusiastic to desire to see the sport in perfection, to spend a winter in India, and to study the methods of training hawks and of flying game which Eastern, and especially Anglo-Indian, falconers have brought to so great perfection. As an example of the sport which may be obtained we append a return of the quarry killed by the hawks of two members[1] of the Old Hawking Club during the months of November and December 1888, and January and part of February 1889, chiefly in the neighbourhood of Meerut. Fifteen hawks in all were trained :—[2]

| | |
|---|---|
| Herons | 24 |
| Houbara | 17 |
| Black Ibis | 13 |
| Egrets | 7 |
| White-necked Stork | 1 |
| Bar-headed Goose | 1 |
| Ruddy Sheldrake | 4 |
| Common ,, | 2 |
| Mallard | 31 |

[1] Mr. B. H. Jones and Captain Biddulph.

[2] Of these hawks, three shahins were brought to England, one of which had killed no less than seventy duck of various sorts out of the above score. This falcon, one of the red variety, was successfully flown at grouse, partridges, and magpies in England and Scotland, and lived till 1891, through two severe English winters.

| | |
|---|---|
| Spotted-billed Duck | 12 |
| Red-crested Pochard | 3 |
| Pintail | 1 |
| Gadwall | 18 |
| Shoveller | 24 |
| White-eye | 4 |
| Tufted Duck | 1 |
| Teal | 68 |
| Red-wattled Lapwing | 72 |
| Indian Roller | 12 |
| Various | 7 |
| Total | 322 |

## CHAPTER V

THE SHORT-WINGED HAWKS—GOSHAWKS—HOW OBTAINED—TRAINING—ENTERING—RABBIT HAWKING—VARIOUS FLIGHTS—THE SPARROW-HAWK—MANAGEMENT—BLACK-BIRD HAWKING.

Of the short-winged or true hawks only two varieties are used in England, viz. the goshawk and the sparrow-hawk; the latter is common enough in every country, the former is only an extremely rare visitant to this country. It breeds pretty freely in the forests of Germany, in France, and in Norway, the hawks from the latter country being as a rule the best. They are widely distributed, however, throughout Europe, and varieties of this species are found throughout the world. We know of no authenticated instance of its breeding in Great Britain since Colonel Thornton in his 'Northern Tour' found several nests in the forests of Glenmore and Rothiemurchus, whence he took and trained a young bird. Passage goshawks, which are in every respect infinitely the best, are sometimes taken at Valkenswaard in the same manner as peregrines. Full-grown birds can also be caught not unfrequently in the German and Norwegian forests; such as these will prove very superior to the hawks taken out of the nest, which are spoken of by Bert, who wrote in 1619 one of the best and most practical books ever published on falconry, treating entirely of the short-winged hawks, as 'the cyas hawk upon whom I can fasten no affection for the multitude of her follies and faults.' In ancient times, however, falconers or 'ostringers,' as the trainers of the true hawks were termed, seem to have been in the habit of turning their hawks

into woods to breed. From the 'Colloquium' of Archbishop Ælfric, written about A.D. 995,[1] it would appear that the practice of Saxon falconers was regularly to turn their hawks in the spring into the woods, and to take the young at the end of the summer. With birds like the goshawks, which are not greatly inclined to stray from where they can get food, we can well believe that this plan might answer.

In the 'Paston Letters,' edited by Mr. Gairdner, a correspondence is given between John Paston the younger and his elder brother, in which the younger man prays the elder :—

'I axe no more gods of yow for all the servyse that I shall do yow whyll the world standyth but a gosshawke.' After some further correspondence his desire seems to have been granted, but alas !

> She hathe ben so brooseid with cariage of fewle that she is as good as lame in both hyr leggys, as every man may se at ice. Wherfor all syche folk as have seen hyr avyse me to cast hyr in to some wood wher as I wyll have her to eyer, but I wyll do ther in as ye wyll, wheder ye wyll I send hyr yow agen or cast her in Thorpe wood and a tarsell with hyr for I weit wher on is.

This practice was therefore known, if not common, in 1472, but we cannot find an account of the goshawk having bred in England within the last century.

There is little difficulty in procuring nestlings from France, Germany, or Norway now, though if it be possible to find a keeper skilful enough to snare the young birds some months after they have flown, it is worth while to pay an extra price for them. Goshawks average in value about 5*l.*, females being worth considerably more than males ; they do not require to be flown at hack.

The training of short-winged hawks is not difficult, as they are hardy and easily managed, but it is a laborious task, and requires time to accomplish, nor is it very easy to get a goshawk into such condition that she will fly well and keenly. They

[1] See also the Introduction by J. E. Harting to 'The Perfect Booke for kepinge of Sparhawks, 1575,' printed by B. Quaritch, 1886.

are 'hawks of the fist'—that is to say, they are flown straight from the hand, and do not mount after their quarry; the nature of the flight is a short, sharp dash at their prey, and they either take it or give up the flight in a short distance. They are never hooded except during training and when travelling. It is their nature to lie in wait for prey on some coign of vantage, remaining immovable perhaps for hours, till the chance occurs of a swift dash at the unsuspecting quarry, which rarely escapes. The trained bird, therefore, will learn to look upon her master's hand as the vantage post whence she is to kill, and will soon learn to sit thereon, bareheaded and immovable, but ready to dash like lightning at the first prey that stirs. The art of training her, then, is to carry her day and night, till she is so familiar with her master and his hand that she looks on the latter as her home on which she lives, from which all her sport is obtained, and to which she will return without lure after an unsuccessful flight.

To arrive at this desirable end a great deal of trouble must be taken. The older falconers made a good deal more use of the hood than is done nowadays with goshawks, and took as much pains to break them to stand well to the hood as they did with any other kind of hawk; we believe that they were wise, for the more training these birds undergo the better they will be. However, having procured a goshawk and put upon it jesses of stout leather—white horseskin, if kept well greased, is the most reliable—the best plan is to put on her a rufter hood through which she can see a little—a loose old one with a hole bored near the eye is very good—and to carry her for the greater part of the day, and as much of the night as possible, handling her in every possible way, and inducing her to pull at a piece of beef in the same way as is recommended in the case of the freshly-caught peregrine (see Chapter III.) As soon as the goshawk will feed well and keenly through her hood, let it be discarded, but from experience we think that the use of the hood in the early stages of training saves time, and that it should not be left off till the hawk is thoroughly at home on the fist, and feeds thereon without hesitation. When first the hood is taken off it should be done by candle-light, and the hawk should be carried till she recovers her first alarm at being bare-headed. She must then be placed in a dark room, on the perch, and taken on hand therein for half an hour or so in the morning before she is brought into the daylight. As soon as she will sit pretty quietly on the hand, she should be carried at intervals for the whole day. Every time she is taken on to the fist a reward of meat should be given her. She should gradually be taken among all the strange people, sights, or dogs that can be found, and in fact accustomed to everything that is unusual. An hour or two in the village blacksmith's forge, with all its strange sights, sounds, and constantly changing succession of visitors, is admirable training, provided that her food be given her at intervals, so that she may learn to pull away at a meal amongst all these disturbing influences. Colonel Delmé Ratcliffe most wisely advises carrying a hawk in the gas-lit streets of a crowded city—an excellent means of taming her where it can be carried out. In fact, as Bert phrases it, 'She shall be well assured to finde no other perch than the fist, from the time I rise till I goe to bed, when she shall goe with me.'

Very soon, if the hawk be well handled by her master and not frightened by any harsh treatment either by look or by deed—for goshawks watch their carrier's eye and are very sensitive to it—she will become very tame, and show but little fear of strangers. Long ere this stage is arrived at she will have learned to jump to the fist the instant she sees food, and have begun to come to it when held out to her in the expectation of being fed.

She should now be called to the hand in a long string out of doors. It is better that she be set on the ground for these lessons; she will come the more readily, and it will not tend to get her into the habit of taking perch in a tree after a flight—this should always be discouraged. The fist is the home of the goshawk, and she should never be allowed to fly quarry from any other position, however tempting it may be to do so when she is well placed. As soon as she comes readily to the fist the distance may be increased very rapidly, till she will come as far as she can see her master in enclosed country; in fact, if hungry she probably will not allow him to go a hundred yards from her. Goshawks, for all their wild savage nature, when so thoroughly tamed are very affectionate birds, and learn to know their trainer very well. They should be used to a short cry or call when they are coming to the fist, and it will often bring them up when in a wood or covert where their owner cannot see them.

They can now be entered at the quarry they are to fly; females are generally used for rabbit hawking, and this is on the whole the best purpose to which goshawks can be put in England. A few live rabbits must be obtained, and having carried the hawk for an hour or two, and when she is sharp set, a rabbit must be offered her. She will almost certainly take it, when it should be instantly killed by the thrust of a knife, and the hawk well fed on it. The next day she will be ready to fly a bagged rabbit in a good place, and then may try a wild one. Should she fail to take it, it will be wise to give her an easy bagman, feed her on it, and make a fresh essay next day.

Rabbits lying out in old pasture give the best and most dashing flights, especially where there are a few bushes, &c. for them to dodge in. Great sport may be had in summer evenings, when the rabbits feed a long distance out from the covert, by creeping between them and the wood, when one or more will be seen to squat, and may be taken in detail and captured, each one so noiselessly as not to alarm the others. In fact, a good goshawk in full training is very deadly indeed. The number killed by her need only be limited by the time her master spends on her, and the more she has flown the more trustworthy she will be. In 1877 we killed 112 rabbits in two months with one goshawk, never using her more than three days a week. During this period ten was the greatest number taken during an evening walk, but we have known sixteen and seventeen killed before the hawk was tired. Good sport may be obtained by using a ferret to bolt the rabbits, but care must be taken lest the goshawk take the ferret and kill it. A good female will kill pheasants; they are best flown among hedge-rows or in a very open plantation, and should they gain covert

Goshawk with rabbit in her foot

in front of the hawk they will not dare to run, but will lie very close. The goshawk will 'make her point,' i.e. shoot up again in the air, very accurately at the spot where the pheasant has put in, and when she is called down to the fist the bird may be freshly found by a spaniel and will generally be taken at the second flight.

Hares may be taken by female goshawks in precisely the

same way as rabbits, to which they should be at first entered. The next attempt must be at a leveret, found in a good place, and if it be taken, an old hare may be attempted; but a hawk must be kept entirely to hares, for one that is frequently used for taking rabbits will soon learn to refuse the more powerful quarry.

A good hawk will always get her quarry fast by the head, when it is almost powerless in her grip, which is tremendous. We have often seen a goshawk with one foot over the head of a rabbit, plant the other across his loins and, almost before we could stoop down to kill poor bunny, he has turned over dead, killed almost instantaneously by the simple grip of the hawk's terrible feet. A very stout glove must be worn when carrying a goshawk, or the hand will not only be injured, but the whole arm numbed by the pressure of her claws.

The male goshawk is very much quicker than the female, and will take pheasants well. Young partridges, too, he can take, but old ones will generally outfly all but the best. Few male goshawks can take rabbits regularly; they too often fail to hold them, and so get disappointed. Waterhens and coots, when they can be driven from the water, may be killed to a certainty. Wild ducks or teal, if they can be stalked, will be taken as they rise; but if once on the wing the goshawk has no chance with them. Grouse, where they lie well, have been caught in this way. In fact, a goshawk in really good 'yarak,' or flying condition, can be used like a fowling-piece—he will dash at and kill almost anything that rises within reach of him, provided he can overtake it within a certain limited range. Thus, in the list of 'various' quarry that have been killed by one goshawk, now in training, we find (besides her legitimate quarry of rabbits and hares) pheasants, partridges, wild duck, rats, squirrels, waterhens, stoats, blackbirds, &c. Of actual performances on the part of a male goshawk in recent years, we are informed by Mr. Riley, of Putley Court, Herefordshire—a gentleman who has been markedly successful with short-winged hawks in a county well suited to their capabilities—that he took with his male goshawk (an eyess) in 1886, 26 partridges (all well-grown stroug birds), 10 pheasants, 16 rabbits, 5 landrails, 12 waterhens, and one stoat; and with a female bird, in the same year, he killed 136 rabbits, 4 ducks, 3 waterhens, a pheasant and a stoat—good work, indeed, for two hawks, and, as regards the male bird, better than has been recorded for some time past. They grip their prey firmly on taking it, and are seldom inclined to 'carry.' Goshawks, though not capable of emulating the fine flights of the falcons, are able to show a great deal of sport in a country where the higher branches of falconry are impossible. Like a good fox-terrier, there is no more delightful companion in a morning's stroll round an ordinary English country-place than a goshawk in good form on the fist of a man who knows how to work her. If she be not required, she is no trouble; but if a good chance occurs, almost any game that is likely to be met with can be killed with her.

The determination of a goshawk is something surprising; we have seen one drive downhill at a rabbit, and as it leaped four feet in the air to avoid the stroke which grazed it, turn over and catch it from underneath while in the air, rolling afterwards down a steep bank head over heels, but never leaving go her hold. It is not uncommon to see a rabbit captured at the mouth of a burrow, and hawk and all disappear under ground; but when she is lifted out, however much she is knocked about, the rabbit is in her foot. No covert will stop them, and they dash between the bars of a hurdle or through a meuse like a flash of light.

Goshawks, though easily tamed, if sufficient trouble be taken with them, require experience and a considerable knowledge of condition to be induced to fly well. They must be a little lower in condition than most other hawks, but require a good gorge every fifth day, lest they lose strength. It is better to give them washed meat than to shorten unduly the quantity of food, and when being got into flying order they may be given washed meat for as much as a week at a time. It is not possible to lay down fixed rules for their management, as the tempers of individual hawks differ so much. It is easy for the falconer who is constantly carrying his hawk, and calling her to his fist, to judge if she be keen and fit to fly or not. If she be slack-mettled or sullen, he can judge of the cause and govern himself accordingly. It is useless to fly a hawk unless she be in perfect 'yarak.' If not in good order, even the best of them will take perch and sulk, appearing absolutely unconscious of live rabbits, pigeons, or other lures, a few feet below her. This sulkiness is a great drawback to the use of goshawks, but it is the effect of imperfect or insufficient training; and the same hawk which one day spoils an afternoon by her sulky refusals to fly will, two days afterwards, behave to perfection, and perhaps continue to do so for weeks, if properly handled. Nay, even at the height of their 'sulks,' we have seen them leave their perch, with live and dead lures below them, and follow their master who has made as though he were leaving them! When in true 'yarak' the feathers are set up, as if the hawk were cold, the crest is erect, the hawk immovable, gripping the fist with a grasp of iron, yet noticing the movement of every living thing and ready to dash at it. When not fit to fly her feathers lie close to the body, she constantly utters a chirp or twittering cry, and will bate *from* the fist, but not *at* everything that moves. When in this condition it is hopeless to fly her.

Even when in good 'yarak' a goshawk must be carried for an hour or two to get her into flying order on every day that she is wanted. If left idle for a day or two, more work will be wanted. An hour or two of carriage will work a transformation in a hawk that obviously was not fit to fly in the morning. Thus a goshawk will require more time to be expended on her than a team of four or five peregrines when once they are in condition, and two goshawks are as much as any one man can manage if he be required to keep both in flying order.

Goshawks can be kept in-doors upon the screen and out-of-doors on the bow-perch (see Chapter VII.) They are dangerous brutes with other hawks, and must be kept well away from them at all times. If convenience admit of it, they should not be kept in the same house as peregrines, for, if by any accident they get their leash untied, they may kill every other hawk in the mews. Very much more can be done in India with goshawks than in Europe, because—first, there is so much greater a choice of quarry to fly them at; and, secondly, labour is so much cheaper that a man can be told off solely to attend upon each bird, by which means they are kept tamer and in more constant 'yarak' than an English falconer in charge of many other hawks can find time to do.

In Colonel Delme Radcliffe's work on the Falconidæ used in India he gives the list of quarry at which he has flown goshawks as follows:—'Hares, cranes, geese, ducks, teal, houbara, florikin, pea fowl, jungle fowl, partridges, crows, kites, mynas, a great variety of other birds, and ravine-deer.' With a list such as this it is no wonder that the goshawk is very highly esteemed, or that her price is sometimes as high as *20l.* Goshawks seem, from some illustrated works in our possession, to be very popular in Japan, and to be flown chiefly at pheasants, cranes, and wild fowl. They are carried on the left hand, as in Europe, and appear to be rarely hooded, and usually taken from the nest.

We take from 'Falconry in the British Isles' the following description of the goshawk:—

The colour of the young goshawk differs considerably from that of the mature bird. During the first year the whole of the under portion of the body is of a rusty salmon-colour, marked with long lanceolate streaks of blackish brown, while the upper part is liver-brown, each feather being margined with reddish-white. At first the eyes are grey;[1] this colour gradually changes with age to lemon-yellow, and eventually becomes orange; the cere is waxen yellow, with tarsi and feet of a deeper tone. At the first change the whole of the under-plumage becomes light grey, striped transversely with narrow bars of a dark brown colour, the top of the head, back, wings and tail becoming of a uniform brown, with five distinct bars of a darker colour on the latter. There is also a

[1] In very old [illegible] the colour of the eyes changes to a deep fiery red. [illegible] hawks do not deteriorate [illegible] with age [illegible] three or four [illegible]

streak of light grey over each eye, speckled, as are the cheeks, with minute brown splashes. The bars on the breasts of the adult birds differ considerably in width in different individuals. The under tail coverts are pure white.

The sparrow-hawk, or 'spar-hawk' of our ancestors, is the commonest species that is used in hawking; it is familiar to everyone who knows anything at all of the ornithology of this country. Being a true or short-winged hawk, its training and management are almost identical with that described in the foregoing pages as suitable for the goshawk. But, as the sparrow-hawk is a more delicate bird, the severe discipline as to diet which is necessary for the goshawk cannot be resorted to in her case. They require a great deal of carrying, but must be well fed, as much as possible upon birds, and should be given a mouthful or two in the morning without any castings, as well as the usual meal at night. They are birds of a highly nervous organisation, and when first taken on hand will seem to be, and in fact are, so absolutely paralysed by terror as to lose all use of their legs. Nothing is to be done but to replace them on the fist as often as they fall off, and so steadily to inure them to being carried, and then to follow out the course of training as before described.

Although delicate and rather liable to fits, the sparrow-hawk is full of dash and courage, and has not so sulky a temper as that with which her larger congener is cursed. Instances of their dashing through windows to get at caged birds are so common as to be hardly worth recording, and during the present year a sparrow-hawk belonging to Mr. Riley took and held a pheasant nearly full-grown and three times her own weight. In fact, they are most sporting birds, and well worth training and using in a country which does not admit of the higher forms of falconry.

Sparrow-hawks can easily be flown at hack in the same manner as is prescribed for peregrines and merlins, but there is no advantage in doing this; birds brought up in a large room or loft will fly quite as well as those that are hacked.

Moreover, they can be well entered at birds while yet in the loft, and before they are taken in hand to train. The males and females must be kept in different lofts, or the former will probably be killed, and in any case they must all be highly fed. It will be found that one, or at most two, of these hawks will take up the whole of a man's time, and it is better for the falconer to restrict himself to one good bird than to attempt too much by trying to train several.

The female sparrow-hawk will take partridges—even full-grown ones—fairly well. In early September she will kill many. Formerly they were of no little account for killing landrails, which were far better for the table when thus killed than if they had been mangled with shot. The best sport to be had with them is at blackbirds and at thrushes in large old hedgerows, and this is really an excellent flight, requiring much skill and management. Two assistants are advisable, and, the hedge being beaten and a blackbird marked down into it, the falconer, hawk on hand, should make a détour, and having got well round the bird, should advance close to the bush where it is concealed, while the beaters, one on each side of the hedge, advance towards him. The blackbird is thus well between the two fires, and if the beater on the opposite side to the falconer is a little in advance of his fellow, and uses his stick well, the blackbird is certain to be forced away between the falconer and the advancing beater, and so affords a fair good chance in the open. Thrushes are more active and not so easy to take.

Sparrows and similar small birds may be taken by the male or 'musket,' but upon the whole he is not worth training. If the female be used for small birds, almost any number may be killed by her, but the sport is not very good—and if she is to fly blackbirds, she must be kept to them and not allowed to fly at easier quarry, or she will become slack-mettled. The late Sir Charles Slingsby—whose melancholy death by drowning (caused by the overturning of the Newby ferry-boat when he was crossing the river Ure during a run with his hounds) is fresh in the memory of all hunting-men—was an excellent falconer, and especially clever in the use of this little hawk. We have witnessed his skill on various occasions, but the only record we can find of his performances was a score of forty-seven blackbirds with one hawk in 1853. His friend, Mr Bower, was also exceedingly successful with these hawks, and (we quote from 'Falconry in the British Isles') in 1857 he killed 327 head between August 23 and October 20—mostly, however, sparrows. In 1858, with another hawk, he killed, in nineteen hawking days, 46 blackbirds, 36 thrushes, 17 partridges, 11 sparrows, and 1 starling—total, 111; the best day being 6 blackbirds, 3 thrushes, 2 partridges, and 1 sparrow. And in 1861 Mr. Bower killed 126 birds in twenty-seven days, with a young sparrow-hawk which was in flying order by July 27, the score being—68 blackbirds, 42 thrushes, 5 sparrows, 3 greenfinches, 7 partridges, 1 wood-pigeon, 1 sundry. He had an excellent hawk in 1865; but, though we witnessed some of its performances, we have no record of the result. But Mr. Bower was, no doubt, the best and cleverest hand with these delicate little hawks that has attempted to use them during the present century.

For a good many years after 1866 nothing much has been done with the sparrow-hawk, until about the year 1883, when Mr. Riley—whom we have mentioned above as having done very good work with goshawks—commenced also to fly sparrow-hawks in Herefordshire with great success. Commencing with a hawk which took 34 head in the first season in which he attempted the sport, he in the year 1887 killed with one hawk 51 blackbirds, 4 thrushes, 3 partridges, 1 pheasant, and 2 small birds—total, 61. Mr. Riley informs us that he only uses one beater, and that he frequently lets the hawk take her own stand in trees, and beats the hedge up to her. Mr. Bower's practice was always to have two assistants, and to so place himself that he could ensure the hawk a fair chance at the blackbird as it crossed the open; he never allowed the hawk to fly except from his hand, and he never let her go except when she had a chance to kill. Except when he had an inferior hawk, he was most careful never to allow them to take a small bird; but with one that was not good enough for blackbirds (and very many are not) he would kill as many sparrows, &c., as he pleased. Mr. Bower and Mr. Riley concur in using the

Sparrow-hawk on bow-perch

lure occasionally to call their hawk out of trees; but Mr. Bower's hawks would nearly always (unless half-fed) come to his hand with or without food, and this is the proper way to manage short-winged hawks.

Sparrow-hawks are rather delicate and very liable to fits; the best recipe to preserve them in health is to feed high, work hard, and protect them from cold draughts and damp. If fed high without work, they will probably have fits; but if worked too hard without condition to bear it, they will be sure to do so. They are best kept on the bow-perch, and indoors on the screen. They must be flown with very short jesses of rather stiff leather, for ordinary jesses are very apt to become entangled in hedges, &c., and when on the perch a short leash or strap, four inches long, should connect the ordinary leash with the swivel, so as to give them room to jump on the perch without recoiling on to their long tails, which are ever apt to suffer in confinement.

In conclusion, sparrow-hawks are the very best of all hawks for the beginner who lives in an enclosed country to try his hand at; they cost nothing to procure, and, if failure be the result, the loss is not great. If the beginner has the patience and perseverance to master the peculiar temperament he has to deal with, he may be sure that his further efforts in the art of falconry will be made infinitely easier to him by this experience; and, if he succeeds in training a good hawk, he may have a considerable amount of sport with her, as the preceding records will show.

# CHAPTER VI

CELEBRATED FALCONERS—SCOTCH, DUTCH, AND ENGLISH CLUBS—THE FALCONERS' CLUB—COLONEL THORNTON—THE LOO CLUB—THE OLD HAWKING CLUB—AMATEUR FALCONERS—FAMOUS HAWKS—RECORDS OF SPORT.

The histories of those individuals by whose skill and knowledge any sport, science, or art has been maintained will always be interesting to those who at a distance of time may follow in their footsteps. A few pages describing the men who in recent times have kept the art of Falconry not only alive, but have now and again fanned its glowing embers into a blaze, will no doubt prove of interest to the student of the sport.

For a history of the falconers of the last century we would refer our readers to the introduction to 'Falconry in the British Isles.' We will 'take up the running' from the point where that work has abandoned the task. Among the chief friends of John Anderson the great Scotch falconer, who was born in 1745 and died in 1833, was one Ballantyne, who was the steward at Lord Bute's residence, Dumfries House, in Ayrshire, and who had at one time acted as falconer to the Earl of Eglinton. Ballantyne, like his friend, loved a hawk, and his boy Peter was trained to carry one as soon as he could stand erect. Peter Ballantyne was born in 1798, and at the age of twenty was apprenticed to his father's old friend, John Anderson, who was at that time falconer to the Renfrewshire Subscription Hawks. Mr. Fleming was the manager of this club till his death, and the head-quarters of the hawks was at his seat, Barochan Castle. For some years after Mr. Fleming's death, Anderson and the hawks, with Ballantyne to assist him, continued at Barochan; but for the last two years of his professional life he was in the service of the Earl of Morton at Dalmahoy. It was during the time of Peter Ballantyne's apprenticeship to him that he visited London in a fancy dress of the period of James I., on the occasion of the coronation of George IV., in order to present to the king a cast of falcons on behalf of the Duke of Athol, who held the Isle of Man on that ancient feudal tenure. Very quaint indeed was Ballantyne's description of his master's appearance in this 'get up,' and the old picture at Barochan, which has been engraved (though impressions are scarce), fully justifies the language applied to it by Anderson himself.

After Anderson's retirement in 1832, Ballantyne entered the service of Lord Carmarthen under John Pells, senior, at Huntly Lodge, Aberdeenshire. Both passage hawks and eyesses were kept, and great sport was obtained both at herons and at game. The finest flight was that at the woodcock, which could then be obtained in perfection among the young plantations on Deeside. From Pells Ballantyne learned the Dutch method of training hawks, of making hoods, and of using the swivel and jesses in lieu of the old heavy varvels, and by combining both systems was able to become the successful falconer that, so far as game hawking is concerned, he undoubtedly was.

After leaving Lord Carmarthen's service Ballantyne entered that of Sir James Boswell, where he had charge of greyhounds as well as hawks. At Sir James's death he was employed by Mr. Ewen of Ewenfield, Ayr, and it was in that gentleman's service that he was most successful, and showed the great sport that is recorded in a previous chapter on game hawking. On Mr. Ewen's death he became falconer to Mr. Oswald of Auchincruive, in whose service he died in 1884, a falconer to the last, at the age of eighty-six.

Though he failed a little for the last year or two of his life, so lately as 1880 he was able to show good sport, and probably never flew a better hawk than the falcon 'Pearl,' which was then in fine form; but even at the time of his death he had one hawk in training, which died on the same day as himself.

A notable family of Scotch falconers have been the Barrs. William Barr, the father of the family, was by profession a game-keeper, but having been bred in the good days when a falcon or two was a necessary part of the appanage of a north-country gentleman, he had learned the rudiments of management, and acquired skill enough to train eyesses for game very successfully. His sons all learned the business with aptitude. William, the eldest, was a clever falconer with eyesses, and for some years made a living by exhibiting his trained hawks at racecourses and similar places, and flying them at pigeons—a description of hawking which cannot however be sufficiently condemned as being degrading to those who practise it, and a prostitution of what is essentially a genuine wild sport. William Barr emigrated to Australia in 1853, and is we believe still alive. Robert Barr, the third son, was trained under his elder brothers William and John, was for a time in the service of Captain Salvin and of the Maharajah Dhuleep Singh, and eventually became falconer to the Old Hawking Club. He remained in their service for about seven years, and then entered that of the Marquis of Bute, dying soon afterwards, in the year 1871.

John Barr, the second son, was, however, the falconer who will be best remembered of the whole family, probably also as the cleverest professional falconer of this century. John Barr may be said to have been the first of that school of falconers who have been able to combine all the different methods of the various countries where hawking is practised. Brought up under a Scotch falconer, he was from childhood familiar with the method of rearing and training eyesses. As a lad he travelled through Italy and Syria, with the Maharajah Dhuleep Singh, and associated regularly with the professional falconers of the East, observing their system and bringing his own energy and cleverness to bear upon it; while year after year he visited Holland to assist in the catching of hawks, and whatever the Dutchmen could teach him was at his disposal. A real lover of hawks, active and intelligent, it is no wonder that he more thoroughly fathomed the mysteries of catching, taming, and training a hawk than any man we have as yet met. There was no quarry that he had not flown at, no kind of hawking that was not familiar to him.

From 1857 to 1865 he was with the Maharajah, during which period he may be said to have trained every variety of hawk used in falconry, and to have taken every quarry that can be killed by means of hawks. After this he became head falconer to the Champagne Hawking Club, whose head-quarters were at the camp of Châlons. A good deal of sport was shown by Barr at rooks, herons, magpies, curlews, &c. In 1869 the club was broken up, but the hawks were kept on by the Comte de Aldama, and though Barr subsequently brought them over to England, he was still, we believe, in the Count's service. At that time he had several excellent hawks in training, some of whose performances have been referred to on page 286. In 1869 John Barr, with his nephew, James Barr, also a falconer, made a successful visit to Iceland to capture gerfalcons, which, mainly owing to John Barr's skill, resulted in his bringing home thirty-three, though he was, of course, a perfect stranger to the country, and probably had not at that time seen a wild gerfalcon. He was next engaged by Lord Bute to take the place of his brother Robert, who had recently died, but he only remained for a short time in his lordship's service, and after that he gave exhibitions of trained hawks at various places, chiefly the Welsh Harp at Hendon, after the fashion of his brother William. In 1872 he became head falconer to the Old Hawking Club, and showed very good sport on the Wilts downs. In 1873 he had an exceptionally good team of passage hawks, and we may remark that he was the only falconer we have seen who succeeded in taking peewits in the spring with a trained hawk. He was next engaged by Captain Dugmore, who organised the Falconry Club, to be described hereafter. At this time Barr had three under-falconers, and flew hawks in Ireland, on

Epsom Downs, in the grounds of the Jardîn d'Acclimatisation at Paris, and at the Alexandra Palace, near London. It was not, however, during this period that Barr's talents as a sportsman and a falconer had the best scope for their display. In the summer of 1876 he was sent by Captain Dugmore to Norway to catch gerfalcons. Here the old talent came out, for though unfamiliar with the country, he came back, after an absence of but eight or nine weeks, with ten fine falcons, and as many goshawks as he cared to bring. At catching a wild hawk or at recovering a lost bird Barr had no rival; he seemed to know instinctively where the hawk would be, and what she would be about at the time when it suited him to search for her, and somehow or other he generally came back with a hawk on his hand. In 1879 Barr entered the service of Mr. Evans, of Sawston, Cambridgeshire, and in 1880, after having successfully trained and flown some passage hawks at rooks in the spring of that year, he died at the age of thirty-nine. As skilful in the mews as he was in the field, and that is no light word, it will be many years before such another falconer is found to ensure success to the sport of which he was so ardent a lover.

With the Barrs and Ballantyne the ancient line of Scotch falconers seems to have died out, and though many an intelligent ghillie and keeper has shown an aptitude for the science, and, with the opportunities at their disposal, might soon have developed into falconers, yet, for the first time we believe in the history of sport, there is at the present time no Scotch falconer of note now practising the art.

The Scotch school was, as we have previously said, always the exponent of the management of eyesses and of game hawking. For many years, therefore, the Englishmen who cultivated the higher flights at the rook, the heron, and the kite, with passage hawks, were dependent upon the Dutch falconers for their servants. We are indebted to Professor Schlegel's 'Traité de Fauconnerie' for an account of the more celebrated of these clever trainers and managers of hawks.

Jan Daams, born at Valkenswaard in 1744, entered the service of Lord Orford about the year 1772.[1] After Lord Orford's death he was engaged by Colonel Wilson, at Didlington in Norfolk, and in 1808, while waiting at Cuxhaven for a passage to England after one of his annual voyages to Holland to procure hawks, was arrested by Louis Bonaparte, then king of that country, and was made to re-organise the mews at Het Loo, which had been abandoned since the departure of the Statholder William V. in 1795. There he stayed until King Louis's abdication in 1810, when he was summoned by Napoleon to take charge of the hawking establishment at Versailles. This was suppressed in 1813, when Daams returned to Valkenswaard, and died in 1829.

Frank van der Heuvell was born at Valkenswaard in 1766, and when very young was apprenticed to Frank Daams, nephew of Jan Daams. In 1780 he entered the service of the Elector of Hesse, where he remained till in 1785 he was engaged at Versailles under M. de Forgès, Lieutenant de Chasses to Louis XVI. In 1792 the royal establishment was suppressed, and he returned to Valkenswaard. Two years later he joined Colonel Thornton, with whom he stayed till 1799, when he was hired by Lord Middleton, and in 1804 entered the service of Sir Robert Lawley. Subsequently he engaged with Colonel Wilson from 1820 to 1828, when he went back to Valkenswaard. In 1840 he was taken on by the recently formed Loo Hawking Club, and he died in 1845.

Jan Peels, a pupil of Jan Daams, and with him at the time of his detention at Cuxhaven, was also a native of Valkenswaard. After making several voyages between Holland and England, he returned to the latter country in 1808 (when his master was carried off), and was engaged by Sir John Sebright and others. About 1814 he entered Colonel Wilson's service, and was sent for heron hawks to Holland. He returned to England in 1815 with Jan Lambert Daankers (who had

[1] See also 'Hawking in Norfolk,' Appendix to Mr. Southwell's edition of Lubbock's *Fauna in Norfolk*.

been his fellow-pupil under Jan Daams, and died in 1816), and continued to make annual trips till 1827, being for part of that time in the service of Mr. Downes of Gunton (see Sebright, 'On Hawking'). He was subsequently enagaged by Lord Carmarthen, afterwards Duke of Leeds, and then by the Duke of St. Albans, in whose service he died in 1838.

JAN BOTS, a pupil of Daankers, first came to England as an assistant to Frank van der Heuvell in 1821. From 1828 to 1838 he was regularly at Didlington, but on the death of Lord Berners he went to Baron Offemont in France. In 1840 he was engaged by the Loo Hawking Club, and continued in its service until 1852, making in that time one expedition or more to Norway to take gerfalcons.

ARNOLD BOTS, brother of the preceding, accompanied him on his voyages to England from 1829, and was also one of the falconers to the Loo Club.

JAMES BOTS, a third brother, was also in his youth employed at Didlington, and he subsequently entered the service of Colonel Hall at Weston Colville. He then returned to Holland, and was employed by the Loo Club. He established himself at Valkenswaard, where he kept the Valken Inn. He occasionally visited England, and died about the year 1869.

John, the elder son of Jan Peels, was born in England, and adopted the English form of surname, Pells. He succeeded his father in the service of the Hereditary Grand Falconer of England, the Duke of St. Albans. When the present Duke gave up all active participation in the sport of hawking, Pells was pensioned off, and continued to train and fly hawks at Lakenheath, in Suffolk. In 1845 he made an excursion to Iceland, to procure gerfalcons, and brought home fifteen, eight of which were trained at Loo. He was an excellent falconer, well known to many of the present generation, and always ready to impart his knowledge to beginners. He died in 1883.

ADRIAN MOLLEN—almost the last of the old Dutch falconers—was a native of Valkenswaard, and a pupil of Jan

Bots, when in Lord Berners's employ from 1833 to 1836. In 1837 he entered the service of Prince Trautmansdorff, near Vienna, when he trained hawks, principally for game and for the flight at the thick-kneed plover. During his stay he procured from Hungary a nest of young sacres, two tiercels, and a falcon, which he trained for game. Occasionally, but rarely, he saw a wild sacre when flying his hawks. In 1841 he returned to Holland, and became head falconer to the king, flying his hawks at Loo and working with the falconer employed by the Loo Hawking Club. After the abandonment of the annual hawking at Loo, Mollen returned to Valkenswaard, and since then, aided by his two sons, has annually caught, and in many cases trained, what passage hawks are required by English or other sportsmen. Of his skill and ability all falconers are aware.

Paul Mollen, brother of the last mentioned, was under Adrian Mollen when he was at Loo. After the breaking up of the king's stud of hawks he obtained employment at the Zoological Gardens at Antwerp. About the year 1860 he was engaged as falconer and attendant on his aviaries by Lord Lilford. A few years ago he retired, and lives at Oundle in Northamptonshire.

This closes the list of a race of falconers which Sir John Sebright well describes as 'sober, industrious men,' as well as clever and patient trainers of hawks. To their skill and care the art of modern falconry owes much, and it is to be regretted that men of this stamp have almost ceased to exist.

We have treated above of Scotch falconers and of Dutch falconers—both masters of the art—practising in England under English masters; but as yet we have named no English falconer. Singularly enough, from the days of Colonel Thornton up to the time of the present generation no Englishman professionally has attained eminence in the science of falconry. In Colonel Thornton's 'Northern Tour' (1804), his chief factotum seems to have been 'William Lawson, Head falconer and Inspector-general,' and from the Colonel's account he seems

to have been an old and highly valued servant. We believe he was an Englishman. But we have to pass from that date to 1870 before we again find an Englishman similarly well qualified and in a position equally of trust, in the person of John Frost, head-falconer to the Old Hawking Club. Being the son of a keeper to Mr. Newcome, of Feltwell, Norfolk, Frost was brought up from childhood among hawks, and had the opportunity of learning the intricacies of the art, not only from Mr. Newcome himself, but from Robert Barr (to whom he acted as under-falconer at one time), and John Pells, who lived at Lakenheath, hard by. In 1872 the present writer engaged him for the Old Hawking Club as under-falconer to John Barr, and in 1873 he was promoted to the post of head-falconer, which he filled to the year 1890. During that time he annually visited Holland to train the freshly-caught hawks of the Club, and under Mollen and his assistants had the opportunity to master the Dutch school of falconry, just as his education under the Barrs started him with an acquaintance with Scotch methods. Those who have seen the sport shown by the Club hawks when under his charge on Salisbury Plain and Yorkshire, in Kildare, Cork, and Wexford, in Sutherland and Caithness, will know that the art of falconry had in him an able English exponent. His death, at the early age of thirty-six, occurred in September 1890, at Langwell in Caithness, where he was engaged in flying his hawks on the moors of the Duke of Portland, one of his employers. Those only who have participated in the sport shown by the hawks under his care will realise what a loss the ancient science of falconry has sustained by the death of one so capable of demonstrating its practice both in the field and in the mews.

Even in the last few weeks of his life he had the greatest success in the difficult sport of grouse hawking, killing, although in failing health, ninety-six grouse between August 12 and September 6 with four hawks only. He lies buried at Berriedale.

It is not too much to say that, with the exception of John Barr, Frost has had no rival as an 'all-round' falconer during the present century, and it is hard to say what perfection the sport, as adapted to modern times and modern methods, might not have attained under his intelligent care and unfailing keenness. As a first-rate sportsman he excelled, and with dog, gun, or hawk was equally good. With an education and an intelligence not commonly met with in persons of his station, he was not only an admirable servant, but an interesting companion, clever at all sports, and as such, and as a friend, he will be most regretted by all those who knew him best. Fortunately Frost was not the only English professional falconer; his brother, Alfred Frost (in the service of Mr. T. J. Mann), George Oxer (formerly falconer to Mr. St. Quintin), now in the service of the Old Hawking Club, both trained under John Frost, are as able to train and fly hawks as either Dutchmen or Scotchmen of fifty years ago. James Retford, falconer to Major Hawkins Fisher, is a pupil of John Pells the younger, and is an able falconer, as also is Cosgrave, now falconer to Lord Lilford, and Peter Gibbs, falconer to the Hon. C. W. Mills, M.P.; and E. Dwyer, in the service of Major Bingham Crabbe. But with this short list our account of living professional falconers must close, though other men beside these no doubt exist, well able to train and fly a hawk to the satisfaction of their employers.

Like many other sports hawking has, especially of late years, been most successfully carried on by means of clubs, or establishments maintained by joint subscriptions. One of the first of these institutions was the Renfrewshire Subscription Hawks, to which John Anderson was falconer, and which had its headquarters at Barochan Castle, the seat of Mr. Fleming, who seems to have been the master of the hawks until his death about 1812. After that event the hawks seem to have remained at Barochan for many years with Anderson still as falconer, and Sir John Maxwell of Pollock as master. They would appear to have been given up about 1830.

A larger and more ambitious establishment was maintained at about the same date under the management of Colonel Thornton, and is described by him in his 'Northern Tour' by the name of the 'Confederate Hawks of Great Britain;' but it was more generally known by the name of the Falconers' Club. Lord Orford was the president of the club, and apparently its manager, both before and after the reign of Colonel Thornton. The date of the formation of this club is not certain, but it would seem to have been started in 1770 or thereabouts, and to have been maintained on a high scale, chiefly for kite and heron hawking. The falconers were almost entirely Dutchmen, and the hawks used passage hawks. From the chapter on Hawking in Norfolk, in Stevenson's 'Birds of Norfolk,' we take the following ancient advertisement, which gives a good idea of the transactions of the club:—

Swaffham: February 5, 1783.

HAWKING.

EARL OF ORFORD, MANAGER OF THIS YEAR.

The gentlemen of the Falconers' Society are hereby acquainted that the hawks will be in England the first week in March, and will begin kite and crow hawking immediately on their arrival. The quarters are fixed at Bourn Bridge, Cambridgeshire, forty-eight miles from London, until the first April meeting, when they will go to Barton Mills and Brandon until the 31st May, when the season will finish.

The hawks to be out every Saturday, Monday, and Wednesday in each week at ten o'clock, provided the weather is favourable.

Subscribers are desired to pay in their subscriptions for this season on or before the 20th March, to Messrs. Coutts & Co., Bankers, in the Strand, London.

N.B.—The cage consists of 32 Slight falcons, 13 German hawks, and 7 Iceland falcons.

The 'German hawks' were probably goshawks, but the number of these birds seems very large. 'Slight' falcon was a term often used for the peregrine at that date. Colonel Thornton appears to have taken the management of this club in 1772, and to have resigned it in 1781, when Lord Orford took his place. In that year a handsome piece of plate in the form of a silver-gilt urn, with a hawk killing a hare, well modelled on the top thereof, was presented to the Colonel by the club. (This urn was exhibited in 1889 at the 'Sports and Arts' exhibition at the Grosvenor Gallery by the present Lord Orford, who purchased it from a descendant of Colonel Thornton.) The inscription on the urn, and the list of names which is engraved on it, are interesting as recording something of the progress of the chief hawking establishment of a hundred years ago, and the names of those who patronised the sport at that date. The inscription runs as follows :—

Col. Thornton, the proposer and manager of the Confederate Hawks, is requested to receive this piece of plate from George, Earl of Orford, together with the united thanks of the members of the Falconers' Club, as a testimony of their esteem and just sense of his assiduity, and of the unparalleled excellence to which, in the course of nine years, he has brought them, and when unable to attend to them any longer, he made them a present to the Earl of Orford. Barton Mills, June 23rd, 1781.

MEMBERS OF THE CLUB

Earl of Orford
Mr. Sturt
Mr. Snow
Mr. Smith
Mr. Stephens
Earl Ferrers
Hon. Thos. Shirley
Sir John Tancred
Mr. A. Wilkinson
Mr. B. Wrightson
Mr. Drummond
Sir Cornwallis Maud
Duke of Ancaster
Mr. Williamson
Mr. Baker
Mr. W. Baker
Mr. Pierse
Mr. Chaplin
Mr. Vaughan
Mr. R Wilson
Mr. Musters
Mr. Barrington Price
Mr. Daniel
Hon. W. Rowley
Lord Mulgrave
Mr. E. Parsons
Captain Grimstone
Captain Yarburgh
Earl of Leicester
Mr. Stanhope
Mr. Leighton
Mr. Francis Barnard
Mr. Nelthorpe
Mr. Potter
Col. St. Leger
Mr. Serle

MEMBERS OF THE CLUB—*continued*

| | |
|---|---|
| Mr. Coke | Mr. Parkhurst |
| Duke of Rutland | Mr. Molineux |
| Duke of Bedford | Earl of Surrey |
| Mr. Lascelles Lascelles | Sir William Milner |
| Mr. Parker | Sir John Ramsden |
| Mr. Tyssen | Mr. Royds |
| Mr. Molloy | Sir Richard Simonds |
| Mr. Affleck | Earl of Lincoln |
| Mr. St. George | Marquis of Graham |
| Earl of Eglinton | Mr. Parsons |

Lord Orford remained manager of the Falconers' Club till his death in 1792. After his death the control of the establishment passed into the hands of Colonel Wilson of Didlington, who subsequently became Lord Berners. The hawks were kept at High Ash, near Didlington, but as kites became very scarce the heron was the chief quarry. The club seems to have been carried on and the hawks maintained, to some extent at any rate, by subscription up to the date of Lord Berners's death in 1838. Several sketches were made by Sir E. Landseer of the hawks at Didlington, one of which, with the date, 'Didlington, June 30, 1831,' is in the author's possession.

Previously to Lord Berners's death herons had become comparatively scarce at Didlington, and what was of even more importance, the ground over which hawks could be followed had become very circumscribed, owing to the breaking up of the heath land and bringing it under the plough. Hence it occurred to the members of the club that they might find better sport further a-field, and instead of bringing their hawks from Holland over to England to fly at a quarry becoming more and more scarce, they might go over to Holland to their hawks, and in that country turn them to better advantage. A prospecting party was formed of Mr. Stuart Wortley and the Baron d'Offemont, with the result that in 1839 the Loo Hawking Club was formed. Mr. E. C. Newcome, of Feltwell, who had for several years been the backbone in the field of the English Club, became secretary of the new Anglo-Dutch institution. In 1839 he appears on the list of the club as its solitary member, but in 1840 a goodly number of members was enrolled, and at their head were the Prince of Orange, with the Princes Alexander, Frederick, and Henry of the Netherlands—of Englishmen, the Duke of Leeds, Rev. W. Newcome, Mr. Jerningham, Lord C. Hamilton, Lord Suffield, Mr. E. Green, Mr. J. Balfour, and Mr. Knight were early members—and thus the Hawking Club was established at the Loo under the protection of his Majesty King William II., and under the presidency of his Royal Highness Prince Alexander of the Netherlands.

With the establishment of the Loo Hawking Club there came to an end the old Falconers' Club of England, which for some sixty-six years had maintained the sport with no little success and prestige. It had carried on the art of falconry from the days when the kite and bustard were quarry readily found on our wolds or warrens, till the heron was the only flight left of those which were deemed most worthy of pursuit. But from its ashes a worthy successor had arisen, and the Loo Club was destined to carry the sport to a pitch of excellence never before achieved. The establishment of the club consisted as a rule of twenty-two falcons, that of the king twenty-two more with their attendants, and with such a staff success became merely a question of opportunity. The sport that was shown has been related in the chapter on heron-hawking, to which branch of falconry the club solely confined its operations. In the eight seasons during which it lasted nearly 1,500 herons were taken by hawks, and never has hawking been managed so skilfully or on so princely a scale. Of the hawks that were most successful the best were a falcon called 'Bull-Dog,' which had the character of rarely needing to make more than three stoops at any heron. Mr. Newcome used to speak of this falcon as the best heron hawk he had ever met with. Next to her came a famous cast of falcons, 'Sultan' and 'De Ruyter,' which after their first season as club hawks became Mr. Newcome's own property. This cast of hawks, always flown together, took in 1843 fifty-four, and in 1844 fifty-seven herons, besides many rooks in England. 'De Ruyter' was ultimately lost at Feltwell while rook hawking, but 'Sultan' adorns the splendid collection of stuffed birds which Mr. Newcome formed at Hockwold, set up as his hands alone could do it. Besides these a ger-tiercel called 'Morock' was noteworthy.

Among the Englishmen who were members of the club we find, besides the names already quoted, those of Mr. Stirling Crawford, Lord Alvanley, Lord Chesterfield, Mr. Thornhill, Mr. Fred. Milbank, Lord Strathmore, Hon. C. Maynard, Hon. C. L. Fox, and Hon. C. Fitzwilliam. In 1853 the club came to an end; the royal patronage was withdrawn, and its head-quarters at Loo ceased. For the next ten years after that date the maintenance of falconry in England was due chiefly to the efforts of Mr. Newcome, who, himself the ablest and most skilful amateur falconer of the present century, was ever ready to assist beginners or to further the sport of those who were already entered to the sport. Few of the mature falconers of the present day do not owe something of their success to his kindly assistance and advice, or to his experience, which was ever at their disposal. During this period Mr. Newcome, who could not always procure passage hawks from Holland, succeeded in taking herons on the passage with one or two eyess falcons, a feat never before achieved, but possibly never attempted, nor perhaps one of special difficulty, since a really good eyess is as good as the average passage hawk, but it is necessary to train and to discard many before one sufficiently good is obtained. At this time also Mr. Newcome practised game hawking—of which, however, he was never very fond—and was also very successful with merlins at lark hawking, which sport he ranked next to the flight at the heron.

In 1863 the Hon. C. Duncombe, with Robert Barr as his falconer, commenced rook hawking on Salisbury Plain, conjointly with Major Fisher; and the year following, finding that the management of the hawks, which was left on his hands, was more than he could attend to, a club was organised which grew and prospered as the present Old Hawking Club. The original members in 1864 were:

| | |
|---|---|
| The Hon. C. Duncombe | Mr. E. C. Newcome |
| Lord Lilford | Mr. Amherst |
| The Maharajah Dhuleep Singh | Col. Brooksbank |
| | A. E. Knox, Esq. |

Robert Barr continued as falconer, and the chief sport of the club was then, as now, shown on the Wilts downs in March and April, rook hawking. A little heron hawking was done in Norfolk in May after the hawks returned thither each year, and some good work was done at grouse, chiefly in Perthshire on moors taken by the Maharajah Dhuleep Singh. In 1871 falconry in England sustained a severe blow by the death of Mr. Newcome at the comparatively early age of sixty, and under that shock and other difficulties, the fortunes of the club for a brief while were at a low ebb. But in 1872 it was reorganised on a rather larger basis. The Wiltshire downs were again visited, and in that autumn a peculiarly fine team of passage hawks was got together. John Barr had been engaged as falconer, and the present writer succeeded Mr. Newcome as secretary and manager. The area of operations became somewhat extended. A first-class team of hawks, eyesses, and passage hawks has ever since 1872 been maintained, suitable for every description of hawking. The annual two months' visit to the Wiltshire downs has been kept up as the leading feature of the club's sport; and the great kindness and liberality of a large body of owners and occupiers of land on the open downs of Salisbury Plain has enabled the club to establish itself on a tract of country wide enough to show sport every day without doing damage to anyone. Besides this, the hawks and their falconer are at the disposal of any member of the club who desires to use them during any part of the year, and thus the green jackets of the members and their servants have become well known in Kildare, in Wexford and in Cork, in Sutherlandshire and Caithness, in Yorkshire and in Hants, in fact wherever hawking could be carried on in the United Kingdom, while it is only the lack of time and leisure that has prevented them from carrying the sport yet further afield in response to numerous invitations. Of the sport which has been shown we have treated to some extent under the various heads of game and rook hawking. The total number of head of quarry killed of all sorts is very large, but perhaps the return of the year 1887 may serve as a specimen of the sport carried on by the club; it was as follows:—

| | |
|---|---|
| Rooks | 209 |
| Magpies | 13 |
| Grouse | 95 |
| Black game | 2 |
| Partridges | 114 |
| Rabbits | 112 |
| Pheasants | 5 |
| Hare | 1 |
| Various | 25 |
| | 576 |

During the year 1890 244 rooks were killed in the spring and 95 grouse between August 12 and September 6, when game hawking came to an end temporarily, owing to the death of the falconer, John Frost.

During the period of its existence the club has owned many hawks of marked excellence. One of the first that is worthy of mention was an eyess tiercel called 'Druid,' trained in 1864, which, after a visit to Ireland and being entered to magpies, was flown regularly at rooks for some three seasons on Salisbury Plain, as we have already stated when treating of rook hawking.' We have not known an eyess tiercel to repeat this feat since the days of 'Druid,' though in recent times Mr. St. Quintin has trained and flown one or two at gulls that would in our opinion have been equal to any performance that a tiercel is capable of.

In 1872, among others of a remarkably good team of hawks one falcon called 'Empress' was trained, and for general excellence has hardly been surpassed. Her record of 63 rooks in one season has not yet been beaten. She was flown for three seasons, and died from an accident. In 1876—a remarkably stormy spring—a passage hawk called 'Bois-le-duc,' from the name of the place where the hut at which she was taken is located, formed part of the consignment sent to the club. Probably this falcon is the best that has been trained since the days of the famous 'Bull Dog' of the Loo Club. Troublesome at first to enter, when once she took to rooks she killed no less than 60, missing but one flight. It seemed impossible to give her slips that were too long or for a gale to blow strong enough to stop her, and the magnificent style of her flying and stooping left nothing to be desired. She was flown for five seasons, in three of which she made the highest score of rooks killed against any of the other hawks, and eventually was given away as a pet. Another excellent servant was the falcon 'Elsa.' This falcon is especially remarkable for her excellence at all sorts of quarry. A passage falcon trained in 1886, she killed by far the highest score of rooks in her first three seasons, and was not far behind the best in 1889 and 1890. While in her second season she was entered to grouse, and has each year since then proved herself to be one of the most perfect game hawks that it is possible to fly, steady, tractable, and as high a mounter as can be procured. In the spring of 1890 she killed 35 rooks, and in the autumn 31 grouse, nor does the flight at the one appear to interfere in the least with her keenness to take to the other quarry when the time comes. In all 186 rooks and 123 grouse have been killed by this falcon, besides many sundries. 'Elsa' was lost at Langwell in the autumn of 1891.

'Vesta,' an eyess falcon from Culvercliff, Isle of Wight, has been spoken of when describing game hawking. As a grouse hawk she is nearly perfect for killing, but lacks a little of the perfect style of the passage hawks with which she has been generally flown. This falcon was flown chiefly at grouse (though a great number of sundries were killed by her, as well as partridges in one or two years). For nine successive seasons she visited Scotland, and her average score for each season is 33. She died in the winter of 1890.

The remarkable score made in 1882 by an eyess falcon, 'Parachute,' is recorded when treating of game hawking in Chapter II. This was a very steady high-mounting tractable falcon, easily worked, and thus very deadly. She was in 1882 two years old. Nor must the ger-tiercel 'Adrian,' trained in 1878, be forgotten when speaking of hawks perfect in style.

Of tiercels two very good passage hawks were trained in 1873, 'The Earl' and 'The Doctor.' These tiercels were the only two trained hawks with which we have succeeded in taking wild peewits in March. Many excellent magpie and partridge hawks have been trained, among which 'Cabra' and 'Meteor' will long be recollected by members of the club. 'Shamrock' and 'Shillelagh,' two Irish tiercels (eyesses), were flown in the autumn of 1873, in Kildare and Wexford chiefly. These two formed an almost perfect cast of magpie hawks, and with them the smallest field could kill a magpie. It was beautiful to see how perfectly the two little hawks understood the whole game, and to watch how they divided the labour, one always mounting high and remaining steady at a lofty pitch, so as to dominate the magpie and command every point by which he could escape, while the other at a lower pitch would drive at the quarry every moment that the white wing fluttered, and either drive him below the fatal pitch of his comrade or else seize him for himself. These tactics never failed, and the two hawks rarely omitted to adopt them, and would exchange *rôles* as often as flights were found for them. A year or two afterwards a cast of tiercels, 'Buccaneer' and 'Meteor,' killed in thirteen days 44 magpies on similar ground. Such performances as these have no doubt been equalled over and over again by hawks belonging to private individuals.[1] They are set down here simply as a record of what has been done with hawks within our own knowledge, and in order to prove what can be done in the way of modern falconry by anyone who will devote that time and care to it which is necessary for the attainment of excellence in any kind of sport.

The members of the Old Hawking Club in 1890 were as follows :—

| | |
|---|---|
| Lord Lilford | Duke of St. Albans |
| Mr. F. Newcome | Duke of Portland |
| Rev. W. Newcome | Hon. E. W. B. Portman |
| Mr. W. H. St. Quintin | Col. Watson |
| Earl of Londesborough | Mr. A. Newall |
| Mr. B. H. Jones | Hon. G. Lascelles, *Manager and Secretary.* |

HONORARY MEMBERS

| | |
|---|---|
| Hon. Cecil Duncombe | Col. Brooksbank |
| Hon. G. R. C. Hill | Mr. F. H. Salvin |

The objects of the club have ever been to promote falconry, first, by keeping up a first-class establishment of hawks for every description of hawking ; secondly, to train young men and boys as falconers under an able man ; and, thirdly, by every year getting a fresh lot of hawks and by drafting out at the end of each season all but a few favourites of very high class, to keep up the supply of well-trained hawks available for the public. In this way many beginners have been assisted when first taking up falconry, by obtaining a perfectly trained hawk at about her original cost price, and even if they have found that an edu-

[1] In 1883 a remarkable tiercel called 'Destiny' was caught at Valkenswaard and trained by George Oxer for Mr. St. Quintin. He was flown regularly for seven seasons, and was one of the most beautiful fliers that we have ever witnessed. During his career he killed 88 partridges, 40 magpies, 64 sea-gulls (assisted by a second tiercel), and 30 'sundries,' which include grouse, blackbirds, pheasants, curlew, landrails, rooks, &c. This is an apt illustration of the amount of fine sport which can be obtained by means of one good hawk if in proper hands and well cared for.

cated hawk is not as easy to handle as a barrel-organ, still they have been able to make a better start than by those crude efforts at 'training a hawk for themselves' which result in the death of the subject to be trained and the hopeless disappointment of the trainer.

A club on rather similar lines was started in France in 1866 under the title of the 'Champagne Hawking Club,' with M. Alfred Werle as president, other members being M. Pierre Pichot, Comte de Montebello, Vicomte de Grandmaison, Comte Alphonse de Aldama, Count le Couteulx de Canteleu, &c. John Barr was head falconer, and the country mainly resorted to was in the plains near Châlons. A large establishment was kept up, and a sincere desire was shown to follow the best traditions of falconry; but in 1869, owing to various circumstances, the club came to an end, though the establishment was maintained for a year or so longer by the Comte de Aldama. But the good which the club did in reviving falconry in France may be traced by the existence in that country of more than one excellent and able falconer who might perhaps never have taken to the sport had it not been for the fillip administered at a critical moment by the organisation of so good an establishment as that of the Champagne Club.

In 1878 an English club was promoted on an ambitious scale by Captain F. S. Dugmore under the title of the Falconry Club. The head-quarters of the club were fixed at the Alexandra Palace, Muswell Hill, near London, where the hawks, sometimes forty in number, were kept on view and were occasionally flown to the lure or at bagged pigeons for the public amusement. Branches were proposed to be established in France, Ireland, Spain, Holland and Belgium; four or five falconers were engaged, and a large number of hawks of all kinds ordered and procured. The scale of operations was so large as to be unwieldy, and the method of carrying out the scheme did not prove successful. A certain amount of sport was shown at rooks on the Epsom Downs under the management of Mr. J. E. Harting, who acted as secretary and devoted much trouble and time to the perfecting of the arrangements, but after a brief period of life the club was broken up and the establishment scattered.

Besides clubs, there are various private establishments in the United Kingdom, as well as many amateurs who keep a few hawks which they manage themselves, in some cases, with marked ability, and show very great sport on a small scale.

A private mews has for very many years been kept up by Lord Lilford, whose falconer was, as stated previously, Paul Mollen, and subsequently Ed. Cosgrave. Falcons have been successfully taken on the passage in the autumn as they migrate over Northamptonshire, and indeed we believe the hut placed there has rarely failed to secure one or two when the attempt has been made in earnest. Although the country about Lilford is not particularly well suited for the sport, Lord Lilford stands high as one of our oldest and ablest falconers, and the ancient sport owes no less in these modern times to his munificence and energetic support than it did in the days of a former generation to the support of Lord Orford or Berners. It is not too much to say that the maintenance of falconry of the higher class in England during the last hundred years is due to the three noblemen named above, together with Mr. E. C. Newcome. At the present day the sport is wider spread; fresh enthusiasts spring up from year to year, and falconry no longer depends, as for so many years it did, upon the maintenance of one single establishment which in its turn was dependent on the liberalities of its principal patron.

Among amateur falconers Mr. W. H. St. Quintin, of Scampston Hall, Yorks, has been very prominent. He has had special success both in game hawking and in the flight at seagulls, and is seldom without a cast or two of tiercels of superior excellence. For many years his falconer was George Oxer, formerly under-falconer to the Old Hawking Club, who has now returned to that establishment as head falconer, his place being taken by young Charles Frost.

Major Fisher's establishment is one of the oldest now in England. He has principally devoted himself to game hawking, especially at grouse, but has annually visited the downs in the spring for a brief season at rooks. For the first years of his hawking career Major Fisher chiefly confined himself to eyesses, of which he trained some very superior hawks, especially those taken from Lundy Island. But of late years he has adopted the passage falcon for game as well as for other flights, although his original predilections were in favour of eyesses alone for this flight; and we have the Major's authority for saying that he has found the passage hawk as superior for game as he had already proved her to be at other quarry, especially in the case of a famous falcon called 'Lady Jane Grey,' which he has flown for some eight seasons. His falconer for many years past has been James Retford.

Another well-known establishment is that of Mr. T. J. Mann, of Hyde Hall, Sawbridgeworth, who with Alfred Frost for his falconer has had much sport in Norfolk and Herts both with peregrines at rooks and game, and with a famous goshawk known as 'The Shadow of Death.'

Colonel Watson and Mr. Bingham Crabbe have also a joint mews in Ireland, with E. Dwyer as falconer, now located in Ireland. And in that country lives also a veteran falconer, Mr. W. Corbet, of Rathcormack, Cork, to whom many a beginner is indebted for assistance. Mr. Corbet had a fine acquaintance with the numerous eyries of Ireland, and in some years reared and hacked a great number of hawks, which were often at the disposal of those to whom he thought they would be of good service.

The Hon. C. W. Mills has also a mews of hawks at Mulgrave Castle, Yorks, under the charge of Peter Gibbs, but the principal work done hitherto has been with the goshawk at rabbits.

Besides these gentlemen, many amateurs as stated above train their own hawks, among whom may be quoted the veteran Mr. F. Salvin, one of the authors of 'Falconry in the

British Isles,' Mr. A. Newall, Major Anne, and Mr. E. Riley, whose successes with the short-winged hawks have already been referred to. Nor is the church ill-represented among the ranks of falconers, for the successes of the Rev. W. Willimott in the difficult branch of gull hawking have been mentioned when describing that sport, while all readers of the 'Field' are familiar with the writings of the Rev. G. E. Freeman, under the nom-de-guerre of 'Peregrine,' dealing chiefly with game hawking with eyesses, and with the training of merlins.

Even this brief list of the better-known amateurs will show that English hawking is in no moribund condition. Very rarely does a sportsman who has once taken it up abandon it during his life, and though from the nature of the sport, and of the country requisite for it, it can never become generally popular, we believe that as it is already the most ancient, so it will continue to be one of the most enduring of the field sports in which mankind takes delight.

# CHAPTER VII

GENERAL MANAGEMENT — MEWS—BLOCKS — PERCHES — BOW-PERCH — BATHING — CONDITION — FEEDING — CASTINGS — IMPING—MOULTING—VARIOUS DISEASES—GENERAL HINTS.

THE first consideration of a falconer will naturally be to provide himself with a 'mews,' or place to keep his hawks in. Almost any stable or loose box will do for this, and elaborate buildings are rather to be shunned. The requirements are: first, that it be well ventilated, but quite free from draughts; second, that it can be made dark at any time. The best mode of ventilating is what is known as a 'Tobin' tube, by which plenty of air is admitted without either light or draught, combined with a ventilator in the roof which can be closed. When the place is made dark, hawks will remain still, and can be left for the night without any fear of their jumping or fidgetting during the early morning hours. The 'mews' should be kept as dry as possible, and for this purpose one of the little slow-combustion stoves known as a 'Tortoise' stove is exceedingly useful, and, though anything like coddling hawks is undesirable, still it is a good plan when they are getting no exercise at all to give them a little extra warmth, and the stove keeps the whole place dry. The perch may be arranged in the mews just as is most convenient to the shape of the building; a very good plan is place it round the house, parallel with the walls, and not less than three feet from them. It should be four feet high, and is best made of a rough larch pole with the bark on it. In any case it must not be too smooth, lest the hawks slip off it.[1] On the under-side of the perch is nailed a piece of stout canvas, (whence it is often called the screen). This is best nailed firmly along the pole, with the use of leather washers to prevent the canvas from tearing at the nail-holes. At intervals of about eighteen inches can be worked large eyelet holes, through which the leashes can be passed, so as to tie round the perch. If it is preferred, the nails can be put in at intervals of about eight inches, so as to allow the leash to be passed between the canvas and the perch; but by the first-named plan the canvas will last twice as long. The object of the screen is, first, to make sure that a hawk that has bated off the perch will certainly attempt to regain her position on the same side that she came off from, and so will not get her jesses twisted round the pole; secondly, it enables a hawk that is not very active, to struggle to the perch again by getting a hold with her claws in the canvas. This perch is in universal use indoors and is perfect for passage peregrines, merlins, or the short-winged hawks; but eyess peregrines, being less active, cannot safely be placed on the perch at first, though most of them will gradually become used to it. A sick hawk should never be placed on any perch from which it can possibly be hung.

A bed of sand, three inches thick, should be placed below the perch, and that part which is foul must be removed every morning. If sand is not procurable, sawdust can be used; but in that case great care must be taken lest any of it find its way on to the hawk's food, especially if it be deal sawdust, which contains turpentine.

In fine weather hawks must be kept in the open air as much as possible, and every day, before they are flown, should be placed out at least for an hour or two to 'weather.' If put out for this purpose by seven o'clock in the morning they should be well weathered and ready to fly by eleven o'clock at latest, and

[1] If a padded perch is required, the best and most durable method is to cover the pole with Brussels carpet turned the reverse side out; it will be found to answer every purpose and to come cheap in the end.

those which are so inclined will have bathed and got thoroughly dry; but when hawks are being flown every day, and perhaps late in the day, they cannot be so fed as to be ready early the next morning, and therefore, when the same lot of hawks are being daily used, the sport must take place in the afternoon for the most part.

The blocks on which hawks are kept in a garden or on a lawn are made in different ways, but the best pattern is the simplest and the cheapest of all. Take a plain simple log of wood with the bark upon it, saw into lengths fourteen inches long and six inches in diameter; drive into the base thereof an iron spike ten inches long, the end of which is then sharpened so as to be driven into the ground and thus hold the block firmly. Into the centre of the top drive an iron staple, to which the leash is to be tied, and for a few pence a block is produced that cannot be surpassed for all practical purposes. Hardwood of any kind is the best, for fir decays, loses its bark, and rots from the staple, which may thus wax loose. Birch with the bark on it makes a very neat, pretty-looking block, and a very durable one; while holly, if it can be obtained of large enough size, is almost imperishable and very neat. Both blocks and perches have been devised of various and more or less complicated forms. Blocks which revolve and blocks which do not; with fixed staples and with revolving rings (which have been known to break, and which invariably jam). Blocks of the shape of wine-glasses on stems, of wine-glasses without stems, and of wine-glasses upside down, are all recommended by their various inventors; but the only advantages we could ever see in them are those which are obtained by the turner and the carpenter, who are able to charge roundly for their manufacture!

Short-winged hawks, and also merlins, are better kept on the bow-perch which is figured on p. 323. This is best made of a simple piece of hazel or ash, shaved on the lower side to make it bend readily, and kept in its position by a stout piece of iron wire bent round the bow and securely fastened. The ends of the bow should be shod with iron, so as to be driven into the ground, and a stout iron pin, at least ten inches long, must be run on to the wire and driven into the ground in the centre of the perch as an extra safeguard. A ring, large enough to run over the perch with *perfect* freedom, is put on to the bow before the wire is made fast, and to this the hawk's leash is tied. So long as this ring is large enough to run freely there is no fear of the hawk ever becoming fast or hung up in any way.

An iron perch similar to the bow-perch, and figured on p. 353, has been invented by Capt. Salvin. In this perch a small space for the hawk to sit upon is padded with leather. It is a very useful handy perch for travelling, and answers well, but for permanent use at home the old wooden bow is a more natural and comfortable resting-place for a hawk. A canvas screen is sometimes fitted to the inside of the bow-perch on an inner bow of wire, between which and the perch the ring runs. We do not know that there is any special advantage in this arrangement, for if the running ring be large and loose enough it will never jam, and the hawk cannot get entangled by any possibility.

The blocks are best placed upon grass and frequently moved, and in very dry weather it should not be closely mown, or feathers will suffer. Where space is confined and blocks cannot be daily moved, it is a good plan to cut a circle in the turf all round the block and fill it with sand, which should be changed at least every other day; hawks may be kept neat and clean in a very small garden in this manner.

Peregrines and goshawks can be kept out of doors in almost all weathers, but with valuable birds we think it is better to keep them in the mews at night, and when this is done it is wiser not to put them out in cold windy weather or in gales with rain. Simple cold without wind rarely hurts hawks, and to wet they are almost impervious, unless it is accompanied by a gale; but it is not the nature of a wild hawk, hardy as she is, to expose herself to the full stress of bad weather, and it is not right to tie hawks down in a place where they cannot obtain the shelter their own instinct would teach them to provide for themselves.

The author of 'Falconry: its History, Claims, &c.' recommends the use of a lean-to shed against a wall, closed at the ends but open in front, as a sheltered and convenient place to

Young goshawk on Captain Salvin's bow-perch

keep hawks. From lack of opportunity we have never ourselves tried this form of an open-air mews; but we can well believe that it would answer extremely well, both in summer and winter, for eyess hawks, though for passage hawks during the earlier stages of their training it is obviously unfitted.

Hawks must not be exposed to the full heat of the sun in midsummer. We have known more than one killed in this way.

As a rule, cats, foxes, &c. will never meddle with hawks on their blocks, but stray dogs must be guarded against. In 'Falconry in the British Isles' it is stated that turkeys and peacocks will attack hawks that are tied; they may possibly be dangerous, but we have never known a case of the kind, and have kept hawks on a lawn with peacocks and turkeys running among them for a long time. But we have known these birds, and very many others, to attack a hawk that had brought down her quarry close to them and was busily engaged in killing, and no time must be lost by the falconer in 'making in' to his hawk under these circumstances.[1]

A bath should be offered to each hawk every fine day in summer, and twice or thrice a week in winter. Some hawks, especially eyesses, will not fly at all till after they have bathed. A large tin milk-pan makes a very fair bath, but a shallow round tub of wood about two feet six inches in diameter and four inches deep is better, especially if the edge be wide enough for the hawks to perch on before they enter the water. It is a good plan to sink the bath in the ground.

When travelling, flower-pots inverted make capital blocks, and the falconer will have a store of stout iron pins with a ring in the head to which he can tie his hawks down. These pins should be at least ten inches long and five-eighths of an inch in thickness. Hawks travel on the 'box cadge' described it Chapter I., and if brailed they can be carried about by rail or otherwise with no more trouble than a hamperful of pigeons. A temporary perch can generally be rigged up in some stable, and it is a good plan to have canvas ready prepared, in short lengths, and with a strap and buckle to fasten it to the perch,

[1] Carrion crows, where several are collected in one place, will often make a determined and combined attack upon a falcon, that has killed in their vicinity, in order to drive her from her quarry. We have once seen magpies attempt to do the same.

by which means any pole is made into a good screen perch in five minutes.

In training hawks so as to make the best of their powers, the most important matter for the trainer's consideration is that of *condition.* And this in hawks, as in most other animals from which severe exertion at a high rate of speed is required, is arrived at, by the greatest amount of work which can be given without such fatigue as results in staleness, so that the muscles may be thoroughly developed and the wind clear, while at the same time the utmost quantity of firm flesh is carried that is consistent with the entire absence of fat, internal or external, more especially the former. Birds, however, lose flesh rapidly, and alter from day to day much quicker than larger animals, and the falconer will anxiously feel the breast and the rounded muscles under the wing almost as often as he takes a hawk on hand. The practised touch will tell to a nicety the state the bird is in. Game hawks, as a rule, will fly in higher condition than rook or heron hawks, and peregrines generally in fuller flesh than goshawks; but individuals vary much, and nothing but experience will teach the falconer the proper condition of each hawk. It is always easier to take flesh off than to put it on again, and, therefore, it is better to err in the direction of high condition than in the other. The heavier a hawk is the more strongly can she fly, and the more fatal is her stoop. A wild hawk, whose powers no trained bird can hope to emulate, is generally 'as round as an apple,' but then she has only to fly exactly when it suits herself. It is the essence of the falconer's art to make his hawk fly just when it suits him to see her exert her powers, and, therefore, if at all 'above herself,' she may, though in perfect health, decline to work for him, become independent of lure or call, and even soar away till she is lost to her owner ere she is hungry enough to obey him. The ancient maxim is a wise and true one which says that 'a fat hawk maketh a lean horse, a weary falconer, and an empty purse.' Yet a half-starved hawk is not worth a rush, though she may be docile enough for anything, and 'Medio tutissimus ibis' must be the falconer's motto. Hawks are fed but once a day except in the case of merlins or sparrow-hawks, which usually have a light meal given to them in the morning, even before flying. These little hawks must always be kept in high condition, and are too delicate to undergo much discipline. They should also be kept as much as possible on their natural food, i.e. small birds, if plenty of casting be given. We have never known a hawk injured by being fed upon shot birds, but of course one would prefer that a hawk should not swallow lead if it can be avoided.

For a stud of the larger falcons birds cannot always be procured in sufficient quantities to feed all the hawks, and beef will form the staple diet. Mutton is good when lean enough, as also veal. When hawks are doing but little work, it is a good plan to let them pull hard at a very tough piece of beef, and so, as it were, earn their food by work; but where a lot of hawks have to be fed, time is not always available to do this. In such cases the meat should be well chopped up into a mince, and it is a good plan to sprinkle a little fresh water with it, and so mix it all up into a kind of pudding. For young, delicate, or moulting hawks a new-laid egg may be beaten up in lieu of the water. Nothing makes feathers come down broad and strong so well as a diet of egg given occasionally; it also gives to the feet and cere, that rich yellow colour which is always to be seen in wild hawks. Fresh butter will also, to some extent, produce this effect.

The quantity of this food which is to be given to each hawk must, as we have said above, be regulated entirely by the disposition of each bird. Speaking generally, about two-thirds of a crop may be given daily. But in every case, whether a hawk is being lowered in condition or not, a 'gorge' or full crop should be given at least once a week. The gorge should be followed by a very light feed on the next day, and indeed the quantity given to hawks should not always be regular in amount, but may vary according to circumstances or discretion. This state of things is precisely what a wild falcon has to submit to, when from bad weather or scarcity of quarry she is unable to kill, for a day or two at a time, and consequently has to put up with short commons.

But when a wild hawk kills and is hungry she will always eat as much as ever she can, and for this reason not only must the gorge never be neglected, but also no hawk must be kept on small feeds for many days together, however intractable she may be, or she will certainly lose her powers of digestion and with them her health. It is in a difficulty of this sort that 'washed meat' proves to be an aid so valuable to falconers. Washed meat is simply fresh meat that has been soaked in fresh water for from twelve to twenty-four hours according to circumstances. Before use it is taken out of the water and thoroughly squeezed till all the juices are extracted from the meat. The object of this is that the falconer may be able to give his hawk a full crop of food which she shall digest very rapidly and which shall at the same time add but little to her condition. By this means the powerful digestive organs are kept at work, but the hawk gains no flesh, and is in fact reduced more and more in condition without being starved. Washed meat is very valuable in the case of a hawk that has been flying well for a long time, and is fed highly, but needs a little discipline to render her obedient; it is also useful in entering a hawk to a quarry which she does not readily take; but it is a thing to be used with care and discretion, and only under special circumstances and for a special purpose.

'*Rangle*' or small stones is also a valuable 'conditioner. For a falcon the stones may be of the size of good large peas; smooth pebbles off a gravel walk are very good. Four or five may be given at a time, either over hand, to a gentle hawk while sitting on the fist, or else the hawk may be cast and held by an assistant and the stones given by the falconer. If the hawk is fed lightly in the morning and the stones given at night, they will be found in the morning to have been thrown up thickly coated with slime and mucus. Their effect is to cleanse the interior of the hawk, and render her clean and fit to fly, and for one that has lately moulted or has been idle for a length of time they are almost indispensable. No ancient saw is more true than that which says—

> Washed meat and stones makyth an hawk to fly;
> Long fasting and much casting will cause an hawk to die.

Some writers advise that rangle should be placed within reach of the hawks on their blocks so that they may voluntarily take it. No doubt they will do so at times, and this is a capital plan to adopt where hawks are standing idle—as when moulting—for a long time together. But when they are being regularly flown the falconer should, in our opinion, know precisely what his hawks are taking, and should regulate it himself with the greatest exactitude; nothing should be left to chance, but day by day the food and other means for producing good condition should be carefully administered in accordance with a preconcerted plan for each individual hawk. Rangle should therefore be given by hand.

Among all these arrangements *castings* will hold an important place. Castings are the mouthfuls of fur, feathers, bone, &c. which are freely swallowed by a hawk every time she breaks up and devours any quarry she has killed. These indigestible substances are ejected, generally within twelve hours, in the form of a large oval pellet, the condition of which is a sure test of the health of the hawk. In a healthy bird the pellet should be firm, dry, and perfectly sweet; if it is soft, intermixed with mucus or with bits of undigested meat, the bird is out of health.

It is not natural for hawks to be kept long without casting. In fact, in their wild state they get it at every meal, and therefore when they are being kept for a long while on butcher's meat some steps must be taken to supply them with it. The natural form, that of a bird's skin and feathers, is the best. The skin of the whole of the head and neck of a pigeon turned inside out and dipped in blood is as good as anything; rat's skin forms excellent casting, and the heads of ducks or poultry are good.

Sometimes no natural casting can be procured; in such a case tow dipped in blood or woollen threads form a fairly good substitute. A hawk should never go more than a week without castings, and they are never in such good health as when they are fed daily upon birds and given an abundance of casting (or allowed to take it naturally) at every meal.

There is yet one recipe for bringing a hawk into good flying order which we have tried ourselves when all others have failed, but with qualified success. It is an Indian method, and it may be here remarked that the Eastern falconers are always prone to the use of drugs in the conditioning of their hawks, more so than European falconers have ever been. In the case of some varieties of falcon, e.g. the education of the sacre to fly the kite, the administration of drugs is an integral part of the training, and the composition of the physic is a secret handed down from generation to generation of falconers The prescription we refer to is a well-known 'dodge,' and is as follows: Take, say, 4 oz. of sal-ammoniac, boil or melt it into a solid mass in fresh butter in an iron ladle over a fire; as it cools squeeze over it the juice of a lemon to remove any grease which has not been strained away. Feed the hawk, which is to be doctored, for three days upon well-washed meat, giving a three-quarter crop each day, then leave her absolutely without food for twelve hours. Take of the sal-ammoniac a piece as large as a filbert, wrap it neatly round with cotton-wool, and administer it over hand. In about twenty minutes she will cast the cotton-wool thickly covered with a mass of greasy fat. If this be floated off into hot water, it will be found to consist of the whole of the fatty lining of the stomach, and the quantity is sometimes very remarkable. About two hours after this casting give the hawk some three mouthfuls of warm blood or very fresh meat. In the evening let her have half a crop of well-washed meat. The day after she is fit to fly, and may be fed as usual; the greater part of her internal fat is gone.

The effect of this removal of the inner lining of the stomach is to induce a condition of ravenous hunger, while the hawk is not weakened by that starvation which alone could produce a similar effect. But the treatment is a powerful one, and must be used with extreme caution. Especially the drug must only be administered in settled fine weather; a sudden change to cold or wild weather will destroy the bird when thus physicked; nor will a hawk in low or weak condition withstand so drastic a treatment—it will in itself lower her quite enough. We have adopted it in the case of old self-willed hawks that were in high condition and good fliers, but had become, as such hawks sometimes will, independent of lure or discipline, uncertain as to doing their best when hooded off, and inclined to soar away. The effect has always been to reduce the hawk to absolute obedience, and to bring her under perfect control; but though sometimes keen to fly, we think there has always been a loss of dash and courage attending the effect of the physic. One or two have been made very ill, and occasionally a hawk has been killed by it. On the whole, it is a device infallible in its action, but dangerous to use and not well suited to our climate. It is sometimes highly successful, but must be used with discretion, and in our opinion the more of this quality that the falconer himself possesses, the less he will use of sal-ammoniac for his hawk.

After keeping his hawks in good health a falconer's chief care should be to maintain their feathers in the most perfect order. Without these hawks clearly cannot fly, and the loss of even one important flight feather means as much to a falcon as an impost of 10 lbs. extra does to a racehorse. Feathers, however, are but frail things, and in spite of all care accidents to them will happen. Travelling, both on the box cadge and still more so in hampers, is a fruitful source of injury, and in killing rooks on dry hard fallows in March and April hawks often get a good deal knocked about. In every case a broken feather should be mended at once. So long as the whole wing is intact, it presents but one outer edge to strike against hard substances, with the combined strength of all the feathers to bear the force of the blow; directly a gap

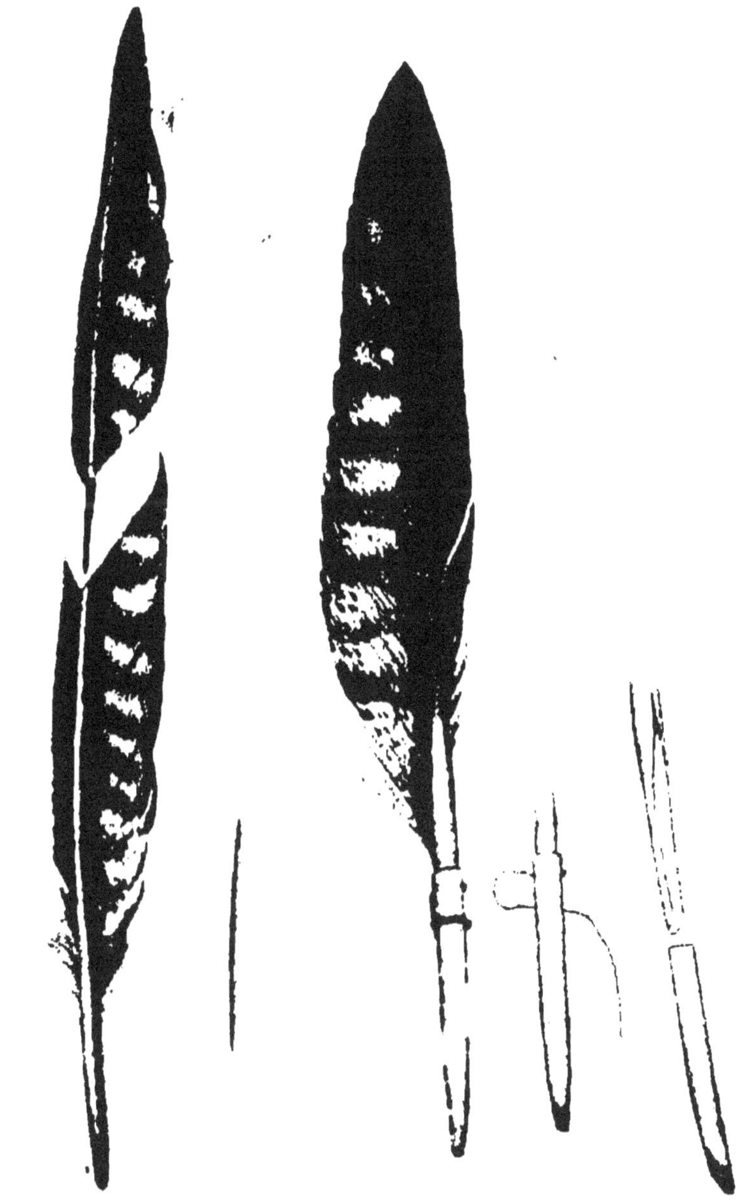

Process of 'imping' a feather

Process of 'sewing in' a feather

appears there are two more of such outer edges, and a blow that catches either of the feathers singly will be sure to break it, though the wing, if intact, would have had the strength and elasticity to resist such injury. In this way the mischief that begins with a single feather will spread till the hawk becomes a ragged creature, so much knocked about as to be past repair. A broken feather should therefore be replaced without delay. When a feather is merely bent and frayed it will straighten itself perfectly if dipped and held in hot water. If, however, it is actually broken, it must be carefully 'imped.' The simplest and easiest way to do this is to cut the feather, across, about half-way up, slantingly, and, having selected from the stock, which every falconer is careful to maintain, the corresponding feather which has formerly belonged to a hawk of the same age, species, and size as the one now under treatment, it must be cut at such an angle as to precisely correspond with the feather in the hawk. An 'imping needle' is now thrust into this feather (see last page), and both ends are then pushed up till they meet. The needle having been dipped in brine will rust a little and hold so firmly that it would be easier to pull out the feather itself, in many cases, than to pull the joint apart.

Imping needles are merely three-sided needles, sharp at both ends, which are filed out of soft steel wire; different sizes must be prepared for different kinds of hawks. Some care is requisite to get them made of the proper temper, as if too soft they bend, but if tempered too hard are apt to be brittle.

Sometimes a feather is broken so near the quill that there is nothing solid to hold the needle. In such a case it must be mended thus. Cut off the broken stump just where the shaft of the feather merges into the quill, leaving that part only in the bird. With a sharp-pointed penknife slit this quill on the under side from the point where the quill enters the flesh up to the broken end. Having selected the proper feather to replace the broken one, cut its quill into the form of a rather elongated pen, running the whole length of the quill, but of course without a nib. Slide this pen into the stump of quill which remains in the bird's body. Being split, it will admit it easily, and the feather can be pushed home so as to exactly replace the broken one. Then take a needleful of waxed silk, and pass it through the double quill just below the joint, whip the silk a few times round the feather and over the joint, pass the needle back through the feather above the joint, and finish off. To mend a feather well in this way requires some skill, but if it is well done, and great care taken that the feather lies exactly right, viz. at the same angle as the others in the wing, it will be impossible without the closest examination to tell whether the hawk has a mended feather in her body or not. Sometimes a feather broken at the quill is repaired by inserting a plug of wood or of the stem of a larger feather into the quill and mending on to this with an ordinary imping needle, the plug being held fast by cobbler's wax. Of course, for all such operations as these a hawk must be securely held by an assistant. The proper way to do this is as follows: Tie a knot in the corner of a silk handkerchief and throw it on to the hawk's back as she sits on the perch, so that the knot is at the nape of her neck and the sides of the handkerchief fall over her shoulders. Take her round the middle with both hands so as to wrap the silk well round her, and lay her on a soft yet firm cushion on the operating table; then let the assistant hold her with both hands, confining her legs and wings, his thumbs lying in the channel of her back, and exercising enough pressure to keep her from struggling; the cushion protects her breast from injury and the silk preserves her feathers from being frayed.

'*Coping*' is the necessary shortening of both beak and claws, and is done best with a sharp penknife and a pair of nail clippers. Claws only require to be dealt with in the early stages of training, when hawks are prone to use them to the detriment of the falconer's hands. It is also well when two hawks are flown together not to allow the claws to be very sharp, for fear of an accident in case of 'crabbing.' The beak, however, requires constant attention. In a wild state, no doubt, hawks counteract the growth of the horn by the incessant wear and tear of tough pulling at their food, the breaking of bones, and pulling up of rough skin; but when domesticated and fed principally on soft food the beak is apt to grow fast, to become soft and unsound, and to split. It must be watched with care, and on the appearance of any split or scaling off must be well examined. All the rotten part must be carefully pared away till the root of the crack is arrived at, if not at the first, then at the second or third operation.

Moulting is a period when hawks require special care, both to get their frames into the most vigorous condition, so as to ensure the growth of strong broad feathers, and also to avoid risk of injury to the feathers in the blood when they are very soft and easily damaged. With care, however, hawks can be flown at all stages of the moult, especially at a quarry, such as game, which they are very fond of, and at which they can be used when in very high condition. Eyesses usually commence the moult much earlier than passage hawks—why this is so we cannot tell. As a rule, a healthy eyess will throw her first feathers—which will be the seventh in the wing—then the two centre or 'deck' feathers of the tail early in May or even in April. Such a hawk if well fed will get through the more important stages of her moult and be ready for use, even if she has a feather or two to throw, by August 12. Passage hawks, on the other hand, do not generally begin to moult till July, and very often not till August. Such hawks as these can very well be flown at game in the earlier stages of the moult without their powers being very much affected. Occasionally, however, a falcon will lose a fortnight or so in the latter part of September, owing to the wide gaps in her wings, for this will render it difficult for her to overtake grouse, which are then very strong. It is better to let her rest for a time than to risk her being frequently disappointed.

We have, however, successfully flown passage hawks at

game year after year, from August 12 up to about October 10, and then put them down to moult, or rather to finish moulting, and have taken them up at the end of February, in time for the spring rook hawking, perfect in every feather: this we consider to be the best method of managing passage hawks, and the means by which the most work can be got out of them. The last feather thrown is the first or outside feather of the wing. Very great care is necessary to avoid injury to these feathers as they come down, which they do very slowly. Very quiet tame hawks will moult very well on the block, but when they are put down to moult late in the season or where they are of a wild, excitable nature the best plan is to turn them into a warm loft or loose box, as large and as light as possible; the windows should be protected by *perpendicular* bars, to which the hawks cannot cling, and so break their feathers, and all corners or inconvenient perching-places should be rounded off or protected. Two or even three hawks of the same sex[1] may be moulted in one loft in this way. Their food should be securely tied to small boards, so that it may not be dragged into corners, and should consist as much as possible of birds, with their feathers on to form castings, and of rough food such as rats, rabbits, fowls, or pheasants' heads, and similar things—the less butcher's meat is used the better. A hawk should always be turned into the mews with new, or, at any rate, very sound jesses on her in order to avoid any struggle with her in replacing unsound ones when she is first taken up, wild and full of flesh.

According to the ancient writers, hawks appear to have suffered from as many and as complex diseases as human beings, and the pharmacopœia employed was as extensive and as filthy in the one case as in the other. In modern times our practice is more simple, but it must be owned that some of the diseases of our hawks baffle our skill. We propose, first, to treat of such complaints as have been found curable, and

[1] Except goshawks, which can never be trusted near any other hawk of their own or another kind

afterwards to deal with those for which we cannot with confidence recommend remedies.

*Croaks* or *kecks* is a very common disease: it is caused by a cold, frequently induced by a low state of condition, and answers nearly to an ordinary cough in beasts or human beings. The noise, however, from which the name is derived only appears when the hawk is exerting herself, as by bating or flying. For physic give half a chili, or three or four peppercorns daily, for two or three days. Keep the hawk constantly pulling at rough food, such as pigeons' backs, fowls' heads, and the like, so that she may constantly be feeding, and yet always exerting herself a little; finish off each day with a crop of light food, such as rabbit's or tender meat; every third day give a cropful of 'warm blood,' such as a freshly-killed pigeon, and as the hawk gets better give her plenty of flying to the lure. This ailment often hangs about a hawk for a long time, but if she can be kept up in condition and in good heart it will gradually die out.

*Frounce* is a canker of the interior of the mouth, and occasionally spreads to the throat, when it is apt to prove fatal. It is caused generally by damp, and sometimes by feeding hawks upon foul meat. The symptoms are, a frothing at the mouth and difficulty in eating, and if the hawk's mouth be opened the whole of the tongue and palate will be seen to be covered with a whitish scale or scab. As much of this scale

as can be removed without making the parts bleed should be scraped away with the edge of a quill or a knife, and the exposed part dressed once a day with burnt alum mixed with vinegar. In ordinary cases this will effect a cure in a few days, but if the canker spreads downwards and into the throat it will be found impossible to cure it. Lunar caustic will sometimes prove effective.

*Inflammation of the crop* is a serious complaint, and causes the hawk to throw up the contents of her crop in an undigested form shortly after feeding. If not taken in time it will prove fatal. About three grains of powdered Turkey rhubarb must be given without castings and on an empty stomach. A little light warm food should be given, as a freshly-killed pigeon or rabbit, at frequent intervals as the hawk seems able to take it, and the rhubarb dose may be repeated for two or three days (but not more) until the hawk is able to digest a full meal.

The falconer will always examine with special care both the mutes or droppings as well as the castings of his hawks in order that he may judge of their condition of health. The mutes should be perfectly white, of the consistency of cream, with occasionally a black spot in them; if they are thick or with much black in them the hawk is out of order. Green mutes are a very bad sign, generally indicating an advanced stage of inflammation of the crop. For all disorders of this kind rhubarb is the best and safest remedy, but not more than three or four consecutive doses should be given without an interval of some days, or it loses its effect. Sugar candy and manna are also useful and harmless laxatives. Hawks are liable to fits, both epileptic and apoplectic, especially when very fat and suddenly excited or frightened. We cannot recommend with confidence any remedy except keeping the hawk perfectly quiet and feeding her lightly, getting her as soon as possible into better condition.

Hawks that are taken too young from the nest or that have been much exposed to cold when taken are sometimes seized with *cramp* in the legs; this will completely paralyse the limbs and render the bird useless. Indeed, in bad cases we have known the bones of the leg dislocated. Mild attacks will sometimes pass off of themselves, but there is no remedy for bad cases.

*Swelled feet* and *corns* are common but troublesome complaints which affect trained hawks. The first and more serious form of the disease is a swelling and inflammation of the whole ball of the foot; the latter are small tumours which appear on different parts of the foot and generally come slowly to a head, open, and discharge their contents in the form of a core of hardened pus. Time is generally the best cure for this complaint, care being taken to diminish every cause by which inflammation can be maintained. Very soft and loose jesses should be put on, and in cases of swelled foot a padded perch and block should be used, or, better still, the hawk kept on a mound of turf, and not on a perch at all. It will be found that she will spend most of her time lying down, so that her feet are relieved of all pressure. Gradually the tumour within the foot will come to a head and the hardened core, at times as big as a hazel nut, work its way out, when all that is necessary is to anoint the open wound with goose-grease or vaseline, and get it to heal as rapidly as possible. Hot fomentations are sometimes used to bring the inflammation to a head rapidly; we cannot speak very highly of this treatment, but in the earlier stages a lotion composed as follows has been found very useful: Brandy, one wineglass; vinegar, one wineglass. Steep in the above a good handful of fresh parsley, keep in a covered jar, and apply with a sponge three times daily.

Many falconers attribute swelled feet to the use of hard blocks or perches, and consider that all such resting-places should be padded. Hawks, however, do not in a wild state get padded perches to sit on, and we do not believe that hard perches really induce the complaint, but more often the constant strain on the feet caused by incessant jumping against the jesses does so. The frequent concussion on a hard perch may no doubt aggravate the evil, but the true remedy is to keep the hawk so quiet as to remove the causes which induce her to bate and jump, or, if necessary, keep her hooded—or even brailed—till she learn to sit quiet.

A simple improvement on the ordinary perch, which appears to be founded on common sense, has lately been devised by Captain Biddulph, one of our most successful Anglo-Indian falconers; it is merely the cutting of a groove half an inch wide and a quarter of an inch deep along the top of the perch, so that pressure is taken off the ball of the foot which rests in the groove. It is probable that this may operate so as to check a tendency to develop swelled feet in some hawks, which, though quiet on the perch, seem to be specially prone to this complaint.

*Inflammation of the lungs* is a complaint which hawks occasionally acquire, and it seems to be near akin to the 'pantas,' of which ancient writers tell us so much; the chief symptoms are feverishness, a peculiar shortness of breath, and quick heaving of the body, especially of the lower part or pannel, as each breath is drawn; the hawk steadily pines away and dies, when her lungs are either found to be in a highly congested state or in some cases are almost altogether gone. We have tried various remedies, but have found none in which we have such confidence as to recommend it to our readers. Latham in his 'Faulcons' Lure and Cure' gives the following as a remedy, if administered in the very earliest stages, and we give it for what it may be worth:—'Take a quarter of a lb. of the best sweet butter and put it into dammaske rose water and there preserve and keep it close. And as you have need to use it, which must be very often, take some of it forth and with the powder of rue and the powder of saffron and a little brown sugar candie mingled well together make a pellet or two and give every morning to your hawk for a week together early in the morning, and keep her very warm.' Each ingredient in this prescription is one that is usefully administered to various birds, and may be serviceable even in so extreme a case as the pantas.

*Blain* is supposed to be peculiar to passage hawks and to be incurable.[1] It takes the form of a large watery blister on the pinion joint at the extreme end of the wing; gradually this stiffens, the feathers become immovable, and the power of the wing so greatly impaired that the hawk is useless. In extreme cases the pinion joint will rot off altogether. The cause is perhaps the sudden inactivity which is enforced upon freshly caught hawks just when they have been using their powers of flight most freely during the migration. We have also noticed that it is most prevalent in very severe winters, and may there-

[1] An eyess was taken with this complaint in the spring of 1892.

fore be in some cases attributable to frost bite. We know of no remedy.

*Parasites.*—All hawks are occasionally subject to lice very similar in character to those which appear on pigeons, fowls, and other birds. Especially when hawks are being frequently flown at rooks in the spring they are apt to get covered with lice, which abound on those birds, especially on any that may have been sitting. The parasites quit the lately killed bird for the living one by scores. They are easily got rid of by either blowing tobacco smoke through the feathers or by giving the hawk a good dressing of tobacco water. Both these remedies are apt to make the hawk herself sick and to throw her out of condition for a few days, and a better plan is to induce the hawks to bathe regularly, even daily in fine weather, and to allow them plenty of time to 'weather,' or to dry and preen themselves. Where this is done very little will be seen of these pests.

Formerly it was supposed that passage hawks would not bathe or even sit on their blocks bareheaded until they had been at least one summer in training. In later times enlarged experience of these hawks, coupled with lessons learnt from the Indian falconers, who use no other kind, whether for game or for the 'high mountee,' have taught us that they can be made in every respect as tame as eyesses ; and there are few passage hawks trained nowadays that are not reclaimed sufficiently to bathe freely at the block before the spring hawking season has even commenced.

A more troublesome form of parasite is known as 'mites.' These are tiny red insects that burrow into the wax-like skin or 'cere' around the nostrils and the eyelids, gradually forming large scabby sores. They are the infallible accompaniment of low, impoverished condition, and often appear in cases of croaks, or even when a hawk has been left out for a night or two and been starved. The true remedy is to feed the hawk into better condition, when the mites will all disappear; but, as they are certainly contagious, and must inconvenience the hawk, they are better removed. This is easily done by dressing the parts with tobacco water to which is added a little spirit. This mixture should be carefully applied with a camel-hair pencil, and the second application generally effects a cure.

We do not give directions for setting broken limbs in hawks, as, though such injuries may be cured in them just as in other animals, it can only be in some very exceptional case that it is worth while to attempt the cure. It is, as a rule, better to destroy the suffering hawk at once in all cases where there is not a fair prospect of effecting a cure, and it is very improbable that a hawk which has met with an accident of such a kind will ever be available for purposes of sport.

A word of caution, in conclusion, to the beginner in falconry—*avoid keeping too many hawks.* Out of the twenty-four hours there are not more than six per diem available for such a sport as hawking. Hawks will fly every day, and are, in fact, all the better for being thus worked. Three or four good hawks will, under ordinary circumstances, provide sport for the whole of each day, and will be much improved by being thus freely used. Where more are kept, except in establishments of the largest size, the result usually is that half of the hawks rest in idleness, deteriorating day by day, and occupying time and attention which had better be devoted to their more useful compeers. To obtain three or four really good hawks no doubt entails a trial of twice that number, and the discarding of the inferior birds. But we strongly urge upon the tyro that he should content himself with one or two useful steady hawks, gradually testing more and retaining those, and those only, which he finds to be of the first class. He will obtain more sport from a single good tiercel than from six or seven moderate hawks, and will benefit both as to his pocket and his leisure time by the abridgment of his establishment.

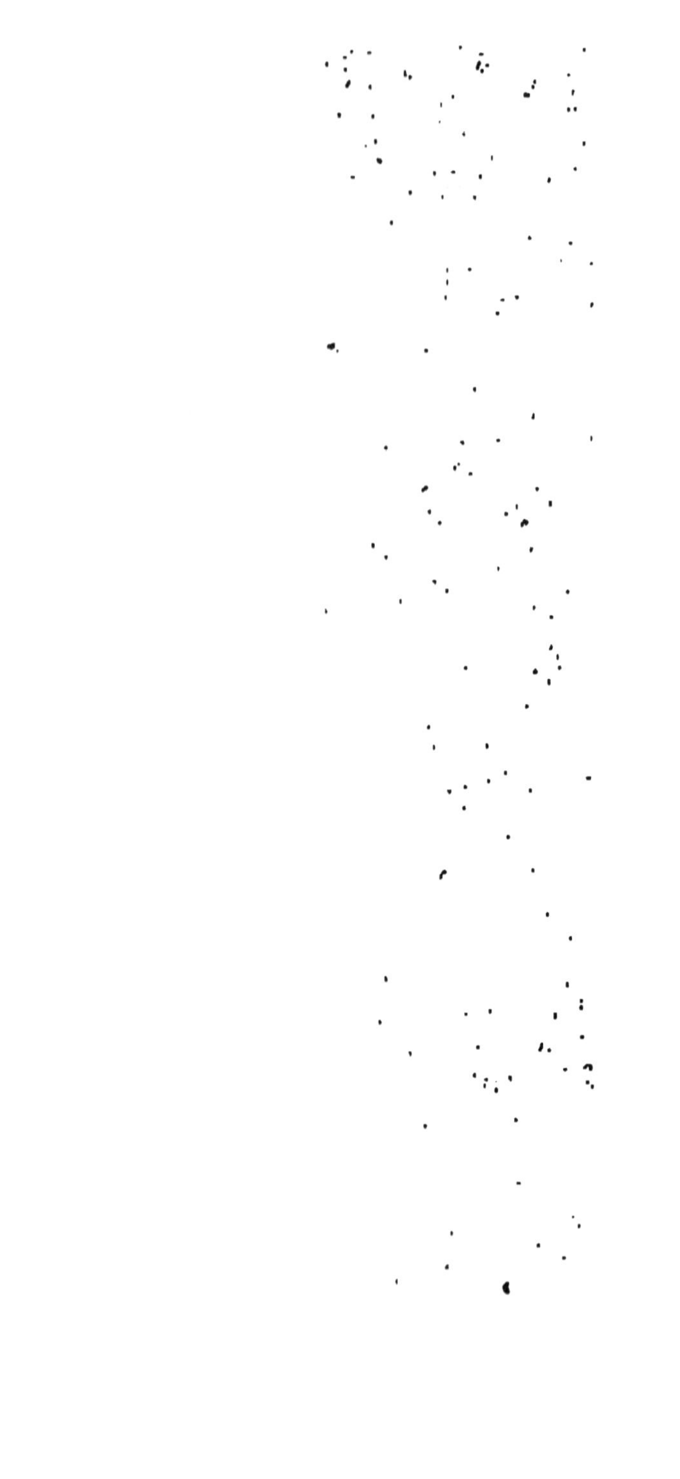

# APPENDIX

## *COURSING SECRETARIES*

| Club | Name and Address |
|---|---|
| Aberdeenshire Club . . | W. Lowe, Don Terrace, Woodside, Aberdeenshire. |
| Abergele . . . . | John D. Jones, Bodergh, Abergele, N.W. |
| Acle Bridge . . . | B. J. Foulsham, Duke's Head, Great Yarmouth. |
| Adderly (Salop) . . | W. Bankes, Market Drayton. |
| Aldford (Cheshire) . . | Richard Brown, Churton, Chester. |
| Altcar Club . . . | H. Brocklebank, 4 Fulwood Park, Aigburth, Liverpool, hon. sec. |
| Amesbury (Open) . . | G. M. Williams, Countess Manor Farm, Amesbury, Salisbury. |
| Annandale (Mid.) . . | A. Chapman, Buckon Hill, Lockerbie, N.B. |
| Appleby (late Burton-upon-Humber) | J. Ashton, 73 Wrawby Street, Brigg. |
| Appleton Wiske . . | F. Hesletine, Appleton Wiske. |
| Ashdown Park . . . | J. H. Laurence, Shrivenham, Berks. |
| Aston Hall (Salop) . . | — Cartwright, Oswestry. |
| Bagley (Salop) . . . | E. Williams, 7 Chester Street, Shrewsbury. |
| Banbridge (co. Down, Ireland) | T. M'Clelland, hon. sec. |
| Bangor . . . . | T. Hampshire, Bangor, N.W. |
| Barnton Club . . . | J. Gray, 6 Bath-street, Portobello, Edinburgh. |
| Berkeley (Open) and Yeomanry | T. Pearce, Berkeley. |
| Bickerstaffe (Lancashire). | R. Anderton, New Hall, West Derby, Liverpool. |
| Black Brae (Londonderry) | Sir T. Lecky, Foyle Hill, Londonderry, Ireland. |
| Blandford . . . . | F. V. Ensor, Dorchester, Dorset. |
| Blenkinsopp (Northumberland) | J. Ord, Fetherstone, Haltwhistle. |
| Bothal Club . . . | Dr. F. Richardson, Rothbury, Northumberland. |
| Border Union . . . | R. B. Carruthers, Huntingdon Lodge, Dumfries, N.B. |
| Bradbury (Durham) . | J. Madderson, Fishburn Hall, Ferry Hill, Durham. |

| Club | Name and Address |
|---|---|
| Bradford Club . . . | J. Tillotson, Bradford. |
| Brandon (Durham) . . | G. Thornton, High Brandon, Durham. |
| Bredwardine (Herefordshire) | C. Farr, Merton Hotel, Hereford. |
| Burnham (Essex) | — |
| Burscough-Bridge(Lancs.) | E. Thorougood, Burscough. |
| Butterwick (Durham) . | T. Towes, Sedgefield. |
| Byer's Green (Durham) . | R. Robinson, Todhills, Willington, Durham. |
| Carmarthenshire . . | H. Cadle, Half-Moon Hotel, Carmarthen. |
| Carmichael . . . . | R. Paterson, Birthwood, Biggar, N.B., hon. sec. |
| Castlerea(co. Roscommon) | T. Clancey, Ballintubber, French Lawn, Castlerea. co. Roscommon. |
| Chaddesden (Derby) . | J. W. Bailey, Wood Farm, Chaddesden, Derby. |
| Chilton . . . . . | E. Salmon, Chilton Buildings, Ferry Hill, Durham. |
| Chirbury (Salop) . . | T. E. Issard, Newtown, Montgomeryshire. |
| Chirk . . . . . | P. O. Gill, Trewern Hall, Oswestry. |
| Cliffe and Hundred of Hoo | Horace Ledger, Cliffe, Rochester. |
| Clyro Club . . . . | W. Price, Baskerville Arms Inns, Clyro, Breconshire. |
| Collingbourne . . . | Reynolds & Rose, Bear Hotel, Devizes. |
| Corrie . . . . . | A. Chapman, Buckon Hill, Lockerbie, N.B. |
| Cothelstone (Taunton) . . | W. T. Gibbs, Manor House, Cothelstone, Taunton. |
| Croome . . . . . | J. Millington, 50 Foregate Street, Worcester. |
| Cross Hands (Gloucestershire) | T. L. Bennet, Combsend Farm, Old Sodbury. |
| Darlington Club . . | W. Watson, Tower Corner, Darlington. |
| Dirleton and North Berwick | J. Hutchison, Woodside, by Hamilton, hon. sec. |
| Docking Club . . . | G. Platten, Sedgford, Lynn. |
| Draycott (Staffordshire) . | J. W. Beech, Taynsley Hall, Stoke-upon-Trent. |
| Dumfries . . . . . | Andrew Lawson, Dumfries. |
| Dunston . . . . . | J. H. Mutimer, Dunston, near Norwich. |
| East Kent (Wye) . . | G. Kennet, Harville, Wye, Kent. |
| East Stirlingshire Club . | J. Morrison, Steeple Land, Falkirk, N.B. |
| Ecclefechan . . . . | J. Irving, Bank, Ecclefechan, N.B. |
| Eccleston and Aldford . | D. F. Chalton, Rake Farm, Eccleston, Chester. |
| Edenderry (Ireland). . | J. O'Brien, Edenderry, King's County. |
| Elemore (Durham) . . | T. Lamb, Brewery, Hetton-le-Hole, Durham. |
| Elm Club . . . . | G. J. Moore, Chambers, Wisbeach. |
| Everingham (Yorkshire) . | H. Myers, Holme-on-Spalding Moor, York. |
| Everleigh (Wilts) . . | J. T. Randoll, 2 Melrose Villas, London Road, Salisbury. |
| Evesham (Worcestershire) | A. W. Morris. |
| Ewerby (Lincolnshire) . | G. Lee, White Hart Hotel, Sleaford. |
| Farcet Fen . . . . | J. Tilbury, Bell and Oak, Peterborough. |
| Felton Park (Northumberland) | J. Adams, Red Lion, Felton. |

| CLUB | NAME AND ADDRESS |
|---|---|
| Great Thurlow (Suffolk) | — |
| Greencroft (Lanchester) . | C. Maynard, 19 Old Elvet, Durham. |
| Hale (Lancashire) . . | E. Rowe, Child of Hale Inn, Hale. |
| Halewood (Lancashire) . | W. J. Eccleshaw, Halewood. |
| Halston . . . . . | G. Cottle, West Felton, Salop. |
| Hawthorn (Durham) . | W. Cowen, Innkeeper, Sunderland. |
| Haydock Park. . . . | R. J. Bury, Haydock Park, Newton-le-Willows. |
| Heatley Warburton (Cheshire) | A. F. Pope, Barton House, Manchester. |
| Herefordshire (West) . | G. Farr, Merton Hotel, Hereford. |
| Hetton (Durham) . . | W. C. Day. |
| Holme-on-Spalding Moor (Yorkshire) | John Brown, Tillingham, Holme-on-Spalding Moor, York. |
| Hook and co. Wexford Club | John Murray, South Street, New Ross, co. Wexford. |
| Horbling (Lincolnshire) . | C. Smith, Spalding. |
| Hull, Beverley, and East Riding Club | C. Greensides, Beverley. |
| Hunmanby (Yorkshire) . | J. Hutchinson, White Swan Hotel, Hunmanby, Yorkshire |
| Ince (Cheshire) . . | A. Howcroft, Moss Hay, Tarvin. |
| Ince Blundell (Lancashire) | John Coke, Birkdale, Southport. |
| Isle of Man . . . . | J. Gore, Douglas, Isle of Man. |
| Kelloe (Durham) . . | C. Maynard, 19 Old Elvet, Durham. |
| Kilkenny Club. . . . | T. Manning, Kilkenny. |
| Kilmarnock (co. Wexford) | L. Murphy, Priest Haggard, New Ross, co. Wexford. |
| Kingscote . . . . | Elias Hobbs, Huntsman Hall, Kingscote, Gloucestershire. |
| Kinver Hill (Worcestershire) | J. P. Hitchings, Wordsley, Stourbridge. |
| Kyle Club . . . . | Jas. Murray, jun., Dumfries Arms Hotel, Cumnock, N.B. |
| Leeds and County . . | J. Allanson, 87 New Briggate, Leeds. |
| Leinster Club . . . | J. Manning, 35 Arran Quay, Dublin. |
| Lichfield . . . . . | J. Trevor, Swan Hotel, Lichfield. |
| Liddesdale Club . . | J. Scott, Newcastleton. |
| Limerick Club. . . . | R. Bourke, Dromlasa, Pallas Green, co. Limerick. |
| Little Crosby . . . | T. Barnes, Little Crosby, near Liverpool. |
| Little Maston (N. Lancs.) | J. Nickson, Talbot Hotel, Blackpool |
| Littleton (Staines) . . | P. Fowles, Staines. |
| Longstock . . . . | J. T. Randoll, Wyndham Terrace, Salisbury |
| Longtown (Cumberland). | S. McClure, Longtown. |
| Louth and Meath Club . | F. W. Leland, Drogheda. |
| Lydbury, North (Salop) . | A. Wright, New Inn, Lydbury North. |
| Maidenhead . . . . | F. Clease, Burnham, Bucks. |
| Malton . . . . . | J. King, Malton. |

| CLUB | NAME AND ADDRESS |
|---|---|
| Market Drayton (Salop) . | T. W. Banks, Market Drayton. |
| Market Weighton . . | F. Brough, Market Weighton. |
| Marlborough (Wilts.) . | H. Partridge, Castle and Ball Hotel, Marlborough. |
| Middle . . . . . | T. Parry, Red Lion, Middle, Salop. |
| Moorhampton (Herefordshire) | T. Packwood, Palmers Court, Holmes, Hereford. |
| National Coursing Club . | R. B. Carruthers, Huntingdon Lodge, Dumfries. |
| Newmarket (Champion) . | J. Williams, Ross Road, Newmarket. |
| North Kent . . . . | W. Hayward, 38 Plumstead Common Road, Plumstead, Kent. |
| North of England Club . | T. Snowdon, 33 Mosley Street, Newcastle-on-Tyne. |
| Northern Club (Holestone) | J. Stevenson, Fourmileburn, Doagh, co. Antrim. |
| Orford, Open (Suffolk) . | W. Wilson, Raydon Hall, Orford, Wickham Market. |
| Ossory Club . . . . | E. Williams, Rathdowney, Queen's Co. |
| Oxfordshire Club . . | W. R. Pratt, 22 Commercial Road, Oxford. |
| Pawlett (Bridgwater) . | Horace Hurman, Auctioneer, Bridgwater. |
| Perthshire Club . . | W. Bartholomew, Auchtertool, Kirkcaldy, N.B. |
| Pilling (North Lancs.) . | W. Jemson, Ridge Farm, Pilling, Garstang. |
| Plumpton (Sussex) . . | W. H. Hollis, 42 Bond Street, Brighton. |
| Powderham (Devon) . | S. Dobell, Louthtown, Kenton, Exeter. |
| Pulborough (Sussex) . | A. Agate, Wareham, Horsham. |
| Purdysbury Club (Belfast) | W. Gibson, 2 Great Edward Street, Belfast. |
| Purslow (Salop) . . | E. Smith, Hundred House, Purslow, Aston-on-Clun. |
| Quebec and Lanchester (Durham) | J. Cockerill, Hamsteds Colliery Hotel, Durham. |
| Riccall (Selby) . . | J. W. Pratt, Riccall. |
| Ridgway Club . . . | J. Mugliston, Lytham, Lancashire, hon. sec. |
| Rochford Hundred (Essex) | W. Whistler, Southend. |
| Rokeby (Yorkshire) . . | R. Hedley, Three Horseshoes Inn, Barnard Castle. |
| Rufford (Lancashire) . | Phillip Ascroft, Rufford, Lancashire. |
| Salisbury and Amesbury . | W. G. Knight 3 Milton Place, Salisbury. |
| Scarboro' (Open and Club) | C. Postill, St. Sepulchre Street, Scarboro'. |
| Scottish National . . | B. Paterson, Birthwood, Biggar, N.B. |
| | Assist. Sec. A. B. Paterson, 13 Walker Street, Edinburgh. |
| Sedgefield . . . . | T. Lowes, Hardwicke Arms Hotel, Sedgefield. |
| Selby (Yorkshire) . . | T. L. Palframen, Shipton, Market Weighton. |
| Sheraton (Hartlepool) . | J. Carter, West Hartlepool. |
| Shotton (Durham) . . | T. Lamb, jun., Hetton-le-Hole, Durham. |
| Sleaford . . . . . | C. Smith, Bristol Arms Hotel, Sleaford. |
| South Essex Club (Rainham) | F. T. Davis, 2 New Road, Woolwich. |
| South Lancashire (Sthprt.) | J. Bell, East Bank Street, Southport. |
| South of England Club . | A. J. Humphrey, Walton Leigh, Addlestone, Surrey. |
| Southern Club (Trabolgan) | A. H. Ledlie, Victoria Hotel, Cork. |

| Club | Name and Address |
|---|---|
| Southminster (Open) . | J. H. Salter, Tolleshunt D'Arcy, Kelvedon, Essex. |
| do. (Local) . | J. Prior, Southminster. |
| Springhill (Dumfriesshire) | J. E. Byers, Greenurne, Gretna, N.B. |
| Stamfordham (Northumberland) | W. Reed, Pen's Close, Stamfordham. |
| Stokesby (Norfolk) . . | B. J. Foulsham, Duke's Head Hotel, Gt. Yarmouth. |
| Stych (Salop) . . . | W. Banks, Market Drayton. |
| Sully (Cardiff) . . . | C. Moir, V.S., Cardiff. |
| Sundorne (Salop) . . | E. Williams, Chester Street, Shrewsbury. |
| Surrey Club . . . | W. Haydon, Tulse Hill, London, S.W. |
| Swansea Club . . . | C. Richfield, Swansea. |
| Sydmonton (Berks.) . | A. Booth, Burghclere, Berks. |
| Tadcaster . . . | Miss Laurence, Londesboro' Arms, Tadcaster. |
| Tarbock (Lancashire) . | W. H. Gregory, Tarbock. |
| Thirsk . . . . | T. Long, Three Tuns Hotel, Thirsk. |
| Tillingham (Essex) . . | W. G. Small, Easthall, Bradwell-on-Sea, Essex. |
| Tintern (co. Wexford) . | M. Power, St. Kearns, Arthurstown, co. Wexford. |
| Tolleshunt D'Arcy . . | J. H. Salter, D'Arcy House, Tolleshunt D'Arcy, Kelvedon, Essex. |
| Upleatham (Redcar) . | G. Clay, Red Lion Hotel, Redcar. |
| Upper Nithsdale Club (Dumfriesshire) | J. B. Little, Sanquhar, N.B. |
| Vale of Avon and South Wilts Club | W. G. Knight, 3 Milton Place, Salisbury. |
| Vaynol . . . . | H. Harwood, Vaynol, North Wales. |
| Walshford Bridge . . | G. O. Sergeant, Hunsingore, near Wetherby. |
| Watford Club . . | H. B. Didsbury, 52 High Street, Watford, Herts. |
| West Cumberland Club . | Dr. J. E. Lace, Frizington, near Whitehaven. |
| Westwick (Durham) . | R. Hedley, Three Horseshoes, Barnard Castle. |
| Westby (Lytham) . . | T. Windebank, Ship Hotel, Lytham. |
| Whitfield (Northumberland) | J. Johnson, Kingswood, Whitfield, Langley. |
| Whittlesey (Cambs.) . | H. Brown, Whittlesey, Cambridgeshire. |
| Widdrington (Northumberland) | H. Annet, jun., Widdrington, Northumberland. |
| Wilton (Redcar) . . | G. Clay, Red Lion Hotel, Redcar. |
| Willington (Durham) . | J. Robinson, Masons' Arms, Willington, Durham. |
| Winmarleigh (N. Lancs.) | R. Thornton, Gibstick Hall, Winmarleigh, Garstang. |
| Woodhouse (Salop) . . | P. O. Gill, Trewen Hall, Oswestry. |
| Woolley Park (Berks.) . | W. H. Fyer, Newbury, Berks. |
| Wye (Kent) . . . | George Kennet, Harville, Wye, Kent. |
| Yorkshire Club . . | E. Dobson, 67 Northgate, Bradford. |

## PUBLIC GREYHOUND-TRAINERS

| Name | Address |
|---|---|
| Abrams, A. | Calne, Wilts. |
| Aldred, John | Blakeley, Manchester. |
| Askew, John | Yaxley, Peterborough. |
| Bamford, John | 210 Latimer Road, London. |
| Barlow, Richard | West Houghton, Bolton, Lancashire. |
| Barnes, George | Cross Street, Beverley. |
| Baty, W. | Cargo, Carlisle. |
| Benn, W. | Lolby Hall Lodge, Wisbey, Bradford. |
| Bullock, T. | Killingworth, Northumberland. |
| Burrows, George | Newton-le-Willows, Lancashire. |
| Burton, G. | Bridge Hotel, Durham. |
| Byrne, H. | Ludlow. |
| Coke, Archibald & Sons | Blundell Arms Hotel, Birkdale, Southport. |
| Cole, Mark | Woodcote Lodge, Epsom, Surrey. |
| Collard, A. J. | Cherry Tree Kennels, Newmarket. |
| Cross, J. | Stratton Heath, St. Helens, Lancashire. |
| Deans, J. | 47 High Street, Musselburgh, N.B. |
| Deighton, W. | 2 Providence Row, Durham. |
| Dixon, J. G. | Wansbeck Place, Morpeth. |
| Elliot, Andrew | North Seaton, Morpeth, Northumberland. |
| Erricker, G. T. | Lawn Cottage, West Molesey, Surrey. |
| Fall, George | Jolly Sailor Inn, Redcar. |
| Fitzgerald, John | Woodside Cottage, Curragh Road, Evergreen, Cork. |
| Godfrey, W. | Great Warley, Brentwood, Essex. |
| Graham, A. | Mallsburn-by-Brampton. |
| Hancock, H. | Stanley Arms, North Stanley, Ripon. |
| Hodd, T. | 4 St. Mary's Terrace, St Anns, Lewes. |
| Hope, William | Croft Stables, Worcester. |
| Horsburgh, Alexander | Idstone, Shrivenham, Berks. |
| Johnson, Henry | Flimby, Maryport, Cumberland. |
| Jolly, E. | Victoria Street, Chorley, Lancashire. |
| Jones, E. | Red Lion Inn, Tarvin near Chester. |
| Jutsum, T. | Beaufort Kennels, Wichlo Place, Brighton. |
| Kellaway, J. | Tyler's Green, North Weald Bassett, Epping. |
| Langley, H. | Mizpap Villa, Exning Road, Newmarket. |
| Liddle, Thomas | South Shields. |
| Little, William | Thorneymoor, Walton, Cumberland. |
| Maxwell, M. L. | British Lion Hotel, Ipswich. |
| May, J. | 4 Henrietta Cottages, Bathwick, Bath. |
| Munro, D. | Brown Street, Stewarton, N.B. |
| Nagnall, Richard | West Houghton, Lancashire. |
| North, W. | Bramley, Leeds. |
| Poole, Jno. | Bridge Inn, Gateacre, Liverpool. |

| NAME | ADDRESS |
|---|---|
| Presdee, C. J., jun. | Sidbury, near Worcester. |
| Reid, Alexander | Strathaven, N.B. |
| Simpson, J. | Gosforth-on-Tyne. |
| Souch, W. | St. John's, Worcester. |
| Stamp, J. | Walkeringham, near Gainsboro'. |
| Stamper, Joseph | Ellenborough, Maryport. |
| Stickley, J. | 54 Ditchling Road, Brighton. |
| Stretton, J. & Son | Stanton Road, Burton-on-Trent. |
| Thompson, J. B. | Victoria House, North Howard Street, Great Yarmouth. |
| Thorpe, Oswald | Kersall Moor, Manchester. |
| Wade, J. | The Guinea, Ridge, Herts. |
| Waterer, R. | Cook's Ferry, Edmonton. |
| Whitelock, G. | Hookstone Lodge, Woodlands, Knaresborough. |
| Wilkinson, Edward | 117 Manchester Road, Southport. |
| Wood, Jesse | Walkergate, Beverley. |
| Wood, John | Ship Inn, Fisher Row, Edinburgh. |
| Wright, Joseph | Horwich, near Bolton. |

## *COURSING JUDGES, SLIPPERS, AND FLAG STEWARDS*

### JUDGES

| | |
|---|---|
| Bell, T. S. | Torrorie, Dumfries, N.B. |
| Betts, Henry | Claibanisam, Ballyroan, Ireland. |
| Blaxland, E. V. | Heath, Leighton Buzzard. |
| Brice, R. A. | White Hart Hotel, Witham, Essex. |
| Bull, E. J. | Tarvin, Chesire. |
| Cherrington, W. | Allscott, Bridgnorth, Salop. |
| Coke, J. | Blundell Arms, Birkdale, Southport. |
| Cottle, G. | West Felton, Oswestry. |
| Cowing, W. | Engineers' Arms, Coronation Street, Sunderland. |
| Cumstive, Richard | Great Eccleston, near Garstang. |
| Dalziel, R. H. | Water Hall, Workington. |
| Dunbar, Valentine J. R. | 36 North Great George Street, Dublin. |
| Fulwell, H. C. | Whitteley, Coventry. |
| Foord, W. | Bobbing House, Sittingbourne. |
| Gardner, J. | Moulton, Newmarket. |
| Gray, J. | 6 Bath Street Portobello, Edinburgh. |
| Goldsbrough, B. | Hutton Rudby, Yarm, Yorkshire. |
| Hay, John | Dovecot, Preston Pans, Edinburgh, N.B. |
| Heatley, S. P. | Whitehouse, Ditherington, Shrewsbury. |
| Hedley, J. | 9 Roseworth Terrace, Gosforth, Newcastle-on-Tyne. |

| Name | Address |
|---|---|
| Huntley, R. . . . | Glebe Farm, Bedlington, Northumberland. |
| Jillings, W. G. . . | Bridgham, Harling, Thetford, Norfolk. |
| Johnston, D. . . | Wall Club, Carlisle. |
| Kemp, Leslie J. . . | Southminster, Essex. |
| Lindsay, G. . . . | Annan, Dumfriesshire, N.B. |
| Maner, H. . . . | Red Bear, Sherburn, South Milford, Yorks. |
| Millar, C. . . . | Old Shildon, near Darlington. |
| Moore, J. J. . . . | Wightwich, Wolverhampton. |
| Myers, H. . . . | Shipton, Market Weighton. |
| Palframan, G. H. . . | Brayton, Selby, Yorks. |
| Roe, P. . . . . | Ballykelly House, Roscrea, Tipperary. |
| Spafford, E. . . . | Hill House, Nasenby, near Grantham. |
| Stephenson, Thomas . | Shipton, Market Weighton, Yorks. |
| Steward, A. A. . . | 23 Park Road, Wimbledon. (Telegrams to Judge, New Wimbledon.) |
| Swarnley, W. H. . . | Boakefield, Ballytose, Athy, Ireland. |
| Vawser, C. . . . | Burton, near Sleaford. |
| Wadhams, F. G. . . | Shakespeare Hotel, Stratford-on-Avon. |
| Warwick, George . . | Greyhound Hotel, Shrewsbury. |
| Watton, E. . . . | Palace Farm, Upton-on-Severn, Worcestershire. |
| Wentworth, N. K. . . | Great Bedwyn, Hungerford, Berks. (Telegrams Gt. Bedwyn Station.) |
| Williams, R. L. . . | 24 Mansfield Chambers, St. Ann's Square, Manchester. |
| Wilson, Frank. . . | Newington Avenue, Alnaby Road, Hull. |
| Wood, A. B. . . . | 29 Rose Lane, Mossley Hill, Liverpool. |

## SLIPPERS

| | |
|---|---|
| Barfoot, R. . . . | Frankton, near Rugby. |
| Birks, S. . . . . | Carr Woodside, Ripley, Derbyshire. |
| Bootiman, J. . . . | Harbottle, Rothbury, Northumberland. |
| Bootiman, T. . . . | Harbottle, Rothbury, Northumberland. |
| Cook, J. . . . . | Winmarleigh, Garstang, Lancashire. |
| Cummings, W. . . | Royal Oak Inn, Preston. |
| Deighton, W. . . . | 2 Providence Row, Claypath, Durham. |
| Dwyer, Edward . . | Cabra, Thurle, Ireland. |
| Groves, J. . . . | Upper Brook Street, Oswestry, Salop. |
| Holesworth, F. . . | South Newbald R. T. O., East Yorkshire. |
| Hoysted, W. J. . . | 34 Northbrooke Avenue, Dublin. |
| Hutchins, G. W. . . | Biggleswade, Bedfordshire. |
| Jeffrey, R. . . . | Chapel Street, Ely, Cambs. |
| Kent, Joseph . . . | Aycliffe, Darlington. |
| Luff, Alfred . . . | Newnham Croft, Cambridge. |
| Magee, E. . . . | Castle Eden, co. Durham. |
| Maltman, J. . . . | Alexandra Place, Barrhead. |
| Moore, E. . . . | Gale's Cottage, Woking Station, Surrey. |

| Name | Address |
|---|---|
| Nailard, A. . . . | Bine's Green, Ashurst, Steyning, Sussex. |
| Penrose, W. . . . | 160 Lifton Street, Southport. |
| Pond, A.. . . . | Cock Inn, Tillingham, Essex. |
| Raper, J., jun. . . | Gilling, Richmond, Yorks. |
| Rimmer, J. . . . | Formby, near Liverpool. |
| Robertson, T.. . . | South Gyle, Corstophine, near Edinburgh. |
| Shaw, F.. . . . | Northallerton, Yorkshire, near Edinburgh. |
| Souch, W. . . . | Worcester. |
| Titchmarsh, V. A. . . | Crystal Palace Hotel, St. Albans, Herts. |
| White, T. . . . | Ramsay, Isle of Man. |
| Wilkinson, Thomas . | 'The Leash,' Lime Street, Southport, Lancashire. |
| Wright, R. . . . | Waverton, near Chester. |

## FLAG STEWARDS

| | |
|---|---|
| Bell, John . . . | Wellington Hotel, Southport. |
| Bettoney, S. . . . | Crosby Street, Maryport. |
| Bootiman, J. . . . | Harbottle, Rothbury, Northumberland. |
| Crozier, H. N. . . | Chelmsford. |
| Cunnington, R. . . | Newmarket. |
| Erriker, G. T. . . | Lawn Cottage, West Molesey, Surrey. |
| Gunton, M. . . . | 11 King's Road, Hay Mills, Yardley. |
| Hicks, B. W.. . . . | North Fields, Stamford. |
| Jolly, E.. . . . | Chorley, Lancashire. |
| Kelsey, Walter . . | Fox Inn, Petergate, Yorkshire. |
| Penrose, W. . . . | 160 Lifton Street, Southport. |
| Reeves, R. . . . | Newbury, Berks. |
| Weightman, H. . . | 61 Bell Terrace Westmoreland Road, Newcastle-on-Tyne. |

## SLIP STEWARDS

| | |
|---|---|
| Bootiman, John . . | Harbottle, Northumberland. |
| Gunton, M. . . . | Waterloo Hotel, Birmingham. |
| Jeffery, R. . . . | Chapel Street, Ely, Cambridgeshire. |
| Jolly, E.. . . . | Chorley, Lancashire. |

## CODE OF RULES OF THE NATIONAL COURSING CLUB

1. THE SECRETARY AND STEWARDS.—For any proposed open meeting a committee of not less than three shall be formed, who, with the secretary, shall settle preliminaries. The management of the meeting shall be entrusted to this committee, in conjunction with stewards, who shall be elected by the subscribers present on the first evening of a meeting. The stewards alone shall decide any disputed question by a majority of those present, subject to an appeal to the National Coursing Club. The secretary, if honorary, shall be a member of committee and a steward *ex officio.* No steward shall have a right to vote in any case relating to his own dogs. The secretary shall declare, on or before the evening preceding the last day's running, how the prizes are to be divided; and shall give a statement of expenses, if called upon to do so by any six of the subscribers, within fourteen days after the meeting.

2. ELECTION OF JUDGE.—The judge may either be appointed by the secretary and committee acting under Rule 1, in which case his name shall be announced simultaneously with the meeting, or elected by the votes of the subscribers taking nominations: but each subscriber shall have only one vote, whatever the number of his nominations. Not less than ten days' notice of the day of election shall be given to the subscribers, and the appointment shall be published at least a fortnight before the meeting. The names of the subscribers voting, with the votes given by them, shall be recorded in a book open to the inspection of the stewards, who shall declare the number of votes for each judge, if called upon to do so by any of the subscribers. When a judge is prevented from attending or finishing a meeting, the committee and the stewards (if appointed) shall have the power of deciding what is to be done.

3. DESCRIPTION OF ENTRY.—Every subscriber to a stake must name his dog before the time fixed for closing the entry,

giving the names (the running names if they had any) of the sire and dam of the dog entered. The secretary shall publish on the cards the names of those who are subscribers but do not comply with these conditions. These nominations shall not be drawn, but must be paid for. For produce stakes the names, pedigrees, ages, and colours, and distinguishing marks of puppies, shall be detailed in writing to the secretary of a meeting at the time of the original entry. Every subscriber must also, if required, state in writing to the secretary, before or during the meeting for which such entry is made, the names and addresses of the parties who reared his puppies; and any puppy whose marks and pedigree shall be proved not to correspond with the entry given shall be disqualified, and the whole of its stakes or winnings forfeited. No greyhound is to be considered a puppy which was whelped before January 1 of the year preceding the commencement of the season of running. A sapling is a greyhound whelped on or after January 1 of the year in which the season of running commenced

4. The colours, sex, names, pedigrees, and ages of all greyhounds, with the names of their owners, and the owners of their sires and dams, shall be registered in a Greyhound Stud Book. The registration fee shall be 1*s.* for each dog registered on or before July 1, and a double fee shall be charged for registration of all greyhounds (other than saplings) after that date to the end of the coursing season immediately following. Any owner may, by payment of 1*l.* annually, compound for the registration of any number of greyhounds *bonâ fide* his own property. The keeper of the Stud Book shall give a receipt for the registration fee of every greyhound, which shall be called a certificate of registration.

5. The Greyhound Stud Book shall be published under the authority of the National Coursing Club, on September 1, or as soon after as possible.

6. Applications for registration of greyhounds shall be made on or before July 1, and registrations applied for subsequent to that date that do not appear in the Stud Book of that year will appear in that of the following year.

7. If the same name has been given to more than one greyhound, the keeper of the Stud Book shall give priority to the dog first registered, and shall add to every other such name, except the one first registered, a numeral commencing with II.

8. All greyhounds whose names do not appear in the Stud Book,

or whose owners cannot produce a certificate of registration from the keeper of the Stud Book on being required to do so by a steward or the secretary of any coursing meeting, shall be disqualified, and shall forfeit all entry moneys which may have been paid, and any stake or prize, or share of any stake or prize won at such meeting, and such entry moneys, stake, or prize or share thereof, won by any dog so disqualified, shall be disposed of as provided by Rule 37 applicable to disqualification.

9. PAYMENT OF ENTRY MONEY.—All moneys due for nominations taken must be paid at or before the time fixed for closing the entry, whether the stakes fill or not, and although, from insufficient description or any other cause, the dogs named may be disqualified. No entry shall be valid unless the amount due for it has been paid in full. For all produce and other stakes where a forfeit is payable no declaration is necessary; the non-payment of the remainder of the entry money at the time fixed for that purpose is to be considered a declaration of forfeit. The secretary is to be responsible for the entry money of all dogs whose names appear upon the card.

10. ALTERATION OF NAME.—If any subscriber should enter a greyhound by a different name from that in which it shall have last been entered to run in public, or shall have been registered in the Stud Book, he shall give notice of the alteration to the secretary at the time of entry, and the secretary shall place on the card both the late and the present names of the dog, and this must be done at all meetings at which the dog runs throughout the coursing season in which the alteration has been made. If notice of the alteration be not given, the dog shall be disqualified. The new name must be registered before the dog can run under it.

11. PREFIX OF 'NS.'—Any subscriber taking an entry in a stake must prove to the satisfaction of the stewards, if called upon by them to do so, that any greyhound entered by him, without the prefix of the word 'Names,' is *bonâ fide* his own property. If a subscriber enters a dog not his own property without putting 'ns' after his own name, the dog so entered shall be disqualified. Every subscriber shall, if requested, deliver in writing to the secretary of the meeting the name of the *bonâ fide* owner of the greyhound named by him, and this communication is to be produced should any dispute arise. No dog purchased or procured for a less time than the entire period still remaining of its public running, or belonging to two or more persons, unless they are

declared confederates, shall be held as *bonâ fide* the property of a subscriber. The names of confederates must be registered with the keeper of the Stud Book--fee, 1*s.* for each name. Assumed names must also be registered with the keeper of the Stud Book—fee, 5 guineas.

12. Death of a Subscriber.—The death of a subscriber shall only affect his nominations if it occur before the draw, in which case, subject to the exceptions stated below, they shall be void, whether the entries have been made or not, and any money received for forfeits or stakes shall be returned, less the proportion of expenses when the amount has been advertised, and when the nominations rendered vacant are not filled by other subscribers. If he has parted with all interest in the nominations, and dogs not his property are entered and paid for, such entries shall not subsequently be disturbed. When dogs that have been entered in produce stakes change owners, with their engagements and with their forfeits paid, the then owner, if entitled to run them in those stakes, shall not be prevented from doing so by reason of the death of the former owner.

13. Draw.—Immediately before the greyhounds are drawn at any meeting, and before nine o'clock on every subsequent evening during the continuance of such meeting, the time and place of putting the first brace of dogs into the slips on the following morning shall be declared. A card or counter, bearing a corresponding number, shall be assigned to each entry. These numbered cards or counters shall then be placed together and drawn indiscriminately. This classification, once made, shall not be disturbed throughout the meeting, except for the purpose of guarding, or on account of byes.

14. Guarding.—When two or more nominations in a stake are taken in one name, the greyhounds, if *bonâ fide* the property of the same owner, shall be guarded throughout. This is always to be arranged, as far as possible, by bringing up dogs from below to meet those which are to be guarded. This guarding is not, however, to deprive any dog of a natural bye to which he may be entitled, either in the draw or in running through the stake. Dogs whose position has been altered in consequence of guarding or of byes, must return to their original position in the next round, if guarding does not prevent it.

15. Byes.—A natural bye shall be given to the lowest available dog in each round. No dog shall run a second such bye in any

stake, unless it is unavoidable. When a dog is entitled to a bye, either natural or accidental, his owner or nominator may run any greyhound he pleases to assist in the course, provided always that in sapling stakes only a sapling may be used, and in puppy stakes none older than a puppy. But if it is proved to the satisfaction of the stewards that no sapling or puppy respectively can be found to run an accidental bye, an older dog may be used. No dog shall run any bye earlier than his position on the card entitles him to do. The slip and the course in a bye shall be the same as in a course in which a decision is required, and the judge shall decide whether enough has been done to constitute a course, or whether it must be run again, and in the latter case the judge shall give the order. If at the commencement of any round in a stake, one dog in each course of that round has a bye, those byes shall not be run, but the dogs shall take their places for the next round as if the byes had been run. A bye must be run before a dog can claim the advantage of it.

16. Slip Steward.—The committee of an open meeting and the members of a club meeting shall appoint, on the first evening of a meeting, a slip steward, whose duty shall be to see that every greyhound is brought to slips in its proper turn, to report to the stewards, without delay, any greyhound that does not come to the slips in time, and any act on the part of the slipper, nominators, or their representatives, which he may consider should be brought to their knowledge. If a nominator or his representative should refuse to comply with the directions of the slip steward, or should use abusive and insulting language towards him, the stewards may inflict a penalty not exceeding 2*l.* on the person so offending.

17. Postponement of Meeting.—A meeting appointed to take place on a certain day may, if a majority of the committee and the stewards (if appointed) consider the weather unfit for coursing, be postponed from day to day: but if the running does not commence within the current week all nominations shall be void, and the expenses shall be paid by the subscribers, in proportion to the value of nominations taken by each. In the case of produce stakes, however, the original entries shall continue binding if the meeting is held at a later period of the season.

18. Taking Dogs to the Slips.—Every dog must be brought to the slips in its proper turn, without delay, under a penalty of 1*l.* if absent for more than ten minutes (according to the report of the slip steward or of one of the stewards), its opponent shall be

entitled to claim the course, subject to the discretion of the stewards, and shall in that case run a bye. If both dogs be absent at the expiration of ten minutes, the stewards shall have power to disqualify both dogs, or to fine their owners any sum not exceeding 5*l.* each. The nominator is answerable for his dog being put into the slips at the right time, on the right side, and against the right dog. No allowance shall be made for mistakes. No dog shall be put into the slips for a deciding course until thirty minutes after its course in the previous round without the consent of its owner. *See Rule* 31.

19. CONTROL OF DOGS IN SLIPS.—The control of all matters connected with slipping the greyhounds shall rest with the stewards of a meeting. Owners or servants, after delivering their dogs into the hands of the slipper, may follow close after them, but not so as to inconvenience the slipper, or in any way interfere with the dogs, under a penalty of 1*l.* Neither must they holloa them on while running, under the same penalty. Any greyhound found to be beyond control in the slips may, by order of the stewards, be taken out of the slips and disqualified.

20. GREYHOUNDS OF SAME COLOUR TO WEAR COLLARS.—When two greyhounds drawn together are of the same colour, they shall each wear a collar, and the owners shall be subject to a penalty of 10*s.* for non-observance of this rule. The colour of the collar shall be red for the left-hand side, and white for the right-hand side of the slips. The upper dog on the card must be placed on the left hand, and the lower dog on the right hand of the slips.

21. The order to slip may be given by the judge, or the slip steward, or the stewards of a meeting may leave the slip to the sole discretion of the slipper. The length of slip must necessarily vary with the nature of the ground, but should never be less than from three to four score yards, and must be maintained of one uniform length, as far as possible, throughout each stake.

22. THE SLIPPER.—If one greyhound gets out of the slips, the slipper shall not let the other go. In any case of slips breaking, and either or both dogs getting away in consequence, the slipper may be fined not exceeding 1*l.*, at the discretion of the stewards.

23. The judge shall be subject to the general rules which may be established by the National Coursing Club for his guidance. He shall, on the termination of each course, immediately deliver

his decision aloud, and shall not recall or reverse his decision, on any pretext whatever, after it has been declared; but no decision shall be delivered until the judge is perfectly satisfied that the course is absolutely terminated.

24. The judge shall decide all courses upon the one uniform principle that the greyhound which does most towards killing the hare during the continuance of the course is to be declared the winner. The principle is to be carried out by estimating the value of the work done by each greyhound, as seen by the judge, upon a balance of points according to the scale hereafter laid down, from which also are to be deducted certain specified allowances and penalties.

25. The points of the course are—

- *a.* *Speed*—which shall be estimated as one, two, or three points, according to the degree of superiority shown. [See definition below (*a*).]
- *b.* *The Go-bye.*—Two points, or if gained on the outer circle, three points.
- *c.* *The Turn.*—One point.
- *d.* *The Wrench.*—Half a point.
- *e.* *The Kill.*—Two points, or, in a descending scale, in proportion to the degree of merit displayed in that kill, which may be of no value.
- *f.* *The Trip.*—One point.

### Definition of Points

(*a.*) In estimating the value of speed to the hare, the judge must take into account the several forms in which it may be displayed, viz:—

1. Where in the run up a clear lead is gained by one of the dogs, in which case one, two, or three points may be given, according to the length of lead, apart from the score for a turn or wrench. In awarding these points the judge shall take into consideration the merit of a lead obtained by a dog which has lost ground at the start, either from being unsighted or from a bad slip, or which has had to run the outer circle.
2. Where one greyhound leads the other so long as the hare runs straight, but loses the lead from her bending round decidedly in favour of the slower dog of her own accord, in which case the one greyhound shall score one point for the speed shown, and the other dog score one point for the first turn.

3. Under no circumstances is speed without subsequent work to be allowed to decide a course, except where great superiority is shown by one greyhound over another in a long lead to covert.

If a dog, after gaining the first six points, still keeps possession of the hare by superior speed, he shall have double the prescribed allowance for the subsequent points made before his opponent begins to score.

*b*. *The Go-bye* is where a greyhound starts a clear length behind his opponent, and yet passes him in a straight run, and gets a clear length before him.

*c*. *The Turn* is where the hare is brought round at not less than a right angle from her previous line.

*d*. *The Wrench* is where the hare is bent from her line at less than a right angle; but where she only leaves her line to suit herself, and not from the greyhound pressing her, nothing is to be allowed.

*e*. *The Merit of a Kill* must be estimated according to whether a greyhound, by his own superior dash and skill, bears the hare; whether he picks her up through any little accidental circumstances favouring him, or whether she is turned into his mouth, as it were, by the other greyhound.

*f*. *The Trip*, or unsuccessful effort to kill, is where the hare is thrown off her legs, or where a greyhound flecks her, but cannot hold her.

26. The following allowances shall be made for accidents to a greyhound during a course; but in every case they shall only be deducted from the other dog's score:—

*a*. For losing ground at the start, either from being unsighted, or from a bad slip, in which case the judge is to decide what amount of allowance is to be made, on the principle that the score of the foremost dog is not to begin until the second has had an opportunity of joining in the course, and the judge may decide the course or declare the course to be an undecided or no course, as he may think fit.

*b*. Where a hare bears very decidedly in favour of one of the greyhounds, after the first or subsequent turns, in which case the next point shall not be scored by the dog unduly favoured, or only half his points allowed, according to circumstances. No greyhound shall receive any allowance for a fall or an accident, with the exception of being ridden over by the owner of the competing greyhound, or his servant, provided for by Rule 30 or when pressing his hare, in which case his opponent shall not count the next point made

27. Penalties are as follow :—

*a.* Where a greyhound, from his own defect, refuses to follow the hare at which he is slipped, he shall lose the course.

*b.* Where a dog wilfully stands still in a course, or departs from directly pursuing the hare, no points subsequently made by him shall be scored ; and if the points made by him up to that time be just equal to those made by his antagonist in the whole course, he shall thereby lose the course ; but where one or both dogs stop with the hare in view, through inability to continue the course, it shall be decided according to the number of points gained by each dog during the whole course.

*c.* If a dog refuses to fence where the other fences, any points subsequently made by him are not to be scored ; but if he does his best to fence, and is foiled by sticking in a meuse, the course shall end there. When the points are equal, the superior fencer shall win the course.

28. If a second hare be started during a course, and one of the dogs follow her, the course shall end there.

29. Greyhound Getting Loose.—Any person allowing a greyhound to get loose, and join in a course which is being run, shall be fined 1*l.* If the loose greyhound belong to either of the owners of the dogs engaged in the particular course, such owner shall forfeit his chance of the stake with the dog then running, unless he can prove, to the satisfaction of the stewards, that he had not been able to get the loose greyhound taken up after running its own course. The course is not to be considered as necessarily ended when a third dog joins in.

30. Riding Over a Greyhound.—If any subscriber, or his servant, shall ride over his opponent's greyhound while running a course, the owner of the dog so ridden over shall (although the course be given against him) be deemed the winner of it, or shall have the option of allowing the other dog to remain and run out the stake, and in such case shall be entitled to half its winnings.

31. A 'no course' is when by accident or by the shortness of the course the dogs are not tried together, and if one be then drawn the other must run a bye, unless the judge on being appealed to shall decide that he has done work enough to be exempted from it. 'An undecided course' is where the judge considers the merits

of the dogs equal, and if either is then drawn the other cannot be required to run a bye; but the owners must at the time declare which dog remains in. (See Rule 33.) The judge shall signify the distinction between a 'no course' and an 'undecided' by taking off his hat in the latter case only. After an 'undecided' or 'no course,' if the dogs before being taken up get on another or the same hare, the judge must follow, and shall decide in favour of one if he considers that there has been a sufficient trial to justify his doing so. A 'no course' or an 'undecided' may be run off immediately, if claimed on behalf of both dogs before the next brace are put into the slips, or in case of 'no course' if so ordered by the judge, otherwise it shall be run again after the two next courses, unless it stand over till the next morning, when it shall be the first course run; if it is the last course of the day, fifteen minutes shall be allowed after both dogs are taken up.

32. The judge shall render an explanation of any decision only to the stewards of the meeting if required, through them, before the third succeeding course, by the owner, or nominator, or representative of the owner or nominator, of either of the greyhounds engaged in the course. The stewards shall, if requested to do so, express their opinion whether the explanation is satisfactory or not, and their opinion in writing may be asked for and published afterwards, but the decision of the judge, once given, shall not be reversed for any cause.

33. Withdrawal of a Dog.—If a dog be withdrawn from any stake on the field, its owner, or some one having his authority, must at once give notice to the secretary, or flag, or slip steward. If the dog belongs to either of these officials, the notice must be given to the other. When, after a 'no course' or an 'undecided,' one of the greyhounds has been officially drawn, and the dogs are again, by mistake, put into slips and run a course, the arrangement come to shall stand, whatever the judge's decision may be, and all bets on the course shall be void.

34. Impugning Judge.—If any subscriber, owner, or any other person, proved to be interested, openly impugns the decision of the judge on the ground, except by a complaint to the stewards, according to Rule 32, he shall forfeit not more than 5*l*., nor less than 2*l*., at the discretion of the stewards

35. Stakes not Run Out.—When two greyhounds remain in for the deciding course, the stakes shall be considered divided if they belong to the same owner, or to confederates, and also if

the owner of one of the two dogs induces the owner of the other to draw him for any payment or consideration; but if one of the two be drawn without payment or consideration, from lameness, or from any cause clearly affecting his chance of winning, the other may be declared the winner, the facts of the case being clearly proved to the satisfaction of the stewards. The same rule shall apply when more than two dogs remain in at the end of a stake which is not run out; and in case of a division between three or more dogs, of which two or more belong to the same owner, these latter shall be held to take equal shares of the total amount received by their owner in a division. When there is a compulsory division all greyhounds remaining in the class that is being run, even where one is entitled to a bye, shall take equal shares. The terms of any arrangement to divide winnings, and the amount of any money given to induce the owner of a dog to draw him, must be declared to the secretary.

36. Winners of Stakes Running Together.—If two or more greyhounds shall each win a stake, and have to run together for a final prize or challenge cup, should they not have run an equal number of ties in their respective stakes, the greyhound which has run the smaller number of courses must run a bye, or byes, to put itself upon an equality in this respect with its opponent.

37. Objections.—An objection to a greyhound may be made to any one of the stewards of a meeting at any time before the stakes are paid over, upon the objector lodging in the hands of such steward, or the secretary, the sum of 5*l.*, which shall be forfeited if the objection proves frivolous, or if he shall not bring the case before the next meeting of the National Coursing Club, or give notice to the stewards previous thereto of his intention to withdraw the objection. The owner of the greyhound objected to must deposit equally the sum of 5*l.*, and prove the correctness of his entry. Expenses in consequence of an objection shall be borne as the National Coursing Club may direct. Should an objection be made which cannot at the time be substantiated or disproved, the greyhound may be allowed to run under protest, the stewards retaining the winnings until the objection has been withdrawn, or heard and decided. If the greyhound objected to be disqualified, the amount to which he would otherwise have been entitled shall be divided equally among the dogs beaten by him; and if a piece of plate or prize has been added, and won by him,

only the dogs which he beat in the several rounds shall have a right to contend for it.

38. DEFAULTERS.—No person shall be allowed to enter or run a greyhound, in his own or any other person's name, who is a defaulter for either stakes, forfeits, or bets, or for money due under an arrangement for a division of winnings, or for penalties regularly imposed for the infraction of rules by the stewards of any meeting, or for any payment required by a decision of the National Coursing Club, or for subscriptions due to any club entitled to have representatives in the National Coursing Club. As regards bets, however, this rule shall only apply when a complaint is lodged with the secretary of the National Coursing Club within six months after the bet becomes due. On receipt of such complaint the secretary shall give notice of the claim to the person against whom it is made, with a copy of this rule, and if he shall not pay the bet, or appear before the next meeting of the National Coursing Club, and resist the claim successfully, he shall be considered a defaulter.

39. JUDGE OR SLIPPER INTERESTED.—If a judge or slipper be in any way interested in the winnings of a greyhound or greyhounds, the owner and nominator in each case, unless they can prove satisfactorily that such interest was without their cognisance, shall forfeit all claim to the winnings, and the dog shall be disqualified; and if any nominator or owner of greyhounds shall give, offer, or lend money, or anything of value, to any judge or slipper, such owner or nominator shall not be allowed to run dogs in his own or any other person's name during any subsequent period that the National Coursing Club may decide upon.

40. Any person who is proved to the satisfaction of the National Coursing Club to have been guilty of any fraudulent or discreditable conduct in connection with coursing, may, in addition to any pecuniary penalty to which he may be liable, be declared incapable of running or entering a greyhound in his own or any other person's name during any subsequent period that the National Coursing Club may decide upon; and any dogs under his care, training, management, or superintendence, shall be disqualified during such subsequent period.

41. BETS.—All bets upon an undecided course shall stand unless one of the greyhounds be drawn. All bets upon a dog running further than another in the stake shall be p.p., whatever accident may happen. Bets upon a deciding, as upon every other course, are off, if the course is not run. Long odds bets shall be

void, unless the greyhound the bet refers to shall run one course in the stake, other than a bye, after the bet is made. Long odds bets, with this exception, shall be p.p.

42. Bets on Stakes Divided.—Where money has been laid against a dog winning a stake, and he divides it, the two sums must be put together and divided in the same proportion as the value of the stakes.

# INDEX

*Spottiswoode & Co. Printers, New-street Square, London.*

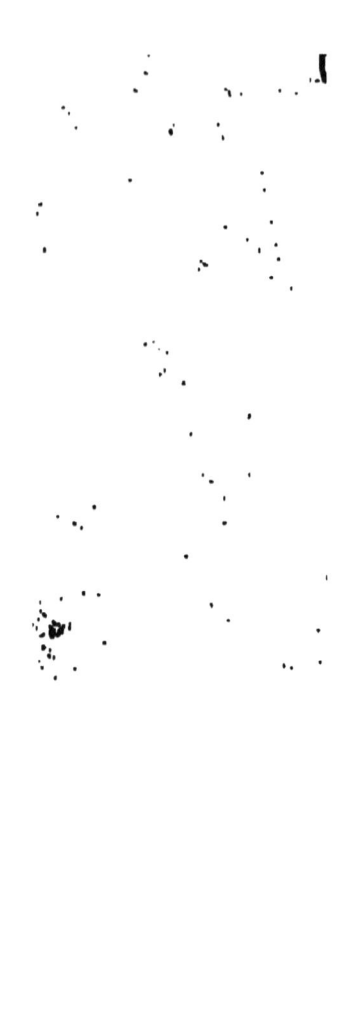

# THE BADMINTON LIBRARY.

Edited by the DUKE OF BEAUFORT, K.G and A. E. T. WATSON.

DRIVING. By His Grace the DUKE OF BEAUFORT, K.G. With 11 Plates and 54 Woodcuts &c. Crown 8vo. 10s. 6d.

FENCING, BOXING, and WRESTLING. By WALTER H. POLLOCK, F. C. GROVE, C. PREVOST, E. B. MICHELL, and WALTER ARMSTRONG. With 18 Intaglio Plates and 24 Woodcuts &c Crown 8vo. 10s. 6d.

GOLF. By HORACE G. HUTCHINSON, the Right Hon. A. J. BALFOUR, M.P. Sir WALTER G. SIMPSON, Bart. LORD WELLWOOD, H. S. C. EVERARD, ANDREW LANG, and other Writers. With 22 Plates and 69 Woodcuts &c. Crown 8vo. 10s. 6d.

TENNIS, LAWN TENNIS, RACKETS, and FIVES. By J. M. and C. G. HEATHCOTE, E. O. PLEYDELL-BOUVERIE, and A. C. AINGER. With Contributions by the Hon. A. LYTTELTON, W. C. MARSHALL, Miss L. DOD, H. W. W. WILBERFORCE, H. F. LAWFORD, &c. With 12 Plates and 67 Woodcuts &c. Crown 8vo. 10s. 6d.

RIDING AND POLO. By Captain ROBERT WEIR, Riding Master, R.H.G. and J. MORAY BROWN. With Contributions by the DUKE OF BEAUFORT, the EARL OF SUFFOLK AND BERKSHIRE, the EARL OF ONSLOW, E. L. ANDERSON, and ALFRED E. T. WATSON. With 18 Plates and 41 Woodcuts &c. Crown 8vo. 10s. 6d.

SKATING, CURLING, TOBOGGANING, and other ICE SPORTS. By J. M. HEATHCOTE, C. G. TEBBUTT, T. MAXWELL WITHAM, the Rev. JOHN KERR, ORMOND HAKE, and HENRY A. BUCK. With 12 Plates and 272 Woodcuts &c. by C. WHYMPER and Captain ALEXANDER. Crown 8vo. 10s. 6d.

MOUNTAINEERING. By C. T. DENT, with Contributions by W. M. CONWAY, D. W. FRESHFIELD, C. E. MATHEWS, C. PILKINGTON, Sir F. POLLOCK, H. G. WILLINK, and an Introduction by Mr. JUSTICE WILLS. With 13 Plates and 95 Woodcuts &c. by H. G. WILLINK and others. Crown 8vo. 10s. 6d.

COURSING AND FALCONRY. By HARDING COX and the Hon. GERALD LASCELLES. With 20 Plates and 56 Woodcuts &c. by JOHN CHARLTON, L. SPEED, G. E. LODGE, &c. Crown 8vo. 10s. 6d.

London: LONGMANS, GREEN, & CO.